HISTORICAL METHODS
in Mass Communication

Fourth Edition

HISTORICAL METHODS

in Mass Communication

―

Fourth Edition

James D. Startt
Wm. David Sloan

VISION  PRESS

HISTORICAL METHODS
in Mass Communication
Fourth Edition

Copyright 2019 by Vision Press

Vision Press
4195 Waldort Drive
P.O. Box 1106
Northport, AL 35476

ALL RIGHTS RESERVED. No part of this publication may be reproduced, stored in a retrieval system, or transmitted in any form or by any means, electronic, mechanical, photocopy, recording, or otherwise, without the prior written permission of the publisher.

ISBN   978-1-885219-84-8

Printed in the United States of America

HISTORICAL METHODS
in Mass Communication

Fourth Edition

AUTHORS

JAMES D. STARTT received his Ph.D. in history from the University of Maryland. He is senior research professor in history at Valparaiso University. He is the author of the books *Journalism's Unofficial Ambassador: A Biography of Edward Price Bell, 1869-1943*; *Journalists for Empire: The Imperial Debate in the Edwardian Stately Press, 1903-1913*; *Woodrow Wilson and the Press: Prelude to the Presidency*; and *Woodrow Wilson, the Great War, and the Fourth Estate*. He also has written numerous articles, essays, chapters in books, and encyclopedia contributions — mostly on the presidency of Woodrow Wilson and on American and British journalism and diplomatic history. He co-edited the first three editions of the popular textbook *The Media in America: A History*, the seven-volume series "History of American Journalism," and *The Significance of the Media in American History*. He served as president of the American Journalism Historians Association in 1997-1998 and in 2000 received its prestigious Kobre Award for Lifetime Achievement. He also has served on its Board of Directors and as chair of its research and oral history committees. From 1986 to 1989 he was Associate Editor of the research journal *American Journalism*.

WM. DAVID SLOAN received his Ph.D. in mass communication and United States history from the University of Texas. He is a professor emeritus of journalism at the University of Alabama. The founder of the American Journalism Historians Association, he served a five-year term as editor of its journal, *American Journalism*. The AJHA recognizes him with its annual "Sloan Outstanding Faculty Research Paper" award. He has published more than forty other books, among them *American Journalism: History, Principles, Practices*; *Media and Religion in American History*; *American Journalism History: An Annotated Bibliography*; *Perspectives on Mass Communication History*; *The Age of Mass Communication*; *The Significance of the Media in American History*; *The Early American Press, 1690-1783*; *Great Editorials*; and *Masterpieces of Reporting*. His book *The Media in America: A History* is the most widely used textbook in the field of communication history. He is co-editor of the series "History of American Journalism." He has written numerous articles and papers on history and journalistic writing and has been recognized with several research awards for his work in communication history. In 1998 he received the AJHA's Kobre Award for lifetime achievement. He has served as national president of both the AJHA and Kappa Tau Alpha, the mass communication honor society. On its ninetieth anniversary, KTA selected him as one of the five most important members in its history.

ACKNOWLEDGMENTS

We appreciate the contributions of numerous colleagues and assistants in the preparation of the third edition of this book.

We are grateful to the many professors who shared their insight and thoughts about historiography. We particularly want to thank Prof. Ford Risley, editor of *American Journalism*, for explaining that journal's process for evaluating manuscripts, and Prof. Greg Borchard, editor of *Journalism History*, for providing material related to his journal. Likewise, we thank Prof. Erin Coyle of Louisiana State University for providing material about the judging process for research papers submitted to the annual competition of the American Journalism Historians Association.

For earlier editions of the book, graduate students at the University of Alabama were especially helpful in checking sources. We particularly want to thank Lisa Mullikin Parcell, Susan Thompson, Jimmy McCollum (all of whom are now professors), Laurie Lattimore, Lisa Daigle, and Pamela Harris. Several librarians and other staff members at Valparaiso University — particularly Rebecca Byrum, Donna Resetar, Ruth S. Connell, Stephenie Umbach, Susan Wanat, Ellen B. Meyer, and Judith K. Miller — helped us to clarify our understanding of the vast expansion of library and computer technology. Dr. William Horne, then of the Telecommunication and Film Department at the University of Alabama, offered valuable suggestions and criticism for our original discussion of mass communication sources in Chapter 5. We appreciate their enthusiasm for this book and have benefited from their counsel and expertise.

Finally, special thanks go to Michael Stamm of Michigan State University, the co-author of the book's third edition. His expertise was invaluable for discussions of such matters as contemporary philosophical considerations in doing historical research.

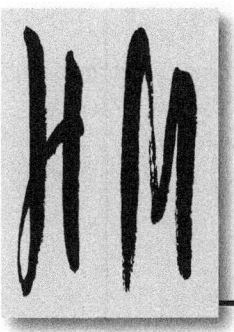

PREFACE

At the outset of a journey, it is helpful to know where one is going. So, here at the beginning of this book, we want to offer a word about what it does and what it does not do. As for what it does do, it is based on the fundamentals of historical research. We believe the only way one in mass communication can do historical research well is to adhere to the basic principles and procedures that good historians in all fields follow. We thus emphasize such matters as evidence, primary sources, the need to be aware of present-mindedness and to avoid bias, reasoning grounded in reality, and familiarity with the literature. The book eschews the vague "philosophical" and "theoretical" and "grand theory" recommendations that have at times been faddish with some communication historians. Likewise, while taking account of the quantitative methods drilled into graduate students in theoretical communication programs, it attempts to keep those methods in perspective as only one limited part of research necessary in history.

The concept underlying this book is that historians and students must have a knowledge of the well-prescribed methods that have proven themselves. It therefore is offered as guidance for communication historians who wish to improve their skills and for students who wish to learn the fundamentals of historical research.

We have approached the study of communication history as primarily history rather than primarily communication. It is our belief that the broader perspective brings to communication historians a greater recognition of the potential value of their research.

Communication historians today are much better at methods than when this book's first edition was published three decades ago. For communication history to reach its full potential, however, it must move beyond the sometimes poor standards of scholarship practiced in that field of study. By associating themselves with the broad study of history, communication historians will become more aware that their research must meet the high standards required of historical study. No less should be expected or accepted.

CONTENTS

Acknowledgments	vii
Preface	ix

1 THE NATURE OF HISTORY — 1

History as a Form of Knowledge	4
History Among the Disciplines	9
The Purpose of History	16
History and Communication History	19

2 INTERPRETATION IN HISTORY — 25

The Nationalist School	28
The Romantic School	29
The Developmental School	31
The Progressive School	35
The Consensus School	37
The Neo-Conservative School	40
The Cultural School	41
The Cultural Studies School	44
Gender and Minority Schools	46
The Necessity of Interpretation	49

3 THE FUNDAMENTALS OF GOOD HISTORY — 51

The Criteria of Good History — 52
Present-Mindedness — 56
The Historian Between Past and Present — 58
The Open Borders of Knowledge — 63
Psychology in History — 66
Quantification in History — 70
Postmodernism in History — 76
Cultural and Critical Studies — 79

4 BASIC PROCEDURES AND TECHNIQUES — 83

Preliminary Reading — 83
Topic Selection — 85
Organization — 88
Focusing the Study — 88
Notetaking — 92
The Library as a Reference Tool — 93
A Working Bibliography — 97
The Internet as a Reference Tool — 98
Archival Research — 100

5 HISTORICAL SOURCES AND THEIR EVALUATION — 103

Primary and Secondary Sources — 104
Evaluation of Written Records — 109
Types of Sources — 122
Using Communication Sources — 137
How Much Research is "Enough"? — 143

6 SEARCHING FOR HISTORICAL MATERIALS — 145

Online Library Searches — 145
Libraries vs. Archives — 147
Bibliographic Sources and Reference Works: A Selected Listing — 150
Mass Communication Sources — 180
Computerized Bibliographic Searches — 185
The Library Physical Card Catalog — 186

	The Library Online Catalog	190
	The Historical Researcher and Bibliography	191
7	**HISTORICAL RESEARCH ON THE INTERNET**	**193**
	Benefits of the Internet	193
	Limitations of the Internet	195
	Types of Material on the Internet	199
	How To Find Material on the Internet	203
	List of Recommended Websites	206
8	**EXPLANATION IN HISTORY**	**235**
	Clarification of Purpose	235
	Interpretation in History	239
	Explaining Causation	243
	Theory and Historical Explanation	247
9	**WRITING**	**253**
	The Historical Narrative	254
	Unity of Composition	259
	Constructing an Effective Historical Composition	261
	Checklist for Proofreading	276
10	**PRESENTATION AND PUBLICATION**	**279**
	Conference Presentations	280
	Journal Articles	203
	Book Publishing	290
	Scholarly Paper Conferences	292
	Journals Publishing Articles on Communication History	293
11	**BIBLIOGRAPHY**	**295**
	The Study of History	295
	Conducting Historical Research	297
	Communication History Research	299
	Conducting Historical Research on the Internet	300

Communication Research Methods	301
Research in Related Disciplines	302
Approaches to History	305
Approaches to Communication History	308
Writing and Forms	311

12 INDEX 313

HISTORICAL METHODS
in Mass Communication

Fourth Edition

THE NATURE OF HISTORY

An interest in history permeates Western civilization. The past finds its way occasionally into the thoughts of most people. It fascinates others. For some, the study of history becomes a life's work. Of those, some are especially drawn to communication history. They have selected for study a subject that has played an integral part in the world's and in this nation's past. For two centuries, American historians have been studying communication; and all signs indicate that, rather than declining, the interest in communication history is on the rise. That interest raises the question of why study history, or, more specifically, communication history.

Besides the simple enjoyment they derive from studying history, communication historians, and students as well, give various answers to such questions. Coming from professional backgrounds in such areas as journalism and advertising, some want to learn from the past so that they may be better practitioners in their professions. Oriented primarily toward the present rather than the past, some examine the past to help them find the roots of present practices. Others pragmatically believe they can learn mistakes of the past so that they can avoid repeating the errors, while others think they can use the past to help prepare for the future.

All these views may have some validity, but historians find that the study of history is valuable primarily in other ways. First, it helps us to understand the past as it really was. Although historians may first approach the past for some other reason, with continued study they find that it has intrinsic value in itself. They wish to study the past for its own sake. Second, the study of history can help us understand people. Conditions and times may change, communication technologies and publishing and broadcasting enterprises come and go; but human nature, the human character, human relationships, and the human spirit endure. Third, it can help in understanding the present. Its value, however, is not simply in helping discover the paths by which the present emerged, but in revealing particulars from the past that may serve as comparisons with the present, as lenses through which to consider our own times. Fourth, the study of history is valuable for the intellectual stimulation it provides. Professional communication schools today emphasize courses of study to prepare students for careers, but the true value of education lies in gaining knowledge and in developing a critical intellect. The study of history, requiring as it does rigorous and mature thinking, helps nurture the intellect as few other disciplines can do.

> "Today is not worth living if we do not examine and learn from the past." — Maurine Beasley, author, *Eleanor Roosevelt: Transformative First Lady*

For the study of history to provide its benefits, though, it must be done properly. The purpose of this book is to guide communication historians and history students in the methods of proper research. It is structured in such a way as to assist both the beginning researcher and the experienced historian. Students doing their first historical study will find instruction in the fundamentals of sound research necessary for all projects beginning with the most elementary, while established historians will find material and discussion of matters that advanced researchers must consider. It also is intended to assist historians who come to communication from other fields by providing reference material and assistance on problems specific to communication history. Communication researchers who are not historians also will find much to contemplate as they attempt to expand their knowledge of methods that can be used fruitfully in their own studies.

Historical research in communication, which began in the early 1800s, is the oldest form of research in the field, but it also is the most modern. Other methods of research from the social and behavioral sciences appeared in the first half of the twentieth century and became popular in communication studies in the second half. At first, researchers greeted them confidently as the ways to answer all questions. But as researchers matured and the methods lost their newness, scholars began to subject the methods to more critical scrutiny. The methods lost some of their sheen, but the scrutiny also refined them. Researchers are now more aware of the limitations of behavioral and social science methods, and they recognize that much refinement still is needed. Historical methods, being as old as they are, for generations have been subjected to similar scrutiny and refinement. But they, unlike methods in the social and behavioral sciences, are long past their infancy, and historians through long practice have tested them. Those that were usable, they refined. The useless, they discarded. The result is that historical research now is based on an assorted but cohesive set of tested and

Chapter 1: The Nature of History

> "Knowing media history is essential to understanding modern media practices and values. Our professional forebears took risks, made mistakes, and promoted innovation. It is the media historian's privilege to study and share their contributions." — Butler Cain, University of North Alabama

proven methods. While mature compared with many other methods, historical methods at the same time are forward-looking. Historians have not been oblivious to the methods that other researchers use and have readily adopted those refined, proven methods as they have shown themselves useful to the study of the past. Incorporating the most recent research devices, historical study therefore has remained at the forefront of contemporary methodology.

Historical research also possesses an intrinsic capacity, unlike other methods used in communication research, to study almost the total range of the human experience. It is not so esoteric as other fields of theoretical communication research. The methods of social and behavioral sciences cannot fully study the lives of humans, but historical research can incorporate most other communication research methods. Combining them with methods unique to the study of history, it is not as limited or as limiting as other communication research methods and therefore can come closest to helping us understand humankind in its full dimensions. History, therefore, is the most comprehensive form of study among the various fields of communication research, for it brings together the methods, findings, and insights of the others and shapes them into a coherent explanation of humankind.

The vast range of methods used in history, as well as the broad expanse of the fields it covers, forces one to realize that historical study is neither simple nor easy. It requires much from the historian, considerably more than is normally expected from other communication researchers. The rigor of method and amount of work necessary cannot be overstated. Foremost, historical study demands an absolute desire to find the truth. Commitment to a philosophy, an ideology, an ism, a theoretical framework must take a backseat. The notion of whether we can know the "truth" has come under fire from postmodernists and others in the last several decades, but in historical study a commitment to anything other than an honest desire to find the truth conflicts with the proper role of history.

Furthermore, history requires unsurpassed rigor. Historians must bring thoroughness and tirelessness to the effort of collecting and analyzing source material. The task may sometimes require hour upon hour of research to find the minutest detail. Historians also must have or must develop an acute thinking ability. Unlike communication researchers who use social and behavioral research methods, historians rarely have mathematical formulae and statistical systems on which to rely. In analyzing and evaluating research material, they must depend on their own mature judgment, critical mind, and incisive analytical ability. Yet they are not allowed the loose judgments that communication researchers in cultural and critical studies sometimes employ. They may not simplistically impose their values on the past. While harshly analytical, they must be judicious in their treatment of the material and the people whom they study. The search for historical truth requires that they deal openly and fairly with their subjects.

> "If you have ever wondered why someone did what they did or why something happened when or how it did, then you are already an historian." — Lisa Parcell, co-editor, *American Journalism: History, Principles, Practices*

Finally, historians must have a power of imagination. The cold facts of history alone are nothing more than cold facts. They remain dead unless subjected to the thoughtful, imaginative mind of the historian who can perceive relationships among the materials and meaning in them. It is the duty of the historian to breathe life into them. Piling data upon data is not enough. As the historian Page Smith, winner of the Bancroft prize for his biography *John Adams*, commented in regard to researchers who amass research but never bring life to it, "Research is too often a substitute for thought, for bold speculation, for enlightening generalization."[1]

In summary, historical research cannot be based on vague, haphazard, lackadaisical method. It must be founded on rigorous, proven methodological procedures and an incisive mind.

History as a Form of Knowledge

Everyone thinks about the past. The habit is a human indulgence. In fact, the reasons an individual contemplates the past are endless. To some, interest in history is a matter of genealogical curiosity about their own family; to others, a matter of civic pride or patriotism. For yet others, it is a matter of interest stimulated in a person or aspect of the past by film, fiction, or some experience of life. Perhaps those courses in history, taken by choice or by compulsion in school, can claim some credit for stimulating a historical interest. Let us hope at least that they did not dull interest, for history is a natural form of thought for modern humans. As such, it can be a burden or an inspiration, a curse or a blessing, a cause of confusion or a source of confidence. History lends itself to both use and abuse. The past is also the object of attention for those men and women who call themselves historians, people who devote their professional lives to a serious study of its many facets. These scholars believe their labor is as important as truth and hope

---

[1]Page Smith, *The Historian and History* (New York: Alfred A. Knopf, 1964), 145.

Chapter 1: The Nature of History

> "Without a look at the past, we have no vision for the future. History tells us not only where we have been, but also where we need to go." — Bernell Tripp, author, *Origins of the Black Press*

that it will set a standard for others in their treatment of historical knowledge.

Modern historical consciousness began with the Renaissance, but the origins of history can be traced back much further. It can be argued that written history in the West originated among the Sumerians in the third millennium B.C. But the historical thought they recorded in their *King Lists* and other documents bore little resemblance to modern historical thought. It was devoid of rational evaluation and was little concerned about how things changed over time. The historical events they recorded simply appeared ready-made, the work of powerful gods. It remained for the Hebrews first to think of historical time as linear rather than cyclical (that is, as moving from beginning to end rather than as repeating itself, as the ancient Greeks perceived it). Still, we normally credit the Greeks, despite their cyclical concept, with inventing the study of history. In a sense, historians today still work under the timeless shadow of Herodotus and Thucydides, those two Greek writers who gave birth to history as a literary form. It has survived as a subject of commanding importance to this day, although it had to endure inhospitable medieval centuries before emerging in its modern form.

What do these two founders have to do with the study of communication history today? The answer is: quite a bit. Herodotus, "the Father of History," opened *The Persian Wars* by explaining that he was publishing his "researches ... in the hope of ... preserving from decay the remembrance of what men have done...."[2] Few historians have written better or told a better story or conveyed more of a sense of humanity than he. Curious about the Persians as well as the Greeks, Herodotus conducted a careful inquiry into the people and cultures involved in the famous war of which he wrote. Although he intended his history to be humanistic rather than mythical or theistic, his interest in cultures led him to include myths and tales when he believed them to be part of the whole epic he was describing. His subject, however, was the deeds of humans. Thucydides, on the other hand, seems more modern. He turned to documented records for his classic study *The Peloponnesian War*. As he tells us early in that masterpiece, he measured the accuracy of his evidence against the "most severe and detailed

---

[2]Herodotus, *The Persian Wars,* trans. George Rawlinson (New York: Random House, The Modern Library, 1942), 3.

tests possible."³ Both Herodotus and Thucydides sought to produce an account of a singular event worthy, they thought, of contemplation then and in the future.

These two ancient historians provide many clues regarding the nature of history. From its inception in their hands, history has been a record-based account of the human past. It is a form of inquiry that asks questions about the actions of people and elicits answers based on evidence. In that process there is a story to be told and truth to be found.

Most of all, Herodotus and Thucydides alert us to the fact that when historians deal with the study of the past, they assume that it

> "I used to think the world of fiction owned the methodology of time travel. Now, it never fails to mystify me how the reading of a newspaper story from a distant era packs the power, energy and, yes, magic to transport a scholar into the thoughts that shaped those words, and even among the people for whom those words were written." — Leonard Teel, author, The Public Press, 1900-1945

possesses certain characteristics. What are these characteristics? That short question can produce a long answer. Nevertheless, it is possible to offer a brief response to it by suggesting that historical study contains at least three elements: (a) evidence, (b) interpretation, and (c) narrative. Let us consider each for a moment.

First, take the matter of *evidence*. Since the time of Herodotus, evidence has been the basis for history. Without it one does not have history. A major portion of the historian's effort must be devoted to proper use of evidence. When modern historians speak of evidence they have a certain kind of evidence in mind. This evidence is collectively called "the record." Thus history can be described first as a fact-based account of what real people in the past did or failed to do. It is restricted to the study of the human past and accordingly is viewed as an investigation apart from the natural past, the geological past, the mythological past, the theistic past, or the prehistoric past. Furthermore, the evidence historians use is that which has been screened and tested to assure as much accuracy as possible.

Regarding the matter of *interpretation*, references to history as the reconstruction of the past actually refer to reconstruction as an interpretive act. When historians reconstruct something from the past, think of the material that is never available for the process. How much of the past has been lost forever? How little we know even about great events, figures, and movements that occurred in

³Thucydides, *The Peloponnesian War*, trans. R. Crawley (New York: Random House, The Modern Library, 1934), 14.

Chapter 1: The Nature of History

times past! Ask yourself: How much do we actually know about many of the famous publicists of the last few centuries, and how much of that does the record prove beyond doubt? Complete sources providing answers to all one might wish to know about some past figure or event are seldom, if ever, available. Sometimes governments, institutions, or individuals place restrictions on records. In other instances, the desired record may never have been made in the first place. Consequently, historians cannot find all the information they might wish to know about human motive and opinion and many other things. Records may have been too bulky or too expensive to keep. Sometimes historical records have been lost or destroyed. Communication historians encounter this problem frequently.

The problem of incomplete records hinders probes even into the recent past. Take the case of broadcasting, one of the most significant developments in communication history. As historian Michele Hilmes remarks of early radio, "much of what was actually broadcast — the sounds and stories actually experienced by listeners — went out live, unrecorded, and with little record keeping. Many — the vast majority — of broadcast hours are lost forever."[4] In his book *So It Was True: The American Protestant Press and the Nazi Persecution of the Jews*, a study for which one might suppose a full record of print materials would exist, Robert W. Ross similarly laments that this was not the case. "All of the periodicals were not available for all of the years between 1933 and 1945," he explains. "Some published in 1933 became victims of the Great Depression and either went out of business or merged with other existing periodicals."[5] On the other hand, think of the amount of published material that he had to distill in order to write that book. The goal of historians should be to compile as full a record as possible. They should not assume, for example, that the fact that periodicals went out of business means they are lost from the historical record. Files may still exist somewhere. Yet, the point we can gain from Hilmes and Ross is that even the recent past is not fully documented.

Although the historical record is incomplete, consider the vastness of the total past that remains in the record that is left, collected, and passed from generation to generation. One cannot know it all equally. Nor can one make it all a part of historical explanation. Historians select information from the record to include in their studies. Communication historians, because of the extent of

---

[4]Michele Hilmes, *Radio Voices: American Broadcasting, 1922-1952* (Minneapolis: University of Minnesota Press, 1997), xvi.
[5]Robert W. Ross, *So It Was True: The American Protestant Press and the Nazi Persecution of the Jews* (Minneapolis: University of Minnesota Press, 1980), 305.

records they use, face problems of selection all the time. Consequently, one only has to reflect upon how historians make conscious decisions about the use of evidence to understand that problems of its availability and selectivity guarantee the interpretive nature of their inquiries.

Anyone who has tried to write a serious account of some past occurrence can appreciate the interpretive nature of history. The writing of history involves constant decisions about finding meaning in the record of the past and explaining that significant part of the total available record to an audience. All "facts" of history found in the record have explanations attached to them. Take President Woodrow Wilson's first presidential press conference as an example. He held it on March 15, 1913, just eleven days after his inauguration. The simple fact of that conference tells us little. Historians ask and answer a number of questions about such facts before employing them as part of their explanations. In this case they might ask: How and why did this meeting originate? Was it intended to serve the interest of the president, the press, or the public? What did it accomplish? Was it a success or failure? How does it fit into larger historical themes such as the nature of the relationship between the presidents, or the presidency, and the media? As one observes historians such as James E. Pollard and George Juergens address these questions in their studies, it becomes clear that the simple "facts" of history, in this case that of the first regularly instituted presidential press conference, do not stand alone. They are loaded with explanation.

Thus fact and interpretation, however scrupulous and honest the historian may be in the search for the truth, go together. The early twentieth-century British journalist C. P. Scott used to say, "Comment is free, but facts are sacred."[6] Whether or not one agrees with Scott's statement, it cannot be applied to history. Comment should not come easy. Historical interpretations must arise from facts, for history is a study in which fact and opinion are bound together in more ways than one might suppose. Historians select the evidence as they assemble it into their accounts and finally offer a general explanation by way of shaping an overall understanding of the subject.

Finally there is the element of *narrative* to consider. By speaking of the narrative element in history, we are not referring to those majestic narrative histories produced by nineteenth-century historians but rather to the narrative element that is bound up in the writing of history. Since the time of Herodotus, the element of "story" and its telling have been an integral part of history. They re-

---

[6]Quoted in Sir Linton Andrews and H. A. Taylor, *Lords and Laborers of the Press: Men Who Fashioned the Modern British Newspaper* (Carbondale: Southern Illinois University Press, 1970), 13.

Chapter 1: The Nature of History

main central to historical writing today and help to give history a distinguishable form. The influential twentieth-century historian G. R. Elton once explained, "... if it cannot be told as a story it can no longer be called history.... The story may be short or long, simple or complex, but the element of story has to be there if what he [the historian] is producing is to be history."[7]

History Among the Disciplines

These characteristics will be covered at greater length later. But even this brief introduction suggests that history is a distinctive study. Yet it shares a common body of information with other subjects, and college courses in history are found in various other academic departments. To make matters even more confusing, a number of courses other than history contain a historical component. The problem stems from perceptions of how knowledge should be divided and from considerations regarding curricular design and structure. Before undertaking serious historical inquiry, students of communication history should understand the reasons for the varied placement of history in a university curriculum as well as the qualities that characterize historical study. So, let's review a few fundamental considerations.

Most American colleges base their curriculum on areas of knowledge known as *disciplines*. Each has its own type of information and regimen of inquiry. For example, history and geography are disciplines. The various disciplines are accommodated by departments for purposes of teaching, research, and administration. Beyond that, disciplines are grouped together into larger subject fields or divisions. These aggregate subject fields normally are designated the arts, the biological sciences, the humanities, the physical sciences, the social sciences, and the professional programs. There is usually a methodological similarity among the disciplines in each division, but that is not always the case. Some disciplines pose no difficulties regarding where they fit into the larger aggregate groups. Political science, for instance, readily can be designated a social science. History, however, defies such clear classification, as does communication. For example, the Department of History at the University of California, Irvine, is in the School of Humanities rather than the School of Social Sciences. At the nearby University of California, Los Angeles, the Department of History is in the Social Sciences Division rather than the Humanities Division.

The difficulty regarding the placement of history is twofold. First, it involves

[7]G. R. Elton, *Political History: Principles and Practice* (New York: Basic Books, 1970), 176.

not only those courses traditionally classified as "history" but also various types of other courses that are difficult to place because of problems of staff, program continuity, and sometimes competition between departments. Communication history exemplifies these difficulties. The first part of the problems deals with the proper classification of history itself. Does it belong among the humanities or the social sciences? Second, should a course in communication history be taught in a history or a communication department, and how should it be taught? The answer to the first part of that question is simple. It can be placed in either department. It might even be cross-listed as a course for which one may receive credit in either department.

FIELD	DISCIPLINE
Arts	Creative writing
	Dance performance
Biological Sciences	Microbiology
	Physiology
Humanities	Literature
	Philosophy
Physical Sciences	Astronomy
	Geology
Social Sciences	Political science
	Sociology
Professional Programs	Business administration
	Advertising
	Journalism
	Public relations

The important thing is not where it resides as a course but how it is perceived and taught. If it is called history, one might reason, then it should be taught as history. Remember, scholars other than historians deal with the past, but only historians deal with the past as history. For instance, political scientists studying presidential elections might extend their investigations to past presidential elections, a topic that interests historians, too. When studying such material, political scientists proceed in their own way. They use their own methods, and their work is judged by the accepted standards of political science. Their work is significant and stands on its own merits as political science. It is not history, nor is it judged as history. So it is with the field of communication. Many aspects of the work of scholars in that field lead them to make probes into the past. Valuable as that work may be, one should realize that it is not history if it fails to manifest the distinguishing characteristics of history. If it doesn't, then another name should be found for it, for names convey substantive meaning.

There are other considerations that underscore the need to classify communication history as part of history. Its subject content is so integrated into the

Chapter 1: The Nature of History

context of society that it is impossible to isolate one from the other. Indeed, communication history engages the larger history of the past at so many points that it would appear artificial to classify it as anything other than history. In the first volume of *The Information Process*, Robert W. Desmond claimed that "the history of the press itself is a part of the social history of mankind in his search for information and understanding." Desmond's purpose in compiling his comprehensive survey of world news was to "repair ... [an] omission in the social history of man, and to establish its relation to political history."[8] His purpose was as suggestive as it was laudatory, for the story of how people have communicated by the various vehicles of mass media throughout time cannot be removed from history without damaging its integrity. But for communication history to reach its potential as history, it should have the hallmarks of history.

Before proceeding further, several qualifications should be made about whatever designation we choose for a subject such as communication history. First, to some extent any distinction is artificial. Sometimes it is simply the result of the academic curriculum design. Subjects have to fit somewhere, and compromises are made in the process. Second, since all of the humanities and social sciences are worthy studies and all frequently borrow from and contribute to the others, it little behooves practitioners of one field to indulge in scoffing and derogatory comments about areas of study other than their own. Human nature being what it is, such comments are common enough, but they only impair the effort to understand a particular discipline. In a sense, every major discipline exists in close association with others as auxiliary fields. These qualifications should be kept in mind as one attempts to distinguish between the various disciplines.

Now let us return to the matter of the positioning of history. Should it be considered as part of the humanities? It can be if the term *humanities* is broadly defined. If it is used in reference to the study of humankind in its many dimensions, then history qualifies as a humanities. Moreover, since history contains a definite artistic element and deals with some of the great statements of people's achievements, it can always qualify on those grounds as one of the humanities. But if the definition of humanities is narrowed to mean only an organized study of great achievements in literature, philosophy, and perhaps the fine arts, then history fits less well. Although the works of historians such as Herodotus, Thomas Babington Macaulay, and Francis Parkman are great literary achievements, the study of history usually encompasses more than a consideration of only such

---

[8]Robert W. Desmond, *The Information Process: World News Reporting To the Twentieth Century* (Iowa City: University of Iowa Press, 1978), xii.

masterpieces. It pushes out into a vast area of people's actions in social, economic, cultural, and political realms. It is the nature of, the conventions of, historical probes into the world of the past that defines history's place among the humanities. In fact, the assistant director for research and publications of the American Historical Association, the largest history organization in this country, has recommended that history be placed among the humanities. "Including history in the social sciences," he argued, "no longer accords with our self-understanding as a discipline." In support of that position, he pointed out that "with few exceptions, the search for 'laws' and principles in human history is over, a point perhaps emphasized by the fact that quantitative history is increasingly rare and often relegated to the footnotes."[9] Thus, historians today generally consider the relationship between history and what might be called the pure humanities close and compatible.

Is there a similar compatible relationship between history and the social sciences (more recently the behavioral sciences)? They share a number of common interests. Both historians and social scientists study things in the past. They both deal with analysis, explanation, and generalization. Both employ research methods in their work, aim for precision, and are concerned with the verification of conclusions reached. To be sure, they tend to go about these tasks in different ways, and the tasks themselves do not necessarily mean the same thing to the one group as to the other. By methodology, for instance, a historian usually has something quite different in mind than a social scientist has. To make matters more confusing, many communication historians studied social and behavioral sciences in graduate school and remain influenced by those fields. Furthermore, some historians think of themselves as social scientists, particularly, but by no means exclusively, those interested in social history. On the other hand, many social scientists think of themselves as behavioralists, whereas most historians do not. Social scientists, however, do not compose a monolithic group. Some of their scholarly interests are more traditional than they are behavioralist. The various disciplines of the social sciences continue to define and redefine themselves. So does history.

What then are the differences? In answering that question, keep in mind the variety of interests found among social scientists and the diversity of the definitions of their individual disciplines. It is, consequently, only fair to speak of tendencies in much of their work and how they differ from those found among his-

[9]Robert B. Townsend, "Assessment of Research Doctorate Programs: Testimony delivered to NRC [National Research Council] Committee," *Perspectives: The Newsmagazine of the American Historical Association*, September 2002, 18.

torians — who are by no means of one mind regarding the nature of history. Social scientists, for instance, tend to think of themselves as scientists. The tendency is most pronounced among behavioralists.

Do historians think of history as a science? The question is, of course, an old one that carries us back to nineteenth-century debates about the nature of history. It is correct enough to think of history as a science if *science* is loosely construed to mean a rational investigation in which generalizations will be advanced based on evidence and if it is thought of as a study that is concerned with establishing truth.

History and science, however, differ in significant ways. Scientists can experiment in the laboratory and subject the experiment to a type of verification impossible for historians to use. Scientists seek laws. Historians hope to generalize, and their generalizations are usually qualified. The scientist can measure, but measurement is not always within the province of the historian. Can the historian measure the impact that a war, a revolution, or an idea made upon the mind of someone or some group of people who lived in times past? The scientist deals with prediction, but history is not predictive in nature. Historians do not claim that their study of the past allows them to predict the future. They study what people have done, thus helping one to understand what people can do, but they do not predict what people will do. Scientists claim to observe data objectively. Historians are objective, too, but they are also frequently subjective. Historians become involved in the past as they endeavor to understand the mood of a time or the nature of someone's personality or many other intangibles of the past. The material of history, concerned about things such as cultural forces, social contexts, and human beings of the past, is simply different from that of science. It yields a different type of understanding than that which the scientist seeks. So historians differ from scientists — and also from social scientists to the degree that the latter think of themselves as scientists.

In fact, differences between social scientists and historians are numerous. Consider the following statement that the political scientist David Easton made in explaining the study of political behavior. "There are," he contended, "discoverable uniformities in political behavior. These can be expressed in generalizations or theories with explanatory and predictive value."[10] Such a study of political behavior, indeed, would be scientific, but it would have little to do with a historical inquiry. Easton, of course, did not speak for all political scientists, just as the present writers do not express the opinion of all historians. But the thrust

---

[10]David Easton, *A Framework for Political Analysis* (Englewood Cliffs, N. J.: Prentice Hall, Inc., 1965), 7.

of his comment does underscore a definite difference that exists. There are others. The aim of history is the desire to understand complexity, contingency, and human agency more than it is to develop generalizable theories of human behavior. As contrasted to historians, social scientists tend to be more interested in constructing models, in quantification, in factor analysis, in establishing regularities they perceive present in their data, in linking together theory and research, and, when discussing the past, in using it to substantiate theories of social concepts.

Historians, on the other hand, study particular things in the past. More than social scientists, they place great stress on original sources and on narrative in their accounts; and unlike social scientists, they accept intuitive insight as a viable element in their inquiry. More than social scientists, they try to position themselves at some point in the past and to grasp how something or someone appeared from that perspective. Perhaps most of all, the understanding they seek differs from that which social scientists seek. As the historian John Lukacs points out, history is about human understanding, and that "is a matter of quality, not quantity.... The purpose of [human] understanding differs from the scientific purpose of certainty, and of accuracy.... Human understanding of other human beings is always, and necessarily, imperfect."[11] Yet, acquisition of knowledge about real people who once lived and engaged life lies at the core of the purpose of history.

Any consideration of how history relates to the humanities and social sciences and where it should be positioned is useful. It helps to sharpen one's understanding of the nature of history and helps to define what history can and cannot do. The novice tackling a serious historical investigation for the first time would be well advised to read a few of the better known statements on the subject by historians.[12] History is sometimes perceived in part as one of the humanities and in part as one of the social sciences since it contains elements of both art and science.

But is such a hybrid definition correct? Both science and art were known

---

[11]John Lukacs, *At the End of an Age* (New Haven, Conn.: Yale University Press, 2002), 55.

[12]Among the better books on the subject are the following: Joyce Appleby, Lynn Hunt, and Margaret Jacob, *Telling the Truth About History* (New York: W. W. Norton, 1994); Edward Hallett Carr and Richard J. Evans, *What Is History?* 2nd ed. (Basingstoke, U.K.: Palgrave, 2017); G. R. Elton, *The Practice of History* (New York: Thomas Y. Crowell Company, 1967); Eric Hobsbawn, *On History* (New York: The New Press, 1997); H. Stuart Hughes, *History As Art and As Science* (New York: Harper and Row, Publishers, 1964); and Arthur Marwick, *The Nature of History*, 3rd ed. (Basingstoke, U.K.: Palgrave, 2000).

when Herodotus and Thucydides wrote. Yet they thought of their investigations as unique studies. As we have previously seen, history has a number of distinguishing characteristics. They are all clues to its separate identity. The renowned English historian R. G. Collingwood once observed that the "prime duty of the historian" is found in "a willingness to bestow infinite pains on discovering what actually happened."[13] The object of that discovery is some particular thing of the past. History, it should be remembered, is the study of human deeds. It is about real human beings who lived in the past, their lives and sayings, successes and accomplishments, and their sufferings and failures. It is also about particular events and movements and the change that occurs within them. Since no other study of human experience has these hallmarks, one is led to conclude that historical study can be distinguished from all other fields of investigation. It can be understood as an autonomous approach to the past.

However scholars view the various disciplines, one must be careful not to adopt a perspective that is artificially limited. The restrictive view adopted in the mid-twentieth century among some communication scholars and in graduate communication training, that the research methods of social and behavioral sciences are the only truly legitimate ones for the study of communication questions, endangers inquiry. All research methods have some value, and only the scholar of narrow perspective would argue that only his or her method is correct in all cases. Indeed, some communication scholars firmly grounded in current social and behavioral science methods ignore the fact that their preferred methods can address only a limited range of topics and suffer their own weaknesses. Communication researchers, including historians, must be familiar with all methods that can help shed light on problems and answer questions.

A variety of methods are used in communication research, but the historical method has a number of advantages. First, unlike specific social and behavioral science methods, it can be used to study a wide range of problems covering many aspects of the human condition. Second, while social and behavioral science methods generally are limited to an examination of situations that presently exist, the historical method provides the only adequate way to study topics from the past. Third, while social and behavioral sciences tend to view the human mind as being mechanistic, the historical method assumes a freedom of thinking apart from the behavioral or biological mechanics of the brain to account for the diversity of human thought and action. Fourth, the historical method, while not mechanistic, is more systematic than methods found in ideological areas such as

[13]R. G. Collingwood, *The Idea of History* (London: Clarendon Press, 1946; reprinted, London: Oxford University Press, 1956), 55.

cultural and critical studies. Fifth, the historical method can and should make use of all other methods when they will help study the problem at hand, including the techniques used in behavioral and social sciences.

But the fact that the historical method is so versatile should not mislead historians into thinking it is easier to master than are other methods. If anything, the opposite is true. The historical method requires more rigorous thinking than any other. While the communication researcher working, for example, with opinion surveys may use established methods to draw a random sample or to determine margins of error, the historian frequently must make sound judgments without such formalized mathematical equations. Historical research, therefore, requires the development of a critical mind that must be able to evaluate a wide range of material, subject it to intense scrutiny without the aid of formulae, and arrive at thoughtful conclusions.

The Purpose of History

Without exaggeration, one can say that people have found purpose in history since the Greeks invented it. For the Romans it was an inspiration for their imperial confidence and vision. Medieval monks and scholars produced various works that kept alive Western civilization tradition. And, even if they bent it to their own purposes, who can doubt that it offered the society of their day a historical vision? Following the Middle Ages, history grew in prominence as a form of knowledge until the nineteenth century, when it entered its golden age. Whether written as a national epic, biography, science, or a revelation of historical destiny, its purpose was not questioned. It was central to the age. Never before or since has it enjoyed such prominence. The literature of that century is crowded with the great works written by historians across the Western world.

Today, people continue to pursue history as a subject worthy of serious investigation. They do so for different reasons. In the United States, for instance, early twentieth-century Progressive historians used history to undergird their ideas of enlightened democracy that were so important to their hopes of reforming contemporary society. More recently, "new left" historians attempted to radicalize history and make it an instrument of social revolution. The Marxist historian Herbert Aptheker claims that history must serve the needs either of the oppressed or the oppressors. To that comment, the well-known Lincoln scholar Richard Current responded: "Though that may be good Marxism, it may also represent the fallacy of the excluded middle. Surely there are historians who try, not wholly in vain, to write and teach for the sake of neither oppressors nor op-

Chapter 1: The Nature of History

> "Students unfamiliar with history sometimes roll their eyes at the mention of it, believing it's a task of memorizing names and dates. This is not only an unfortunate idea, but a wrong one — analogous, I think, to saying the pyramids of Egypt are simply rocks in the desert."
> — Greg Borchard, author, *Abraham Lincoln and Horace Greeley*

pressed but for the sake of historical truth."[14] He provides an important clue with that comment, for most American historians are neither new leftist nor Marxist nor devotees of any special school of history. Most simply pursue their studies hoping to produce a significant, convincing, honest, authentic, and engaging account.

If in the last hundred years, with many new competitors in the field, history has failed to retain its nineteenth-century position, it surely has held its vitality. It remains today a major form of knowledge pursued both as a popular and professional study. It continues, moreover, to enjoy a flourishing existence in schools and colleges and constitutes a significant genre of writing.

Yet, it is still possible and profitable to inquire into history's purpose. Like all subjects and forms of investigation, history has its detractors as well as its supporters. Moreover, in a culture such as ours in which present-mindedness, practicality, vocationalism, and materialism are so pronounced, the questions sometimes raised about the value of historical study fail to surprise us. Such questions find their logical answers in an understanding of the purpose of historical study.

What is it, then, that historians hope to do when they make their inquiries into the past? The first part of the answer to that question is simple. They hope to explain particular things of the past with fullness and truth. They hope to capture and relate the thought and feeling of a time past as they are associated with the problem under consideration. The meaning sought cannot be imposed from without. Such study, therefore, can subordinate itself neither to political or social ideology, nor to religious or anti-religious passion, nor to deterministic theories, nor to the social scientist's "models," and still be history. History investigates things that have happened and seeks to comprehend them in their fullness of meaning. In that manner it hopes to be informative about human behavior, about how people have related to one another, and about how they have interacted with the conditions of their time.

Indeed, it is possible to perceive a number of purposes in a study of particular things of the past pursued from the inside out. Within the context of the

[14]Richard N. Current, "Fiction as History: A Review Essay," *The Journal of Southern History* 52 (February 1986): 87.

problem under investigation, it affords the opportunity to be informed about the nature of humankind and historical truth. The purpose of history is neither to justify an action of the past nor to offer facile judgments about it nor to suggest careless analogies between past and present. It is rather to provide reasonable explanations for the complexity of evidence for some part of the past. As such, its purpose involves the painstaking willingness to search for the truth of a past situation and, by doing so, to set a standard of excellence for conducting an inquiry.

> "Thinking of history not only as names, dates, demographics, records and documents — the hard facts — but also as the consciousness of the people at a given time gives our research much more significance as we help provide understanding of the past and present and possibly the future." — Kenneth Campbell, University of South Carolina

By their separate inquiries, historians contribute to the authentic record of human experience. But is that record worth the effort? What use does it have for society? Consider the proposition that history has purpose from a slightly different angle than that found in the previous discussion. Most historians believe that their discipline provides information important for identity and background. It helps us to know ourselves both individually and collectively, and it provides knowledge valuable in helping us to understand the world as we find it.

By way of example, consider a few events much studied by historians. The revolution that began on the battlefield in 1775 gave birth to our American republic. No one expects it to experience another revolution of that sort. Since it probably will not recur, should it be studied? Can Americans living more than two centuries after the event be informed about themselves as a nation by studying this event? Or, consider the Nazi movement that surfaced in the 1930s to disrupt Western society and to occasion one of history's bloodiest wars. No one expects a Nazi revolution to happen again in Germany or elsewhere, though it is always possible that it might. Should that terrible historical event be studied? Everyone hopes for international peace. Is there any profit to derive from studying the causes of previous wars or the success and failure of peace settlements? They will never occur again in exactly the same way they did in the past. The creation of the modern state of Israel in 1948 set off a series of conflicts that continue to this day. Would knowledge of the relationship between Israel and its neighbors since the Hebrews settled in the region more than 3,000 years ago — not to mention knowledge of the why and how of the establishment of the modern Israeli state and Arab opposition to it — help one to understand the nature of that conflict today? Or, take the case of Britain, the first country to industrialize in the modern world. Can we benefit from a knowledge of what the results of that industrialization were and what policy measures were made in an effort to cope with the problems inherent in the new industrialized order? One could ask hundreds of questions of this type, and their answers surely suggest that history has a purpose for anyone who hopes to be a responsible and informed person, particularly in a democratic society.

The purpose of history involves the significance and particularity of the object studied. Its significance is suggested by the historian's conviction that something selected from the past for study has an ongoing importance. Its particularity stems from the idea that history investigates things in context and things about particular problems, people, places, and times.

Scholars involve themselves in historical investigation for many reasons. Some seek to close gaps in some important segment of the existing historical record. Others may aspire to advance a new idea. Whether the aim is to supplement or to supplant previous historical knowledge, they don't assume they will produce final answers. They know they will never learn all there is to know about their probes into the past. The object of the historian's quest is to provide an honest understanding of something in the past based on the best evidence available. The past, of course, is a vast domain. No one can know it all. Serious-minded specialists, moved by their own particular interests, select what amounts to slices of the past to study.

The great variety of history now becomes apparent. Some specialists choose to work within the framework of an established period limited by time and place. One might, for instance, be drawn to a study of nineteenth-century America or to twentieth-century Europe. Others are drawn to national history or to area studies, and yet others to special topics such as reform or industrialization. Biography attracts some; social groups, others. Some incline toward economic studies; others, toward political, diplomatic, cultural, religious, or military ones. There are viable historical dimensions to practically every major contemporary entity or institution, and they too attract the historian's attention. All historians pursue special interests of some sort.

History and Communication History

Communication history is one such specialized study. Nevertheless, the more one inquires into its nature, the more it can be understood as a part of the mainstream of history. In a sense, it is more general than communication research, which mostly deals with current problems and tends to employ the methodology of the social and behavioral sciences. Communication history can be broadly defined as part of history because its subject matter is integrated into the general currents of history and cannot, with integrity to its subject, be separated from it.

Communication history is a vast area of study that can accommodate numerous interests. For instance, within its scope fall a great variety of subjects related to the news media in the past. Communication historians are concerned with these media in terms of their content and audience and the various forms they have taken. They are interested also in the development, control, and effects of those media as well as with the people who have influenced their existence. The media's influence on opinion interests communication historians, as well as the influence that society has had on the media.

It is, in fact, difficult to place boundaries on communication history. Its study is an invitation to investigate not only the media in the past but also subjects such as literacy, technology, advertising, readership, publicity, propaganda, public opinion, and freedom of expression. Communication historians are interested also in opinion-policy relationships. Their studies, consequently, deal with many aspects of how people communicated and how communications interacted with society in the past.

Communication history pursues a certain dimension of the past. It examines something that happened in the past and cannot be understood if separated from the context in which it occurred. Historians interested in this variety of history must inform themselves about "historical time." They have to acquire a sense of the particular time in the past associated with their inquiry. They must acquire knowledge of the personalities, events, and forces that influenced not only the object of their investigation but also those that influenced the particular time in which it existed. Can one understand figures such as William Cobbett, William Lloyd Garrison, James Gordon Bennett, P. T. Barnum, Sarah Josepha Hale, Nellie Bly, Edward R. Murrow, or Frank Capra without knowledge of the times in which they lived? The more one appreciates the many dimensions of communication history and the way they connected to so many aspects of the past, the more it becomes clear that communication history has a place in the mainstream of social, economic, cultural, and political history.

Some scholars have recognized this claim for many years. A century ago, the American historian James Ford Rhodes wrote: "The story of the secession movement of November and December, 1860, cannot be told with correctness and life without frequent references to the *Charleston Mercury* and the *Charleston Courier*. The *Mercury* especially was an index of opinion and so vivid in its daily chronicle of events that the historian is able to put himself in the place of those ardent

Chapter 1: The Nature of History

> "Historical research is a combination of knowledge and experiences. Knowledge of the events tells you WHAT happened, while the life experiences of the people involved tell you WHY something happened." — *Bernell Tripp, author, Origins of the Black Press*

South Carolinians and understand their point of view."[15] How many other occurrences of the past can be vivified and given meaning by use of the media as records?

Let us consider just one additional example. It is perhaps the most famous case of its kind, and it demonstrates that to construct the historical record without including a place for the media would grossly distort the record. The case deals with the Spanish-American War. In explaining that war, historians place a special emphasis on the role newspaper sensationalism played in causing it. The newspaper war between Joseph Pulitzer and William Randolph Hearst, some reason, helped to cause war between Spain and the United States. Other interpretations of causation notwithstanding, this contention has some merit. To understand it, however, one needs to know a good deal about the nature of the press and the society at that time. Who and what forces were involved in the sensational press? Was "yellow journalism" a thing of the moment, or had it been long in coming? Our questions cannot be limited to the press alone, for the press exists in society. Accordingly, we must know something about the public of that time. Why was it so receptive to sensational journalism? Then, there is the factor of government to consider. Did the influence of the sensational press reach into the chambers of political power? If so, can that influence be documented? Once one has answered such questions, then alternate explanations for the cause of the war can be sought and studied in order to place the factor of the press in its proper perspective. To remove that factor from consideration, however, would damage the history of the event under investigation.

Historians are interested in communication history for many reasons. Just as the media today help the public to gain understanding of current issues, so the media of the past enlighten historians about past public problems. Today's media influence the public's perception of the present world. So it was with the media in the past. Media are a part of the past that cannot be removed from it. To some degree, they have always reflected public whim, taste, and opinion, and to some degree they have shaped public and individual perceptions and opinions about aspects of society too numerous to mention. Have they been a mirror of society, a source of entertainment, a branch of commerce, or a forum for news, opinion, and business? Obviously they have been all of these things, though the

[15]James Ford Rhodes, *Historical Essays* (New York: Macmillan, 1909), 70.

mix varies according to time, place, and circumstances. Mass media are essential elements in modern political life. What modern revolutionary movement has neglected them? Or, consider modern democracy. Its history is bound up with the media. In a democratic society, journalists have the responsibility to report and interpret news and to watch authority from the perspective of the governed. They exist as an irreplaceable unit in the public debate. Consider how important the media were to the revolutionary mentality that emerged at some point before the start of the American War for Independence. Think of the role the media played in every great issue (expansion, slavery, reform, isolation, entrance into wars, civil rights, etc.) that has permeated this country's history.

The record of the mass media, consequently, is one of the richest of historical sources, and it deserves the serious attention of historians. In order to study these media as parts of the past, historians must acquire a workable knowledge of their characteristics at a particular time in the past. How were they organized? What roles did they play, and why? Take the case of one medium, the newspaper. Historians need to know much about a newspaper to understand it as a historical source. Who produced it, and how and why? What type of influence did it have, and why? Was it known equally for all of its contents? Were there restraints placed upon its opinion, and did that opinion conform to some outside interest? There are, of course, many other questions that can be asked about a newspaper as a historical source or as an object of historical inquiry. Such a medium — and it is but one among those that attract the attention of communication historians — must receive the same scrutiny that historians devote to other historical sources and subjects.

Historians, however, are not the only group to have a special interest in communication history. Journalists and other mass media practitioners have a special interest in their professional predecessors. As the distinguished British journalist and writer Sir Linton Andrews contended, there is much for one to learn from the career and lives of key figures in journalism history, even those whose work falls within recent generations. It is important, he said, to know what made them journalists? What qualities made them excel? What did or do they see as the proper function of the press? Have they expanded its influence? Have they made it more powerful for ensuring the public good?" Once these questions can be answered, he explained, "the better equipped we shall be to face present challenges in the world of communication."[16] He might have added that one does not have to read far into the history of today's media to discover that many of its successful practitioners have themselves had a lively curiosity

---

[16]Andrews and Taylor, *Lords and Laborers of the Press*, xx.

about their own predecessors.

It stands to reason that communication professionals themselves should have a natural curiosity about the development of the field of which they are a part. As in any other craft or profession, it is valuable to have a knowledge of how things were done previously, to have an awareness of problems that once existed (and perhaps still exist) and how they were handled, to have a grasp of past successes and failures, and to have an understanding of how the forces of modernization such as technology have influenced its development. Principles and problems, potential and pitfall can all be underscored by such knowledge. At the very least, knowledge of what others have done before helps one to understand what it is possible to do.

The appeal of communication history is many sided and well deserved. Like any other division of historical study, its record goes back into time. In order to comprehend that record, in part or in full, one must also understand the historical setting with which it is associated. If the media have influenced society, they surely have been influenced by society. The interaction between media and society has to be one of the fundamentals of communication history.

There is, however, another fundamental to grasp. If communication history is to reach its potential and acquire the stature it deserves, it must reach the standards of excellence of any serious historical investigation. In ensuing chapters those standards will be discussed along with many practical matters. They all contribute to the construction of sound history. But first, let us consider how previous historians approached the subject of mass communication history.

INTERPRETATION IN HISTORY

History is more than the story of what happened in the past. It is not simply an account of certain events occurring on certain dates and of certain individuals doing certain things. Dates, names, and places provide the raw data for history. Any time, though, we advance beyond such basic details, we soon realize that history well researched and effectively told does more than provide chronologies and lists. If we attempt to determine, for example, whether a particular person or an event had an impact on American media or if we attempt to explain what that impact might have been or the extent of the impact or its value, we immediately find that history is no longer a simple statement of what happened. It has become an attempt to explain what happened.

In that task of explaining, however, historians have not always shared the same views. One historian might approach a subject from a starting viewpoint that varies either in small or large degree from that of another. Thus, in the two centuries that American historians have been writing about the history of communication in this country, they have given accounts that differ widely. One historian might condemn the party press for its partisanship, while another might praise it for its contributions to the American political system. One historian might rebuke the media for propaganda during World War II, while another might salute them for contributing to Allied victory. Such differences can frustrate students who wish to have the "true" history of communication, but they actually provide one of the most valuable features of historical study. Differing perspectives among historians result in pictures and explanations that are multi-dimensional rather than flat, multi-colored rather than monotone.

The most valuable historical writing is, in a sense, always interpretive. Every time a historian selects material or advances a generalization based on that material, interpretation occurs. Every time one attempts to explain causation or to probe into the nature of change, one interprets. Without interpretation, historical study remains superficial, with no probing beneath the surface of facts to determine why events occurred and why people acted as they did. With no attempt to determine why, historical study provides mere chronology.

Yet, interpretation should not be predetermined. Good historians do not set out with a theory and marshal facts to fit it. The best history is always a search for truth. As facts are gathered to find the truth, they may lead to a theory, but theory never should be used to determine facts. Interpretation arises instead from the gathered facts. Spurious historians ask how they might select and interpret facts to fit their theory. The result is, at best, didactic history. It offers little benefit except to those historians who have a particular view to propound. Historians should gather all the relevant facts and then ask what conclusions may be drawn from them.

> "Doing historical research is like fringing a shawl. You start by pulling a thread. Then you pull more threads until you've exhausted the possibilities. The creative work starts when you start tying all those threads together in a certain pattern to create, in the case of the shawl, a decorative edging. In the case of historical research and writing, you tie the threads together to create your interpretation of what all those individual threads mean when you put them together." — *Debra van Tuyll, author, The Southern Press in the Civil War*

It is the need for interpretation that accounts for the periodic rewriting of various episodes in history; but we still may ask why historians, if previous ones have done a good job, periodically reinterpret communication history. The answer is that differing interpretations arise for four primary reasons. The most important is that historians' attitudes are influenced by the conditions and beliefs of the times in which they write. Successive generations of historians tend to view the past in terms of the ideas of their own time — and it goes without saying that every generation believes that it knows more than the previous generation. As present views and perspectives on communication change, so also do our understanding and explanations of communication history, and we believe we have a more penetrating and accurate view than previous generations did and thus can offer better explanations. The existing conditions of mass communication — not to mention politics, social and economic conditions, and a multitude of other aspects of the surrounding culture — thus have helped determine the ways historians have looked at the past. In effect, the way in which they ex-

Chapter 2: Interpretation in History

plain history reflects, to some degree, the culture of their own times. Historians are not immune to those conditions that shape their own day.

At the same time, historians within the same generation bring to their study different beliefs and assumptions. Therefore, historians writing at the same time take the same body of material and come to differing conclusions about the past.

The third reason is that new material from the past is being discovered constantly. One would think that generations of study of the press in the American Revolution would have exhausted the resources, but then a historian turns up letters in a depository heretofore overlooked. Or a student of the penny press of the 1830s discovers copies of a newspaper long forgotten. Or another scholar examines radio program transcripts in a university archives never before seen by historians. Or, as so often happens, a historian thoroughly reads the files of a newspaper that others have taken for granted and provides a whole new insight into the paper and its era. The new information makes possible a fuller insight than has been possible before and sometimes provides a startling new explanation that turns on head long-held assumptions.

The fourth reason for new interpretations is the availability of new research tools for examining the past. A new generation of scholars may be trained in new techniques of inquiry. In the 1970s, for instance, many historians began to use quantitative methods in their studies and then computer technology as it became available. They borrowed both methods and theories from social scientists and, to some extent, from historians in other countries and applied them where feasible in their investigations. As a result, historians today have heightened awareness of methodological options of inquiry, and their studies reflect that diversity.

Thus, the idea that history is a static account of dead details from the past is made meaningless.

Based on their perspectives or interpretations, communication historians may be grouped into several schools. Awareness of these schools of history is essential. It helps historians to delineate the changing nature of earlier accounts of their subject, to grasp the reasons that explain that change, and to respond to the broad achievements of previous scholars. By understanding these schools, students not only may recognize why historians present such diverse explanations of the past, but they also may draw from the various schools those perspectives that seem best to explain history, apply them to one's own study, and thereby provide a fuller, deeper explanation in one's work.

Generally speaking, interpretation of mass communication history in the United States has gone through these broad stages: Nationalist, Romantic, Developmental, Progressive, Consensus, Neo-Conservative, and Cultural.[1] In recent years a growing number of historians have taken an activist stand on topics dealing with women and minorities, and they comprise a separate school. Others have adopted the views of the Cultural Studies approach to the study of contemporary communication. Although a handful of historians have written within Critical Theory, Marxist, and other schools, historians in the following schools have provided by far the most extensive work.

> **Major Schools of Interpretation**
> 1. Nationalist
> 2. Romantic
> 3. Developmental
> 4. Progressive
> 5. Consensus
> 6. Neo-Conservative
> 7. Cultural
> 8. Cultural Studies
> 9. Gender and Minority

The Nationalist School

Historians of the early nineteenth century, writing during an era in which pride in American progress and achievements was popular, took a nationalistic approach and explained the mass media, primarily newspapers, and journalists as influential and important patriotic organizations and figures who contributed to the progress of the nation and its institutions. These Nationalist historians looked on the history of America as the advancing revelation of the nation's leadership role in the world's improvement. To them, America was the nation chosen to lead in the fulfillment of humankind's destiny: greater and greater freedom and liberty.

Influenced by the ideas of the Enlightenment, with its emphasis on natural rights and progress and the people's role in determining their government, these historians displayed a particular interest in the subject of freedom of the press. Working within a framework of the unfolding advance of humankind and its social and governmental institutions, they attempted to place the progress of freedom of the press within an overall story of the developing liberty of Western civilization and of the American people in particular. Most Nationalist historians wrote about freedom of the press in terms of the political splits of early America, between colonists and British authorities and between Patriots and Tories. Their attention centered on the colonial and revolutionary periods, when Americans had struggled to free themselves from British rule, and they virtually ignored the early years of American independence. Fulfillment of human freedom, they believed (unlike many of today's historians), had been accomplished with the sep-

---

[1]For detailed accounts of the schools of interpretation, see Wm. David Sloan, *Perspectives on Mass Communication History* (Hillsdale, N.J.: Lawrence Erlbaum Associates, 1991).

aration from England. They pictured the sides in the conflict over freedom as those who advocated the natural rights of liberty and those who supported authoritarian government.

Isaiah Thomas, America's first journalism historian, expressed the Nationalist interpretation of the struggle in classic Enlightenment terms. He had been a leading Patriot printer during the Revolution. In *History of Printing in America*, published in 1810, he explained that "the rulers in the colonies of Virginia in the seventeenth century judged it best not to permit public schools, nor to allow the use of the press and thus, by keeping the people in ignorance, they thought to render them more obedient to the laws, and to prevent them from libelling the government, and to impede the growth of heresy, &c."[2] Like Thomas, most other Nationalist historians viewed the history of the press in terms of America's struggle for freedom and the advance of humankind against repressive British authority. They identified the great forces in that history as liberty and progress, with the new American nation serving as their cradle.

The Romantic School

Even as the Nationalist interpretation continued strong throughout the nineteenth century, in the 1830s the influence of Romanticism began to alter it. Romantic historians shared their predecessors' belief in the progress of humankind, in liberty as the ultimate goal of history, and in America's special role in leading the world to that goal. The press, they believed, was one of the institutions of primary importance in the advance of civilization, and they considered the United States as the high point in its development. But they added a new flavor to history. The Romantic movement in the arts — with its emphasis on vivid pictorial descriptions and narrative, its fascination with the past, and its accentuation of the role of great men in history — greatly influenced these historians. They thought of history as one of the literary arts, and they mainly wrote narrative biographies in a romantic style designed to appeal to large audiences. Most Romantic historians were men of leisure who had spare time to pursue historical study as an avocation, men of the professional classes, or journalists who had an inclination toward historical study. Frequently, they had known their subjects or had participated in the episodes about which they wrote. Personal reminiscences therefore often served as the basis for their histories. While the Romantic historians usually were amateurs, many attained a high degree of chronological

---

[2]Isaiah Thomas, *History of Printing in America* (Worcester, Mass., 1810; reprint ed., Barre, Mass.: Imprint Society 1970), 7.

accuracy and literary quality.

Primarily from New England and New York, Romantic historians took as their predominant subject printers and editors from those same regions and described them as men larger than life who imprinted their newspapers with their own characters. Since Romantic historians typically were gentlemen from socially and politically elite families, they especially favored printers and editors who respected established values and traditions. They frequently told the history of the press against the panorama of politics. Tending to be conservative, they reacted negatively to the shift away from the aristocrats' participation in government that had occurred with Thomas Jefferson's and Andrew Jackson's elections to the presidency. As a result, they tended to treat conservative printers and editors (Federalists and Whigs) favorably, while blaming Jeffersonian Republicans and Jacksonian Democrats for the exclusion of men of higher principles from public office and for their replacement by men who pandered to the desires of the mass public.

The Romantic interpretation was readily apparent in the work of Joseph T. Buckingham. A journalist who, among other achievements, founded the *Boston Courier*, a Whig newspaper, in 1824, he had worked with many of the journalists about whom he wrote and was intimately acquainted with many of the episodes. One of the earliest histories of the American press, his *Specimens of Newspaper Literature: With Personal Memoirs, Anecdotes, and Reminiscences,* published in 1850, combined narrative history with autobiography. Composed primarily of pleasant and anecdotal descriptive biographies, it emphasized journalists whom Buckingham had known and extracts from their papers, most of which were in New England.

Romantic historians' predilection for respectability was typified by another major work of the mid-nineteenth century, James Parton's *Life and Times of Benjamin Franklin*. Published in 1864, it provided one of the earliest biographies of an American journalist. Sometimes called the father of American biography, Parton drew a revealing contrast between Benjamin Franklin and his older brother, James. He especially praised Ben's competence as a businessman, editor, and owner of the *Pennsylvania Gazette* and lauded his success in making it the best newspaper in colonial America. His achievement was based on his talent and respectability. But for his brother James, Parton had few kind words, in contrast to most recent historians, who have praised James for his defense of freedom of the press against encroachments by the political and religious establishments. Parton was a critic of radical movements in American history and thus was not inclined to agree with James' attitudes and practices. He criticized James' *New-*

Chapter 2: Interpretation in History

England Courant for being the first American newspaper based on sensationalism and roundly condemned it for its sarcasm and ridicule of civil and religious authorities.

By the time Parton's biography appeared, however, a change was taking place in American journalism, and with it a change in historical interpretation.

The Developmental School

In 1833 Benjamin Day founded the *New York Sun*, America's first successful general-interest penny newspaper. It created a revolution in journalism, in attitudes about what the nature of newspapers should be, and in historians' views about communication history. From this changed perspective emerged what came to be the predominant, most pervasive, and longest-lived approach to communication history, the Developmental interpretation. Beginning with the publication in 1873 of Frederic Hudson's *Journalism in the United States, from 1690 to 1872*, the Developmental interpretation has provided the underlying assumptions of most histories of American mass media and continues today as a commonly held perspective.

It is based on the concept of the professional development of the press, viewing the history of journalism as the continuing improvement of journalistic practices and standards. While other interpretations have been strong at various times, the concept of the developmental progress of the media has been persistent since the last decades of the nineteenth century. In addition to working as an independent interpretation, it also has operated in combination with the other interpretations and frequently served as an underlying assumption of historians in the other schools. Thus, Nationalist historians, for example, thought of the development of the press as an aspect of the progress of humankind, while Progressive historians in the twentieth century evaluated the press as it developed as an instrument of reform. In its purest form, however, the Developmental interpretation has been based on the concept of the professional progress of the press. How the press became a journalistic instrument was the primary concern of Developmental historians. Like other historians, they tended to view the past in terms of the present, but they attempted to explain and evaluate history by its contributions to present journalistic standards.

Hudson's *Journalism in the United States* was the first survey history of American journalism written after the appearance of the penny press in the 1830s, and in its interpretive basis it provided the approach that most later historians used. Hudson had been managing editor of the *New York Herald*, the newspaper that more than any other emphasized news over opinion as the proper function of newspapers and that had been the most successful mass newspaper in American history. Assuming that such characteristics were the appropriate ones for newspapers, he tended to explain earlier journalism in terms of how it performed in accordance with the successful practices of the *Herald* and how those practices had developed in the past. His Developmental perspective can be made clear by an examination of his evaluation of the party press, which immediately preceded the penny press in American history.

With his news-oriented background, Hudson evaluated earlier newspapers in terms of how they conformed to the concept of a newspaper as a news medium and as a journal popular with the masses and independent of influence by political parties. He concluded that the party press, although important and influential in politics, was primarily partisan in nature, that it was vituperative, and that the partisan period was a negative one for journalistic development. The primary problem, he said, was that politicians controlled the press and prevented it from developing professional standards. Newspapers had been necessary to build a solid political foundation for the nation, but journalism "had not yet become a profession." The press "was a power with the people," but it ultimately failed because "it was managed by ambitious political chiefs, as armies are maneuvered by their generals." During the party period, Hudson admitted, the press had progressed in some areas, but "its views and opinions on public affairs were the inspiration of politicians and statesmen.... Editors ... were bound to party. Independence of opinion and expression, outside of party, was political and financial ruin." Despite such problems in journalism, Hudson could see with the historian's hindsight that the penny press would emerge soon, and thus he observed that "the world was moving, and its soul was marching on."[3]

As mass communication began to professionalize in the late 1800s, interest in its history began to grow. As a result, historical studies increased in number. Although differing on a few particulars, they largely echoed Hudson's themes. Most later historians came out of the mass communication professions, and beginning in the twentieth century many taught in professionally oriented college programs in journalism, broadcasting, and advertising. Because of their professional perspective, they considered the penny press, with its emphasis on news, mass appeal, and political autonomy, to have been the origin of the "modern journalism" of their own times. They believed the professional standards that had developed over time to be the appropriate and proper ones for the media,

---

[3]Frederic Hudson, *Journalism in the United States, from 1690-1872* (New York: Harper and Row, 1873), 142.

and they began to apply even more universally the concept of professional progress in the history of communication.

The Developmental interpretation had a pervasive impact on historical assumptions because most textbooks for college courses in communication history were cast in terms of the professional framework. With textbooks such as James Melvin Lee's *History of American Journalism*, published in 1917, and Willard Bleyer's *Main Currents in the History of American Journalism*, published a decade later (1927), the Developmental interpretation became entrenched in historical thinking. Studied by generations of students and future historians, they tended to reinforce the explanation that the history of American mass communication was the story of how the media evolved in their professional characteristics. Developmental historians focused often on determining the origins of media practices and on the individuals who had made contributions to media progress. Textbooks and other studies, being generally positive about the professions in mass communication, also exercised a major importance by providing a favorable view of the American media and reinforcing a pro-media outlook among communication students and professionals.

Although Bleyer's was the most widely used of the early textbooks,[4] it was superseded by Frank Luther Mott's *American Journalism*. Through its three editions (1941, 1950, and 1962) Mott's book provided the basis for the historical study by most journalism students for four decades. The foremost practitioner of the Developmental interpretation, Mott primarily concerned his study with documenting the progress of journalism and its practices. The concept of progress provided the thematic structure for his entire narrative, and he established it with his treatment of America's earliest newspapers. Viewing the past as the story of how journalism had reached its modern state, he titled his narrative of the colonial press "The Beginners, 1690-1765." The chapter illustrates the essence of the Developmental interpretation.

Mott detailed such topics as the earlier European patterns upon which American publications were based, pamphlets and other forerunners of the newspaper, and early episodes involving freedom of the press. Among the journalistic "firsts" he chronicled were the first American newspaper, Benjamin Harris' *Publick Occurrences Both Forreign and Domestick*; "the first continuous American newspaper," John Campbell's *Boston News-Letter*; and the appearance of entertainment and the first American newspaper crusade, both in James Franklin's *New-England Courant.* To these were added narratives of such items

---

[4]Bleyer's book, we should add, was not staunchly Developmental but instead mixed Developmental ideas with a mild Progressive interpretation.

as the "first American newspaper consolidation," the "first serial story in an American newspaper," the "first titled series in an American paper," the first illustration, and so on.

While Mott appreciated the fact that colonial newspapers operated under unsophisticated journalistic conditions, he tended to explain the early press in terms of later standards. Thus, he observed that the *Boston News-Letter*, because of its content and writing style, "seems very unexciting to a modern reader" and that Campbell's "theory of the presentation of foreign news [emphasizing a chronological historical record over recency] gave little consideration to timeliness." Methods of newsgathering, page appearance, the job of the editor, the absence of editorial pages, and other such aspects of the colonial press — Mott explained them all with an implicit comparison to later practices.[5]

In general, Mott evaluated the colonial press as relatively crude by the standards of his time but found satisfaction in the fact that it had provided a solid foundation for later journalistic practices and achievements. While he found much lacking in the toddler attitudes and performance of many early printer-editors, he believed some — such as James Franklin with his attempt to free the press from control by authorities, Benjamin Franklin with his several innovations, and the Bradford family of Pennsylvania with their high standards for printing and their sense of the role of the press — had recognized what journalism was supposed to be and had made contributions to the quality and development of the American press. He gave to subsequent chapters titles such as "The Dark Ages," referring to the party press, and "Sunrise," referring to the advent of popular penny papers. Mott's work provided the apex of the Developmental school, and most later historians labored in his long shadow. To a large extent, they provided elaboration or extension of his ideas. After World War II, several events contributed to the expansion of the professional concept of the news media as entities that ideally should be autonomous from outside authority and independent of the rest of society. Influenced much by the media's role in such episodes as the civil rights movement of the 1950s and 1960s, the Vietnam War, and the Watergate political scandal, Developmental historians — while retaining the concept of professional progress — sometimes viewed history as a clash between the media and established institutions such as government, religion, the military, and big business. Thus, whereas Progressive historians, for example, emphasized the media as a means of working within society to

---

[5]The quoted material is taken from Frank Luther Mott, *American Journalism: A History of Newspapers in the United States Through 150 Years: 1690 to 1940* (New York: Macmillan, 1941), 3-70.

achieve social and political change, Developmental historians tended to emphasize such historical trends as press freedom and media-government relations in which the media confronted other units of society. In their attitude toward nationalism, the newer Developmental historians differed markedly from their predecessors. Earlier historians had viewed nationalism positively and the media as contributors to it. Recent historians sometimes have seemed anti-nationalist. The devotion of the media, they believed, should be to journalistic ideals rather than to a nation. Thus, they showed considerable concern with such issues as the media's autonomy in the area of national security, press freedom during wartime, and the media as propaganda agents for governmental activities.

The Progressive School

Contrasting with the Developmental interpretation, a fourth school — that of Progressive history — emerged around 1910. In place of the Developmental school's professional progress explanation of history, Progressive historians substituted a concept of ideological conflict. The Progressive school grew, in part, out of a change that had taken place in the study of American history in the late 1800s. Professional historians began to replace the gentlemen historians and amateurs; and, under the impact of discoveries in the natural sciences, they began to think of the study of history as a science rather than as an art. While professional journalists continued to write many of the historical works, many communication historians in the early 1900s were educators from the emerging departments of journalism at various universities. Because American universities opened their doors to everyone, the new professional historians came from various levels of society. Representing various geographic regions, they began to shift some of the emphasis away from journalism in New York and New England to that in other sections of the country.

Influenced by the ideas of such Progressive American historians as Frederick Jackson Turner, Charles A. Beard, Claude Bowers, and Vernon L. Parrington, reform-oriented communication historians began to view the past as a struggle in which editors, publishers, and reporters were pitted on the side of freedom, liberty, civil reform, democracy, and equality against the powerful forces of wealth and class. Theirs was a black-and-white, conservative-vs.-liberal, bad-guy/good-guy dichotomy. They believed the primary purposes of the media were to crusade for liberal social and economic causes and to fight on the side of the masses of the common, working people against the entrenched interests in

American business and government. The fulfillment of the American ideal required a struggle against those individuals and groups that had blocked the achievement of a fully democratic system. Progressive historians often placed the conflict in economic terms, with the wealthy class attempting to control the media for its own use. Progressive historians, as earlier historians had done, viewed history as an evolutionary progression to better conditions. They thought in ideological terms, perceiving the media as an influential force in helping assure a better future. Sympathetic with the goals of the Progressive reformers of the early twentieth century, these historians wrote in such a way as to show the media as tools for social change, progress, and democracy. They explained the past in cycles of democratic and journalistic advance, which occurred when the media improved in serving the masses in America. They praised journalists and episodes that had contributed to greater democracy, while criticizing those favoring an elitist society and political system.

While Progressive historians reevaluated every major period in American communication history, works by three historians in the 1920s and 1930s epitomized their ideological approach and their use of history to change conditions of their own time. The first was Oswald Garrison Villard. Deploring what he considered to be crass materialism on the part of most of the American press, he argued that the best newspapers were those that led the fight for improved social conditions. In *Some Newspapers and Newspapermen*, published in 1923, he claimed that newspapers too often had deserted their leadership role in molding public opinion and instead appealed to public tastes in scandal, racial hatred, and social animosities — all because owners thought the best way to make money was to appeal to public passions. He described, for example, Adolph Ochs' *New York Times* as racist and a promoter of discriminatory separation between blacks and whites. In *The Disappearing Daily*, published in 1944 as a revision of his earlier book, Villard argued that fighting crusades was more important than providing news, and he scorned the trend toward pictures, features, and a generally soft approach to news. Believing that the role of the media was to keep a wary eye on the government in order to protect the public, he claimed that too few newspapers championed enough causes. The problem with American journalism, he concluded, was that newspapers treasured profit more than principle.

The second historian, George Seldes, in two major works in the 1930s, attacked wealthy owners' self-serving use of their newspapers. In *Freedom of the Press*, published in 1935, he argued that big business' control of the media was destroying press freedom. A pro-business oligarchy owned and manipulated the American press, he claimed, and its intent was to destroy the democratic foundation of the American political system. No section of journalism went untouched. Advertisers, public utilities, big business in general, and propagandists colored and suppressed the news and corrupted both the media and the public. The Associated Press, Seldes declared, always sided with authority, no matter how corrupt, while the *New York Times* spoke without exception for the conservative status quo, and William Randolph Hearst advocated privilege and possessed no social conscience. Seldes denounced the media for their opposition — despite the great need for social reforms — to the rights of organized labor, support of child labor for purely financial reasons, emphasis on scandal, invasion of privacy, interference with trial by jury, and critical treatment of the American Newspaper Guild (the reporters' labor union). He concluded that a majority of American newspapers published propaganda simply because to do so was profitable. Thus, it was impossible to have freedom of the press and unconcealed truth. Seldes followed his first work with *Lords of the Press* in 1938. Employing the same theme of the pernicious effect of wealthy moneymakers' ownership, he argued that the media typically were ultra-conservative and failed to ensure fair news treatment of labor or social and economic reforms.

One of the most trenchant Progressive attacks on the conservative media came from Harold L. Ickes, Secretary of the Interior under Franklin Roosevelt and director of the Public Works Administration. In the 1939 book *America's House of Lords*, a caustic criticism of publishers who opposed Roosevelt's New Deal, Ickes argued that the shortcomings of the press resulted from modern publishers being businessmen more interested in running their newspapers as business enterprises than journals of news. Publishers, he said, imparted to their papers an upper-class outlook and sought to make them profit-seeking businesses rather than public-spirited agencies concerned with social good. As a result, the emphasis on business endangered the free press that a democracy requires and led to a lack of fairness in newspaper pages, unreliability, suppression of information, and fabrication of news.

The Consensus School

While the Progressive interpretation greatly influenced the study of American history in the first half of the twentieth century, the fact that America faced major crises during that same period encouraged a diametrically opposing interpretation. With the nation confronting external threats from world war and domestic problems caused by the Great Depression, a number of historians presented a picture of America and its mass media that was characterized by basic agreement on fundamental principles. These Consensus historians reasoned that America's past was marked more by general agreement than by conflict and that Americans, rather than sundered by class differences, tended to be more united than divided. While Americans from time to time might disagree on certain issues, their disagreements took place within a larger framework of agreement on underlying principles — such as a belief in democracy, human freedom, and constitutional government — that overshadowed their differences. Generally, Consensus historians claimed that American history was not marked by extreme differences among groups. In their hands, the Progressives' villains such as industrialists, businessmen, and media owners were molded into important people who made constructive contributions to America, while Progressives' heroes such as reformers and the labor press were painted as less idealistic and more egocentric.

Forsaking the excessively critical attitude that had characterized much Progressive writing, Consensus historians tended to emphasize the achievements of the United States and its mass media, with the intent of showing a national unity among Americans. The Consensus outlook had a major impact on the interpretation of numerous aspects of communication history. It explained the American Revolution and the press' role in it, for example, as democratic rather than economic or social, as Progressive historians had argued. It viewed the media's role in America's entry into World Wars I and II in terms of the general agreement among Americans that involvement was necessary. Consensus historians viewed the media's performance during the wars positively, crediting the media and government for providing adequate information in a way that helped make possible the defeat of democracy's enemies. They praised many media owners, whom Progressives had castigated for their conservatism, as entrepreneurs who had made the American media system into the freest and most effective in the world. In these explanations as in others, Consensus historians generally approached communication history from the viewpoint that the media should work with the public and government to solve problems rather than create divisions by emphasizing problems and conflicts.

The foremost advocate of this interpretation was Bernard Bailyn. He expounded the argument first in his 1965 work *Pamphlets of the American Revolution, 1750-1776* and then elaborated it in *The Ideological Origins of the American Revolution*, the 1967 winner of both the Pulitzer Prize and the Bancroft Prize for history. Pamphlets provided the most important forum for the expression of opinion during the revolutionary period, according to Bailyn. They revealed that the American Revolution, rather than being a class struggle, as Progressive historians claimed, was above all else an ideological, constitutional, and political struggle. Colonial leaders feared that a sinister conspiracy had developed in England to deprive citizens of the British empire of their long-established liberties. This fear lay at the base of the ideas expressed in the pamphlets. Those ideas then became the determinants in the history of the revolutionary period by causing colonists to change their beliefs and attitudes. Colonial writers challenged British authority and argued that "a better world than had ever been known could be built where authority was distrusted and held in constant scrutiny; where the status of men flowed from their achievements and from their personal qualities, not from distinction ascribed to them at birth; and where the use of power over the lives of men was jealously guarded and severely restricted."[6]

The Consensus viewpoint tended to be especially strong at those times when the United States faced grave dangers. Thus, a number of studies of the media during World War I, for example, appeared in the years surrounding World War II. Consensus historians believed that the media should aid in defeating the threats and solving the problems that the nation faced. To them, history revealed that the media had performed best when they contributed to national unity. They believed that the media's endorsement of America's entry into both World War I and II had been responsible and reflected the consensus of the American people and that the proper role of the media during the wars was to support the aims of the nation. Against the Progressive argument that propagandists, profiteers, and reactionary publishers misled the public and led America into the wars, Consensus historians declared that the position of the media mirrored the opinions of the majority of the American public and that the enormity of the threat from America's and democracy's enemies fully justified media support of the war effort.

Consensus historians also broke sharply with the views of Progressive and recent Developmental historians on the issues of freedom of the press and government control over information. While other historians sometimes argued that freedom of the press should be absolute or that cooperation of the conservative media with government posed the danger of compromising liberal, honest journalism, Consensus historians believed absolute freedom and independence of the media could result in an irresponsible journalism that ultimately could endanger the nation and the democratic system that made press freedom possible. To merit freedom, Consensus historians argued, the media must perform re-

[6]The quoted material is taken from Bernard Bailyn, ed., *Pamphlets of the American Revolution, 1750-1776* (Cambridge, Mass.: Harvard University Press, 1965), "Introduction."

sponsibly in relation to the rest of society, with the welfare of the nation as a whole rather than of the media alone of primary importance. This view led Consensus historians to the natural conclusion that restrictions on media freedom during wartime may be acceptable and that such restrictions — because of the circumstances under which they are implemented — do not abandon the concept of freedom in a democratic philosophy.

The Neo-Conservative School

Similar in some respects to the Consensus interpretation — indeed, sometimes mistakenly classified as part of it — has been the Neo-conservative approach to history. Beginning in the 1920s, it provided an abrupt departure from the interpretation of Progressive and some Developmental historians. Its reinterpretation has been most evident in a number of biographies of media owners. Progressive historians had portrayed owners as selfish, conservative profiteers. Neo-conservative historians argued that owners often had made lasting constructive contributions to the media and that they symbolized some of the fundamental positive aspects of the American character. Whereas Progressive historians had viewed most owners with suspicion, Neo-conservative historians described them as individuals of high principle.

For many historians in the Neo-conservative school, a primary goal was to celebrate the achievements of American industry. Following the leadership of scholars in the prestigious Harvard Graduate School of Business Administration in the 1920s, historians approaching the industrial history of the American media from this perspective argued that owners were not predatory profit seekers but farsighted, thoughtful entrepreneurs whose contributions to the American media system were considerable. Owners' paramount goals were not to accumulate money but to bring new efficient methods of management to the media industries and in the process to serve better the information needs of the American public. In considering the business history of the media industries in this way, these historians also rejected the Progressive critique of media owners as enemies of democracy and freedom. They argued instead that owners, by providing efficiency and larger operations, gave America the best media system in the world and thereby actually contributed to greater democracy and freedom.

The most highly acclaimed work from these historians was Gerald Johnson's *An Honorable Titan*, published in 1946, a biography of Adolph Ochs, publisher of the *New York Times*. Ochs, Johnson said, was one of the financial giants of the late 1800s who had so much to do with making industrial America what it was. Unlike many of the industrialists who were materialists and rogues, however, Ochs was an honorable businessman committed to the ideal of the newspaper as a public institution: impersonal, reliable, responsible, and devoted primarily to serving the public with news. Daring and honest, he made the *Times* successful through faith in traditional values, hard work, common sense, and self-reliance. Believing journalism's first obligation was to inform the public, he refused to be influenced by advertisers and maintained a low editorial profile. His journalistic career exemplified principle, and the history of the *Times* under his direction provided a story of advancing journalism. Ochs, Johnson wrote, broke with the personal journalism of the past, while shunning the sensational techniques of Joseph Pulitzer and William Randolph Hearst. In emphasizing serious news, rather than sensationalism or opinion, he adapted the *Times* to conditions of his era and of the future and thus laid the foundation of modern quality journalism. As the *Times* quickly acquired a reputation for excellence, its owner gained a reputation for honor, character, and integrity.

The Cultural School

The seventh major school of interpretation — that of Cultural history — gave little attention to any such ideology, neither conservative nor liberal. Its fundamental premise is that the media operated in a close interrelationship with their environment. The major works in the Cultural school were written by university professors trained in communication history and often in communication and social and behavioral sciences. The impetus for the Cultural interpretation may be traced to a work on urban sociology by Robert E. Park, one of the members of the prestigious Department of Sociology at the University of Chicago. In "The Natural History of the Newspaper," published in 1923, he argued that the evolution of American journalism resulted from its interaction with the surrounding culture. The press, he said, was "the outcome of a historic process in which many individuals participated without foreseeing what the ultimate product of their labors was to be. The newspaper, like the modern city, is not wholly a rational product. No one sought to make it just what it is. In spite of all the efforts of individual men and generations of men to control it and make it something after their own heart, it has continued to grow and change in its own incalculable ways."[7] The primary factors in determining the nature of the newspaper, Park stated, were the conditions of the society and the system in which the press

---

[7]Robert Park, "The Natural History of the Newspaper," *American Journal of Sociology* 29 (November 1923): 273.

operated.

While some historians in other schools had attempted to explain the media as institutions somewhat separate from society, Cultural historians considered the media as a part of society and therefore influenced by various factors outside the media themselves. Thus, such questions as what factors accounted for the founding of newspapers and radio stations and under what financial conditions the media operated began to involve the historians' interest. Whereas most historians had assumed the media had a major influence on society, Cultural historians were interested in the reverse effect: the impact of society on the media. This perspective accounted for a major change in historical outlook. Until the 1950s, media influence was so widely accepted that historians often had based their studies on the concept of influence. With behavioral research studies in the 1950s beginning to suggest that the persuasive power of the mass media was limited, historians largely downplayed the idea of direct persuasive media influence on society and substituted for it the concept that the media themselves were a product of social influences.

The changed perspective on influence had other effects. One result was a virtual disappearance of the "great man" explanation of communication history. Rarely did Cultural historians frame their studies around the role that an individual had played in shaping the media. More and more studies also shifted their focus from the media giants in the Northeast to journalists on the frontier and in other sections of the nation. The emergence in the Midwest of the major doctoral programs in journalism education, followed by other programs in the South and West, was responsible for some of the shift in interests. Studies of communication on the frontier began to give particular attention to the environmental conditions in which the media operated and their effect on the media. The frontier studies' emphasis on surrounding factors demonstrated a clear shift in the thinking of historians.

The most productive historian of the Cultural school was Sidney Kobre, who in a number of works attempted to explain the mass media as a product of environment. Labeling his perspective as "sociological," he argued that the development of American journalism could be explained best in terms of how the media had been influenced by economic, political, technological, sociological, geographic, and cultural forces working on them from the outside. In his 1945 article "The Sociological Approach in Research in Newspaper History,"[8] the fullest treatise on Cultural interpretation, he declared that without consideration of such factors,

---

[8]Sidney Kobre, "The Sociological Approach in Research in Newspaper History," *Journalism Quarterly* 22 (1945): 12-22.

Chapter 2: Interpretation in History

media history could not be understood. Kobre applied his sociological approach to explain media history in five major books: *The Development of the Colonial Newspaper*, published in 1944, *Foundations of American Journalism* (1958), *Modern American Journalism* (1959), *The Yellow Press and Gilded Age Journalism* (1964), and *Development of American Journalism* (1969). In the first, a study of the years 1690-1783, he attempted to show how "the changing character of the American people and their dynamic social situation produced and conditioned the colonial newspaper." The first American newspapers were products of economic, social, and cultural conditions, including city growth, the public's desire for political and commercial news, and the need of business for an advertising medium. The public's and printers' ideas about political self-determination, a new American philosophy then taking shape, greatly affected the character of colonial newspapers. Colonial publishers, Kobre argued, "altered the character of their products to conform to ... transformations in society.... Expensive machinery, large personnel and extensive office buildings and plants were not necessary. Given these economic and technological conditions, a free press was easily secured for the people."[9]

In *Modern American Journalism*, Kobre studied the twentieth-century media from the same perspective. Emphasizing the development of the modern news media in terms of their interaction with their environment, he argued that gigantic forces such as population changes and growth, industrialization, labor organization, and a spirit of social reform transformed America in the first half of the century and thus drastically altered the nation's media. As the media mirrored the changes in economics and society, they changed to conform to new conditions. Thus, there developed a greater emphasis on interpretive journalism and newspaper column writing to explain a complex society to readers. Journalism schools and associations of journalists grew in importance as their profession grew more sophisticated. Technological developments in radio and television altered traditional media practices. Because of rising costs of labor and newsprint, publishers consolidated newspapers and formed chains to save money and to buy production material on a larger scale, mirroring similar developments in such other businesses as grocery store chains. Unlike Progressive historians, Kobre thus explained — as did several other Cultural historians — the business growth of the media as harmonizing with the tremendous changes in industrial, social, and economic conditions of the twentieth century. While the harmonizing frequently occurred in dynamic ways, Kobre concluded that changes in the me-

---

[9]Sidney Kobre, *The Development of the Colonial Newspaper* (Pittsburgh: Colonial Press, 1944).

dia were natural results of the social and economic environment.

The Cultural Studies School

A notable impetus in encouraging studies from a new perspective came with James Carey's 1974 article "The Problem of Journalism History." It appeared in the inaugural issue of the journal *Journalism History*. In calling for a "cultural history of journalism," Carey argued that historians should focus on a "ritual" view of communication, on the relationship of mass communication to human "consciousness," and on journalism's "symbolic meaning." Carey was himself not a historian but instead worked in the realm of philosophy. He drew his ideas from a wide range of philosophical areas, one of which was cultural studies. Scholars who have drawn on his ideas usually have added their own, and thus the Cultural Studies school of interpretation incorporates a variety of approaches. In general, however, historians in the school believe that mass communication plays a significant role in determining the ideas of the culture in which it operates.

Historians studying journalism, Carey said, should be concerned principally with the "way in which men in the past have grasped reality." The role the press played in that process of grasping reality, he argued, is the key to journalism history. "The task of cultural history is the recovery of past forms of imagination, of historical consciousness. The objective is not merely to recover articulate ideas or what psychologists nowadays call cognitions but rather the entire 'structure of feeling'.... By culture," he explained, "I ... mean the organization of social experience in the consciousness of men manifested in symbolic action. Journalism is then a particular symbolic form.... Cultural history is not concerned merely with events but with the thought within them. Cultural history is, in this sense, the study of consciousness in the past."[10]

Because Carey's ideas have been influential with many scholars, they deserve particular scrutiny. First, it should be observed that whether they hold

---

[10]James Carey, "The Problem of Journalism History," *Journalism History* 1 (1974): 3-5 and 27. Along with proposing his "cultural history" approach, Carey also popularized the idea that a "Whig interpretation" had "exclusively dominated" the writing of journalism history. He borrowed the term that Herbert Butterfield had coined in 1931 to identify a view among British historians that political ideas had been advancing toward those of the modern era. Carey's use of the term identified an approach to journalism history that resembled in some respects that of the Developmental school discussed earlier in this chapter.

true is virtually impossible to determine. In fact, there's no way to prove they do or don't. One can discuss them or muse about them, but whether it is possible to document a connection between mass communication and human consciousness in the past is not at all certain. Indeed, Carey's ideas are almost impossible to study within the context of history using historical methods. They can provide a stimulus to thinking about the possible role of communication in the past, but one is hardly able to document them. Carey himself didn't do any historical work that attempted to apply his ideas to history making rigorous use of primary sources. His most determined effort to provide an account of the past involved the role of the telegraph in the nineteenth century. The account, though, relied mostly on secondary sources, and even with that approach Carey tended to focus not so much on his major concepts of communication as ritual, symbolic meaning, or how humans in the past grasped reality. Instead, he mainly dealt with the effect of the telegraph on communication.[11]

Individuals working from the Cultural Studies perspective have produced studies dealing with a variety of matters. Book-length accounts have treated such topics as how "new media affected traditional notions of space and time," professionalism and ethical standards in society, violence as a cultural norm, media coverage of murder and its relationship to such questions as where one fits into a changing community, American culture's preoccupation with success and anxieties over it, and news as an expression of knowledge and what is knowable. Other historians in the school are overtly ideological. Their approaches draw less from Carey and more from such philosophical perspectives as critical theory, postmodernism, feminist theory, ethnic studies, Marxism, liberation theory, and a host of others. Their research tends to focus on the content of mass communication, with the researchers then drawing conclusions about what the content meant to the audience or about the social values that the content presented.

For the most part, those trying to use Carey's ideas or others in Cultural Studies in the study of history, particularly those making the boldest claims, have not been trained as historians but have backgrounds in such areas as cultural and critical studies or philosophy as taught in schools of communication. As a result, they tend not to employ the methods of history rigorously or to exercise the historian's normal caution about drawing connections. A few have done well-researched studies of media coverage of events in the

---

[11]James Carey, "Technology and Ideology: The Case of the Telegraph," Chapter 8 in *Communication as Culture: Essays on Media and Society* (Boston: Unwin Hyman, 1989).

past but then have drawn their main conclusions without providing the documentation necessary to support them. Most writers in the field are inclined, not confined by evidence, to jump to big conclusions.

In fact, Carey himself, even though not a historian, recognized the enormity of the problem of documenting his ideas. In his 1974 article he wrote that it is extremely difficult to "get hold of" the "felt sense" of the past. On a level that is less challenging than that which Carey proposed, we can get a sense of the problem if we think about the cause-effect relationship between mass communication and audience members. Primary source material is scarce that indicates that someone in the past changed his or her mind because of the mass media. There are instances of individuals saying something such as "From the first time I went to see a movie, I was captivated," but it is rare to find individuals leaving records stating something as simple as the fact that media content persuaded them to change their minds about a public issue. The problem becomes thornier when historians attempt to deal not with such matters as views about public issues but with human consciousness. Historians who have adopted Carey's concepts have made the task even more difficult by the expansiveness of their reasoning. Rather than focusing on individuals, they have attempted to explain the structure of feeling of society as a whole, or at least of a sizable portion of it. Thus we can conclude that works in the Cultural Studies school offer interesting concepts to think about but may or may not be offering a valid explanation of the past.

> "On close inspection, the secondary literature can be a minefield. Who draws uncritically from the works of others risks adding error to his or her work and, far worse, perpetuating and further cementing flaws in the historical facts and interpretations. As Ronald Reagan said, 'Trust, but verify.'" — *Frank Fee, University of North Carolina*

Gender and Minority Schools

Since the 1970s, an approach that has been especially popular has focused on women and minorities. Since then, approximately one-fifth of all history research articles appearing in journals in communication have focused on those topics. Of course, both those topics have a long historiography, but recent decades have seen much greater attention to them and a perspective that emphasizes women's and minorities' struggles' against discrimination. Some of the works have been written from Romantic, Developmental, Cultural, Cultural

Studies, and even Consensus interpretations and fit into those schools as discussed earlier in this chapter. The Developmental, Cultural, and Cultural Studies works, however, have tended to employ an obvious liberal ideology (with a bias against tradition and the status quo), and historians writing with those approaches have contributed a considerable body of works on the topic.

The distinctive approaches of recent years have, however, exhibited what have been called "Feminist" and "Militant" perspectives.[12] A variety of factors provided the impetus for those approaches. Among them, one can point to such elements as the civil rights movement and the protests against the Vietnam war of the 1960s (a time when many later communication historians were students on college campuses), the women's and feminist movements, instances of apparent mistreatment of minorities (such as the Los Angeles police beating of Rodney King in 1991), a growing emphasis in academia on ideology, and an increasing number of women and minorities who worked as college professors, many of whom specialized in communication history.

Even though many histories of women and the media had been written starting in the 1800s, the Feminist school produced more works than any other school. It focused on the discrimination women faced and overcame and on the feminist media in general. Some Feminist historians adopted some of the Developmental perspective for their work as they explored feminist issues as factors in the professional development of women in the media. Some dealt admiringly with women who overcame discrimination to become notable media professionals. Other Feminist historians took a more critical approach and condemned the male-dominated media for their treatment of women.

Marion Marzolf typified the Feminist approach in one of the school's early books, *Up From the Footnote: A History of Women Journalists* (1977). She complained that earlier historians had unjustly overlooked the historic role of women in the media. "Historians," she said, "skip over these early women printer-editors, usually passing them off as accidents created by the early deaths of husbands or fathers." In providing a history of women in media from colonial times to the 1970s, she gave particular attention to women who faced discrimination. For instance, women took over male jobs during World War II, but when the war ended and the male employees returned, female journalists were forced to return to writing "women's" news. "Once again you could count the number of wo-

---

[12]For extensive discussions of both approaches, see Julie K. Hedgepeth, "Women in Media, 1700-Present: Victims or Equals?" chapter 7, and Bernell Tripp, "The Black Media, 1865-Present: Liberal Crusaders or Defenders of Tradition?" chapter 12, in Sloan, *Perspectives on Mass Communication History*, 91-103 and 172-85.

men in the newsroom on one hand and their beats were likely to be education, health, welfare or features," Marzolf said. "The wartime lesson that 'women could do anything' had contained an unspoken but powerful tag end — 'in an emergency.'"[13]

Similar to the approach of Feminist historians, a number of historians writing about minority groups and the media argued that the story was essentially one of discrimination and attempts to overcome it. That view was particularly evident in histories of Native Americans and African Americans.

Historians dealing with Native Americans focused mainly on the frontier press. They claimed that white editors' belief in racial superiority toward and hatred of Indians encouraged violence toward them. For example, in a series of articles and the book *Let My People Know: American Indian Journalism* (1981), Sharon Murphy declared, "Long before television and films, the print media of the 19th Century did their part to foster inaccurate images of Indians. In fact, much of news reporting about Indians was done in advocacy fashion, encouraging or at least condoning the savage treatment of Indians."[14] Indian journalism developed in response to stereotypes presented in the white press and as an attempt to provide communication channels for Native Americans themselves. Indian newspapers, Murphy explained, "served as watchdog, teacher and advocate, promoting literacy, reporting on encroachments by white civilizations and commending the heritage and accomplishments of the Indians."[15]

Similarly, some historians of African Americans and the media presented a critical picture of white control and discrimination. They considered the black media as part of the "Black revolution," as instruments of political protest and societal reform. Battle lines were clearly drawn — on the one side, white politicians, editors, and businessmen who conspired to withhold from African Americans the rights and advantages that white Americans enjoyed; and on the other side, crusading black publishers and editors dedicated to promoting political, as well as economic and cultural, equality.

In *Issues and Trends in Afro-American Journalism* (1980), for example, James Tinney and Justine Rector presented a fervent argument for a black press immersed in American politics. They noted the opposition that black publishers faced throughout history and the subsequent problems, such as being arrested

---

[13]Marion Marzolf, *Up From the Footnote: A History of Women Journalists* (New York: Hastings House, 1977), 3, 74, 75.

[14]Sharon Murphy, "American Indians and the Media: Neglect and Stereotype," *Journalism History* 6 (1979): 39.

[15]Sharon Murphy, "Neglected Pioneers: 19th Century Native American Newspapers," *Journalism History* 4 (1977): 79.

and having their homes burned and their offices dynamited. Believing the modern black press had capitulated, they criticized it for its "moderatism." Despite this accusation of a new conservatism, they concluded that the black press had never given up in its "defense of equality and in its stand against white racism."[16] Most historians were not as militant as Tinney and Rector, but they generally held the view that the story of African Americans and mass communication was a fight against discrimination.

The Necessity of Interpretation

Understanding schools of interpretation is essential to the historian. All of the schools discussed here have their strengths and weaknesses; and exponents of each have demonstrated different concerns, approaches, and ideologies in the way they have approached the writing of history. It is important for students of communication history to consider these historiographical trends. By understanding trends in writing about the past, students will better be able to develop their own approaches to doing history.

Historians have two primary jobs. One is to describe the essential nature of the past. The other is to explain why that essential nature was as it was. Interpretation helps provide explanation. Without explanation, history is dry if not dead. The presentation of data without explanation of why or to what effect offers little insight or understanding. Explanations grow out of historical perspectives. Without a perspective in which it is based, historical writing tends to wander. It is a traveler with no road map or destination — who takes one road or another and never arrives anywhere because he or she had no place to go.

While the historian or student may find none of the interpretations discussed in this chapter fully satisfying, and while none is without faults or offers the full answer in the search for historical understanding, without them or other interpretations, historical study would offer little more than accumulations of data. Not only is an understanding of interpretation invaluable in understanding the histories that have been written, but it also is essential to the historian who wishes to add to our understanding of communication history and make significant contributions to historical study.

---

[16]James S. Tinney and Justine J. Rector, eds., *Issues and Trends in Afro-American Journalism* (Lanham, Md.: University Press of America, 1980), 1, 7.

THE FUNDAMENTALS OF GOOD HISTORY

The quest for excellence in communication history is by no means new. More than half a century ago, Allan Nevins, a journalist turned historian, called attention to many of the problems that account for the thin and uneven quality of writing in "this branch of history." Nevins, then president of the American Historical Association, urged that journalism history be held to the same standards as other branches of history, but observed, "of such history we have as yet the barest beginning."[1] Since that time, the level of communication history has improved, yet it is still uneven.

The craft of history includes people from many different backgrounds. Politicians, diplomats, generals, journalists, and others join academicians to compose its ranks. So it is also with communication history. Some communication historians were previously practicing journalists. Some are academicians. Moreover, academicians who are interested in communication history come from various scholarly orientations. Such diversity, of course, attests to the widespread interest in the subject, but it also can cause problems. Criteria for excellence in scholarship can differ from field to field.

What then are the standards of excellence that communication history should embrace? In the 1850s when that gifted churchman John Henry Newman undertook to found a Catholic University in Ireland, he realized that an explanation of the principles of a university would help mitigate doubts and opposition regarding the creation of such an institution in Dublin. He developed that expla-

---

[1]Allan Nevins, "American Journalism and Its Historical Treatment," *Journalism Quarterly* 35 (1959): 412.

nation in a series of lectures that became the basis for his much heralded *The Idea of a University*. Those lectures rested on the fundamental proposition that a Catholic university must first be a good university. Such a premise applies to communication history since the first prerequisite of any serious history is that it be "good" history. Assuming that it is absurd to have the creation of poor history as a goal, the foregoing proposition seems simple and correct enough. In fact, it delivers us to the edge of a serious and long debated problem.

To define "good history" is a dubious task. History has no single methodology. Its practitioners hold many different persuasions about the discipline. To define that which such diversity characterizes, indeed, would be presumptuous. Nevertheless, people who wish to engage in a serious pursuit of history, particularly those whose scholarly background lies in another field, should know about the standards of excellence that are generally recognized in the field of history.

In the case of those interested in communication history, we shall assume that they have or will acquire knowledge of the mass media as institutions. They also should deepen their understanding of the schools of communication historians mentioned in the previous chapter. A knowledge of the history of historical writing will help illuminate the principles and controversies associated with history as a major dimension of human inquiry. They should become familiar with the life and works of at least a few of the master historians, and they should be familiar with the historical literature already written about their field. Furthermore, as they pursue their scholarly interest in communication history, an introduction to the basic standards of history will be of value. The first part of this chapter focuses on those standards as they are generally perceived today. In the final sections, we shall consider some matters related to the ongoing effort to expand or change historical methodology.

The Criteria of Good History

Purists, of course, might quarrel with anyone's delineation of the hallmarks of "good" history. Yet historians do recognize and attempt to comply with a number of basic standards. Following are seven of these standards, which we believe describe fundamental elements of good history. In each case, we have provided a brief elaboration by way of introduction. We will say more about them later.

1. *Topic Definition.* Although this task may appear uncomplicated, it is one of the most difficult of all those involved in historical research. A topic should be chosen according to the established rules of selection. It should be clearly

Chapter 3: The Fundamentals of Good History

> "Doing 'good history' means peering under every leaf, kicking each stone out of the way, opening each door, and peering through every window — from the outside, as well as the inside. Good historians question everything and follow all leads until they hit a dead-end. Even then, they hate to give up the hunt for sources and artifacts." — Kim Mangun, author, *Making Utah History*

defined and significant. It must make sense in terms of time and space, and it must have continuity of content. To satisfy these requirements, one has to shape, limit, and sometimes reshape the boundaries and purpose of an investigation.

2. *Bibliographic Soundness.* A well-developed bibliography is essential to any serious historical work. Given the abundance of historical literature, establishing a proper bibliography can be a problem. All varieties of secondary literature that are germane to the topic should be compiled. Standard authorities on a subject must be included as well as all monographic and periodical literature that bears direct relation to the topic. The bibliographic search might well carry one across disciplinary borders.

3. *Research.* Evidence is the foundation of history, and research involves finding it, evaluating it, and reconstructing a segment of the past based upon it. When historians speak of producing a well-researched study, they mean one that rests upon primary sources, with secondary sources employed only with discretion as the circumstances of narration merit. The evidence for historical study, its sources, may be found in either published or unpublished form, but sound history stands upon sound research. Three basic activities are involved in research: (1) compiling a complete body of sources, (2) evaluating those sources by understanding their explicit and implicit meaning, and (3) explaining the relevance of those sources to the account one produces. Researchers must master all three of these activities to achieve quality in their work. To do so requires time, patience, imagination, knowledge, and discipline. Good history depends on one's ability to find and to analyze evidence.

4. *Accuracy.* There can be no substitute for accuracy in both the research and the writing of history. In regard to research, one must attempt to reach the truth of the matter. Did Dr. Samuel Johnson witness or manufacture those parliamentary speeches he reported in the British press? He once admitted that he had only visited the gallery in the House of Commons one time. If he did not hear them, then who heard them and related them to him? Were they faithful reports or invented ones? In communication history sources, one frequently encounters exaggerated reports, examples of views shaping news, and even invented inter-

views. The publisher Frank Munsey complained to the *Louisville Courier-Journal's* Henry Watterson that newspapers in the years before World War I lacked sincerity and were full of inaccuracies. Public figures in that era often charged that news reports about them were inaccurate throughout and that interviews with them were fabricated. If such problems were not enough challenge to accuracy, some researchers add to the problems by their own practices, such as using theory to interpret their sources and shape their accounts.

> "As with any academic study, historians are writing arguments, admitted or not. We must persuade readers that our narratives are legitimate. And we can only do so through expert use of source evidence." — David Vergobbi, University of Utah

What is truth in such cases? In research, one must try to reach the truth of the matter, to understand circumstances related to it, and to analyze the elements of a given problem as exactly as possible. In short, one must establish not only the authenticity of data but also its meaning.

Accuracy is also the cornerstone of good historical writing. It must govern one's presentation of evidence and handling of generalization as well as the details of writing such as sharpness of particular references; the correct use of names, titles, and offices; the selection of the precise word or phrase of description; and the proper employment of quotations, figures, and footnotes.

5. *Explanation.* This activity involves such matters as the explication of sources, but such explication is only one aspect of explanation. It includes other tasks. There will be facts to explain, generalizations to form, and interpretations to offer. The quality of one's work depends on how well one explains the component parts of the subject under investigation as well as the full subject itself.

Explicating the sources of history can be more involved than often supposed. That is especially true when dealing with personal documents. There is much to understand about them before they are ready for use. Suppose the document is an unsigned or undated letter, or even just a fragment of a letter. The problem becomes one of identity, and in resolving it historians act as detectives. They search for clues, some of which may be physical such as the quality of the paper used. Or was there anything unusual or revealing about it? Other aspects of searching for identity involve the contents of the document. For instance, what hints can be derived from people, places, and sundry items mentioned in a document? Establishing meaning in a signed and dated document has its own challenges. Again consider a personal record. What was its purpose? Can possible contradictions in it be reconciled or at least understood? What was the mood of its author? Did the document represent a shift in the writer's attitude? If so, that must be explained. In short, historians must become familiar with their sources to the degree that they clearly understand them and can explain them to readers with equal clarity.

6. *Historical Understanding.* Occasionally in our discussion to this point, we have made reference to *historical understanding.* That term merits special attention, for it is central to good history. It may well be the most illusive of all the elements in history, but its presence enhances all good historical writing. By historical understanding one can mean having understanding of the circumstances and personalities pertaining to a study. The term also can be taken to mean an understanding of historical activity, cause, and change. It can mean an understanding of life as it was in the past. So in their effort to understand some figure or episode, historians probe beyond the documents as such into contextual information. Sometimes this exercise involves closing gaps in the documented record or making connections. Sometimes it involves reconstructing settings.

To achieve understanding, one must develop an awareness of *time* regarding circumstances now vanished. "What distinguishes history from other humanistic disciplines," wrote Trygve Tholfsen, "is overriding interest in the role of time in human life."[2] Historians often speak of the need to avoid "present-mindedness" — that is, viewing the past in terms of the present. Historians stress the need to recapture the sense of the spirit of the times surrounding a study, to comprehend the feelings, persuasions, and emotions that once were real, to grasp how things happened in some past age, or to comprehend the nature of the forces that conditioned life in the past. Communication historians must be able to comprehend past ideas and thinking. An understanding of time, therefore, lies at the core of historical understanding. Without it there will be little comprehension of the reality that surrounded past figures and events.

7. *Writing.* The narrative element is essential to history and is another one of its distinguishing characteristics. It cannot be equated with excellence in popular writing or even in journalistic writing, genres that adhere to their own standards. Historical narrative should be carefully crafted in terms of the elements of good writing and in terms of the elements of history. The latter involves the ability to integrate into the narrative the previous six attributes of history introduced in this section. To be sure, it relies on factual record and must be faithful to it, but the historical narrative also tells a story. "Good history," Lester Stephens reminds us, possesses literary qualities; and "history which is drab, pro-

---

[2]Trygve R. Tholfsen, *Historical Thinking: An Introduction* (New York: Harper and Row, Publishers, 1967), 247.

saic, and devoid of aesthetic value often merits the little attention it is likely to receive."[3]

Present-Mindedness

The danger of present-mindedness is so serious that it deserves elaboration. The historian should try to understand the past on its own terms. As we mentioned in the previous section, present-mindedness is the problem of viewing the past in terms of the present. To the extent that historians judge the past by the values of their own time, they do a disservice to history.

Cautioning against present-mindedness is not to suggest that the study of history has no value for the present. It does. The past can, for example, help us understand the present; and, to a lesser extent, the present may be able to help us understand the past. But historians should not be so caught up in the present that it creates a problem. If a historian is concerned too much with such matters as today's "proper" professional practices, contemporary ideology or political biases, twenty-first century concepts of freedom of expression, or any one of many other contemporary perspectives, those concerns can lead to a misunderstanding of the past. If historians are more interested in, for example, how the mass-communication occupations today should be practiced than in history for history's sake, their concern about the present can translate into efforts to impose the views and standards of our own time on the past. The result is that historians can view the past simply as a stepping stone to the present. They therefore will fail to understand the people, events, and times of the past. One can easily imagine how values and concerns of the historians' own time can distort history and our understanding of it.

For purposes of illustration, consider some examples of how present-mindedness shows up in historical study of communication. The problem is especially strong with historians who think of communication history as the story of the origin, practice, and progress of certain occupational principles and practices. In journalism, for example, concerns include such matters as the gathering and re-

> "Be aware of present mindedness. Do not judge people of the past by the standards of today. First, the times and customs are not the same. Second, it is easy to judge with hindsight. Also, do not assume that words used in the past have the same meanings as today." — *Lucinda Davenport, Michigan State University*

---

[3]Lester D. Stephens, *Probing the Past: A Guide to the Study and Teaching of History* (Boston: Allyn and Bacon, Inc., 1974), 13.

Chapter 3: The Fundamentals of Good History

> "Do you want historians fifty years from now interpreting our times without understanding what life was really like for us? It's our duty to understand the context, the 'spirit of the times' we're writing about." — Lynne Flocke, author, 'False' Ideas and the First Amendment

porting of news, objectivity and partisanship, and independence from government. Some historians find those features to be the important aspects of history for one reason: because they are the ones that professional journalists and professors consider the cornerstones of proper journalism. One of the harmful effects of such occupationally oriented present-mindedness is that it gives us a one-dimensional, linear view of history in which characteristics advance in a line of progress to the present. We can see present-mindedness at work with communication historians in dealing with several forms of ideology, such as the press versus the government, the media and the treatment of gender and race, and the role of materialism and economics as motivating forces, to name just a few.

Today's ideas on press freedom form another potential trap. Most communication scholars have a bias toward the need for a free press. Such an outlook may be natural, since most communication historians come from a media background and made their professional careers in modern fields devoted to the notion of freedom of the press as we understand it today. Thus, they tend to focus their interest on great "victories" that they believe advanced press freedom. Contrast that view with the view of scholars from other branches of history, who don't seem to have such a fixation on press freedom as a sole concern. Hence, they tend to have a broader approach to the context in which the media operated. Rather than focusing narrowly on, for example, court battles, they are more inclined to look at press freedom broadly within the context of the people, thought, and culture in earlier eras. That approach offers the advantage of helping us better to understand the nature of press freedom as it existed at specific times in the past.

Fortunately, historians have means to protect against present-mindedness. The first is simply to be aware that it exists and that it presents a danger in historical study. Then they need to recognize that they themselves naturally have a contemporary perspective and to determine what their values are, divorce themselves as much as possible from the present, and make a determined effort to consider the past in the context of its own times. As historians think about their research projects, they can ask such questions as these: "What values of today do I need to be aware of that might relate to the historical topic that I am studying, and how are they different from those of the past? ... If I put myself in the shoes of, say, editors in 1750, will I see the press of the era with a different outlook? ... How did people of an earlier age think of mass communication? How did their views differ from those of today?" The goal is to understand mass communication as it truly was — and not to imagine that it was merely a crude model of what it has become in our own time or that it should be judged by today's values that perhaps did not exist in the past.

The Historian Between Past and Present

Can there be truth in history? The same question can be asked of journalism. In the case of the latter, there is always a wide array of variable factors to consider such as the disposition of the journalist involved, the nature of news, the demands of the audience, the imperfect quality of sources, and the pressure to make journalism interesting and a paying business enterprise. Is the result propaganda or truth, and if it is somewhere between the two, is it presented as such? Even in the case of today's investigative reporting, there are limits to the time, expense, and effort that can be spent in researching a story. Journalistic writing, by its very nature, can only imperfectly reproduce the full reality of a current episode. Suppose the journalist had the time of the historian to research and publish. The accuracy of the investigation might, indeed, be improved by a more extensive use of sources and perhaps the benefits of detachment. But sources are never perfect, and the detachment of time has to measure against the loss of the sense of the moment. Consequently, if journalists find truth elusive in their explanation of all but the most obvious reportable data, it can be argued that historians might also. The problem revolves around a double axis. In part it relates to evidence; in part, to the investigator.

Historians, like journalists, often despair at the limits of evidence. They frequently need more evidence, or more explicit evidence, to resolve a particular problem of understanding data. Even in this day of the growth of archives and the Internet and the abundant accumulation of printed and other evidence, one must wonder if the historian is forever at the mercy of the evidence that happens to survive. Today more documents are being produced than in previous times. The computer, Internet sites, recording devices, plus those indispensable photocopying machines have provided a mass of records. Have they increased the accuracy of sources? The same technological culture that produced them also produced the greater means for people to communicate with one another without making that communication a matter of record. The same revolution that gave us speed of communication also increased privacy concerns and potential

Chapter 3: The Fundamentals of Good History

> "As in every other endeavor, assumption is the enemy of good historical research. Assumption is especially insidious because it begins with present-mindedness — the implicit expectation that the previous generations did what we do and for the same reasons. Often they approached similar problems from very different perspectives. Our job is to find out what those were." — *Frank Fee, University of North Carolina*

secrecy. Much like journalists confronted with such present circumstances, historians have to deal with evidence that is far from satisfactory. Are there gaps in the record? Can substantive contradictions found in them be reconciled? And, even if the record is complete, is it a biased account of truth? How many individual experiences become embellished with dramatic flourishes when recollected? In our own time, if we have witnessed a remarkable broadening of the definition of historical sources, which we have, we also have failed to experience an end to the inherent problems of sources.

The rules of evidence can help one to handle such problems in a fair way. They cannot guarantee, however, that the outcome will be at one with truth, nor can they assure that all people in all ages will understand the evidence in the same way. Consequently, the fact of partiality of record permeates the nature of history.

Based on this imperfect record, the historian proceeds to advance explanations. By necessity, what part of them is incomplete? How much is hypothetical? What part is artistry or, in extreme cases, even artifice? Complete truth can be known about hardly anything other than the merest superficial elements associated with past episodes. When historians pursue the "how" and "why" of past episodes and when they discuss facts (as opposed to data) and ideas of times gone, they have to acknowledge an appropriate sense of restraint regarding conclusions. It is a function that becomes a part of their professional judgment and a part of the tone of their narratives. It would be unrealistic for any audience to expect the full truth about a segment of the past from historians and arrogant of historians to claim they had discovered it. What can be expected is that they be truthful to the greatest extent possible, that they work to understand the past on its own terms, and that they demonstrate judgment that is honest, perceptive, and balanced. There is, then, a definite personal element in history related to the historian's stance between past and present and to his or her limited knowledge of both spheres.

This personal element deserves further attention for a number of reasons. Like journalists, historians are products of their own social environments. They can never completely escape the conditions that shaped and continue to shape them. They all have emotions, persuasions, and ethical standards, some of which are shared in part with others of similar background and some of which are uniquely their own. Religion, nationality, geography, class awareness, gender, race, ideology, education, occupation, knowledge, and experience help define human perceptions. To what extent do these perceptions become habits of thought, perhaps even biases, either recognized or not, that enter into the writing of history, thus imperiling the reconstruction of the true past? One cannot easily forget the comment of the elder British statesman A. J. Balfour about Churchill's multi-volume account of the First World War: "Winston has written an enormous book about himself and called it The World Crisis."4

> "Nevins said the historian must be able to 'walk around' the characters of historical research for a three-dimensional understanding of who they were. In order to understand the mindset of the time period, historians should also be able to walk around in the shoes of the historical characters and experience life from their perspectives." — Bernell Tripp, author, Origins of the Black Press

History is, after all, a reconstruction by an individual of things past. How much of ourselves do and should we put into it? Modern historians, particularly those cast in the Rankean mold of scientific history, may have extolled the goals of impartiality and objectivity for history, but others have pondered either the possibility or plausibility of such well-intended aims. In more recent years New Left and radical historians, like those journalists who prefer advocacy to objectivity, have rejected such neutrality in favor of a more active search for and development of history as a tool to employ in solving present problems and changing society. In the process, if they are able to reconstruct an accurate version of the past, they have enhanced history. If not, as David Hackett Fischer observed, they become "methodological reactionaries."5

In fairness, it must be admitted that radical historians do not hide their opinions. Among historians of the mainstream, that has not always been true. Some writers in previous generations produced histories based on their conviction that they were on the side of truth and thus have subordinated history to cause. Today's scholars writing from the perspective of cultural and critical studies do the same thing. Furthermore, present-mindedness has distorted much his-

---

4Quoted in Arthur Marwick, *The Nature of History*, 2nd. ed. (London: Macmillan, 1970), 135. Churchill himself had said, perhaps tongue in check, "History will be kind to me, for I intend to write it."

5David Hackett Fischer, *Historians' Fallacies: Toward a Logic of Historical Thought* (New York: Harper & Row, Harper Torchbooks, 1970), 314.

torical writing, as has historians' tendency to view history from the perspective of the mass communication professions rather than as detached observers. Most communication historians have judged the past by their own generation's standards.

Nevertheless, let us return to the fundamental question: What part of themselves do and should historians put into their history? The presence of the personal factor is manifest in all of history from its inception to the final act of composition. It is, in fact, one of the strongest links between history and journalism. The well-known foreign correspondent Herbert Matthews once explained: "That a journalist has, at all times, his bias and sympathies is certain, since he is only a human being. That those feelings color his choice and presentation of news, without his being conscious of it, is also obvious.... It all boils down to the impossibility of achieving perfection or complete precision, and we journalists could write as many books on that subject as the philosophers have written."[6] Much the same comment could be made of historians. They reveal preference in choice of topic, in their selection of evidence, and in the words they employ to describe and explain their subject. The demands of narrative and explanation force historians to become a part of their scholarship.

Historians interpret past figures and events for the present, and in doing that they not only evaluate sources but also exercise judgment. At some points in their reconstruction of past happenings those judgments may be value judgments. Then it is only fair to ask, whose values? Who was right in the partisan press wars of the early 1800s or in the ideological conflicts of the muckraking era? What was the good life for one group in society may have been exploitation or oppression for another group. The freedom of the press rights that were given to newspapers may have been denied to radio in the 1930s. Was that proper? Or, what serves the purposes of the news media may hinder the conduct of government. In the epic of civilization's past experiences, one can find many contradictory, even irreconcilable, convictions, honestly held in their day. They may have appeared as manifestations of national, religious, class, economic, racial, gender, political, professional, environmental, or generational differences and peculiarities. Moreover, who can doubt that standards change, culture evolves, opinions shift, styles come and go, and commitments rise and wane. Such uncertainty is part of the complexity of the past, and historians must explain such things. They are also expected to reflect upon it, to put the best of their thought into it.

[6]Herbert L. Matthews, *The Education of a Correspondent* (New York: Harcourt, Brace and World, Inc., 1946; reprint ed., Westport, Conn.: Greenwood Press, 1970), 59.

Should that reflection involve them in moral judgment? No one expects contemporary history to be a moral narrative, but one might expect it to reflect judgment that goes beyond explanation as such. There are, indeed, ethical and moral dimensions of past human behavior. Every age has its obscene, criminal, and evil elements. Should historians avoid comment on such things? There was an Adolf Hitler, and genocide did occur, as have many other terrible acts in history.

Simply to explain dramatic failings in human conduct stops short of saying whether it was right or wrong. As C. V. Wedgwood, who probed this matter with restraint matched by wisdom, observed: "... from explaining an action we move insensibly towards justifying it, and from thence towards a general blurring of moral issues and a comfortable belief that circumstances are always to blame, and men and women are not.... This outlook steadily and stealthily fosters the conviction that nothing is good or bad in itself but only in relation to its surroundings."[7]

That observation touches the nerve of the issue. Historians, like all writers who describe the human experience, make moral judgments all the time in their use of language (e.g., one person's order is another's oppression). Would it not be better to recognize the habit and discipline oneself to handle it with discernment and precision? Moreover, when it comes to unethical acts in the past of a dramatic sort (as contrasted with mere differences of opinion over such matters as, for example, politics), the historian's audience expects reflection about such matters. Historians have a responsibility to provide that, not to overdo it, but to do it with a broadness and a sense of honesty that will enhance meaning about significant questions while remaining ever mindful of their commitment to the search for truth. Thus, the historian needs to be alert to assure that one's judgment about values is not merely personal bias. We could all justify our biases by simply thinking of them on a loftier plane as defensible value judgments. With that approach, all biases would be acceptable because they would be equal. Handling value judgments well requires a great deal of maturity and wisdom.

Finally, let us remember that history can be a source of inspiration to some people. That being the case, the historian's responsibility includes being ethically responsible. There is a great deal of common sense in Barbara Tuchman's statement that "to take no sides in history would be as false as to take no sides in life."[8]

---

[7]C. V. Wedgwood, *The Sense of the Past: Thirteen Studies in the Theory and Practice of History* (New York: Collier Books, 1967), 48.

[8]Barbara Tuchman, "The Historian's Opportunity," *Saturday Review* 25, February 1967, p. 31.

Without the historian acting as a responsible interpreter of past happenings, it would be difficult to have a deep awareness of self, to be intellectually honest, to seek understanding of the past on its own grounds, and to recognize that there is a time and place for ethical judgment. Historians stand between past and present and must engage both with imagination, integrity, and a sense of responsibility. The creation of that delicate balance represents one of the greatest challenges in historical scholarship. As one authority on the relevancy of history to the present writes: "A mastery of the techniques of scholarship does not necessarily ... guarantee good history, which is also the matter of the human equation, the sum total of the man or woman using the techniques."[9]

The Open Borders of Knowledge

All historians wish to have the fullest grasp of their subject that they can acquire. To that end, they traditionally have been informed by many specialties of knowledge such as diplomatics, heraldry, genealogy, theology, economics, political theory, geography, linguistics, epigraphy, paleography, and statistics. Quite naturally, too, they have had a long reciprocal relationship with the social sciences.

The relationship between geography and history, for instance, is pronounced. These two collateral studies logically intersect at many junctures. Geography explains the physical setting in which history resides and enlightens one about nature's violent and quieter influences on humankind. Knowledge of geography is as important to historians writing today as it was to their counterparts hundreds of years ago. At the very least, as W. Gordon East observed in his thoughtful volume *The Geography Behind History*, history raises "the familiar questions Why? and Why then? but also questions Where? and Why there?"[10]

Historians, of course, understand that communication is interwoven with the geography of humankind from the earliest times. Trade, transportation, and communication are bound together over time in many ways. When the great historical studies are written on that theme, who can doubt that geography will be present in them? Surely the development and practice of communication, and of media themselves, have been influenced by climate, habitat, town settlement and growth, and urban development as well as by the earth's physiographical features — subjects on which the geographer can inform the historian. The same

---

[9]Carl G. Gustavson, *The Mansion of History* (New York: McGraw-Hill Book Company, 1976), 334.

[10]W. Gordon East, *The Geography Behind History* (New York: W.W. Norton & Company, 1965), 4.

thing can be said of communication history and technology, economics, politics, and numerous other specialized areas.

The discipline of anthropology has also been influential on historical scholarship in recent decades, particularly in the ways that anthropologists provide frameworks for understanding the significance of culture. As anthropologist Clifford Geertz argues, "human behavior is ... symbolic action," and he suggests that the task of the analyst is to try to grasp the meaning of those symbols. For communication historians, Geertz's work offers a valuable framework for understanding the perspectives of the historical actors they study. "The whole point," Geertz argues, is to seek "access to the conceptual world in which our subjects live so that we can, in some extended sense of the term, converse with them."[11] Similarly, anthropologist Benedict Anderson's concept of the "imagined community" has proven useful to communication historians. For Anderson, the circulation of mass-produced books and newspapers after the invention of the printing press spurred the creation of the modern idea of the nation as an idea shared by a people in a "deep, horizontal comradeship." Media, Anderson reasons, formed the basis for peoples' understandings of themselves as a part of a spatially dispersed public that "imagined" itself as a common group. For communication historians, such reasoning suggests ways of understanding the meaning and significance of a variety of media messages and forms.[12]

Important differences, of course, both in style and substance exist between history and the social sciences. An extensive literature exists on that point, and this is not the place to review it in depth. Suffice to say, the differences are real enough, but they do not apply totally. Indeed, there are many points of convergence between the studies. Historians and sociologists, for instance, may use a common body of information for different purposes, perhaps less so today than a generation ago. Yet an overlapping between the two occurs at point of contact with many topics. Communication historians today profess a new interest in many things about the past such as public opinion, literacy and readership, advertising influence, sensationalism, the media and violence, gender and media, newsroom organization and social change, to mention only a few current topics that also interest sociologists. They are interested also in how people behave in groups and in the mass. To proceed in investigating such topics in communication history without knowledge of what sociologists have said about them would

[11]Clifford Geertz, "Thick Description: Toward an Interpretive Theory of Culture," in *The Interpretation of Cultures* (New York: Basic, 1973), 10, 24.
[12]Benedict Anderson, *Imagined Communities: Reflections on the Origin and Spread of Nationalism* (London: Verso, 1983; reprint, 2006), 7, 44.

be unwise. The same, of course, can be said of sociologists who explore the same questions, for there is a definite historical element in any sociological explanation. By making that statement, one is not suggesting that history become sociology or that sociology become history. The point is simply that two disciplines can overlap in terms of subject, and at those points it is logical to expect intellectual interaction to occur.

Communication historians explore subjects that frequently fall between the disciplines. Consider again history's convergences with sociology, a borderland familiar enough to communication historians. Today, for instance, one topic that attracts historians' attention is the subject of riots that occurred in the past. It attracts the interest of sociologists, too. More is known about riots in America between the 1740s and the 1770s and between the 1830s and 1850s than those of the intervening decades. Only recently have historians focused on American riots between 1780 and 1830. Newspapers of that era, so important as a source to both the historian and the sociologist, we are told, "seldom covered riots: politics and trade were much more important than local news ... [and] local news which detracted from the commercial reputation of a community was especially taboo."[13] Communication historians have helped to explain that particular circumstance, and they will no doubt have much more to say on this topic and similar ones that social historians are bringing to the surface. In doing so they will want to know about the questions sociologists have asked of such phenomena and the varieties of explanations they offer about them. The findings of social psychologists on the subject should interest them, too.

In order to understand the individual and collective experience of past periods, communication historians need an understanding of time and place. As all historians, they also need to be broadly informed about their subject — not only about the media themselves but about the many sides of knowledge regarding them at any given time in the past.

In fact, communication historians operate in an extremely fluid area of history. Since the media have influenced and have been influenced by so many facets of modern life, their history is multi-sided. So too is most history that is worthy of consideration. To understand the media in history, historians must be able to comprehend a good deal about business, technology, ideology, politics, public opinion, national power, international relations, etc. So, again we see them pursuing topics across disciplinary borders from a historical base.

Moreover, there is the individual in communication history to consider. Was

---

[13]Paul A. Gilje, "'The mob begin to think and reason': Recent Trends in Studies of American Popular Disorder, 1700-1850," *Maryland Historian* 12 (Spring 1981): 31.

Joseph Pulitzer, for instance, an average man? Quite to the contrary, he was an extraordinary man of tattered nerves, many maladies and eccentricities, and a genius as a publisher. How can a communication historian grasp, let us say, Pulitzer's driving and inexhaustible energy? In fact, in writing about the behavior of correspondents in battle or the shaping of public opinion in a nation at war and many other subjects, communication historians can sharpen their comprehension of the subject by knowledge of what psychologists and sociologists have said about such questions.

If the goal of writing communication history is to write good history, then one must be broadly informed about the various dimensions of the subject being studied. As we have indicated, communication historians may have to stray into divisions of knowledge related to history but in many respects different from history. How far and in what manner should they travel along these lines? Before proceeding further, however, we must consider methodological challenges that, beginning mainly in the 1960s, called into question norms associated with the practice of history.

Psychology in History

First, let us consider the use that some historians wish to make of psychoanalysis. The desire to probe deep into the mind and behavior of individuals and groups in the past, in fact, has been alive in history since the days of its inception in ancient Greece. So it might be reasoned that some form of psychological thinking has long been alive in historical inquiry.

What historians have come to call *psychohistory*, however, goes beyond the limits of the more informal previous use of psychological generalization because it is a response to the development of psychology as a modern field of behavioral research. It also reflects the intention, which can be traced back to the nineteenth century, of some historians to make historical inquiry more scientific in nature. Since many people today consider whatever is "scientific" to have a high degree of objectivity and intellectual sophistication, one can understand the desire to use science to increase the accuracy and truth of history. In his much heralded presidential address to the American Historical Association in 1957, William L. Langer encouraged historians to deepen their understanding by exploiting "the concepts of modern psychology," by which he meant psychoanalytical thought and development.[14] Many decades have elapsed since Langer's ad-

[14]William L. Langer, "The Next Assignment," *American Historical Review* 63 (January 1958): 284.

dress, and during that time historians have revealed a heightened interest in psychoanalysis as a useful tool in their inquiries. The most notable use of psychoanalysis in communication history is Richard Hofstadter's *The Age of Reform* (1955), which attempted to describe muckrakers of the early 1900s as motivated by "status anxiety."

During this same time, apprehensions about applying psychoanalysis to history surfaced and could not be dismissed. Part of the reason is that a number of important psychological biographical studies, such as Erik H. Erikson's *Young Man Luther* (1958) and Sigmund Freud and William C. Bullitt's *Thomas Woodrow Wilson: Twenty-Eighth President of the United States: A Psychological Study* (1967), contained, in the judgment of many historians, serious flaws.[15] Even Hofstadter, one of the most prestigious American historians of his generation and an advocate of applying psychological analysis to history, was criticized for his handling of psychological theory in *The Age of Reform*.

The reasons for the historian's apprehension of psychohistory, however, go beyond criticism of particular works. They deal with perceived differences between psychology and history and the difficulties of applying the former to the latter. Communication historians should consider these apprehensions about psychohistory as well as the reasons for using it, for they frequently operate in an area of history that calls for an illumination of personality, persuasion, and motivation. Their work often necessitates the ability to recapture the emotional edge of a historical moment; and, one must admit, in dealing with the mass communication practitioners of the past, they have more than their fair share of eccentric personalities to decipher.

Basic to historians' uneasiness regarding the practice of psychohistory are concerns about approach and evidence. To begin with, they tend to suspect that a psychological approach to history imposes prefixed theories on human actions in the past. Thomas A. Kohut, a scholar trained both in history and psychology, in an examination of this question observed: "... the psychohistorical method relies on theory, particularly psychoanalytic theory, to provide understanding and explanation. Figures and events from the past are not comprehended or

---

[15]For an example of the many reviews on the Freud and Bullitt study of Wilson, see A.J.P. Taylor, "Silliness in Excelsis," *New Statesman*, May 1967, pp. 653-54. Erikson's study of Luther received considerable criticism from historians, though the more thoughtful of their critiques also recognized Erikson's achievement. See, for instance, Roland H. Bainton, "Psychiatry and History: An Examination of Erikson's *Young Man Luther*," and Lewis W. Spitz, "Psychohistory and History: The Case of Young Man Luther," in Roger A. Johnson, ed., *Psychohistory and Religion: The Case of Young Man Luther* (Philadelphia: Fortress Press, 1977), 19-88.

made comprehensible on their own terms but are understood and explained primarily by psychological theory. Too often, when employing the psychohistorical method, the historian comes to the past with an understanding and explanation already in hand; the understanding and explanation do not emerge from the past itself but are the products of a theoretical model."[16]

Traditional historians are no strangers to theoretical thought about the past. Most historians have ideas in mind about and possible answers to questions they intend to pursue when they approach their investigations. Furthermore, they approach their study with an awareness of the modes of thought of their own society. They should not, however, seek to impose a theoretical model on the past. To the greatest degree possible, they believe that the past should be allowed to speak for itself. Accordingly, historians are committed to understanding particular events and figures of the past as much as possible on their own terms. The application of psychological theory to past experiences can mar historical explanation since to be historical an account must emerge from the evidence of the past itself.

Beyond these considerations about approach there is the matter of causation to consider. Historians tend to see particular experiences of the past in their full complexity and usually depend on a mixture of motives to explain human action. Psychological interpretations can suggest an unhistorical reductionism in causative explanations. Or, as scholars such as Jacques Barzun suggest, they may place too much emphasis on tracing the attachments and behavior of adulthood to the circumstances of one's youth.[17] The matter of causation in history logically leads away from such tendencies and toward hard evidence.

The question of evidence in psychohistory involves several considerations. Again there is the problem of psychoanalytic theory to confront. Historians use evidence of the past, but, as Kohut once again cautioned, "psychohistorians, when they rely on theory, also accept evidence from the present to validate their interpretations."[18] Their theories, he noted, are normally derived from contemporary evidence rather than from past evidence. His observations — and they are not those of a detractor of psychohistory — deserve close attention, since evidence lies at the core of historical inquiry.

Some historians believe that every age is unique. Conditions of one time are

---

[16]Thomas A. Kohut, "Psychohistory as History," *American Historical Review* 91 (April 1986): 337-38.

[17]Jacques Barzun, *Clio and the Doctors: Psycho-History, Quanto-History and History* (Chicago: University of Chicago Press, 1974), 72-73.

[18]Kohut, "Psychohistory as History," 337-38.

Chapter 3: The Fundamentals of Good History

> "Understanding a person in history means researchers place themselves inside that person to understand the decisions he or she made. Learn what was done for entertainment or information, how people treated each other, types of housing and furniture, and what bread cost compared to weekly or monthly incomes, for example." — Lucinda Davenport, Michigan State University

never repeated. Therefore, ideas and theories fashioned under the conditions of one time may be erroneous when applied to those of another. Surely it would be careless to suppose that people in the past were the same psychologically as people are today or will be in future generations. Their psychological responses to fear, anxiety, and suffering were influenced by a variety of social and cultural realities that were particular to their day.

A number of recent studies have shown that human behavior has changed over time. They underscore the credence of the traditionalist historian's concern about the autonomy of a past period. But is that autonomy complete? It is difficult to quarrel with the conclusion of Peter N. Stearns and Carol Z. Stearns that psychohistorians need to pay greater attention to the fact of "change in emotional behavior over time ... while admitting that certain psychological findings probably do describe human realities that may be immune to change." To that they add: "After all, we are animals with biological constraints; it is curious that many historians and social scientists have ignored biological factors in their studies of emotion."[19] Current treatment of mental disorders, which is based on medicine as well as on therapy, tends to confirm their point.

Moreover, it would be reckless to assume that the record of the past with which the historian normally works is similar to that which psychoanalysts handle in the routine of their work. The clinical relationship is missing. The historical "patients" cannot be questioned, and the records they leave behind are far from complete. In many cases those records are spotty. Perhaps they were randomly kept in the first place. Or, perhaps they were carefully chosen for posterity. Consequently, although the psychohistorical method may be a valuable tool, it has limitations.

Nevertheless, within limits, historians have come to appreciate psychoanalysis as useful in probing human conduct in the past. They agree that it is not the one and only tool, that it must be substantiated by sufficient historical evidence, that what it produces must be placed in realistic perspective, that the psychoanalytic interpretation is simply an interpretation that might help to explain

[19]Peter N. Stearns with Carol Z. Stearns, "Emotionology: Clarifying the History and Emotions of Emotional Standards," *American Historical Review* 90 (October 1985): 824.

a particular past human action, and that the lack of psychoanalytic training is a problem for most historians. Still, the reasons for accepting properly applied psychoanalytical thought as a tool of historical inquiry are compelling. Historians, after all, are interested in human behavior, in human motivation and reaction. They should prepare themselves to understand these things as sharply as they can. Suppose, for instance, in the course of a study they become convinced that a person in that study was mentally ill. Knowledge of psychoanalytic explanations of mental illness would be useful in such cases.

But beyond that type of extreme instance, psychological generalization can help the historian to elucidate past human behavior. Historians are not interested, as a practicing clinician would be, in the proper treatment for the patient. Rather they are interested in understanding human action and reaction in the past and describing it with sophisticated accuracy in their explanations. Feelings and emotions were realities in a given past human episode and must be understood in their fullness.

Regarding the traditionalist's concern about the use of psychological theory in history, current literature on historical methodology suggests two conclusions. First, it is not a tool for all historians to use. Second, those who decide to use it need to understand it and should consider it only one of the methods they employ in their scholarship and as one of the factors to consider for purposes of explaining thoroughly examined historical material.

Quantification in History

Now let us consider the use of quantitative methods in history (also known as quantohistory or simply as quantification). Communication historians should study the debate surrounding their use since many people active in the field, but by no means all, approach the study with a background in communication research, a field that is much involved in quantitative methodology and other skills associated with the social and behavioral sciences.[20] Many were introduced to

[20]One study found that between 1989 and 2002 about one-third of history articles published in research journals in the field of mass communication used mainly quantitative methods. (See Lisa Daigle, "A Citation and Methodological Analysis of Media History," paper presented at the 2003 Southeast Symposium of the American Journalism Historians Association.) That finding reveals the impact of the fact that most doctoral programs in communication, which focus much more on behavioral and social science than on the humanities, emphasize quantitative methods of research. Most graduates of communication doctoral programs are therefore more familiar with quantitative methods than with standard historical methods.

Chapter 3: The Fundamentals of Good History

> "Be wary of any researcher who insists his or her own method is the only one suited for mass communication study. It is fashionable among many quantitatively oriented researchers to dismiss all other methods as 'unscientific' and so without value. This is hogwash." —
> David Davies, author, The Postwar Decline of American Newspapers, 1945-1965

quantitative methods in their graduate communication research courses.

Should those methods be applied to communication history? Richard L. Merritt in his study of the growth of American nationalism in the eighteenth century and others have demonstrated that quantification can be applied with success.[21] There are, in fact, a number of places in communication history where one can use quantitative techniques to advance and sharpen understanding of a subject. They can be of use, for instance, in probing into the social, economic, and demographic aspects of the field. In grappling with the statistics of publishing, circulation, and readership, these techniques are of obvious value. The same can be said about efforts to comprehend the currents of historical public opinion. Quantitative methods can sharpen the process of textual analysis and aid in the development of collective biography. But, useful tool though it may be, like any other new historical source or technique, quantification has not shown that it can or should replace traditional methods.

It is natural enough that a number of contemporary historians find this methodology attractive. Interest in quantification in history increased as a new interest in social and economic factors grew among historians. Naturally the growth of statistical sources in recent generations and the advent of the computer with its capacity to store, index, and manipulate vast quantities of data were bound to foster interest in this method.

Quantification, of course, can have several meanings. To some, it means the simple counting of figures of enumerative data, an old tradition in the practice of history. Others perceive it as a procedure by which such data can be tested in ways more common to social scientists than to historians. This second group of historians finds quantification a systematic method for historical scholarship, an invitation for historians to use hard data to test the validity of their generalizations and to develop explicit designs in the manner of the social scientist. These advocates are themselves divided. William Aydelotte, for instance, deems quantification an appropriate method for studies that lend themselves to it. Others, like Lee Benson, are attracted to it as a means by which history might acquire a

[21]Richard L. Merritt, "The Emergence of American Nationalism: A Quantitative Approach," *American Quarterly* 17 (Summer 1965, supplement): 319-34.

genuinely scientific methodology and thereby become itself a social science. It is easy to understand why quantification, therefore, has been the source of controversy among historians.

The reaction of historians to this assault has been varied. In part, it must be admitted, the responses of those among them who were suspicious of quantification were reactions to that which they intuitively disliked simply by means of their own professional temperaments. As C. Vann Woodward noted, they saw "their authority challenged, their humanistic values threatened, their canons of criticism ridiculed...." Besides, they found little comfort having "their cherished classics derided as 'soft,' impressionistic and unscientific."[22] Then, too, did not quantifiers practice the techniques of the social sciences and perhaps even hope to use them to carry history away from its traditional moorings? Nevertheless, as more traditionally minded historians have adjusted themselves to the presence of quantification in historical research and perhaps even admit its usefulness in analyzing certain evidence, some fundamental questions regarding it remain.

Essentially these questions reflect three concerns: sources, object, and narration. Regarding sources, most historians maintain that a great deal of historical data is such that it cannot be quantified and that too great a reliance on statistical data will lead to distortion. Personal feelings and social and cultural forces and pressures are as important to historians as so-called "hard" data. Can such things be measured? At the very least they suspect that an emphasis on quantification could lead to greater concentration of the already disturbing stress on recent history, since statistical data is less abundant and reliable for the more distant past. There is also reason to question if quantifiers too readily choose their data because of its recurrent or serial relationship to other data. But much historical data defies placement into well-delineated categories and series. Moreover, the warning that "historical facts are unique in character, space, and time" does indeed restrain historians "from trying to fit them into a rigid theory or fixed pattern...."[23] Quantifiers rely on material that has the capacity to be measured. That thought led Arthur Schlesinger, Jr., to suggest the often repeated argument "that almost all the important questions [in history] are important precisely because they are *not* susceptible to quantitative answers."[24]

[22]Quoted in Richard E. Beringer, *Historical Analysis: Contemporary Approaches to Clio's Craft* (New York: John Wiley & Sons, 1978), 193-94.
[23]Carl Bridenbaugh, "The Great Mutation," *American Historical Review* 68 (January 1963): 325.
[24]Arthur Schlesinger, Jr., "The Humanist Looks at Empirical Social Research," *The American Sociological Review* 27 (December 1962): 770.

Chapter 3: The Fundamentals of Good History

> "The rapid growth in the importance of the computer during the second half of the twentieth century made many fine changes, but it also had the effect of making the word cheap and the number dear. At the same time, the perceived importance of history in a person's education sadly began to lose out as the modern university's interests turned away from the past and toward the technological, numerical future and its profit potential." — Sam Riley, author, *Magazines of the American South*

A particular approach that has been popular among communication historians in the last few decades is content analysis. Because some have relied almost solely on it for their research, it has created several misconceptions and problems. The popularity of content analysis stems from the fact that doctoral programs in communication have emphasized quantitative methods for social and behavioral research, and content analysis seems to historians trained in these programs to be the method most adaptable to historical research. In essence, content analysis is seen as a method for the objective, systematic, and quantitative description of various characteristics of communication. Some historians use it simply to count the number of various items that appear in a publication and then group them according to similarities.

Often, historians have used content analysis alone as the means of research for particular studies. From it they not only have described the nature of the content but sometimes have attempted to imply various reasons underlying history, including writers' and publishers' motivations. Content analysis, however, can do only one thing: describe content. It cannot show, for example, a cause-effect relationship, and it cannot establish motives. It does not prove, for instance, that because a newspaper had a conservative editorial policy its publisher's motive was to gain advertising from conservative businessmen. To be generous to content analysis, however, we should add that it can suggest what motives or relationships might be. But once they discover such a hint, historians should not rush to a conclusion. They should examine other historical sources, such as diaries or private correspondence or business records, that will broaden the evidence.

By itself, content analysis is inadequate to provide the research material necessary in historical study. It provides only a part of the raw material the historian must use. Historical study requires thorough examination of not only the content of newspapers, for example, but of private papers, relevant political or religious or economic material, demographic data — and on and on. The point for historians is this: Content analysis can do nothing more than describe content, which is, after all, only one small aspect of the historical process. It cannot go beyond the material itself; and — this point is particularly important for the communication historian — it can *never* answer the question of "Why?"

The remaining two concerns about quantification relate closely to the first. Regarding the object of history, traditionalists are quick to point out that history must recreate real life. That deals not only with elements of historical setting but also with motives of the individual and of the many in the past. Suppose it is possible to explain that people acted in one way or another economically. One still wants to know if they were motivated by economic rationality. Did the newspapers that supported slavery in the nineteenth century or the magazines that published muckraking articles in the twentieth assume their positions for solely economic reasons? There are, moreover, other cultural and social motives to consider. Most important of all, do the mathematical models of the quantifiers, which grow more involved as the data grow in complexity, convey a sense of what it was like to have lived and to have been moved to action in some previous time? Even when history deals with the many, historians must strive, as Carl Bridenbaugh observed, to "show them as individuals whenever [they] can." That was what he had in mind in his 1962 presidential address to the American Historical Association when he warned historians not to "worship at the shrine of the Bitch-goddess, QUANTIFICATION."[25] Though vigorously put, his point merits pondering.

> "History is empirical because it is guided by evidence. It is not a 'qualitative' endeavor, in the sense that that word implies more interpretation than fact. For historians, the interpretation follows the facts, not vice versa." — *Ed Caudill, author, Darwin in the American Press*

The final concern about quantification is the simplest to explain but equal in importance to the previous two. Will reliance on quantification impair the narrative element in history and its ability to communicate to a wide audience? Peter Laslett's outstanding study of pre-industrial England, *The World We Have Lost* (1965), stands as proof that this need not be the case. Most communication historians who rely on quantification have, unfortunately, made their texts read more like clinical reports than historical narratives. It should be remembered that good historical writing does more than provide a description of the method by which the research was performed and of the findings it revealed. Mechanical structure and style is one of the injuries content analysis and other social-science research methods have inflicted on some historical writing in communication. A few historians rely so exclusively on content analysis that their article

[25]Bridenbaugh, "The Great Mutation," 326.

manuscripts and papers consist mostly of a detailed description of the method employed. However, while research methods, whether quantitative or traditional, are critical in historical study, all that is needed in the narrative — even if a technique such as content analysis took a year to complete — is a brief summary stating the most essential details.

The problem for writing created by quantitative methods in communication history appears to be a result of the uncertainty that some communication scholars have about the academic and "scientific" validity of their field. Although standards of research have improved in recent years, communication historians still sometimes feel compelled to defend the adequacy of their methods. The solution for raising the acceptance of communication history as an academic discipline is the study of historical methods — and a mastery of them. Through such study, communication historians may one day be so rightly confident of the soundness of their methods that they will know it is evident from the results they present. Research methods should be so good that the excellence of the study will be evident from the findings that are narrated, rather than from a minute detailing of how the methods were performed.

Nevertheless, the quantifiers have a strong argument, if quantification is understood as part of the aggregate whole of history. There are quantitative as well as non-quantitative elements and characteristics of the past. Quantification has the potential to expand and sharpen historical knowledge. The work of Lawrence Stone, Charles Tilly, Peter Laslett, and a number of other non-communication historians has proven that proposition. On a smaller research scale, some communication historians have used quantitative methods effectively in examining such topics as journalists' professional attitudes, the origins of sensationalism, and the shift in American newspapers from foreign to domestic news. As a method, quantification has much to offer in understanding that part of historical evidence that can be handled by mathematical means. It can help historians to examine vast amounts of historical data and to search that information for characteristics, uniformities, and variations.

Based on their own explanation of their methodological principles and on the contribution their studies already have made to history, it is only fair to conclude that quantifiers can and do provide enlightenment on a wide range of historical problems including some of general historical interpretation. Several leading exponents of the method have offered this perspective: "What is attempted in quantitative research, as in other research, is not full knowledge of reality but an increasingly closer approximation to it.... These techniques, even if they cannot produce the ultimate, can at least bring us increasingly closer to a position that we can urge with a certain amount of assurance."[26]

Historians can and should acknowledge the value of quantification as well as its limitations. "History is still basically a humanistic study," as Lester Stephens reminds us, "and quantification is useful to historical research only insofar as it helps us to understand human beings in the past."[27] With that thought in mind, its present usefulness can be confirmed as well as its promise for the future.

Postmodernism in History

Toward the end of the twentieth century, another intellectual movement, usually known as "postmodernism," emerged to challenge orthodox ways of thinking about and writing history. The meaning of the term "postmodernism" has often remained obscure, and for many it has been a "notoriously slippery label." Many take it to be synonymous with poststructuralism or deconstruction.[28] While it has taken root more among literary and cultural theorists than among historians, it does represent a critique of the practice of historical thinking and writing and, as such, has occasioned a vigorous response from historians. With origins traceable back at least to the nineteenth-century philosopher Friedrich Nietzsche, twentieth-century postmodernism entered the United States mainly from France, most notably through the work of Michel Foucault and Jacques Derrida in the wake of the Vietnam War. The waning of the Cold War, the rise of multiculturalism's questioning of the norms of national identity, and the challenges to mainstream history by social historians all provided additional incentives for intellectuals to embrace some form of postmodernism.[29]

In some respects, the postmodernist challenge is another episode in the old struggle between historians who contend that their studies are objective and those who believe studies are relativist. That being the case, it can be said that the postmodernists favor a more critical form of relativism that questions long accepted conventions of historical methodology. Some postmodernists claim that historical objectivity is impossible and that truth about the past is unattain-

---

[26]William O. Aydelotte, Allan G. Bogue, and Robert William Fogel, eds., *The Dimensions of Quantitative Research in History* (Princeton, N.J.: Princeton University Press, 1972), 11.

[27]Stephens, *Probing the Past*, 109.

[28]Joyce Appleby, Lynn Hunt, and Margaret Jacob, *Telling the Truth About History* (New York: W. W. Norton, 1994), 200.

[29]Richard Rorty, "Deconstruction," in *The Cambridge History of Literary Criticism*, vol. 8, *From Formalism to Poststructuralism*, ed., Raman Selden (New York: Cambridge University Press, 1995), 193-96.

able. Postmodernist scholars, in the words of one critic, "embrace an extreme skepticism which denies the possibility of historical knowledge altogether."[30] Given the paucity of evidence about human experience, the selectivity of the historian choosing among that evidence, and the fact that interpretations are always shaped by the subjectivity of the analyst, many postmodernists believe that an "accurate" representation of the past is impossible.

Central to the position of the postmodernists are their ideas that the real world of the past can only be known through texts, that texts have no fixed meaning, that readers determine the meaning of texts, and that archival material is simply another type of literature or text. In Foucault's view, in which his own ideology played a considerable role, texts about the past, whether literary or historical, were simply fictive narratives that reflected an exercise of power by the culturally dominant group in society. That idea appeals to extreme multiculturalists, who turned to history in pursuit of their "identity politics."[31] It also encouraged fragmentation in history.

Postmodernists emphasize language and practice a type of "literary determinism."[32] Derrida, in particular, led the way in advocating the deconstruction of texts, arguing that a virtually infinite number of possibilities exist for textual interpretation and that texts never mean what they say. Critics have pointed out a paradox in deconstructionists' thinking: that should we accept their claim that texts never mean what they say, then we must assume that their own statements do not mean what they say. Of course, postmodernists dispute that point. Taken to its logical conclusion, though, Derrida's claims would reduce history to an understanding of language governed by postmodernist criteria. Accordingly, there is no truth to be discovered in history. The world of the past can only be known through the prism of present culture. In such contentions, the postmodernists' relativism is apparent; and since they dismiss the idea of objective history, they represent a triumph of a subjective approach to the study of the past. Critics note that postmodernists, who claim that there can be no absolute truth, do believe there is one, and only one, valid approach to history: theirs. Moreover, along with claiming that historical narratives are really literary ones, some postmodernists contend that efforts to provide coherence or unity to a fragmented past are meaningless at best and propagandistic at worst.

Other postmodernists are more moderate in their contentions, and there are substantial differences among historians working in this vein. Nevertheless,

[30]Richard Evans, *In Defense of History* (New York: W. W. Norton, 1999), 210.
[31]Ibid., 169-70; and Appleby, Hunt, and Jacob, *Telling the Truth About History*, 292.
[32]Appleby, Hunt, and Jacob, ibid., 230.

if their ideas are considered together, they represent a serious criticism of the premises upon which most historians base their work, and it has forced historians to sharpen their senses of their craft and discipline.

History is a record-based, inductive, and empirical study. Most historians remain confident that evidence is the foundation of history and that, although the record of the past can be questioned and interpreted, it cannot be denied. Myths associated with it may be punctured and understandings of it may vary, but evidence remains the bedrock of historical inquiry. No historian would claim that absolute truth about the past is attainable, that those who author serious studies of the past do so with pure objectivity, or that the past can be known in its totality. However, that does not mean that every evaluation of the evidence is equally accurate or that all views of the past are equally right or wrong. To believe otherwise would place histories denying the Holocaust on par with valid studies of Nazi Germany, to cite an obvious example. Nor does the inability to know the past completely mean that historians are satisfied to write accounts of unconnected bits and pieces of the past. Recognizing that any quest for objectivity is tempered by their own subjectivity, they seek to understand the record of times past and to allow it to serve as proof in their inquiries. The same thing cannot always be said about the intellectual candor of postmodernists. In the words of several contemporary authors, historians today insist on the "human capacity to discriminate between false and faithful representations of past reality." The historical objectivity that guides historians in the process, they argue, is a "qualified objectivity" based on the interaction between "the inquiring subject and the external object."[33] This pragmatic approach to history is grounded in the assumptions that curiosity about the past begins in the present and that this curiosity should lead to analyses based on the record of the past. Aware of their own subjectivity, historians then do their best to create accounts that are faithful to that record.

Similarly, postmodernist ideas about historical narratives are unconvincing to most historians. Rejecting the notion that their accounts are literary narratives to be judged by ideological rhetorical criteria, they contend that their narratives are record-based exercises in critical thinking and causal explanations that offer coherent explanations of their subjects. Nor do they see their narratives as confined to the particularity of the object under investigation. To the contrary, they hold that particular things in the past must be placed in context and that an effort must be made to show how they connect to other things. Furthermore, while admitting that they make linguistic choices in constructing their

[33]Ibid., 259 and 261.

narratives, they hold that, rather than being mere subjective discourses about the past, their narratives are object-focused, realistic endeavors to generalize about the truth of the past, as far as it is possible at a given time to perceive the truth. Ironically, the postmodernist criticism of historical writing has increased historians' attention to narrative, which remains the preferred means by which historians communicate with their audience.

In the longer view, the postmodernist challenge has not undermined the pursuit of history but has in fact enriched it. Some historians have found ways of incorporating postmodernist insights into their work in productive ways. Others, while rejecting postmodernism, have been encouraged to be more attentive to the subjective nature of their work and to think deeply about the nature of the objectivity they profess. Such scrutiny can only enhance history. It has forced historians to be more self-critical, and as Richard J. Evans has observed, "it has shifted the emphasis in historical writing ... back from social-scientific to literary models and, in so doing, has begun to make it more accessible to the public outside the universities (and indeed to students within them)."[34]

Cultural and Critical Studies

Specifically for communication history, some of the problems with postmodernism can be seen in cultural and critical studies. That approach has some popularity in communication academic circles, particularly among scholars coming out of "communication studies." At the hazard of over-simplifying, it can be observed that most scholars in communication history who employ cultural and critical studies do not have training primarily in traditional history but come from academic backgrounds such as critical theory, social criticism, gender studies, sociology, and communication philosophy.

In the terminology of cultural and critical studies, *culture* refers generally to the values and beliefs that members of a society share and, more specifically, to the social meaning that derives from, among other things, media content. When researchers have adopted the tenets of cultural and critical studies for history, they have tended to assume that media content is a mechanism whereby social meaning is imparted to society, that social norms reflect media content, and that the media serve as a means to achieve "hegemony" by reinforcing the views of society's dominant groups.

As with postmodernism, ideology is one of the distinctive characteristics of cultural and critical studies. The field "tends to focus on the power that the

[34]Evans, *In Defense of History*, 216.

researchers believe is embedded in media content," explains Sean Baker, one of its practitioners, "with messages viewed to be agents of social control that have a significant impact on people and culture itself.... The beginning assumptions relate to ideological dominance, political economy, structuralism, poststructuralism, psychoanalysis, feminism, and postmodernism. The ideological framework assumes that dominant social ideas and beliefs are manifested in content and that these messages support the status quo."[35] The fundamental ideology is that society's dominant group (or groups) uses the media to maintain its control over society in order to promote its own values and protect its own position. Such an ideology is, for cultural and critical studies, the equivalent of a commonsensical truth without an alternative. Thus, researchers usually do not attempt to investigate whether such a situation exists but rather tend to analyze how the hegemonic process functions. As a consequence, it can be said that historians who come out of cultural and critical studies usually are inclined to know their conclusions before they start their research.

Cultural and critical studies researchers use a variety of methods. They include such tools as ethnography and reception studies, both of which focus on the audience. The most common method, however, is textual analysis. In that methodology, researchers may use a number of sub-methods — such as, for example, "auteur analysis" (which examines texts that a single person or media corporation creates) and "discourse analysis" (which considers language a social practice and examines such matters as the structural aspects of language, including grammar, and its ideological use). Cultural and critical studies often use the terms *textual analysis* and *content analysis* interchangeably. However, one should not confuse the content analysis of cultural and critical studies with quantitative content analysis used in empirical research in social and behavioral science. Cultural and Critical analysis is more subjective and interpretive.

Unlike the traditional practices of historians, which involve examining a variety of types of sources, cultural and critical studies' textual analysis examines only media content. In that, it must be admitted, it resembles some work by traditional historians who examine media content alone and don't supplement it with other types of sources. After examining media content, those historians then draw conclusions about it, such as, for example, how

---

[35] Sean Baker, "Cultural and Critical Studies," chapter 19 in *Research Methods in Communication*, 3rd ed., Shuhua Zhou and Wm. David Sloan, eds. (Northport, Ala.: Vision Press, 2015), 311 and 312.

Chapter 3: The Fundamentals of Good History

> "Great work always begins with a great question. Never approach a research project with a conclusion in mind. You might have a hunch, but you don't have an answer. Go into the archives willing to be surprised. The best findings are the ones you didn't expect." — *Tracy Lucht, author, Sylvia Porter: America's Original Personal Finance Columnist*

the *New York Times* covered a particular event. Cultural and critical studies researchers, however, take their reasoning a step further. Rather than contenting themselves to describe media content, they jump from content to explanations about what it *means* to the audience. In explaining how the audience interprets content, researchers don't do what would seem to be the logical thing: to ask audience members what the content means to them or, in historical research, to find and examine primary sources left by audience members. Instead, the researchers claim that media content is too complex for audience members to understand and that researchers, by virtue of their training, are more qualified than the audience members to understand what media content means to the audience.[36] When researchers cite other types of source material, it frequently is secondary literature — rather than primary sources — published by other researchers who share the same perspective. As one can imagine, such a mindset allows researchers to conclude anything they want. The check on runaway conclusions is the process of review by other cultural and critical studies academics. Since, though, researchers in the field tend to share the same mindsets, the standard ideas gain a strong foothold and continue to be repeated.

Shades of cultural and critical studies can be seen in the approaches of the "symbolic meaning" philosophy of the Cultural Studies school of historical interpretation discussed in Chapter 2 in this book. Cultural Studies tends to be less militantly ideological than cultural and critical studies, but the latter, in that it has defined methods, is more methodologically rigorous than much research in history from a Cultural Studies perspective. Historians in Cultural Studies usually begin with their philosophy and then rely mainly on a lax examination of media content and secondary sources to explain what the content meant to the audience.

Such approaches may suit researchers who wish to use history to support their own ideas, but historical research as traditionally practiced attempts to keep the historian's prejudices in check. Thus, such approaches as

---

[36] Ibid., 316.

deconstruction and cultural and critical studies seem, at their core, antithetical to good history.

Good history, we can conclude, should manifest many qualities. In contemplating them, we are reminded of its diversity. The variety of people who find the study significant enough to involve themselves in the labors of doing history continue to enhance and expand the study. The fascination that attracts them to historical scholarship should not be lost. It is one of history's richest resources. In the words of C. V. Wedgwood, "the mansion of history" has many rooms. Enough, Wedgwood said, "to accommodate all of us."[37] To continue that metaphor, one can add that the mansion has many entrances and a sturdy foundation. History remains history, a form of inquiry with acknowledged standards but one that features elasticity in scope and method. It continues to bear kinship to the humanities and to experience a "love-hate" relationship with the social sciences. Seeking to recapture the human element in the past, its practitioners still recognize the importance of audience and stress the communicative element, the art, that has so long been one of its distinguishing characteristics. They still try to comprehend the past on its own terms as far as is possible and to pursue the truth of a past episode, restrained always by the uncertainty inherent in all the larger aspects of the subject. History continues to depend on the historian, on that person's integrity, imagination, historical grasp, and professional inclination. Communication historians should consider the reasons that make Gene Roberts and Hank Klibanoff's *The Race Beat* — the winner of the 2007 Pulitzer Prize — such a fine history.[38] Its excellence as a piece of history is due less to the fact that it reflects or fails to reflect new techniques available to historians than to the fact that it successfully engages the accepted standards of good history.

> "The mansion of history" has enough rooms "to accommodate all of us." — C. V. Wedgwood, in Gustavson, *The Mansion of History*

---

[37]Quoted in Gustavson, *The Mansion of History*, 1.
[38]Gene Roberts and Hank Klibanoff, *The Race Beat: The Press, the Civil Rights Struggle, and the Awakening of a Nation* (New York: Alfred A. Knopf, 2007).

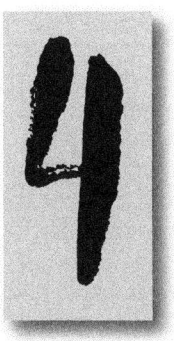

BASIC PROCEDURES AND TECHNIQUES

How should one begin a project in history? Let us assume the project is one of considerable length — a seminar or convention paper, a journal article, or a longer work: a thesis, a dissertation, or even a book. There are basic procedures to follow. At the start of a project, however, one must ask: What is it that I want to do with this study? How can it be done? What are the practical considerations to take into account? What will make it a worthwhile study? With such questions in mind, one can appreciate the fact that beginnings are never easy. There is vastness to confront and manage. Mistakes made at this point can haunt one throughout the entire study. They can even ruin it. In this chapter we shall consider some basic procedures to follow at the outset of a project.

Preliminary Reading

When students and scholars contemplate research in history, they already have started to think about a subject to investigate. From either general interest or previous courses or studies, they have acquired at least a semblance of knowledge about a particular subject. The task they face now is that of sharpening the knowledge they have. The approach is to start reading at the general level and then work downward to literature narrowly focused on the topic.

General reading about the subject in its larger historical setting is a logical place to begin. How much of this general or preliminary reading is necessary? The answer depends on the person involved in the task. We all approach research with varying degrees of knowledge about a field that attracts our interest. Even the seasoned scholar can drift from one historical area to another. Consequently, preliminary reading can be just as necessary for someone who has spent years in serious historical scholarship as for the student beginning a major research project for the first time. Let us, however, focus our attention on a student trying to start work on a research project in communication history. Recent textbooks that include the subject to be investigated provide a sensible first source to consult. A student's advisor can offer guidance about which ones to use, but in the case of communication history, a textbook in that area, such as *The Media in America: A History*, and one in general history, such as George Brown Tindall's *America: A Narrative History*, can be recommended. Since the media do not exist alone in time, the duality suggested in this recommendation will become a major feature of the ensuing research.

> "Remember to keep an open mind, prepared for the possibility that the literature you read and the evidence you find may lead you in directions more interesting and rewarding than you assumed at the beginning. This process of discovery is at the heart of successful research." — *Steve Ponder, University of Oregon*

The idea of beginning by using textbooks will cause some eyebrows to raise. Indeed, if one already has a firm grasp on the larger aspects of a research subject, this step might be skipped. But even in cases where there is an absence of such knowledge, purists can argue that a textbook might shape one's perception of a subject. Why not go to the sources and form your own perceptions? The point is logical and laudable, but unrealistic. By this time in a student's education, general perceptions of the subject already have been formed. That is one reason for the choice of a particular subject in the first place.

Moreover, throughout the course of a research project, one will interact with what other scholars have said on the subject. It can, therefore, be helpful at the start to know how previous historians have shaped the subject and how they have presented it to the general audience. For that reason, familiarity with the "schools" of historiography explained in chapter 2 of this book takes on great importance.

Where to go from here? An appropriate next step would be to locate and study several books germane to the topic under consideration. Let us say that the topic is "The American Press and the Beginning of World War I" (a topic that probably would need refinement). An excellent selection would be Leonard Teel's *The Public Press, 1900-1945* (2006), which is volume 5 in the seven-volume "History of American Journalism" series (1994-2006). Since the topic would most likely involve some aspect of American foreign relations, a logical next step would be to consult appropriate chapters in a survey of that subject, such as

George C. Herring's authoritative *From Colony to Superpower: U.S. Foreign Relations Since 1776* (2008). However, indispensable as these volumes may be, they are only an early part of a bibliographical search. Researchers should continue their general reading on the communication aspects of their topic by checking bibliographies of communication histories and by pursuing bibliographic leads cited in the textbooks consulted. In the case of the press and World War I, that would connect them with studies on censorship, propaganda, war correspondence, etc. They also should consult their advisors about authoritative communication studies that cover the subject in part. No doubt, in this instance, they would be directed to Robert Desmond's *Windows on the World: World News Reporting 1900-1920*, the second volume in his three-volume survey of news-reporting history.

How long should one spend on preliminary reading? In a sense, it lasts for the duration of a study. But when should one move on to the next stage? Bear in mind that any manual (including this one now in your hands) oversimplifies divisions between stages for purposes of illustration. Still, it can be recommended that once you gain familiarity with the general dimensions of your subject (e.g., recognition of its basic political, economic, social, institutional, and biographical aspects), you are ready to proceed with further study. The next step involves defining a precise topic within the chosen area.

Topic Selection

A perfect topic is a rarity, particularly among those that students choose toward the beginning of their investigations. There are no guaranteed criteria for all occasions regarding selecting a topic, but the following suggestions are worth considering:

1. *Ability*. Researchers must ask themselves if they have the necessary skills needed for an investigation. If not, are they willing to acquire them? One would have to have knowledge of the Russian language, for instance, to investigate the Soviet press during Lenin's time. Communication history can involve so many aspects of life and society that the range of expertise regarding language, economics, politics, religion, and many other things related to it is also great. Without the expertise that will allow you to understand the topic in its historical setting and to understand sources, the topic will suffer. In such cases, one is well advised to select another.

2. *Workability*. Is the topic workable in terms of availability of sources? Remember, history depends on evidence, and that evidence must exist in sufficient

quantity to provide answers for significant questions that will be asked of it. Moreover, some topics, however fascinating they might be, are unknowable. For instance, what was the source of the sense of humor that President Lincoln displayed so often in his dealings with reporters? Can it be known beyond doubt? In short, selection involves establishing the feasibility of investigating a topic. Curiosity and interest are important, but they can be taken for granted. Feasibility counts.

> "Whether you're choosing the topic for a thesis, dissertation, or book, there is one rule of thumb that you can't afford to ignore. Whatever topic you choose had better excite you enough that it makes you want to get up in the morning. If that's not the case, chances are you will never finish." — Catherine Cassara, Bowling Green State University

3. *Significance.* Is the topic important, and can its importance be demonstrated? Does it relate in an explainable way to things considered consequential in the past? Does it relate to matters that are important for society to know? If not, it is only of antiquarian value and fails to qualify as a viable topic. Moreover, in establishing the significance of the topic to one's satisfaction, attention should be paid to whether it is historically justifiable. Where does it fit into older work on the topic if previous studies have been conducted? Is this one needed? The answer to these questions takes us back to the purpose of history and assumes a bibliographic awareness that must mature as the investigation proceeds.

Once chosen, a topic must be delineated or restricted in terms of time, space, and content. A researcher can accomplish this task by considering the who, what, where, and when of the topic.

1. *Who.* Decide who or what groups or people will be included in the investigation.

2. *What.* Determine what aspect of communication (the issue, one might say) the study will examine. What are the important questions about the subject that have confronted previous historians? Does the topic have unity of its own? Every topic is related to others in close proximity to it, yet the successful topic should lend itself to individual treatment. The extent of that individual treatment might be quite extensive and inclusive. In the end, however, it must lend itself to intelligible explanation on its own.

3. *Where.* Define the precise geographical area of the topic.

4. *When.* Determine a particular span of time to cover. Be sure it has a logical beginning and end.

By such procedures as described here, the researcher should be able to make the necessary and careful initial topic selection. Once made, it is possible

Chapter 4 : Basic Procedures and Techniques

— though doubtful — that the selection will hold until the end of the project. Either common sense or acquired knowledge may dictate topic modification as the research progresses. That adjustment, though sometimes painful to execute, might be needed for the eventual success of one's investigation. Research should proceed with an ongoing concern for the viability of the initial selection of the topic as well as for whatever redefinition of the topic one has made.

> "The research question provides the roadmap for the entire research process: what sources to examine and how to examine them, what to include in your paper and what to leave out. You can't hope to navigate an unfamiliar place without a roadmap, and a research project that doesn't begin with some well-thought-out questions will similarly wander aimlessly about." — *Tom Johnson, University of Texas*

We would recommend that historians (but not necessarily students) look for topics of large scope. Small topics are chosen frequently because they are the only ones that a scholar can find that have not been "done before." They therefore frequently are insignificant and make little contribution to our understanding of communication history. All topics, even small ones, require a large investment of time and work; and one convention paper or one article seems little reward for so much. Thorough familiarity with literature already produced in communication history should suggest important topics that need to be reconsidered or new topics to be studied. Consider, for example, the issues raised by the historiographical schools discussed in Chapter 2 of this book. The point here is not to discourage work on all small topics but rather to emphasize that historians need to understand the value of the subject when starting out. Small topics can be significant if they relate to the "big picture."

However, when searching for a topic, the historian might ask whether it is worthy of book-length treatment. Many topics in communication history need such study. When an appropriate topic is found, it offers several advantages over the smaller one. First, the topic will have to be significant. Second, book-length studies allow for greater exploration of context and supplemental detail. They open the way for fuller development of characters and for greater use of circumstantial evidence. Third, a large topic forces the historian to realize that extensive research must be done. That is an advantage because it requires the historian to do thorough research. Fourth, once the research has been conducted, the historian has the raw material for several papers and articles in addition to a book. Hour for hour, then, time is spent more economically on a large rather than on a small topic.

Organization

Researchers use a number of basic techniques to organize their investigations. As their topics grow, for instance, they create timelines of events and actions. These timelines may be designed to cover the entire chronological scope of the topic or, in more integral detail, any of its component parts. Historians make a practice of creating a number of files to keep for instant references. Files on basic data and on biographical information, for example, can be indispensable tools in a researcher's work. Many also keep a file of ideas, thoughts they have about various aspects of their investigation. By putting ideas about their subject in writing, they sharpen them and, in the process, discipline themselves to think with precision as well as with imagination about their topic. All researchers, of course, will develop their own version of devices such as these, and it is important to anticipate as early as possible in a project the type of information needed to have on instant recall.

An outline is one of the most useful of all organizational devices. It should be designed early in the investigation as evidence is gathered, but it should not be allowed to dominate that evidence. In the end, it will be the *evidence* that determines the outline. The purpose of an outline is structural and functional. It helps one to perceive a possible order and framework for the study. It also helps one to detect gaps in research and to strengthen its continuity. In short, it is a device for integrating old and new subject matter and for providing structure and direction for the project. Remember, however, that the past should be allowed, as far as possible, to stand on its own. Therefore an outline should not be considered a straitjacket for selecting evidence. To the contrary, it should be used as a tentative organizational device, which itself will probably have to be redesigned as the research mounts. Researchers will find it a useful instrument to use in pulling together the diverse but related data collected. As the project evolves, the original outline will undergo numerous changes, gradually becoming a tool for producing a usable structure for the narrative itself.

Focusing the Study

Let us suppose now that a student has begun a serious inquiry into a historical subject. We shall assume preliminary reading and organizational preparation have been done as far as possible at this point. What next? Questions must be asked: What does one want to discover about the topic? Everything? Do certain conclusions seem to fit before one finds the evidence to substantiate them?

> "Focus, focus, focus. Select a subject that interests you. Then narrow your subject and tell us something, an interesting story, that has never been told about that subject." — Anthony Fellow, author, *American Media History*

Everyone with any knowledge about a general historical subject has a hunch about answers to many questions within it. Sometimes it is even a well-known hunch. Nevertheless, in regard to a specific project, a researcher will do well to keep in mind this advice that Sherlock Holmes once gave to the faithful Dr. Watson: "I have no data yet. It is a capital mistake to theorize before one has data. Insensibly one begins to twist facts to suit theories, instead of theories to suit facts."[1] That sound advice should serve as a restraint for students and scholars involved in historical research at least in forming the overarching structural framework of the study and in advancing conclusions.

Nevertheless, every researcher has thoughts about material at first contact with it and has certain questions in mind needing to be answered. In a sense, the process of selection of evidence has already started. Does that mean that distortion also has begun? Topic selection involved selectivity, and now questions to be asked of the material begin to emerge. Will not the simple presence of those questions guide the choice of evidence? Does the use of an outline structure research too much and force an artificial selection of evidence? Moreover, what happens to evidence once one begins to formulate a hypothesis? Might that encourage reductionism or bias the selection and use of evidence?

Understanding the place of hypothesis in historical investigation can be of use in responding to these questions. A hypothesis is a tentative assumption, a proposition to be proven, modified, or rejected. For example, a hypothesis might be: The American press became a tool of propaganda during World War I. Once stated, that proposition would then have to be proven by evidence or changed. "The hypothesis," as Lester Stephens said, "usually plays a more crucial role in scientific investigation than it does in history."[2] Historians tend to refer to the "working hypothesis," by which they mean a concept to use in approaching evidence. It involves the advancing of a possible explanation for evidence as research progresses. By its nature, it is a tentative device subject to accommodation forced by the sway of evidence. A hypothesis may be vague at first, but it is unrealistic to think that hypothesis formation can be delayed. Thought about a

---

[1] Sir Arthur Conan Doyle, *Great Cases of Sherlock Holmes* (Center, Pa.: The Franklin Library, 1985), 7.

[2] Lester D. Stephens, *Probing the Past: A Guide to the Study and Teaching of History* (Boston: Allyn and Bacon, Inc., 1974), 31.

topic begins as soon as the mind starts to contemplate it. It can be recommended, therefore, that attention be given to crystallizing a working hypothesis (or working hypotheses) as part of the ongoing involvement with evidence.

> "To help establish historical significance, ask, 'what's different?' about your topic in relation to its own time or 'what's missing?' in the current literature. Or both." — Meg Lamme, author, *Public Relations and Religion in American History*

It can also be useful to pose the topic in the form of a question rather than a hypothesis. The proposition that "the American press became a tool of propaganda during World War I" might be rephrased as the interrogative, "Did the American press serve as a propaganda tool during World War I; and if so, how, to what extent, and why? If it did not, what role did it serve, and why?" Stating the topic as a question tends less to force a structure on the evidence than a hypothesis does. Such an approach also forces the student to formulate the topic in a concrete and precise form. Concreteness and precision assist researchers in determining what data they find is relevant and what is not. As research progresses, other smaller questions may be raised in precise manner, and each should be answered.

Similarly, when first stating the question to be studied, it is important to determine whether it really is the essential, most important, most interesting question. Both students and scholars are prone to ask questions that actually only scratch the surface rather than those that get to the heart of history and their interest in it. A good way to find the heart is to ask the question "Why?" repeatedly, every time the historian thinks he or she has answered it. Suppose the question of study first proposed is "What were the attitudes about journalism that penny press editors held in the 1830s and 1840s?" The historian should then ask, "Why do I want to know?" The answer might be, "I want to know whether they thought of themselves as journalists who originated modern journalism, as many historians have claimed, or whether they thought of themselves in some other way and, if so, how?" Each "Why?" and its answer moves the historian closer to the essential question and to a topic of real importance in the study of history. Every question has an answer of true significance if only it can be uncovered.

The danger of forcing an artificial selectivity on evidence, however, remains. Researchers can take several precautions to minimize such dangers when dealing with working hypotheses and tentative answers to questions. First, keep in mind that a hypothesis or tentative answer must be in accord with evidence. Conclusions must arise naturally from the evidence, not from a hypothesis. All available evidence must be considered. Indeed, it is contradictory evidence that usually forces modification or even rejection of a hypothesis. Second, do not avoid a basic step in research, that of gaining familiarity with the evidence. If you are dealing, let us say, with the personal papers of a nineteenth-century advertising agent, study those papers to the greatest degree possible. Use your imagination. Let your natural curiosity lead you to examine evidence in the collection that bears little relation to your topic. Try to acquire a sense of such figures on their own terms. Be generous in your note-taking. Include items that inform one about general circumstances of the time as well as those that have direct relation to the topic being investigated. Pursue and clarify questions about the material at hand until you are satisfied that you have a basic understanding of it. It is unrealistic to suppose that in this process of familiarization you will have no hypotheses or potential answers in mind. They should be, however, more tentative than those that emerge as research progresses. Remember that even the latter are only working hypotheses, ideas to be tested against evidence.

> "Always ask yourself, 'So what?' It's not enough to tell a good story; your story must tell us something we didn't previously know about media history." — Karen Miller Russell, author, The Voice of Business

The historian E.H. Carr reminds us how much of historical investigation is an integrated process of research, writing, and modifying the questions one is asking. As he argues, the notion that there are "two sharply distinguishable phases or periods" of historical work is "unconvincing and implausible." It is simply impossible, he says, to write good history by assuming one can read everything necessary on a subject and then sit down to write. Rather, as he describes his own process, "as soon as I have got going on a few of what I take to be the capital sources, the itch becomes too strong and I begin to write — not necessarily at the beginning, but somewhere, anywhere. Thereafter, reading and writing go on simultaneously. The writing is added to, subtracted from, re-shaped, cancelled, as I go on reading."[3] Historians would do well to consider Carr's advice.

Finally, and this takes us back to the purpose of history, recall that the goal of history is "to reconstruct the past as accurately as possible."[4] That goal involves modification of questions, hypotheses, and answers until one becomes convinced that the reconstruction is valid. Any methodological device such as constructing a hypothesis is simply a tool to use. It should not be allowed to master those who employ it.

[3]E.H. Carr, *What is History?* (Basingstoke: Palgrave, 2001 [1965]), 22-23.
[4]Ibid., 32.

Notetaking

Taking research notes is a more involved process than one might expect. It necessitates the mastery of some mechanics as well as thought. Consequently, even in this day of photo-duplicating machines, scanners, and computers, a few comments about this most basic of research techniques are in order. The fundamental rules to follow are these:

1. Always start by citing the source for the note.
2. Along with that citation, include a topical reference on the note.
3. Be consistent in where you place the citation and other references on the note.
4. Develop a method of consistent usage for copying direct quotations, particularly those long ones that will cover several pages of notes. Be certain that you put quotation marks around any words that you take verbatim from a source. This practice will help you to avoid unintentional plagiarism.
5. Make sure that a note is self-explanatory and that it will make sense when viewed a week, a month, or even years later.
6. Enter only one item on each note. Remember that the notes have to be filed in some coherent order.
7. Make accuracy of information a fetish. Double check your notes as you make them.
8. Never write on the reverse side of a notecard or a page of notes.

These rules apply even if you make notes on a computer, rather than on paper, using text files or notetaking software.

The arrangement and storage of notes can be a problem for historians because of the sheer bulk and variety of materials that can be gathered. Therefore, one has to develop some scheme of arrangement. Suppose the topic is "American Filmmakers and the Great Depression." Should notes be arranged according to topic, area, chronology, or person? Should notes reflect the organizational pattern of your project? Or should they be arranged into a collection of material to be employed as needed in the project, and perhaps in later ones too? If the last method is chosen, an effective indexing system will have to be developed.

We mentioned previously that notetaking involves thought as well as the mastery of mechanics. The thought referred to concerns what you attempt to tell yourself in a note. Notes are not only reminders of what you have seen but also a record of your observations of what you perceive in the sources. Some notes may be a paraphrase of lengthy materials. If that is the case, you must become

Chapter 4 : Basic Procedures and Techniques

> "Take notes as you go on any research materials you collect. This will help you find other resources and slowly build an understanding of your topic. The temptation is to photocopy materials and then keep looking; but that's not research, that's photocopying." — *David Davies, author, The Postwar Decline of American Newspapers*

skilled in the art of reducing long items to comments of manageable length. Some notes are your own reflections about either external or internal aspects of the source. Regarding the former, you might wish to know who initiated a series of letters and what their frequency was, or what type of document is under consideration, or how a newspaper that is being used for opinion or news can be described. Regarding reflections about internal aspects, you might wish to write a note interpreting a source or offering some explanation of how the information fits into broader patterns of thought and action. Explanatory notes can be as valuable as ones containing quotations or basic data. They must, however, be an accurate reflection of the source. Finally, be as expansive as possible when taking notes. The broader the note, the better equipped you will be to place the precise topic of the note in the context in which it appears.

Everyone will develop his or her own habit of notetaking and storage. Nevertheless, it can be concluded that notes should be uniform, accurate, and complete. Once you have decided on how to categorize your notes, a helpful practice is to designate folders for each division and sub-division of your study as well as ones for special topics. A system of arrangement and storage, whether in physical files or on a computer, should be logical, clear, manageable, retrievable, and expandable. Normally, sources have to be revisited and notes reexamined as one's own comprehension of the subject grows. The task of notetaking involves you in the central function of historical research, the continuing interaction between historians and their sources.

The Library as a Reference Tool

The informational files that researchers create are useful devices in both research and writing. They provide the exact background information needed for identifying historical figures and defining data in your work. The information for many of these files, along with other items of reference you may need in your study, can be found in your own university library. Answers to all the questions of a general informational sort (e.g., identification of people and references to particular items, etc.) that emerge as one encounters historical records can never be found. Yet, a great deal of such information can be located by an imaginative use of reference tools available in a university library.

The Reference Room of a library will become a familiar habitat for a historian. It is a storehouse of information that enables one to find facts and to locate other information. In fact, the number and type of reference books can appear overwhelming. The Reference Room of any university library will be well stocked with general encyclopedias as well as a number of general historical surveys such as the *New Cambridge Modern History*. They represent, however, only a few of the reference works available for historical research. You also will discover lining the shelves of a Reference Room an array of almanacs, guidebooks, yearbooks, historical and current atlases, historical dictionaries, special subject encyclopedias, registers of events, and companion volumes to particular studies.

Communication historians, for instance, will find the following sources useful:

Erik Barnouw, *International Encyclopedia of Communications* (1989)

Margaret Blanchard, *History of the Mass Media in the United States: An Encyclopedia* (1998)

Robert V. Hudson, *Mass Media: A Chronological Encyclopedia of Television, Radio, Motion Pictures, Magazines, Newspapers, and Books in the United States* (1987)

Derek Jones, *Censorship: A World Encyclopedia*, 4 vols. (2001)

Michael Murray, *Encyclopedia of Television News* (1999)

Horace Newcomb, *Museum Of Broadcast Communications Encyclopedia of Television* (1997)

Donald Paneth, *The Encyclopedia of American Journalism* (1983)

Vilma Raskin Potter, *A Reference Guide to Afro-American Publications and Editors, 1827-1946* (1993)

Richard Schwarzlose, *Newspapers: A Reference Guide* (1987)

David Sloan, *American Journalism History: An Annotated Bibliography* (1989)

Relating to more specialized interests, a number of useful guidebooks can be found in "Historical Guides to the World's Periodicals and Newspapers," a multi-volume series from Greenwood Press. Representative of the series is *Women's Periodicals in the United States* (1995-1996), a two-volume guide edited by Kathleen Endres and Theresa Lueck.

To help you establish the "who," "when," and "what" about people, there are a number of sources to consult. Some are multi-volume standard works and national in design, such as the following:

American National Biography

Current Biography
Dictionary of American Biography
The National Cyclopedia of American Biography
Who Was Who in America
Who's Who in America
Dictionary of American Negro Biography (1982)
Great North American Indians: Profiles in Life and Leadership (1977)
Notable American Women 1607-1950: A Biographical Dictionary (1971-1980)
Notable Black American Men, 2 volumes (1999, 2007)
Notable Black American Women, 2 volumes (1992, 1996)

Yet others have an ethnic or religious focus or are specialized according to region, topic, or occupation. All are valuable sources for communication historians. So too are dictionaries of portraits and volumes on genealogy.

Of special value to communication historians are a number of biography sources devoted exclusively to the mass media. For example, several single-volume sources are available. They include such works as the following:

Joe McKerns, *Biographical Dictionary of American Journalism* (1989)

Eric Newton, *Crusaders, Scoundrels, Journalists: The Newseum's Most Intriguing Newspeople* (1999)

Sam Riley, *Biographical Dictionary of American Newspaper Columnists* (1995)

William H. Taft, *Encyclopedia of Twentieth-Century Journalists* (1986)

Communication historians will want to direct their attention particularly to the extensive biographical series Dictionary of Literary Biography, published by Gale. It includes more than 250 volumes, and each volume contains lengthy articles (sometimes more than ten pages long) complete with bibliographical leads. A number of these volumes are devoted to communication professionals. For example, Perry J. Ashley edited five volumes under the title *American Newspaper Journalists*. Volume 43 covers the years 1690-1872 (1985); volume 23, 1873-1900 (1983); volume 25, 1901-1925 (1984); volume 29, 1926-1950 (1988); and volume 127, 1950-1990 (1993). Sam Riley edited four more volumes on *American Magazine Journalists*. Volume 73 covers the years 1741-1850 (1988); volume 79, 1850-1900 (1988); volume 91, 1900-1960 (First Series) (1990); and volume 137, 1900-1960 (Second Series) (1994). Arthur J. Kaul expanded the series focus on journalists even more with his *American Literary Journalists, 1945-1995* (First Series) (1997).

For a comprehensive listing of biographical sources and other reference works useful in historical inquiry, one might wish to consult Francis Paul Prucha's *Handbook for Research in American History: A Guide to Bibliographies and Other Reference Works* (2nd ed., 1994) or Thomas Mann's *The Oxford Guide to Library Research: How To Find Reliable Information Online and Offline* (4th ed., 2015). Eugene Sheehy's *Guide to Reference Books* (10th ed., 1986) is the classic general guide to reference sources. Robert Balay edited an updated edition of the *Guide* in 1996. In mass communication, one should be aware of Georgia Ludgate's *Mass Communication: A Guide to Reference Sources* (1988) and Eleanor Block and James Bracken's *Communication and the Mass Media: A guide to the reference literature* (1991).

> "Historical research requires a long attention span. If you want quicker research projects, go into the social sciences." — Dale Cressman, author, Television News Pioneer Elmer W. Lower

It is important for researchers to become familiar with key reference sources in the libraries they use most. What sources are available? How should they be used? The first question is easy to answer. Browse around a Reference Room and observe the sources it holds. Take the time to make some notes on the sources that attract your particular attention. Make your own guide for these sources, taking care to include their location and potential use. The books mentioned earlier and the Online Catalog (or, in a few libraries, the Card Catalog), which we shall describe in chapter 6, can help you designate specialized reference works (e.g., special subjects source books and encyclopedias) that you may want to include in your guide. Regarding how these reference works should be used, it is important to study the Preface or Introduction for each work you select. Examine those sections for information on the work's arrangement, scope, and possible bias. Also, note the publication date of the work to see if it is up to date.

A few words of caution are in order about the use of reference works. They are, as the name implies, for "reference." They are aids to research that provide basic information, an introduction to a subject, or particular information regarding definition and description. Consequently, they should not be cited as bibliographic sources in a research paper. (Major historical surveys that might be classified as reference works such as the Oxford and Cambridge histories as well as the more substantive biographical dictionaries are exceptions to this rule.) Reference works such as historical dictionaries, handbooks, and encyclopedias are tools to be used for background research. They are not to be employed as substitutes for historical sources.

A Working Bibliography

What books and sources to consult? That question is central to any research endeavor from start to finish. A bibliographic foundation, for instance, must be established before work can proceed on a topic. After that, the bibliography will grow and will be defined to accommodate the topic as it develops. In chapters 6 and 7, we shall see that there are many tools to use in compiling a bibliography. There is, however, no perfect previously prepared bibliography to serve one at the outset of an investigation. Bibliographies compiled during research have an organic quality about them. It would be more accurate, therefore, to refer to a bibliography during the time of research as a "working bibliography." At the start of a project one compiles such a working bibliography as a guide to books and sources to consult. As work proceeds, some items are disregarded; others, added. The bibliography becomes a record of material to be consulted. Usually compiled on cards or in computer files for purposes of convenience, the working bibliography becomes the basis for the proper "Bibliography" that will appear at the end of the completed study.

A working bibliography, then, is a tool, an evolving record of sources consulted and to be consulted. It should be complete in terms of time and type of sources. Both old and new books should be included. Older ones are worth at least a cursory consideration. Some remain as standard studies. They can contain information not found elsewhere and may have different perspectives on material that can be found in newer studies. Older perspectives at least enhance a researcher's grasp of the historiographical setting of the subject.[5] Regarding type, it is necessary to have a working bibliography reflect the full range of works and sources available. In terms of published works, that usually means major works and documentary collections as well as biographical, monographic, and periodical literature. Beyond that, whatever oral, visual, and written records you intend to consult should be included. Leave nothing to memory. Finally, a working bibliography should be imaginative in its construction. It should include published works in related areas that may be relevant.

As early as possible in their bibliographic work, students will find it useful to identify "standard authorities" who have produced studies on or related to their project. Students may recognize them from a previous course in the field, or they might begin to gain awareness of them from study of bibliographical, historiographical, and review literature, or perhaps they will learn of them from

---

[5]The term "historiography" has several meanings. It is used here in reference to the history of historical writing.

conversation with their advisors. Regardless, they must consult these standard authorities. Sometimes a major historian will have written directly on a topic now selected for investigation from a different perspective. That work should be studied. For example, who would wish to conduct an investigation into the history of the American newsreel in the 1920s without studying Raymond Fielding's work on that subject? Or who would wish to investigate the topic of war reporting in the twentieth century without consulting works by Michael Sweeney? Sometimes a topic fits into a particular larger area of historical investigation. For instance, should one decide to investigate the topic "American Immigrants and the Press in the 1890s," the works of Oscar Handlin and others on the more general topic of American immigration become key sources to consult. These standard authorities should be known, studied, and, if merited, confronted in a new probe into the subject. They represent the most significant scholarly statement on a general subject and sometimes on a particular topic. Most topics, of course, also involve an extensive monographic and periodical literature that one must search for information and interpretations. This literature, too, contains much that is authoritative.

The Internet as a Reference Tool

A new device in an old discipline, the computer has become a fixture in academic life and a tool for which all serious researchers find multiple uses. It can serve historians in many ways beyond its invaluable use as a word processor. A computer can facilitate compiling bibliographies and indexes, it can store and assist in working with numerical data, and it is useful in conducting literary and content analysis. As will be seen in subsequent chapters, the Internet offers historians indispensable tools for bibliographic searches, and it affords researchers many opportunities to gain access to a variety of historical materials not available in nearby libraries and repositories. At this point, however, our intent is to underscore the use that can be made of the Internet as a reference tool.

As previously noted, a library Reference Room is a storehouse of information for historians. Found there is the most complete array of general informational sources that researchers employ in their daily work. Some sources of this type can also be found on the Internet. Listed below is a selection of ones useful for garnering general information.[6] Researchers would do well to consult their

[6]For additional sites for reference sources, see Anne Rothfield, "Online Reference Desk," in Dennis A. Trinkle and Scott A. Merriman, *The History Highway: A 21st century guide to Internet resources*, 4th ed. (Armonk, N. Y.: M. E. Sharpe, 2006). (A fee-based digital

Chapter 4 : Basic Procedures and Techniques

university library's website for links to other online reference sources. In addition, reference librarians can provide valuable assistance for locating and using online reference sources.

Online Almanac Sources

>Infoplease: http://www.infoplease.com
>CIA World Factbook:
>>https://www.cia.gov/library/publications/resources/the-world-factbook/index.html

Biographical Sources

>Biographical Dictionary: http://www.s9.com
>Biography Online: https://www.biographyonline.net
>Encyclopedia of World Biography: https://www.notablebiographies.com
>Wikipedia Biography Portal: https://en.wikipedia.org/wiki/Portal:Biography

Encyclopedia Sources

>*Encyclopedia Britannica* Online: http://www.britannica.com
>Encyclopedia.com: http://www.encyclopedia.com
>Wikipedia: http://en.wikipedia.org

Statistical and Demographic Data Sources

>Historical Statistics of the United States, Colonial Times to 1970:
>>https://www.census.gov/library/publications/1975/compendia/hist_stats_colonial-1970.html
>Social Explorer: https://www.socialexplorer.com
>U.S. National Historical Information System: https://www.nhgis.org

Researchers also will find a great amount of background material about people, subjects, and events on the Internet. Ranging from sites devoted to major historical figures in all genres of communication (such as, for example, Susan B.

version by Trinkle, Auchter, and Larson, updated to 2016 is available through ProQuest.) Also, most libraries have an extensive list of their reference sources online.

Anthony and Enrico Caruso) to particular subjects such as film production techniques, and to events such as Watergate, these sites have much to offer historians. However, it should be understood that material found at these locations sometimes may be of an introductory nature or even superficial. Despite such shortcomings of many Internet sites, computer technology provides a remarkable number of basic informational sources that researchers will appreciate at the start and throughout the pursuit of their inquiries. It also provides various advantages as they undertake to locate both secondary and primary materials.

It should not be thought, though, that computers are without limitations in historical research. They cannot do what historians must do to be historians. They cannot imagine the past, nor can they establish contact with the mind of the past, nor can they perceive the "climate of opinion" of a past age, nor comprehend what it was like to have lived at some other time and place in history. Moreover, they cannot establish truth beyond the quality of evidence that one feeds them, and that evidence, including numerical data, is far from perfect, as we shall see in a later chapter. As two authorities on historical research conclude, "The computer does not think; like any other machine it only follows commands that a thinking being gives to it."[7]

Still, the computer is a valuable tool for historians. It allows them to do certain things, such as quickly locate digitized material from distant places and process massive amounts of data, that otherwise would challenge their time or be beyond their capacity. Like all tools, the computer has its limitations for historical inquiry, and one should remain mindful of them. Nevertheless, because of its potential, historians should familiarize themselves with computer technology and its applications to historical research.

Archival Research

At some point, most historians will enter an archive to do primary research for the first time. Archival research can be daunting, as historians find themselves immersed in many unfamiliar documents needing context and interpretation. Although most collections have descriptive finding aids, in many cases they are simply lists of box and folder contents. The historian is confronted with mounds of evidence to sift through and make sense of, often on a tight time frame and limited budget. To help assure that time and resources are spent well, the following are some tips for beginning researchers planning an archival visit.

[7]Jacques Barzun and Henry F. Graff, *The Modern Researcher*, 5th ed. (New York: Harcourt Brace Javonovich, 1992), 350.

Chapter 4 : Basic Procedures and Techniques

- After identifying a relevant archive (see Chapters 6 and 7 for suggested resources for finding archives), do a thorough investigation of its website. It will outline important policies and procedures with which you want to familiarize yourself before going to the archive. Some archives also offer funding for research travel, and you can find out if you can obtain support for your visit.
- Find out the archive's hours of operation, and see if it has any scheduled closing periods coming up. Some university archives maintain limited hours during school breaks. Others keep extended hours on particular days of the week.
- Once you have discovered specific relevant collections, check if a finding aid is available online. It will help familiarize you with the specifics of the collection and save you time at the archive.
- See if permission is required to consult materials. Some collections are closed to the public without written permission. You don't want to travel all the way to an archive to find that you're not allowed to use it.
- Confirm that the materials you want to consult are held on-site. Many archives keep some of their holdings off-site and page materials only once or twice a day. If materials are off-site, try to arrange to page them prior to your visit. Many archives will page materials for you in advance so that they are available upon your arrival. This procedure can save you valuable time.
- Find out the archive's photoduplication policy. Does it allow duplication of material? Does it place limits on the number of photocopies you may make? Does it permit scanning or digital photographing of documents?

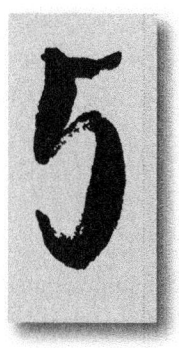

HISTORICAL SOURCES AND THEIR EVALUATION

The foundation of history is evidence. Historical research involves materials and a critical method for their evaluation. Allan Nevins once said that "history was not born — it could not be born — until both these elements came into existence."[1] This chapter deals with both the types of evidence that historians use and the rules employed in evaluating them. Various types of historical evidence can be found in numerous places — in an attic, a cemetery, a courthouse, as well as in a museum, a library, or an archive. Whatever reflects human activity in the past can be part of the historical record. The evidence historians study is much vaster than laymen realize. Fragmented and incomplete as it is, the record of past events and episodes is massive, and without it there can be no history deserving of the name. In Chapters 6 and 7 we will explain how to locate sources of historical evidence. At this point, though, let's look at the main principles involved in understanding and evaluating them.

Communication historians will encounter sources extensive in quantity and varied in scope. It is no exaggeration to speak of the burden of abundance of their sources. Yet, acquaintance with that abundance is both sobering and exciting — sobering because it forces respect for evidence and exciting because it is so suggestive for inquiry. The writing of communication history involves not only knowledge of the media at some point in the past but also an understanding of the general history of the life and thought of that time. The sources for communication history reflect those twin concerns. Accordingly, for purposes of illustration, we shall discuss evidence both in terms of traditional historical types

[1]Allan Nevins, *The Gateway to History,* new rev. ed. (Garden City, New York: Doubleday & Company, Inc., 1962), 66.

and in terms of those particular to mass communication itself. But first, it is necessary to consider two basic categories of historical evidence, those designated "primary" and "secondary."

Primary and Secondary Sources

Primary sources are the raw materials of history. They are contemporaneous records, or records in close proximity to some past occurrence. Or they might be original documents. Secondary sources, on the other hand, rest on primary sources, and they usually are not contemporaneous with the subject under study. The record books titled "Publishers of the U. S. Laws, 1820-70" found in the National Archives contain State Department appointments of various newspapers and their proprietors who were designated to publish the laws. The records of appointments are handwritten and represent a primary source of State Department newspaper patronage. Culver H. Smith's book *The Press, Politics, and Patronage: The American Government's Use of Newspapers 1789-1875* (1977), which uses those records as sources, is a secondary source. Historians give priority to primary records.[2]

The distinction, though, between primary and secondary sources is more involved than one might think. Consider the case of a personal record. An immediately recorded eyewitness account of an event and a written command from an editor to a reporter are examples of pure primary records. Yet, the primary status of a personal record is often not that clear. Is a letter or a diary entry that describes, let us say, an accident a primary source? The answer depends on the physical proximity of the recorder to the accident, the extent of time between the accident and the composition of the written record, and the object of the historian's research. If someone who was in close proximity to the accident observed it and recorded his or her impressions about it immediately, we would classify that record as primary. But suppose the witness did not write about it for several weeks or even for several months? The point at which we would say that it is no longer a contemporaneous record would be a matter of interpretation. Reporters and correspondents may produce pure primary records when they cover events, and, if the records survive in their original form, historians would classify them as primary. But suppose the original records have been destroyed and all

---

[2]The importance that historians accord primary sources can be seen by studying the arrangement of bibliographies in scholarly works. Contemporaneous records, documents, and manuscript collections are placed first to underscore the depth and legitimacy of the research.

Chapter 5: Historical Sources and Their Evaluation

> **"Primary" and "Secondary" Sources**
>
> Primary sources are the raw materials of history. They are contemporaneous records, or records in close proximity to some past occurrence. They might be original documents.
>
> Secondary sources rest on primary sources, and they are not contemporaneous with the subject under study.

we have to consider is a published account. Is it primary? Suppose a reporter did not witness the accident and based his report on the testimony of people who did. Would the report be a primary record? Or imagine that the only record remaining of that accident was a diary comment recorded a week after it occurred or an account of a conversation about it a month later. Would such records be primary?

Although the above examples exhibit varying degrees of immediacy, most historians would accept them as worthy of "primary" classification, particularly if they represented the best evidence remaining of the accident. To say that historians only recognize an eyewitness account immediately recorded as primary is misleading. In practice, they deal with degrees to which a record is primary. They tend to use a flexible definition of "primary" and extend it to include evidence recorded in "nearness" to an event, and they allow reasonable judgment to guide them in determining the time and space requirements needed to establish "nearness."

There is still the matter of the *object* — that is, the purpose — to consider in determining primary evidence. Imagine that the accident referred to above is mentioned in a letter written months after it occurred. That letter may be of only tangential importance if the historian's object were to describe the accident. On the other hand, it would be of great value and considered as primary evidence if the object were to probe into the thought of the person who wrote the letter. The object of the investigation makes a difference. A newspaper editorial, for instance, can be considered either as primary or secondary evidence depending on use. It would be a secondary source if the writer were commenting on an event for which he did not have first-hand knowledge. If, though, the object of the study is the writer's opinion, an editorial would be primary. Moreover, a clearly defined secondary source in one instance might become a primary source in another. A published work by a nineteenth-century historian that would be identified as secondary in most cases might become primary in a study of American historical writing.

Now consider the case of public documents. These records involve yet additional classification problems. Legal and judicial statutes and reports, constitutions, treaties, and other public records are usually considered primary. In many respects, the label fits. Yet, here, too, there are a number of circumstances to contemplate. All public reports, for instance, are not contemporaneous. Some are produced well after the event. Some lack completeness. Treaties between states are public documents, but some have been known to contain secret clauses. Or consider records of proceedings of meetings. If they are unaltered, stenographic records, they are of great value. Nevertheless, sometimes they are modified for publication. Not everything included in the *Congressional Record*, for example, was spoken on the floor of Congress whose proceedings it records. Public documents, then, may or may not be primary; and, even if they are, there are questions regarding completeness and integrity of evidence to ask about them. In fact, all historical records must be scrutinized. Even primary sources, as valuable as they can be, may be inaccurate or biased.

In historical research, a basic maxim is that scholars must ground the study on primary sources. In no other way can one gain a first-hand understanding of his or her subject. In communication history, there traditionally has been an inordinate reliance on secondary sources — on other historians rather than on records left by the historical subjects themselves. If a footnote refers only to a secondary source for evidence — especially to such general survey works as Eric Barnouw's series on broadcast history or to textbooks such as those by Edwin Emery and Paul Starr — it raises a red flag. Such survey works are to a large extent compilations of material produced by other historians rather than original research into primary sources. If the scholar cites Emery's *The Press and America*, for example, as a source, she actually is crediting Emery — whose work is based almost solely on secondary sources — for material Emery probably took from some other historian.[3] Errors often appear in general survey textbooks. The use of Emery as a source therefore automatically raises questions about the quality and thoroughness of the scholar's research. It shows that, at the least, the author is not adequately acquainted with the historical literature on the subject.[4]

The fact that communication historians have based their writing too much on secondary sources has been one of its traditional weaknesses. That problem, along with others that sometimes have led to flawed research, probably is the

---

[3]The Emery book was first published in 1954. It underwent a number of revisions, and later editions were overseen by Prof. Nancy Roberts, a former student of Emery.

[4]Despite the elementary error of using textbooks as sources, a study in the early 2000s found that textbooks were the most cited types of secondary works in communication history research articles. (See Lisa Daigle, "A Citation and Methodological Analysis of Media History," paper presented at the 2003 Southeast Symposium of the American Journalism Historians Association.) The study found, for example, that in the period 1999-2001, five of the six most frequently cited secondary works were textbooks.

Chapter 5: Historical Sources and Their Evaluation

result of the fact that many historians in the field have not been trained in history. Often, graduate study in communication focuses so much on the methods of social and behavioral sciences that students come out of their programs with little grounding in historical methodology. On the other end of the spectrum, some who have gone into the field of history studied at schools where the emphasis was on communication philosophy, with the result that they, like their empirical counterparts, received hardly any education in historical methodology. Communication has many historians of exceptional ability, but the fact remains that many individuals who write about history have had little formal training for it. As a consequence, much work falls short in such basic matters as use of primary sources, thoroughness in seeking and examining them, improper dependence on secondary sources, and even elementary accuracy in citing sources. To complicate the problem, when articles and books are published containing such shortcomings, they sometimes are held up as exemplars of good history, thus encouraging some individuals in the field to perpetuate such practices.

But, we may ask, are such criticisms of work in the field justifiable? A way to address the question is to examine the research basis of the work. Any student should be concerned about that aspect of scholarship. Many articles and books in the field of communication history are models of good history. But one also can find examples of weak historiography, and weaknesses can show up even in well respected works. Consider one example, Michael Schudson's *Discovering the News*.[5] Our intent here is not to engage in a critique of the work but simply to provide an illustration of the need for historians to be rigorous and accurate in their use of sources. In fairness to Professor Schudson, it should be mentioned that he is not trained as a historian but as a sociologist. In the last few decades, though, communication historians have cited his book as frequently as any other monograph and frequently have held it up as an important authority for understanding the essence of American journalism. It is a work that has exercised a major influence on many researchers in the field. In examining its use of sources, though, one finds a variety of problems. For example, a study of the footnotes for one selected chapter finds that about half of the citations are to secondary sources and about thirty footnotes (that is, half of all the footnotes in the chapter) contain errors.[6] Some errors are mechanical — such as wrong page num-

[5]Michael Schudson, *Discovering the News: A Social History of American Newspapers* (New York: Basic Books, 1978). We have selected Schudson's book for consideration — rather than, for example, an obscure article by a beginning writer — because it is so highly regarded.

[6]This discussion of sources is based on an examination of chapter 2, "Telling Stories: Journalism as a Vocation after 1880," 61-87.

bers and incorrect data in the publication information of cited works — while others are errors of substance. Here are some typical examples:

• The chapter begins with a discussion of William Randolph Hearst's notorious telegram to the artist Frederic Remington just prior to the Spanish-American War: "You furnish the pictures, and I'll furnish the war." Schudson uses the anecdote as good evidence of a lack of concern for accuracy in 1890s journalism. Yet, whether the episode ever occurred is questionable, a point Schudson himself admits in the footnote. Earlier historians had cast doubt on the story; and with its importance to Schudson's point, it is an episode that deserves full investigation.[7] The same footnote states that the reporter Irvin S. Cobb called the 1890s the "Time of the Great Reporter," when he actually called it the "Age of the Reporter."

• Shortly into the chapter, a story from the *New York Times* of November 1, 1860, is quoted as saying "The steamship *Fulton*, whose arrival off Cape Cod has been already announced, reached her dock at this port last evening."[8] An examination of the *Times* story reveals that it does not contain such a quotation.

• In another footnote, Schudson cites Richard Hofstadter's *The Age of Reform* as the source for information about reporters' salaries. An examination of Hofstadter's book shows, however, that he took the information from Frank Luther Mott's *American Journalism*.

The primary concern over such source problems is not that they would occur in the work by a sociologist untrained as a historian, but that some individuals in communication history accept such work uncritically. Despite the philosophical appeal that some studies such as Schudson's offer, historians should be particularly concerned about whether the supposed evidence supporting them can be documented. Good history requires much time and effort, more than some scholars wish to invest. Serious historians recognize, however, that history is important and is worth the work.

Despite the fact that using secondary sources for evidence is an elementary error, some communication historians persist in relying on them. For research material, secondary sources should be used mainly as a means of locating primary sources. For example, secondary sources often include references to primary sources, and those references may be used to help researchers locate pertinent primary material for their own studies. Unfortunately, some historians cite the secondary sources themselves as evidence. That is an error that historians

---

[7]See the discussion, on pp. 118-119 in this chapter, of Joseph Campbell's efforts to determine whether Hearst ever sent such a telegram.

[8]Schudson, *Discovering the News*, 66.

should avoid.

When referring to secondary sources, the historian also should be aware that some secondary sources are based on other secondary sources. Thus, researchers should always track down the original secondary source. When they find that a historical study used an earlier work as a source, they should continue checking the citations until the original source (or the secondary source first using the material) is located. That is, they should find the first historian who provided the material. They should not use Emery if Kobre had the same material, not Kobre if Mott had it, not Mott if Alfred Lee did, not Lee if Bleyer did, not Bleyer if James Lee did, not Lee if Hudson did, not Hudson if Joseph Buckingham did, and not Buckingham if Isaiah Thomas did. The point in this list of authors of survey history books is that it is not unlikely that material Emery included might actually have been used first by Thomas and picked up by each succeeding historian. The person who would be a communication historian must become familiar with the basic literature on the field. Reading survey histories should be one of the first things a student does. By doing so, one can at least avoid the misconception that a recent survey history is the best source on the subject. Yet, acquainting oneself with those books provides only a perfunctory beginning for historical knowledge. Whenever historians select a topic for study, they must read all the works that have been written on that topic. One will thus avoid the novice's error of ascribing to Emery or Mott the authority for material on a topic that they treat only cursorily and from secondary sources.

The error of using secondary sources is so serious in communication history that it deserves one final observation. When a historical work cites another historical work as its source, the student using the former should check its citation. Frequently, one will find that the citation is incorrect, that, for example, the page referred to is the wrong one. By checking citations, the student can avoid repeating the mistake.

The purpose of the foregoing discussion is not to rule out secondary sources altogether. They have a place in historical research — if they are used appropriately. We will discuss the matter later in this chapter.

Evaluation of Written Records

Written records are the best known traditional historical records, although there are and always have been other types of sources available to historians. If you understand the principles of evaluation for written records, you can apply them to other types of sources as well.

Two types of evaluation, *external criticism* and *internal criticism*, characterize this process of evaluation. *External criticism* involves establishing the authenticity of a particular record. *Internal criticism* involves matters of credibility and understanding of content. Explanation of record evaluation and the various questions that one can ask of multiple types of written records can be lengthy and detailed. The following discussion of external and internal criticism is intended as an introduction to the subject. All historians could add to it according to the nature and complexity of their own studies.

> **"Criticism" of Sources**
>
> *External criticism:*
> Determining the authenticity of a document – e.g., Was a diary really written by the supposed author?
>
> *Internal criticism:*
> Determining the credibility of a document – i.e., that a particular detail is as close to what actually happened as we can learn from a critical examination of the best sources.

External Criticism

The purpose of *external criticism* is to determine whether a record is genuine. A number of means, some entailing the work of specialists, can be employed in the task. In the main, external criticism involves collation, identification, and textual verification.

Collation. This step is simply the process of comparing various texts. (It should not be confused with the common definition of "collation" as the act of collecting and combining items, such as sheets of paper, in a proper order.) Within the bounds of what is possible and practical, collation with an original record should be made.

Identification. In cases where the name of the author or other data identifying a record is missing, all possible effort must be made to attribute the record to its proper author and to fix it in its correct time. Ghostwritten speeches, for example, need to be attributed to their authors. Writers using pseudonyms need to be identified for a record to be considered authentic.

Textual Verification. To verify the genuineness of a record, let us say a letter to a newspaper, one might examine the spelling of words, the use of language, or particular quirks of punctuation in the letter. It might be compared to other, authentic letters by the same author. Does this particular letter reflect the normal opinions and ideas of the author, and, if not, are there reasons to explain the departure? In some cases, questionable terms or erroneous references to chronological setting might raise doubts about the item. Sometimes authenticity can be decided with certainty, while at other times that is not possible. The process is one of weighing probabilities.

The following examples will illustrate the process. The student also should note that these examples indicate that thorough and painstaking research is required in history.

In 1901 the *New York Sun* published a classic editorial titled "The Oldest Living Graduate." Yet, owing to the *Sun's* practice of writer anonymity, the author of the editorial is unknown. Anonymous authorship frequently confronts the communication historian. Newspapers, especially, have published uncounted millions of unsigned articles. Anonymity presents a difficult problem to historians studying any topic involving authorship by a particular individual. Sometimes, however, by industrious and detailed research, the historian is able to uncover authorship or at least to make an informed guess. As an illustration, let's look at the question of who wrote "The Oldest Living Graduate." As you read the editorial, try to determine the steps you might take to identify its author.

Here's the text of the editorial:

The Oldest Living Graduate
New York Sun; January 30, 1901

The King has no solitary preeminence in never dying. He shares his mortal immortality with another potentate and great public character, the Oldest Graduate. There is always an Oldest Graduate; and always there are heirs waiting for the succession. Mr. BENJAMIN D. SILLIMAN, distinguished and fortunate in so many other regards, was also for some time the Oldest Living Graduate of Yale; and now that honor belongs to Judge Cutler of '29, who lives in Waterbury, where they make the watches. May these be wound up for many a day before he yields his crown to the heir apparent. At 93 the Oldest Living Graduate is or should be but a boy. After waiting seventy odd years for his title, he will be in no hurry to give it up. He should enjoy it to the full, be merciful in his reminiscences, and look with an indulgent pity on the lads of 90 and 91 who want his job.

For, flower unloved of Amaryllis though it be, this honor is greatly prized. The survivor in this Tontine has beaten all his contemporaries at college. He can say to Time, as BERANGER said:

"Old Postilion, hold-up, hold up;
Let us drink a stirrup cup."

It is too much for this glory to go to a man otherwise famous, as Mr. Silliman was or as HORACE BINNEY was. The latter, an illustrious lawyer whose fame is perhaps as dim now as that of most great lawyers who have not held high political office, was graduated at Harvard in 1797, if we remember well, and he was the oldest living Harvard man for some time before be was cut off in '95. An Oldest Living Graduate who has no other fame than that is to be preferred. Such was JOSEPH HEAD of Harvard, of 1804. He lived in some little town. With his bent form, his VAN WINKLE beard, his long staff, he looked what he was as he marched among the younger generations in the yard on Commencement Day, "the oldest living grad-oo-ate," as he pronounced it after the fashion of his rural youth. Good old JOSEPH HEAD, if that was his name! One thinks with kindness of him, and all his predecessors; and of his successors in the procession.

In every college from A to Z something of affection attaches to the college elder and leader of the line. Of ordinary distinction the graduate may grow tired, be it his or that of a classmate. Of the class of 1825 at Bowdoin, of 1829 at Harvard, of 1853 at Yale, it has been possible to hear too much. At Brunswick, 1875, Mr. BLAINE happily expressed the weariness which the constant celebration of the celebrated brings. "I am glad to hear," he said, "that those members of the class of 1825 who are illustrious on earth are happy in heaven."

The graduate whose ambition it is to become the Oldest Living Graduate scorns all loud and easier fames. In seclusion and with perfect modesty of spirit, he sets before himself early the high goal. He accepts philosophically all detriments which Fate and Fortune send. "I am no longer young," he says to himself, "but why should I wish to be? Everybody who stays in the game must get old and how few can become the Oldest Living Graduate? I am not handsome, witty, eloquent, or even popular. I don't have to be, in my business, which is that of living to be the O.L.G. My classmate, HOOKER HAYNES, has made most of the money there is in the world. My classmate, BRATTLE HOLLYOKE, has married most of the rest. I don't need money in my business. BYLES is a Bishop, DWIGHT is a Senator. BILL TRUMBULL is a Trust. I haven't any office. I don't direct anything. I have little property and less hair. But I think I can outlive every man in my class and I mean to do it. Let them last into the nineties if they can. I'll take an even hundred, and one to carry, if necessary."

The young chaps just out of college may not know this harmless ambition at first. They are too young—confound 'em! We remember hearing GEORGE BANCROFT, 60 years after his graduation, imparting the fact to a freshman. The freshman gaped and gasped in wonder. How was it possible for a man to have been graduated 60 years ago. If NEBUCHADNEZZAR had come into the room and tried to sell a book on vegetarianism, that freshman could not have been more surprised. But youth's the stuff will not endure. It doesn't take the truly wise graduate long to find the most reasonable object of desire. He nourishes the gentle vision in his heart. He sees himself a well-preserved ancient of 98, with a face like a BALDWIN apple and still tolerable legs. His gold-headed cane is less a staff than a part of his make-up; 'tis a representative of the monumental pomp of age. He wears, for effect, a tall hat of the fashion of 50 years before. He prides himself on the cut of his frock coat. His surviving hair is soft and white. A perfect gentleman of the old school. "Young gentlemen," says the Oldest Living Graduate, "I ascribe my remarkable health and long life to the fact that for seventy-five years I have never smoked nor drank." "Boys," he says, to a few striplings of 90-odd assembled around the punch bowl, "I attribute my good health and looks to the fact that for eighty years I have taken a nip of good stuff regularly every day. But I never overdid it as you do."

We once knew an Oldest Living Graduate who would walk on the railroad track, although he was nearly a hundred and deaf as a post. This is encouraging for beginners, as it seems to show that the O.L.G. is born, not made by training. Only a very few years ago there happened to live in the same town the Oldest Living Graduate and the next-to-oldest living graduate. They were great cronies and as lively as crickets. But each watched the distressingly robust health of the other with some alarm. "WILLIAM is looking a leetle peaked," JOHN would say; "he oughtn't be out in the cold so much at his age." And both lived in health to the very edge of the hundred. The man who will devote himself with a single mind to becoming the Oldest Living Graduate deserves to be happy.

Now, let's consider the ways one might determine who wrote the editorial. The clues are slim. Stylistic analysis is made difficult by the fact of the *Sun's* policy of anonymity. Since the authorship of editorials never was made known, samples of a writer's editorials cannot be selected to compare with the "OLG" style. The exception is the famous editorial "Is There a Santa Claus?" by Francis Church, the authorship of which the *Sun* revealed upon that writer's death. The "Santa Claus" editorial provides, however, too little evidence to prove that Church also wrote "OLG," and it reveals nothing of the style of any other *Sun* writer.

Stylistic evidence is provided best by the authors of several histories of the *Sun*, the most helpful of which is *Memoirs of an Editor* by Edward P. Mitchell. He served for half a century on the *Sun* staff beginning in 1875. As a member of the editorial staff until 1903 and then as editor-in-chief, he knew individual editorial writers well. During his tenure, the editorial staff included more than a score of writers. Most, however, can be rejected as authors of "OLG" because their specialties were in styles and topics other than the human-interest approach of "OLG" — writers such as Frank Simonds, the military historian, and Henry B. Stanton, a specialist on political affairs.

Based on Mitchell's and other historians' descriptions of styles, the most likely authors were Church, Mitchell himself, William O. Bartlett, Edward M. Kingsbury, Fitz Henry Warren, and Charles Dana, the *Sun's* editor. A check of biographical material reveals, however, that Warren died in 1878, Bartlett in 1881, and Dana in 1897 — all before "OLG" was published. Each of the remaining three *Sun* editorialists wrote with a style that would make possible the authorship of "OLG." Mitchell believed that the range of newspaper subjects should extend beyond hard news and major events, and in style he placed a premium on bright and enjoyable writing. His editorials focused primarily, however, on politics, thus leaving Church and Kingsbury as more probable authors of "OLG." Their writing styles and subject matter, as described by Mitchell, were similar, both resembling that found in the "OLG" editorial. Based on stylistic characteristics alone, however, an answer thus cannot be given on whether the author was Kingsbury or Church, or even Mitchell.

Other details of the editorial may, however, provide clues. The editorial mentions three colleges: Yale, two of whose graduates are named; Bowdoin; and Harvard, with two alumni named. The fifth paragraph names five individuals (Hooker Haynes, Brattle Holyoke, Bill Trumbull, a bishop Byles, and a senator Dwight) without reference to their alma mater. (The surnames "Brattle" and "Holyoke" are notable in the history of Harvard, although not "Brattle Holyoke.") Should it be possible to identify the schools of the five men, the information might provide another clue. A search of *The National Cyclopedia of American Biography*, followed by an Internet search, reveals no listing, however, for any of them; and Congressional records indicate that no one named Dwight served in the United States Senate in the term before or after 1901, the year in which "OLG" was written. On such evidence, it appears that all five individuals may have been fictitious. But George Bancroft, named in the sixth paragraph, was the American historian. He was a Harvard graduate.

Based on the references to the three colleges, it seems reasonable to assume that the "OLG" author may have been a graduate of Bowdoin, Yale, or Harvard. A check of biographical references determines that while Church graduated from Columbia in 1859, Kingsbury graduated from Harvard in 1875 and Mitchell from Bowdoin in 1871. Such may be only coincidence and certainly is not solid evi-

Chapter 5: Historical Sources and Their Evaluation

dence that either Kingsbury or Mitchell was the author.

The Bancroft paragraph indicates, however, that the author heard Bancroft speak to a Harvard freshman sixty years after his graduation. Bancroft had graduated in 1817. Thus, the year in which the episode occurred must have been around 1877, give or take a couple of years, assuming that the author of the editorial, writing in a casual style, was not attempting to be precise. It is not at all unlikely that the actual date could have been two years earlier, 1875, the year of Kingsbury's graduation.

From such piecing together of assorted facts, then, we finally can arrive at the conclusion that the author of the "OLG" editorial probably was Kingsbury. Such effort may seem large in proportion to the simple fact it yields, but it must be done continually by the communication historian, who deals with anonymous authorship on a daily basis.

Remember also that forgeries and invented records exist. Curtis MacDougall in his book *Hoaxes* (1940) and Fred Fedler in *Media Hoaxes* (1989) describe more than 200 falsified newspaper accounts. Any historian familiar with the forged *Protocols of the Learned Elders of Zion* should have little difficulty in remaining on the alert for dishonest records. Alleged to be authentic documents dating back to 929 B.C., the *Protocols* described a cabal of Jewish elders who plotted to rule the world. They were first published in Russia around the time of the Revolution of 1905 probably to justify the anti-Jewish, anti-democratic, and pro-Czarist vigilante groups known as the Black Hundreds. The *Protocols* arrived in the United States during World War I and soon received wide circulation. In 1920 Henry Ford had 500,000 copies printed. He then published a 91-article series, "The International Jew! The World's Problem," in his *Dearborn* (N.Y.) *Independent* newspaper, which the Ku Klux Klan compiled into a four-volume series. The *Protocols* later emerged in Germany to influence Hitlerian propaganda. Back in the United States, the radio commentator Father Coughlin serialized them in his weekly newspaper *Social Justice*.[9]

Forged documents have continued to show up in more recent years. Here are examples:

- In the 1970s Clifford Irving convinced the book publisher McGraw-Hill that the reclusive billionaire Howard Hughes had commissioned him to write an authorized biography. As part of an elaborate and complex deception, he forged three letters he claimed Hughes had written him. On the basis of the letters,

---

[9] Linda Gordon, *The Second Coming of the KKK* (New York: Liveright, 2017), 5 and 50-57; and Peter Vierick, *Meta-politics: The Roots of the Nazi Mind*, 8th ed. (New York: Capricorn Books, 1961), 267-68.

McGraw-Hill gave him a $750,000 advance, Time-Life offered $250,000 for magazine serial rights to the book, and Dell Publishing offered $400,000 for paperback rights. Unfortunately for Irving, as soon as Hughes found out about the planned book, he went public and exposed the hoax.

• In 1983 a similar hoax conned the German magazine *Stern*. Gerd Heidemann, a German journalist, claimed he had obtained copies of the diaries of Adolf Hitler. *Stern* commissioned three handwriting analyses and then paid Heidemann 10 million marks, an amount equal to more than $12 million today. As soon as *Stern* announced publication plans for the first installment, though, skeptics pointed out problems. The diaries were written on modern paper, for example, and were full of errors, and the handwriting was a poor imitation of Hitler's. The official German national archives declared that they were "grotesquely superficial fakes."

• In 1997 David Selbourne, a British historian, claimed he had gained access to and translated into English a journal by an Italian named Jacob of Ancona describing his travels in China four years before Marco Polo arrived. Selbourne refused, though, to make the manuscript available for others to examine. He claimed that its owner had allowed Selbourne to see and to publish it only on condition that he not show it to anyone else or to reveal anything about the owner. As the Associated Press, in an understatement, observed, "This raises questions about authenticity."[10] Little, Brown and Company published the diary in England with the title *The City of Light*; but when it announced plans to publish it in the United States, critics immediately began pointing out problems. One scholar, in reviewing the book, noted that the name *Baiciu*, which the "diary" used for a famous rebel, was "from an 18th-century misreading of an Arabic manuscript — as good a proof as any that something is badly amiss." Similarly, two authorities on Jewish and Islamic history identified an anachronism in "Jacob's" arrival at a *mellah* in the Persian Gulf, a word describing a ghetto that was not coined until the fifteenth century. They compared such a usage as similar to finding the word "Oldsmobile" in the Dead Sea Scrolls. Another reviewer concluded that "By coincidence, much of what Jacob d'Ancona dislikes in 13th-century China is what David Selbourne dislikes in late-20th century Britain." She pointed out rhetorical devices that "Jacob" used that closely resembled those of Selbourne.[11]

[10]Associated Press, ["If authentic, manuscript may tell more of 13th-century China"], 21 September 1997.

[11]T.H. Barrett, *London Review of Books*, 30 October 1997; Doreen Carvajal, "Marco Polo: Is a Rivalry Just Fiction?" *New York Times*, 9 December 1997; and Roz Kaveny, *New States-*

Chapter 5: Historical Sources and Their Evaluation

Anyone familiar with the "Memogate" episode during the 2004 American presidential election knows that dishonest records do exist — and can realize how important it is to assure that documents are genuine. The episode began when CBS anchor Dan Rather hosted a *60 Minutes Wednesday* segment based on photocopied memos claiming that George W. Bush had performed improperly while serving in the Air National Guard in the 1970s. Immediately after the program aired, experts questioned the authenticity of the memos. The typography, for example, was different from what typewriters in the 1970s produced. The memos had proportional spacing and modern superscripts. Analysts found a number of other indications — such as wording that the Air National Guard did not employ in official records — that the memos were fake. *60 Minutes* had rushed the program onto the air without adequately checking out the suspicious documents. CBS initially defended itself and issued a statement standing by the memos' authenticity. After several days of controversy, though, it began an investigation, which determined that the memos "were likely forgeries after all." The consequences were serious. CBS fired the segment's producer and asked three other employees to resign. Following the election, Rather announced that he planned to retire as anchor of *CBS Evening News*.

To demonstrate the problem in historical terms, let us consider how one historian, Jerald S. Auerbach, has called into question the authenticity of one of the best known conversations between an American president and an editor. He probed into the matter in a way that would have pleased any detective worthy of the name. The principals in the alleged conversation were President Woodrow Wilson and Frank Cobb, the editor of the *New York World,* one of Wilson's favorite newspapers. Cobb was a confidant of the President and a frequent visitor to the White House. For years, historians have referred to a particular conversation between Wilson and Cobb that was supposed to have occurred on April 2, 1917, at one o'clock in the morning. At that time, as the story goes, Wilson was preparing to deliver his war message to Congress and expressed many of his forebodings about American intervention to the *World's* editor. He told Cobb about his apprehensions regarding how the war would unleash a spirit of illiberalism among Americans that would be destructive of the things they most valued. In his predictions regarding the meaning of the war, he declared that Germany would be beaten and that there would be a "dictated peace." Wilson's

man, 24 October 1997, p. 45. A convenient summary of the controversy about the authenticity of Selbourne's manuscript may be found at "Jacob of Ancona," Wikipedia, the online encyclopedia, at http://en.wikipedia.org/wiki/Jacob_of_Ancona. Accessed November 28, 2018.

predictions, all of which came true, sound more like the words of one who had already experienced the future than those of one discussing it.

Auerbach's investigation into this alleged conversation went beyond textual examination. He noted that it first appeared in John Heaton's *Cobb of The World*, published in 1924. At that time, the conversation could no longer be validated. Both Cobb and Wilson had died. Then Auerbach discovered that Heaton had not heard of the conversation from Cobb at all. Rather he learned of it from two of Cobb's colleagues, Maxwell Anderson and Laurence Stallings, who collaborated on the antiwar drama *What Price Glory?* also produced in 1924. From them Heaton learned what Cobb was supposed to have said about a conversation with Wilson seven years after it occurred. It was "hearsay evidence twice removed," as Auerbach said. Thus, the rules of evidence led him to suggest that Wilson "never spoke the words so frequently attributed to him."[12] Auerbach also suggested that rather than a record of the President's words, the reported conversation expressed the outrage against war that Anderson and Stallings articulated in the postwar years.

> "Remain skeptical through the entire research process and always look for cross-verification. Question the information in your primary sources as much, if not more, than in your secondary sources." — Bernell Tripp, author, *Origins of the Black Press*

As another illustration of the efforts that historians should make to determine the accuracy of a source, let's look at the search that the historian W. Joseph Campbell conducted to try to determine the authenticity of perhaps the most famous anecdote in American journalism history.

In 1896, William Randolph Hearst, the publisher of the *New York Journal*, sent the reporter Richard Harding Davis and Frederic Remington, the famous artist of the American West, to Cuba to spend a month with the rebels fighting against Spain. They arrived in January 1897 but never reached the insurgents' camps. Remington left for home after about a week.

Legend has it that Remington, seeking to cut short the assignment, cabled Hearst, saying, "Everything is quiet. There will be no war. I wish to return." Hearst is said to have sent a cable in reply, stating, "Please remain. You furnish the pictures, and I'll furnish the war." The original source for the exchange is a book, *On the Great Highway: The Wanderings and Adventures of a Special Correspondent*, written by James Creelman and published in 1901. He had worked as a reporter in Cuba during the Spanish-American War. As Campbell has pointed

---

[12]Jerold S. Auerbach, "Woodrow Wilson's 'Prediction' to Frank Cobb: Words Historians Should Doubt Ever Got Spoken," *Journal of American History* 54 (December 1967): 611.

out, the purported exchange has endured not only as evidence of Hearst's reckless arrogance but of the potentially malign effects of the news media. Many books and articles on media history have quoted it and used it as evidence that Hearst was an irresponsible publisher and that his *Journal* fomented the Spanish-American War of 1898. Determining whether the anecdote is true is therefore of considerable historical significance.

Campbell conducted an extensive investigation of sources and circumstances surrounding the exchange to try to determine its authenticity. In his search, he examined document collections at the Library of Congress in Washington, D. C., Ohio State University in Columbus, the University of California at Berkeley, the University of Virginia at Charlottesville, and Columbia University in New York City.

There are several reasons to doubt the purported exchange. Hearst, Campbell discovered, later denied having sent such a message, and Remington apparently never discussed it. The anecdote's sole original source, Creelman, was in Europe at the time and never explained how he learned about the supposed exchange. Notably, the contents of the respective messages are incongruous, given events in Cuba in early 1897. Specifically, the passages "there will be no war" and "I'll furnish the war" are at odds with the civil war that then raged on the island. Indeed, the war and its privations were the very reasons Remington and Davis were assigned to Cuba. Moreover, it is highly unlikely that such an exchange would have cleared Spanish censors. So strict were the censors that American correspondents covering the insurrection in Cuba often had their dispatches taken by ship to Florida and transmitted from there. Significantly, the correspondence of Richard Harding Davis contains no reference to Remington's wanting to leave Cuba because "there will be no war." Instead, Davis' letters offered other reasons for Remington's departure, including the artist's reluctance to travel through Spanish lines to reach the Cuban insurgents. Davis also said in his correspondence that he had asked Remington to leave because the artist's presence was impeding Davis' reporting.

As a result of his investigation, Campbell concluded that the exchange between Hearst and Remington almost certainly never took place. He has argued that "because the evidence is so persuasive that the purported exchange did not take place, the anecdote deserves relegation to the closet of historical imprecision — at least until proven otherwise."[13]

---

[13]For an account of his investigation into the exchange, see W. Joseph Campbell, *Yellow Journalism: Puncturing the Myths, Defining the Legacies* (Westport, Conn.: Greenwood Press, 2001).

Internal Criticism

Let us consider now the matter of *internal criticism*. It deals with interpreting a record rather than establishing its authenticity. It involves two basic tasks: establishing the credibility of the author and understanding the content.

Credibility. This task touches the real expertise of the historian. To establish credibility of a personal record or a public document, one must have a command of historical contexts and a correct perception of the people or agencies that produced them. Ability and willingness to tell the truth are twin concerns of record evaluation in this instance. Historians have a number of questions regarding someone's ability to report the truth. In judging the credibility of a source, historians ask these three fundamental questions dealing with ability, willingness, and corroboration:

1. Was the source of a detail *able* to tell the truth? Several issues have a bearing in answering the question, such as the following: (a) How near was this person to the event in terms of time and space? For example, was the source an eyewitness? (b) How available was evidence to this person? (c) How competent was this person to understand the event? Competency might involve training, experience, class and cultural differences, or even physical fitness.

2. Was the source *willing* to tell the truth? Regarding willingness, historians apply the basic proposition of intent to clarify. Was the purpose of someone or some agency in producing a record to describe, to interpret, to condemn, to praise, to promote, to propagandize, to publicize, or to persuade? Did the source have some reason *not* to provide an accurate account? Perhaps the source's purpose was to offer a truthful explanation.

3. Is there *independent corroboration* of the detail under investigation? (Are there other sources that confirm the first source?)

Understanding of Content. Here again the historian's command of context is crucial. One must understand a record in order to use it, and there is much in historical records that must be clarified for understanding to occur. Records may be complicated by archaic, colloquial, or technical language. They might contain political, diplomatic, journalistic, or military terminology. Perhaps they include references to titles, ranks, and various terms of social, political, military, or economic gradation. Moreover, some words change in meanings from time to time (e.g., "imperialism," "gay," "correspondent," "printer," "broadcast," etc.). Some vary in connotation according to how they are used and to the person using them (e.g., "freedom of the press," "democracy," "censor," "radical," etc.). Sometimes words have a more restricted meaning than they literally imply (e.g., "freedom," "self-

Chapter 5: Historical Sources and Their Evaluation

> "The history of public relations can be especially hard to study because unless you have the news releases or other materials distributed by PR practitioners, you often can't tell if a news story was influenced by public relations." — *Karen Miller Russell, author, The Voice of Business*

determination," "social order," "discipline," etc.). In all such cases, the real meaning of the words used in the record must be grasped. In essence, historians must understand as far as is possible what the content means. That task involves an ability to use the techniques of textual elucidation plus open-mindedness, imagination, and common sense.

Understanding content, however, goes beyond comprehension of language and expression. It also deals with asking the fundamental question: What type of evidence is contained in this record? What type of information does the record relate? Perhaps it is hearsay; perhaps it is inferential; perhaps it is circumstantial; perhaps it is direct (i.e., a direct proof of fact or a direct reference to something perceived by one of a person's five senses). That basic question, however, does not stand alone. It should be accompanied by several others, such as what does this record leave unsaid and how does this item relate to other pieces of evidence. Diplomatic records and newspaper reports from foreign correspondents, for instance, should be studied in sequence. That is also true of most news coverage and interpretation of prolonged events.

Internal criticism is a fascinating and involved process, and students may wish to sharpen their understanding of its many elements by consulting a volume on legal evidence. Should that be the case, either G. D. Nokes' *An Introduction to Evidence* (1967) or J. D. Heydon and Sir Rupert Cross' *Cross on Evidence* (10th ed., 2015) is a good place to do it.

Four Principles of Source Evaluation

As one can tell from the foregoing discussion, once historians have collected primary materials, they still must make many judgments about which ones are the best. To help in that task of evaluating records as accurate statements of fact, they apply these four specific, important principles:

1. *Time lapse: The closer in time the making of a record was to the event it records, the more reliable it is likely to be.* The assumption is that memory is clearest over a short time span and that it begins to fade with the passage of time. Consider as an instance Benjamin Franklin's account in his autobiography of the circumstances under which his brother James started the *New-England Courant* in 1721. At the time, two other newspapers, the *News-Letter* and the *Gazette*, were

publishing in Boston. Working as an apprentice in James' Boston print shop, Ben surely was aware of both papers. Yet, in his autobiography, published in 1791, he stated that James' friends tried to dissuade him from starting the *Courant* because they thought *one newspaper was enough for the town*. It would be difficult to account for Ben's error in stating the number of newspapers publishing in Boston in 1721 except for the fact that time had dimmed his memory.

> "Many autobiographers and diarists write in a way that casts themselves in a favorable light. It's human nature. Good historians ask themselves, 'Should I trust what this person is telling me?'" — *Mike Sweeney, author, From the Front: The Story of War*

2. *Purpose: The more serious the author's intention to make a mere record — rather than, for example, propaganda — the more dependable the record is likely to be.* A main goal of historians is to determine the factuality of statements, and they concern their investigations with the intent of the authors of documents.

3. *Confidential nature: The fewer the number for whose eyes the record was intended, the more credible it is likely to be.* For example, the statements contained in a diary are assumed (everything else being equal) to be more likely of presenting an accurate statement than an autobiography written by the same person and intended for publication. The principle involved here is that the author would have less reason to fabricate or exaggerate — a weaker motive to paint himself in a good light — in a diary than in a book the public will read. Of course, the principle of confidential nature will not always apply as a universal rule. Sometimes a person may lie even to herself. Still, the principle is generally valid enough that historians place great stock in it. That explains why, for example, they place a high premium on such records as diaries and private letters.

4. *Expertness of the author: The testimony of a well-schooled or experienced observer is more likely to be dependable than that of a novice.* This principle is perhaps the simplest of the four to grasp. It is the common-sense observation that a person who understands a fact — such as, for example, a political convention or a religious conference — is more likely to give an accurate account of it than one who doesn't.

Types of Sources

The sources of history may be of several types. Any categorization of historical sources reflects, however, one's own perceptions of usage and involves some matters of choice. For the purpose of discussion in this case, we shall place the

sources into nine basic categories:
1. Original written records
2. Published personal records
3. Published official documents
4. Secondary written sources
5. Statistical sources
6. Oral sources
7. Pictorial sources
8. Physical remains
9. Internet sources

Communication historians, like legal and military historians, explore and exploit certain types of sources with particular interest. Accordingly, we shall briefly consider each of these sources.

Original Written Records

Into this category fall a wide variety of original sources as they exist in their unpublished state. Many will never be published. Found in libraries, archives, and other repositories, and sometimes kept by individuals, these are the sources that constitute much of the historian's richest raw material. Whether or not particular items found in these sources are primary evidence in regard to the subject of the inquiry remains for the historian to decide. Some of this material, of course, finds its way into published collections, and they are useful. Nevertheless, whenever possible historians wish to consult records in their complete and original form. By studying records in their preserved original state, it is possible to see individual items in relation to surrounding remaining records. An original collection of personal papers, for instance, can reveal many nuances of understanding about its author as a real person.

Let us consider collections of personal papers as a type of original written source. A mosaic of items capable of adding a life-giving dimension to historical study can be found in a well-compiled collection of original personal papers. For instance, in sizable manuscript collections such as the William Allen White Papers or the Josephus Daniels Papers, both of which are located at the Library of Congress, one will encounter the most complete original source records available for the study of these figures. In collections such as these, one will find personal correspondence of all sorts (i.e., routine, general, and special), communiqués of various kinds, memoranda, reports, and a variety of records (e.g., of observation, of conversation, etc.). Here, too, one might find original manuscript versions of published speeches, books, essays, or journalistic writing, as well as manuscript copies of such items never published. Large collections, and some smaller ones too, can contain a great variety of personal records: diaries, journals, notebooks, datebooks, appointment books, itineraries, and address books. Some of the most revealing material found in a manuscript collection is of a miscellaneous variety: family records, financial statements, scrapbooks, picture albums, clippings, and assorted memorabilia. There is good reason why manuscript collections of original personal papers are among the most valued holdings of major libraries; but personal paper collections, small and large, also can be found in many repositories such as special libraries, historical societies, and archives. Some remain in the possession of individual families.

> "Working in the archives is the closest you'll ever get to time travel. The documents, the minutiae, most importantly the language — all re-constitute the atmosphere of that earlier era. Soak it up. And then share the details with readers who weren't able to go on the journey with you." — Joe Hayden, author, *Negotiating in the Press: American Journalism and Diplomacy, 1918-1919*

The type of original material that can be found in archives deserves particular attention. Archives are the repositories of materials pertaining to some type of organized activity and of basic local and national records. In fact, by considering that an archives might be local, state, national, international, organizational, or specialized, it is possible to imagine the vast array of records they contain. Archives hold a variety of types of material. Personal papers can be found in archives. When that is the case, the logic that explains their inclusion in a particular archives is the fact of their "collective significance" to the focus of that archives or to a special collection in it. Archival records, of course, include much more than personal manuscript items. The National Archives in Washington preserves the basic records of the federal government and those of government agencies, commissions, and departments as well as the records of the courts, the censuses, etc. Its holdings are monumental, as are those of many other national archives. On the other hand, archives of a single organization, or those of a particular newspaper, are confined in scope to records pertaining to their own activity. Even they can be far more extensive than one might think. Archival records, then, heterogeneous as they are by their nature, are prime original written sources. They are preserved in a manner that allows them to retain the attributes of their first creation.

Mention should be made at this point of local government records. Since there are more than 80,000 units of local government in the United States, the

Chapter 5: Historical Sources and Their Evaluation

> "No matter how detailed the finding aid, until you open a carton of documents, you can't be sure what type of evidence you have. Sometimes you find a gold mine. Other times it's a lump of coal." — Dale Cressman, author, Television News Pioneer Elmer W. Lower

extent of records produced by the routine of their work tests the imagination. In content they range from records of birth, death, marriage, and divorce to ones regarding matters of property and taxation. Storage is a problem in preserving them. Some are kept in local archives, but most remain in courthouses, town halls, or the office of their origin.

Using such records can be a problem. Researchers may find themselves intruding into the daily work of municipal record keepers. Thus, to achieve the best results in research and to enhance the chances of a cordial reception, researchers should study beforehand the various guides available for the object of their inquiries. They should be as prepared as possible before making a visit.

Such practices can be translated into a basic rule of research: Always be prepared and, whenever possible, use the records in their complete and original form. One should be prepared to visit manuscript libraries, archives, and other places where records are kept. When doing so, it helps to precede the visit with a letter or e-mail of inquiry and intent. Only the most specified and retrievable data (e.g., a birth certificate) should be requested by mail. Such requests should be specific, well defined, and addressed to the appropriate office.

Published Personal Records

Often the correspondence, journals, or writings of an important figure will appear in published form. They are, of course, valuable historical records, but not quite as valuable as they are in their original form. Moreover, historians must consider why such records are published. Did an author keep a diary intended for publication; and, if that is the case, what is its value as a historical record? Was it edited for publication? Perhaps it is of little value. Perhaps it is significant. To diaries published by their keepers, one must apply the rules of evidence as he or she must for any personal record intended for publication. Speeches, public debates, major addresses, and autobiographical and memoir literature are all made or produced with a public audience in mind. Whether or not they are accurate in what they describe or are distortions of truth or apologetic exercises remains for the historian to decide. Nevertheless, even if they are deemed untrustworthy as one type of evidence, let us say as descriptive evidence of particular happenings or verbatim evidence of conversation, they may be valuable as another type. Such records, for instance, may reveal a great deal about the author's personality, values, and perceptions of life. Moreover, what a person remembers years later, even if clouded by the passing of time, is of significance in any attempt to understand that person and can be informative also about historical time.

Published personal records edited by someone other than their author, valuable though they are, can entail problems of usage, too. There are principles to follow in scholarly editing, and knowledge of them will help the historian evaluate the worth of a particular edited selection of personal papers. For a full explanation one might wish to consult the appropriate section in Savoie Lottinville's *The Rhetoric of History* (1976). Suffice to mention here, the author should make no substantive changes in the original record, and its attributes of creation should be retained as much as possible. The criteria used for selection of material should be explained. Most editors of published personal records select items from the original source to include rather than reproducing the full original record. Many published personal records reflect the editors' excellent discernment and perception of the value of sources. Such is the case in Trevor Wilson's *The Political Diaries of C. P. Scott 1911-1928* (1970). Scott, the respected editor of the *Manchester Guardian*, kept extensive diaries and other written records. In editing Scott's political diaries, Wilson used about half of the diaries and appropriate related excerpts from correspondence. "Another editor, " he admitted, "would have selected rather differently."[14] Helpful as Wilson's selections are, the historian cannot help wanting to know about the rest.

Published Official Documents

Here is a source of obvious importance, but it is one that also needs evaluation. In this case, we are using the term "document" to mean an official record authorized by some institution or agency. The records may be the official documents of a government, church, business, institution, or organization, and they may include legal and judicial documents, proceedings of organizations and legislative bodies as well as reports, records, and questionnaires that have been published. A legal published document such as a constitution, a judicial ruling, or a law usually would be considered an unimpeachable record. Such documents can be verified by the original ones. Yet there remains much about those documents to evaluate. Their authenticity may be proven, but it is a more difficult thing to

[14]Trevor Wilson, ed., *The Political Diaries of C.P. Scott 1911-1928* (Ithaca, N.Y.: Cornell University Press, 1970), 12.

Chapter 5: Historical Sources and Their Evaluation

grasp their meaning.

Here we turn to the principles of internal criticism. As an illustration, consider the matter of American law. Since 1791 the American people have had the Bill of Rights as one of their fundamental legal documents. The authenticity of that document and of the Constitution itself is not a matter of question, but the meaning of such documents has been the subject of debate since the earliest years of this republic. A court ruling is a clear pronouncement, but the judicial opinion standing behind it is a matter of interpretation. A law is a clear statement, a binding rule of action for a community; but, as we are reminded by such an obvious example as that of the Alien and Sedition Acts, a social philosophy exists behind laws.

When dealing with such documents, historians want to know not only what a particular one says and whether it can be trusted as a genuine version of the original. They also want to know a good deal about the "why" that lies behind the document itself and the "what" that connects it to a social historical context. Why were the Alien and Sedition Acts passed? What do they tell us about American politics and attitudes of the 1790s? What do they fail to tell us? Or, to skip to the twentieth century, why did Congress adopt the Radio Act of 1927, and what do we need to know about the concept of freedom and responsibility in the 1920s to comprehend the meaning of that law? To comprehend even the best known statutes one must be able to grasp their meaning in terms of time and setting, including the traditions, conditions, and personalities responsible for their presence in history.

Published government documents tend to have a hallowed quality about them. Original documents are even more impressive, but it is the published versions that most people see. Historians must avoid falling into the common trap of accepting without scrutiny authorized government documents, original or published, as valid evidence. They should ponder the "how" and "why" of their composition. As an exercise in understanding government documents as historical evidence, students should take the time to read, for example, the documents produced by the various belligerent powers to justify their involvement in World War I. By itself, the case of each country seems convincing, but when viewed collectively each of those cases is far less persuasive. Only by the use of wide knowledge of historical circumstances and by determined effort to be fair and balanced in judgment of evidence, can one reach conclusions about which country or countries may have been responsible for the war. Yet, think about how much of subsequent history rests upon assumptions regarding responsibility for that conflict — either the way it began or the way it ended.

Government documents are important evidence, but their meaning must be understood in terms of the circumstances and intent of publication. Many government documents, like documents pertaining to other organizations, are published with the honest intent of making information available to the public. Indeed, it would be hard to imagine scholarly work proceeding without such publications. There are two considerations to bear in mind when using them: (1) be aware of the criteria used in selecting them for publication (usually found in the introduction to the first and perhaps following volumes of a set), and (2) particularly in documentary histories (usually single-volume compilations), observe if the document is reduced from its original form. If reduced for publication, such a version of the document would fail to conform to the rule of best evidence.

Secondary Written Sources

Secondary sources, as we have seen, are those based upon primary sources and removed in time from the subjects they describe. They compose a varied category of sources, including (1) pamphlet and periodical literature, (2) major historical studies and monographs, (3) biographies, (4) current affairs literature, (5) official histories, and (6) imaginative literature.

These sources have a definite place in historical research, and that fact should not be forgotten in the historian's effort to employ original sources in a study. The bibliographic searching related to historical inquiry produces a rich yield of secondary literature. It should be studied and used. In fact, historians would be remiss if they failed to use this category of literature. Even imaginative literature has its place in historical research. It can tell us a great deal about the time or age in which it was written and can provide a sense of color and atmosphere that can enhance historical understanding. Thus a novel written in the 1950s about World War II might be a valuable source to use in understanding the mind of the 1950s. Sometimes a novelist can capture the essence of a particular moment or event in history or perhaps the life of an institution. There was, for instance, a good deal of truth about journalism in *Deadlines* (1922) and *Josslyn* (1924), two novels by Henry Justin Smith that in their day were considered classic portrayals of the newspaperman's life that Smith knew so well.

Most of the secondary literature historians will use, of course, will be factual. It might be consulted for general information, for the primary evidence it contains, or for the interpretation it has to offer. It should not, however, be used as a source of primary evidence if that evidence is available itself for investigation. If you do get primary material from it, though, remember that it is evidence that another person selected and perhaps for a purpose other than your own.

Regarding interpretations, naturally you want to know what authorities have said on subjects of their expertise. Moreover, secondary literature can be studied for ideas, for new questions to ask in an inquiry, and for insight into how others have handled particular topics. Journalists, moreover, are often called contemporary historians, and through the years they have been some of the most frequent contributors to that variety of secondary literature called current affairs literature. It can be used to help the historian understand attitudes, for impressions, and sometimes as a type of early history of an event. Secondary literature in its many varieties is a valued body of information for historians, but remember that although the work of other writers can be used to help you understand your subject, your inquiry into that subject must be your own.

Communication historians should remember also that until recently the quality of much of the historical research and writing in their field has been mediocre. Even today, books and articles continue to be published that fail to meet the basic standards of historical research. Too many biographies of journalists have been sentimental and impressionistic portrayals; and too many histories of newspapers have been written, to quote Allan Nevins, "with an eye to pious commemoration or profitable promotion."[15] One has only to think of a fine biography such as David Nasaw's *The Chief: The Life of William Randolph Hearst* (1990) or Gay Talese's *The Kingdom and the Power* (1969), a history of the *New York Times*, to know that there have been exceptions to that statement. Yet it holds as a generalization. Therefore, of all historians, communication historians should adhere to the rules for evaluating secondary literature as a source. Consider a book's author whenever possible. Why did the author write the book? For whom was it intended? Appraise the volume's tone and quality and whether or not it manifests the attributes of good scholarly writing. Are its interpretations well substantiated? If it is a work of current affairs, try to determine if its subject receives reasonable and full treatment and if the opinions expressed are well supported or if, instead, they are statements reflecting whim, emotion, or bias.

Statistical Sources

Earlier in this book we underscored the importance of statistical studies in our discussion on quantification in history. For the sake of perspective, recall that the fascination with figures predated the appearance of the computer. It comes

---

[15]Nevins, "American Journalism and Its Historical Treatment," *Journalism Quarterly* 36 (1959): 411-23, 521. Ibid., 413.

as no surprise that the emergence and growth of computer technology with its capacity for data processing have increased interest in statistics as historical sources. Those sources hold a great potential for many topics in history. They open up new possibilities for the study of local history, for the study of everyday life (as opposed to the history of elites), and for institutional studies. Indeed, political, economic, and social history are all filled with subjects that have statistical characteristics. The growth of databases indicates that the potential for using such sources as historical evidence will continue to expand.

Like all historical sources, statistics must be evaluated before they can be accepted as convincing evidence. Where do statistics originate, and can they be trusted? If they come already gathered for historians, perhaps in a census, they might be less than accurate. The first United States census of 1790 was a far less certain record than ones gathered fifty years later. Newspaper circulation figures of 150 years ago may not be accurate. Perhaps they were padded for purposes of circulation or to attract advertising. Or suppose that the figures the historian wishes to use have to be extrapolated from surviving records. Those records may or may not be trustworthy, and even if the original records of the data attempted to present it according to the dictates of honesty, the person who did the tabulation may not have had the expertise to implement that intention. How well trained were people charged with the collection of data a century or two ago?

It is often claimed that historians make qualitative statements that have quantitative implications (e.g., "many people," "few people"). Such quantitative inferences, indeed, can be sharpened by the careful use of statistics. But the reverse is also true: Quantitative references can have qualitative inferences. It is one thing to use numbers to show that middle-class voters performed in one way or another in a given election. It is quite another matter to define who were the middle-class voters, to explain why they voted the way they did, and to have one historian's definition accepted by other historians. A similar problem of selection might appear in statistical delineation of any group in society. Historians often are interested in using statistics to trace a trend over a period of time. The work involves variables of time, place, and circumstance regarding the figures used. The same is true of comparative examples. There are many variables involved in such comparisons when they are statistical. What constitutes an adequate salary for a reporter in one decade might be inadequate in another, or the amount of profit necessary to make a radio station prosperous at one time or place might be different from that required at another time and place.

We can conclude that the validity of historical statistics involves evaluation of their reliability and selection as well as tests of their suitability for use as sources of comparison or representation. Finally, once they have been verified as usable sources, statistics still have to be explained to readers. That returns us to qualitative techniques.

Oral Sources

As historical sources, oral records can be subdivided into (1) oral tradition and (2) sources of oral history. *Oral tradition* refers to verbal testimony transmitted from one generation to another. Used by social anthropologists before it attracted the attention of historians, it is a study that deals with interpreting the types and means of transmission of verbal traditions. In the study of literature and industrial societies, oral tradition may include riddles, childhood rhymes, legends, folklore, and proverbs. It is, moreover, a source of great significance for reconstructing the history of preliterate societies, and it has risen as a historical methodology as a result of the emerging interest in the history of pre-colonial African societies in the 1960s. Jan Vansina's *Oral Tradition: A Study in Historical Methodology* (1965; ebook ed., 2017) is the most significant explanation of the many procedures involved in this methodology, and anyone interested in applying oral tradition in practice should consult that book.

John Tosh, British historian and African specialist, has pointed out, however, that there are major problems of distortion connected with accepting oral traditions as accurate. The discussion of this matter in his *The Pursuit of History* (1984; rev. ed., 2009) should be used to balance Vansina's. At least, one must consider the possibility that an oral tradition may have been modified or remolded over time and that it may be used today with a particular effect or audience in mind. For instance, it now seems apparent, according to Tosh, that stories were invented in Gambia for Alex Haley, the American writer who went there in 1966 in search of information about his slave ancestor, Kunta Kinte. Later he incorporated that information into his best-seller *Roots*.[16] Oral tradition, then, represents a significant and fascinating historical source but, as is always the case, one that should be used with utmost care.

The term *oral history* refers to the creation of a somewhat different source than that known as oral tradition. Oral history is a less than perfect term that refers to the historical recovery of the remembered but unrecorded past. In some cases (such as legend and folklore) the distinction between oral history

---

[16] John Tosh, *The Pursuit of History: Aims, Methods and New Directions in the Study of Modern History* (London: Longman, 1984), 185-86.

and oral tradition is somewhat blurred. Oral history, however, usually refers to the use of oral sources in a literate society. It is as old as history itself. Herodotus used it, as did a number of medieval and modern historians. Only with the prevalence gained by the written record as a historical source in the late nineteenth century did it fall out of fashion. Interest in oral sources grew sharply in the 1960s among historians as they concentrated more than before on the history of ordinary people, workers, and even the inarticulate struggling poor. Many people have left few written documents. Thus, oral histories are often the only way to get at the histories of such groups. Many recent historians working on traditional subjects also have used them with great success (e.g., T. Harry Williams in his biography of Huey Long, Alexander S. Leidholdt in his *Editor for Justice: The Life of Louis I. Jaffe*, and Gordon W. Prange in *At Dawn We Slept*).

> "World events are lived by humans, and reviewing the recordings and transcripts of the subjective experiences of humans who lived through a flood, a fire, a war, or hard economic times presents history in a more personal form. Through oral history, the past becomes real to us, something tangible that relates to our own experience." — Anthony Hatcher, Elon University

The use of oral evidence has become a major new historical trend, as proven by the establishment of the Oral History Collection at Columbia University and the more recent British Oral Archive of Political and Administrative History at the London School of Economics. The "History Matters" web page "Oral History Online" <http://historymatters.gmu.edu/mse/oral/online.html> provides links to what it identifies as "exemplary oral history sites." They include "American Life Histories" and "Born in Slavery: Slave Narratives," which were gathered as part of the Federal Writers' Project from 1936 to 1940, along with several other sites. The Recorded Sound Reference Center of the Motion Picture, Broadcasting and Recorded Sound Division of the Library of Congress has the largest collection of historical recordings in the world. Dating from the 1890s, the collection of more than two million recordings includes records of all types of music, the spoken word, and radio broadcasts.

Despite their value, oral sources do not of themselves constitute history. Like documents, they are *sources* for historical study. Historians must use them with discernment and in conjunction with other sources.

Many communication historians no doubt are familiar with the practice of interviewing. Those who are not may wish to consider the strategies of historical interviewing in James Hoopes' *Oral History: An Introduction For Students* (1979) and Donald Ritchie's *Doing Oral History: A Practical Guide* (2003). Suffice

Chapter 5: Historical Sources and Their Evaluation

to mention here that the historical interview involves three stages: (1) preparation, (2) the interview itself, and (3) subsequent reconstruction. The first involves background study, selection of interviewees, and the approach to them. The second deals with strategies for conducting the interview. In the last stage, an interview must be transcribed and its validity verified by the interviewer. After that, the interview becomes an authentic record to be tested by all of the means of internal criticism.

Audio Sources

In some cases, historians will work with printed transcriptions of oral histories. In other cases, the materials may be original recordings of interviews. Audio recordings can be particularly rich and evocative historical sources, as they offer historians the opportunity to hear the voices of the past. For example, the interviews that comprise Studs Terkel's book *Hard Times: An Oral History of the Great Depression* (as well as hundreds of other interviews) can be accessed at https://studsterkel.wfmt.com. Most of the recordings communicate a deeper sense of how the Great Depression affected Americans than do the transcribed versions. Besides oral interviews, historians can also find audio sources of music, radio broadcasts, and political speeches to be significant primary materials. Through recordings of music and song, historians can learn much about the popular culture of earlier periods. Through recordings of political speeches, historians can expand their understandings of the appeal of politicians and public figures. Hearing Father Charles Coughlin, for example, can help historians better comprehend both his appeal to Americans in the 1930s and the reasons why many considered him a demagogue. What audio sources can ultimately do is to help historians better understand the mental world of their subjects and learn about the ways people in the past apprehended the sound of the world around them.

Pictorial Sources

Like spoken records, those classified as "pictorial" can provide a corrective to an elitist bias in history. Posters, cartoons, and films, after all, were made with popular appeal in mind. Old photographs are the valued possessions of ordinary people as well as the rich and powerful. Such visual records are, in fact, the exclusive preserve of no particular class or group in society. They are simply revealing sources for the study of modern history. Because of their interest in photojournalism and films of record (e.g., newsfilm, newsreels, documentaries, etc.), communication historians may be more alert than other historians to these visual records as historical sources. The term *pictorial*, however, includes materials beyond photographic and film sources. It encompasses the greater and lesser works of art in their many graphic forms.

To be used as historical sources, pictorial records must first be evaluated. The simplest photograph should be studied for traces of its intent and incidental substance as well as for its main subject. When dealing with the work of a well-known photographer, that person should be studied. What was her purpose? Her approach? Did she have a particular class or cultural interest that her work reflected? Before any extensive use of photographic sources, researchers should become familiar with the works of historians such as Beaumont Newhall; and before employing serious or popular examples of art in their study, they should consult the writings of a reputable art historian. In both cases, such authorities can sharpen one's perception of both content and intent of these sources.

The growth of film archives attests to film as a major source for history since the 1890s. Here we shall refer mainly to fictional films. What can they tell us about past reality? To answer that question the historian must consider a film from three perspectives: production, content, and audience. Critique of evidence is involved in consideration of each of these three perspectives.

Regarding production, the reasons and restrictions accompanying a film's appearance must be analyzed. Did Frank Capra produce *Mr. Smith Goes to Washington, It's a Wonderful Life*, and other films of that genre because he wanted to create "the American dream" or in response to its existence? At various times and places have either official or unofficial censorship or the needs of propaganda influenced the production of certain types of films? How did the ideology of script writers and directors influence films? Perhaps it is possible to make a topical grouping of films. That could be suggestive about what was produced and what failed to be produced.

Regarding content, historians are interested in how films reveal popular attitudes and cultural values and in how they transmit messages.

Analysis of film audiences is the hardest area of film evaluation to penetrate. Nevertheless, in terms of using the film as a historical source, it is important to know about the distribution of a film, the number and type of theaters showing it, and audience attendance and reception. That information requires a great deal of digging, and, unfortunately, all records of such things have not been kept and those kept are difficult to find.

We can conclude by noting that for films to be used effectively as sources, they must be used in a systematic way. Films tend to simplify subjects, and what

Chapter 5: Historical Sources and Their Evaluation

might pass as an accurate film fails to meet the standards historians use in establishing accuracy. Those who wish to use the film as a historical source may wish to consult Paul Smith's *The Historian and the Film* (1976) for a useful elaboration of the subject. Also of use is an enlightening discussion on the subject that John Sayles, a film director, and Eric Foner, a historian, published in 1995.[17]

Physical Remains

This category of sources includes the remaining objects that people created. Although they might in some cases be inscribed (e.g., coins, cemetery markers, various types of engravings, etc.), they display characteristics of things apart from the records of the written or spoken word. Some were made with no intention of preservation in mind (such as a tool). Other objects were constructed to stand for something in a particular society and to endure (e.g., a public building). The category includes relics, mementos, and an array of things people used in work and leisure, as well as buildings, vehicles of transportation, and instruments of technology (such as printing presses and radio receiving sets). Some may be artistic objects. Although these physical remains may be crucial to the study of medieval, ancient, and primitive history, they remain, with the exception of a few areas of interest, supplementary to the pursuit of modern history.

Yet, in their own way, they are valuable to the modern historian. How does one acquire a foothold on the past? The answer, of course, depends on the person, but a contact with the past can be acquired by contemplating those physical objects that remain for us to see. Have you ever visited a historic home or building, strolled the streets of a ghost town, walked through an old newspaper office, sat in an antiquated railway car, or found an old coin? If you have, you no doubt expanded your imagination and perhaps your curiosity about the past and about how men and women lived in some previous time. That is one of the benefits that you can derive from these physical objects. They can also inform you about past styles, fashions, and inventiveness. In the case of, for example, a magazine, these objects inform us about matters of production, design, and distribution. Perhaps physical objects can offer explanations for puzzling references to items you have encountered in your other sources.

Some of these silent remains of the past exist in today's society. Museums, of course, have rescued many specimens of objects out of the past that otherwise would have been lost or perhaps not appreciated. No one who has ever browsed

[17]"A Conversation Between Eric Foner and John Sayles," in *Past Imperfect: History According to the Movies*, ed., Mark C. Carnes (New York: Henry Holt, 1995), 9-28.

through basic museum directories such as Hudson and Nicholls' *The Directory of World Museums & Living Displays* (3rd ed., 1985), or in the case of the United States and Canada, *The Official Museum Directory* (updated annually), can question how rich and ranging a resource museums offer to enhance understanding. Grasping the full meaning of these remaining objects carries us into the domain of specialized studies (e.g., printing, typography, book design, telegraphy, architecture, epigraphy, heraldry, numismatics, etc.). The more you can introduce yourself to the fundamentals of these related studies as they pertain to your inquiry, the more you will perceive in the objects you view or may wish to view.

Internet Sources

In Chapter 7 we'll provide a discussion devoted to sources one can find through the Internet. For the time-being, let's briefly consider secondary sources one can find on the Internet. The Internet offers researchers a wide variety of ever increasing sources. Many scholarly journals have online versions, and there are others published exclusively online. If the latter are properly refereed, these online publications present no problem. They should be judged by the criteria applied to all secondary sources. There are, moreover, a number of archives, government agencies, museums, and universities that maintain Internet sites. When applicable, researchers can mine these sites for a great variety of useful information, to which they can apply the appropriate criteria of either primary or secondary evidence.

However, other types of Internet information can present problems. Since anyone or any group possessing the required software and technical skill can post information on the Internet, researchers must proceed with caution when using these sources. They might contain accurate and useful information on many specialized subjects, or they might contain information posted by individuals or groups with hidden agendas. The producers of the information range from partisan individuals to political action committees to extremists of a variety of hues — in fact, from the whole spectrum of people who have a cause to espouse. Much material on the Internet thus has been put together from motives other than that of providing accurate and unbiased material.

It is therefore necessary for researchers to practice what historians call "information literacy."[18] That practice involves much that they normally do when

---

[18] Jessica Lacher-Feldman discusses the term "information literacy" in "Evaluating Online Resources," in Dennis A. Trinkle, et al, *The History Highway: A 21st-century Guide to Internet Resources* (New York: Routledge, 4th ed., 2006), 24-34.

Chapter 5: Historical Sources and Their Evaluation

applying their rules of evidence. Essentially, it requires a critical analysis of the information source and evaluation of the content. The object of the former is to clarify the nature of the Internet source under observation. Is it sponsored by the government, an institution, or an individual? Study the web address for clues. Is it clear who is the author of the source and what qualifications that person has to discuss the subject of the source? If the Internet source is a Personal Home Page, it might not include the author's qualifications. Consequently, although it might be a source of opinion, it is a questionable one for factual information. Does the source have citations, and if it provides links to other sources, are they reputable and appropriate to substantiate content?

Regarding content, the researcher should study the material for tone and purpose. Is it written in a scholarly or a popular manner? Is the tone reasonable, or is it argumentative and inflammatory? Does it contain signs of a lack of quality control, such as misspelled words or mistakes in grammar? For whom is the source intended? Is its purpose to convey information or to persuade and convert? Are important facts (events, dates, etc.) omitted from the source? Does the content on the website correspond to other information learned about the subject?

Before leaving this topic, it is possible to advance several general rules to follow when using Internet sources. First, one should acquire as much general knowledge as possible about the subject before using Internet sources. Second, keep in mind the basic principles of "information literacy" when consulting those sources. Third, use Internet sources with other kinds of sources. As you try to judge the value of information found on websites, consider such factors as the website's purpose, the intended audience, the depth of the material, the accuracy and objectivity of information, its authorship, the authority of the source, and whether the material is up-to-date. Finally, examine the website itself to try to determine if material found there is credible. You can find succinct checklists for analyzing Internet sources by doing a search for terms such as "evaluating world wide web pages."

Using Mass Communication Sources

Historical sources in communication are more abundant than one at first may realize. They include not only the material researchers most often think of first — old newspaper and magazine files — but personal papers, broadcasting archives, pamphlets, business records, trade journals, and a multitude of other primary sources. Even the familiar sources such as newspaper files are available in greater numbers than researchers often think. References to many of the sources can be found in Chapters 6 and 7 of this book. Historians must acquaint themselves with those and various other references. They also should keep in mind that historical research must be conducted in primary sources and that the array of primary sources they use must be as broad as possible. In evaluating those primary sources, all the criteria already discussed in this chapter apply to evaluating communication sources, but particular points bear emphasizing.

Most historical work in communication probably requires research into media content and other published matter. Historians, however, should be aware of a number of limitations and of proper standards in using such material. Rarely is public material by itself adequate for conducting historical study. A study of newspaper news stories, for example, may allow historians to determine nothing more than the news content of a newspaper. Study of television commercial content may reveal nothing of historical significance beyond a superficial description of the content. Historians should be aware of the limitations of popular methods such as content analysis, as discussed in Chapter 3, which offer only one dimension of the picture necessary in historical study. Published or broadcast materials are necessary but, except for very limited projects, inadequate by themselves as research sources. Historians must consider all possible sources that will help them answer the questions they have posed for study. Office memos, corporate papers, and private correspondence, for example, always should be examined when available.

In fact, communication historians' interests carry them beyond the content of a given report or series of reports. They want to know, for instance, details about news accounts. Were they controlled by some type of authority or shaped by particular circumstances, either of origin or transmission? Researchers need to probe behind the public report itself and into matters of motive and context. They also want to know about circumstances (e.g., reporters' expertise, editorial policies, political ideology, censorship, etc.) that might have a bearing on a given account such as a news story.

> "Reading most journalism history, one would think that only about 20 newspapers, and only large and influential ones, had been published in all of U.S. history — the *New York Times*, *New York Herald*, *New York Tribune*, *Chicago Tribune*, etc. — and that half of them are gone. But if one wants to really understand a nation's journalism, now or in the past, one should study typical newspapers, because that is where most journalists work and what most citizens read."
> — Dane Claussen, Editor, *Newspaper Research Journal*

The career of Walter Duranty is particularly instructive. An Englishman, in the 1920s and 1930s he gained international fame and notoriety as a foreign correspondent for the *New York Times*. Cynical and vain, he became widely known as a brilliant and witty conversationalist and for his flamboyant lifestyle. He began his association with the *Times* as an assistant in its Paris office shortly before the outbreak of World War I. In 1919 it assigned him to Riga to cover the Baltic states, a significant region because of the civil war raging in Russia. His dispatches were emphatically anti-Bolshevik. The Bolshevik system, he wrote, was "one of the most damnable tyrannies in history." However, after Walter Lippmann and Charles Mertz chastised the *Times* for its negative coverage of Russia, the paper reassigned Duranty to Moscow. There he remained until 1934, during which time he gained recognition as an authority on Soviet affairs. He also gained a reputation as "Stalin's Apologist." Not only did his dispatches reflect Soviet idealism, they also painted Stalin as a remarkable, admirable figure and overlooked or excused his brutal methods.

Why did Duranty make such a seismic shift in his interpretation of Soviet news? It had an obvious effect on the news Americans received about Russia. What role did the *Times*' management play in what seems to have been a dismal story of biased reporting? Is it possible that the picture of Duranty promoted by his critics was wrong and that he deserved the Pulitzer Prize he received for his articles on Russia's Five-Year Plan? Or is it possible that his critics were correct? In answering such questions, if a historian consulted only Duranty's dispatches and not the deeper evidence associated with them, the result would be a seriously flawed account.

The fact that published material is public forces another limitation on its use by historians. A cardinal principle of evaluating historical material, as discussed earlier in this chapter, is that the smaller the intended audience, the more reliable the material is. Conversely, the larger the intended audience, the less reliable it is. It is true that the correlation between audience and reliability does not always hold and that a public document may reveal true thoughts. However, the rule should warn historians not to assume that published or broadcast statements necessarily reveal the innermost beliefs of their writers. A private diary, for example, would be better evidence, probably revealing more accurately a source's attitude or motivation than would a newspaper article. The latter might be intended to put the best public light on the source's motives. Historians must continually keep in mind the purpose the source had in putting down in writing any particular thought or uttering it on the airwaves.

Other problems in dealing with published material confront historians. One is distinguishing between opinion and news. Opinion often has masqueraded as news in the media. From colonial times through much of the nineteenth century, newspaper editors made little attempt to distinguish their opinions from news. They frequently interspersed their views with their news accounts. Although the passage of time and changes in newspaper practices lessened the use of news columns for statements of opinion, even today few observers would argue that news is completely objective or unbiased. In fact, the recent trend has been away from objectivity. It is not true that every news item that has appeared in a newspaper accurately described events. Historians usually consider a reporter a reliable source. Contemporary studies show, however, that even today's reporters, most of whom are better trained than their predecessors, make errors of fact or explanation in a large percentage of their stories. Reporters' bias sometimes creeps in. News accounts also often are based on second-hand information rather than a reporter's eyewitness observation. Many providers of information are not trained observers.

Historians should keep such factors in mind when examining news reports and should not necessarily accept statements of fact at face value. One needs to take all possible steps to verify any statements that play a substantive part in one's study. Examining various reports of the same event is one way to do that. The suggestions for determining reliability that the journalism historian Frank Luther Mott made decades ago still are useful for historians today to know. He spelled out a number of tests that communication historians may and should use before they accept material as fact simply because it appeared in print.[19]

The historian also should be careful to avoid attributing all material that appears in any medium to its owner, editor, manager, or any other staff member. Communication historians, regrettably, frequently have been guilty of taking statements from a newspaper and attributing them directly to the editor or to the editor's influence and direction. It is not necessarily true, however, that an editor had the responsibility, even indirectly, for everything that appeared in his or her newspaper. An editor normally did exercise some oversight over editorials; but even so, historians must be wary of assuming that all editorials mirrored an editor's opinions. The problem Horace Greeley had with the views of some of his correspondents, staff members, and co-owners of the *New York Tribune* that his newspaper published should alert historians to the danger of assuming that any editor agreed with everything his newspaper printed. Historians must have good reason to attribute authorship before doing so. Marked files of publications

---

[19]Frank Luther Mott, "Evidence of Reliability in Newspapers and Periodicals in Historical Studies," *Journalism Quarterly* 21 (1944): 304-10.

Chapter 5: Historical Sources and Their Evaluation

and other internal and external evidence should be examined studiously, as discussed earlier in this chapter.

Then there is the personal factor to consider in evaluation of sources. As we indicated earlier in the discussion of internal criticism, this factor is frequently involved. That is surely the case in much of communication history. Let us suppose, for instance, that we are trying to appraise the effectiveness of Edward R. Murrow's *See It Now* series, which was so heralded a television news effort in the 1950s. Suppose the object of the investigation is to attempt to determine why *See It Now*, despite being ably presented, well-financed, and technically innovative, failed to achieve a wide following. By 1958, under the burden of its falling ratings, it left the air. Why the poor ratings?

To answer the question one can turn to a number of written and visual records about the series itself. One can study its content and format plus a number of records about its production. Such records are vital, but they are not sufficient to satisfy the object of the inquiry. Whatever else is of importance in the study, there is Murrow himself to consider. Was his style too serious, too political, or too controversial? Was there something about the sense of urgency that he was able to create or about his "doomsday voice" that failed to attract large audiences in the optimistic 1950s? Had his rhetorical style become dated? How can we explain the penetrating seriousness that he personified? Perhaps his style was the product of his experiences in the 1930s and 1940s and was shaped by occurrences of global consequence — the collapse of European democracies and the rise of fascism. The public records of the program and the various records relating to its production would not inform us sufficiently about such a proposition. Yet they are essential ones in the inquiry, and they will provide indispensable additions to it.

Communication historians, therefore, must probe deeply into private personal records in order to discover evidence about the motive or actions that lie behind the public record to give the latter its full meaning. At least when examining the produced works of media practitioners, historians want to know many things about those people. What were they about as journalists or broadcasters or advertising designers? What were their professional values? Did they have personal commitments that influenced their work? If so, what were they and how did they influence the work? Just as it is difficult to examine a work of literature without knowledge of the author, so it is difficult to analyze a record of mass communication without knowledge of the person or people responsible for it. If communication historians wish their work to reflect the highest standards of historical scholarship, they must seek and study sources both public and private, and they must contemplate and interpret the interaction that exists between the two.

Historians interested in conducting research into broadcast and film material confront a number of particular difficulties. For example, determining authenticity of these materials can be perplexing. When dealing with film, historians should be aware of several problems. A print of a film may not be complete; that is, it may have been altered for various reasons. In many instances, a variety of copies were made. Frequently, the original version as approved by the film's director has been altered, shortened, for example, perhaps to fit a two-hour television slot. Many films made for the theater screen that are reproduced on DVDs or for television have been altered in shape to fit the proportions of the TV screen. Therefore, part of the image on each frame has been eliminated. (To avoid that problem, some directors, such as Woody Allen, have stipulated that their films must retain the original frame proportions if reproduced on DVDs.) Verifying the original hues of some color films is virtually impossible. The color dyes that were used in Eastmancolor film in the 1950s have faded, and even computerized technology used today cannot restore the original colors. Historians also should be aware of projects to add color to motion pictures originally filmed in black and white. Such colorized versions alter the original material and therefore cannot be considered authentic. It also is difficult to measure the original technical quality of silent films because they have been reproduced on different film material and shown on different types of equipment (including projectors that run the film at a different speed than the original equipment did).

A number of other factors must be of particular concern to historians doing research in film or any other type of performed work. They must be careful about ascribing "authorship" for a film. For years, the accepted thinking was that a film's director was its "author." Now the assumption is that films have multiple authors. Films are the result of the ideas and input not only of the director, but of screenwriters, set directors, cinematographers, and others. Historians also must recognize that sometimes a film had multiple directorship — with a second director called in, for example, to handle one special scene — without all directors being named in the film credits. Historians also should consider the question of whether a script for a film (or a broadcast) accurately reflects the actual performed work. Scripts cannot capture fully the performance, and historians wishing to study the performed work should use whenever possible the actual film, broadcast, or recording for study.

Because so many films have been lost and so many broadcasts and performances were never recorded, historians also must be suspicious about whether

Chapter 5: Historical Sources and Their Evaluation

the work that survives truly and fully represents the subject under study. Some early motion picture studios, for example, preserved their material, while others did not. The historian therefore must be cautious in treating material as if it is indicative of the total.

The case of newsreels presents problems of another sort. These productions appeared to resemble news reporting normally associated with the printed media. Did they? Did they present reality or an illusion of reality? Did they convey an accurate representation of events to the viewing audience? Newsreel coverage of the Yalta Conference of 1945, for instance, tended to present an image of harmony suggestive of Allied cooperation near the end of World War II. It contained little substantive analysis of the meeting of the "Big Three," Churchill, Roosevelt, and Stalin. Yet decisions reached there shaped the future of Europe and had other far-reaching effects. Are such newsreels valid records of historical events? What do they tell one about the news media? Raymond Fielding's study *The American Newsreel: A Complete History, 1911-1967* (2006) helps to answer those questions. It also alerts one to the fact that, despite the air of confidence the newsreels radiated and the tone of certainty that characterized their commentary, they contained enough personality impersonation, faked content, and manipulation of news to make their validity questionable.

To historians, however, they are valuable records of one form of news that countless numbers of theater audiences viewed in one era. When using these records, historians must scrutinize their content carefully and compare it to other known and more reliable records of the time. Moreover, in using these films as sources, one would want to know about the circumstances and restrictions that accompanied their production and distribution as well as the purposes they were intended to serve.

While the limitations on evaluating historical material can be frustrating, historians must remember the key attitude with which it must be approached: caution. The historical record, because so much of what happened in the past went unrecorded and is lost forever, never can be complete. Caution and recognition of the limitations, however, will assist historians in treating the material that survives judiciously and insightfully. That treatment, rather than total record, is the standard expected in historical study.

How Much Research is "Enough"?

Concrete research is the foundation of good history. But how much research must be done? There is no simple answer to the question of when one should stop an investigation and begin work on a final draft of an account. All researchers must make that decision for themselves. The following list of questions may help in reaching that decision.

1. Do you feel adequately informed about what other scholars have said about your subject?

2. Are you satisfied with your evidence both in terms of scope and depth? Is it sufficiently exhaustive?

3. Have you studied your evidence in terms of its validity and potential meaning?

4. Do you feel that you understand the historical context of your subject and the various geographical, economic, religious, social, cultural, and political forces that shaped it?

5. Do you understand the people involved in your subject, and have you reached a stage of understanding where little that they do comes as a surprise?

6. As you continue to locate more sources, do you find that the sources contain nothing that surprises you or that you didn't already know?

7. Do you feel as if you understand the period you are studying as though you have "lived" during it?

8. Has your research adequately addressed the purpose of your inquiry?

9. Do you feel that you have addressed all the important questions about your subject? Do you have any questions that still seem in need of answers?

10. Do you feel competent to make judgments about questions, large and small, that are germane to your inquiry?

11. Have you tested your explanations against your own best critical thought, including tracing through possible alternative explanations?

12. Does your inquiry conform to the principles of historical study?

These questions deserve your careful attention because how well you are able to explain your subject will depend on the evidence you've gathered and on the clarity and depth of your thought about it.

SEARCHING FOR HISTORICAL MATERIALS

Research depends on evidence and on access to it. Though that statement is the most apparent of truisms, it is an imperative one to grasp. To gather evidence, researchers might have to spend time at a major research library such as the Library of Congress in Washington, D. C., or the Newberry Library in Chicago or, perhaps, some other similar institution in another country. Or they might have to spend time working in archives such as the National Archives in Washington, the American Antiquarian Society in Worcester, Mass., or the Public Record Office in London. Visits to state and local historical societies may be in order. Some material is in private possession, and researchers may need to locate and use it, too. Even in the case of books and other published or produced historical materials, historians have to learn which ones their own library holds and which ones have to be ordered. The search for historical materials can be an involved problem, but numerous tools are available in a university library and on the Internet to help resolve it.

Online Library Searches

The quest for research materials usually begins at an academic or large public library. Consequently, a word is in order about how to identify items in library holdings.

The most convenient way to begin looking for library material is with WorldCat. It is an online catalog of the holdings of more than 70,000 libraries worldwide. It can be accessed at the link https://www.worldcat.org or with an Internet search for "WorldCat." It contains information about more than two billion items. Using WorldCat, the researcher can identify libraries that hold specific books, journals, and other items in their collections.

Despite the temptation to think that WorldCat provides the solution for all searches, a cautionary note is in order. Even though WorldCat can serve as a guide for locating a huge amount of library material, it does not have a record of everything. Consider magazines, a genre of material that may be of essential interest to many communication historians. Many academic and some large public libraries have extensive collections of bound volumes, with some dating back to the 1800s. A WorldCat search may not identify such collections, and so researchers could overlook a treasure trove of material should they rely solely on WorldCat. A useful principle in searching for material is to recognize that, even if one uses WorldCat for doing most searching of library records, it cannot be a complete substitute for searching in the records of the libraries themselves.

Nevertheless, WorldCat is a wonderful research tool — and it is simple to use. It offers two types of searches: basic and advanced. When one accesses WorldCat, the first web page to open offers its basic search function. One may search for books, DVDs, CDs, articles, or "everything." To conduct a search, simply type in the title of a specific work or enter a generic term, such as "mass media history" or "yellow press" or any other subject. Here, however, we would offer another cautionary note. You should be wary of using a term that is so general that your search will return large numbers of results that are unrelated to your research topic. On the other hand, a narrow search may turn up no works about the specific term you enter. You may need to search using a variety of terms before you find useful material. If you enter the title of a specific work, WorldCat will list libraries that hold the item, ranked (if you enter your Zip Code) by their distance from your location.

WorldCat's first web page also offers a link to its "Advanced search." The advanced mode allows searches defined by keyword, subject, title, author, and other delimiters. It also offers options to search for items by the year or period in which they were published. The "keyword" function allows searches for either individual words or terms. To search for a term, place quotation marks around the term (such as "new journalism"). Otherwise, the search will return results for each word in the term. For example, *new journalism* would find thousands of items that have either the word "new" or "journalism" in their title.

Most libraries have converted the information on their holdings to online records, and one can search the holdings of individual libraries with means similar to those one uses with WorldCat. Using the keyword search option, researchers can gain a considerable amount of information about the holdings in a library that might relate to their topics. Although what the keyword search includes can vary from library to library, it normally scans at least titles, authors, subject headings, and brief notes about a book's content.

Although a library's Online Public Access Computer may limit a search to sources in that library, any computer with access to the Internet allows a much wider search. Researchers may easily consult the online catalogs of other universities simply by visiting their websites. For example, someone at Pacific University can access the library catalogs at Johns Hopkins University, the University of Texas, the University of Wisconsin, and many other schools to search their holdings. Since most of the world's major libraries have opened their catalogs to this means of access, the value of the Online Catalog to historical research is hard to overestimate.

Despite the advantages of online searches, some libraries are not entirely online, particularly small and rural libraries that have not been able to afford to make the transition to online records. Thus, it still is wise, even in the computer age, for the historical researcher to understand the traditional system of the physical Card Catalog. At the end of this chapter, we will include a discussion of how to use it. Even if one does not encounter a physical catalog, the concepts involved in cataloging will help in the understanding of how items are arranged on library shelves.

Libraries vs. Archives

It is possible to find historical materials almost anywhere. Nevertheless, when one speaks of historical materials — the records upon which research in the field rests — it is usually collected, organized, or classified materials that one has in mind. Although some may be held privately, the researcher will find materials of this sort most often in a library or some other institution that involves itself in storing, organizing, and preserving sources of history. Your own university library probably contains many such materials. Not only books but also documents, newspapers, periodicals, etc., are to be found there. In many cases, your library will have an archive or a rare-book collection. Accordingly, researchers can sometimes find materials for their inquiries at their own institutions. In other cases, however, they may have to travel to a library that has manuscript materials or to an institution that holds significant archival materials.

Some archival documents are available in digitized form on the Internet, but they make up only an incomplete part of the total body of primary material that exists. Chapter 7 in this book, "Historical Research on the Internet," discusses how to locate and search archival material on the Web.

Despite all of the online resources available to historians, there are times when the most successful research strategy is a simple, random walk through the library stacks. For a comprehensive discussion of how to locate materials in their own library and in other libraries and archives, researchers should consult Thomas Mann's *The Oxford Guide to Library Research* (2015).

Archival and manuscript records are of prime interest to historians. Before using archival and manuscript materials, a beginning researcher might wish to consult Philip C. Brooks' *Research in Archives: The Use of Unpublished Primary Sources* (1982), which continues to provide a most useful introduction.

But, before proceeding further, a brief explanation of terms is in order, for the distinction made between libraries and archives is not always understood. There is, in fact, reason for the confusion, since some similar items may be found in either a library or an archive. But, although a library might contain or be "the custodian for" an archive, a library is not an archive. A library collects items, some published and some in manuscript form. Manuscript materials may also be found in an archive, but when encountered in a library they are more individualized; and, since they are frequently the private papers of an individual, it can be said that they are also more personalized than records found in an archive. Accordingly, in the William Allen White Papers in the Manuscript Division of the Library of Congress one will find the correspondence, documents, original drafts of published works, and other such items that White, or his family, kept and made part of the collection, or items that the library has added to that collection. Frequently, in such manuscript collections, the materials are uneven. Items may not have been kept with preservation for public use in mind. At the very least, they are the papers of an individual person or thing.

> "There is nothing more thrilling than going through a document collection. If you don't find the hours melting away while you are in the archive, you are in the wrong discipline." — *Dale Cressman, author, Television News Pioneer Elmer W. Lower*

For an archive, to the contrary, it is not the records of an individual that dictate inclusion, but rather how those records fit into the kept materials of an organization or agency, or perhaps a special type of preserved historical record. This is a major difference. One will find in the National Archives,[1] for example, the records of the Committee on Public Information that President Wilson created during the First World War, while the papers of its chairman, George Creel, will

---

[1] A brief explanation of the "National Archives" is in order. In 1934 the United States established a National Archives, the last major nation to do so. Some years later, in 1949, the

Chapter 6: Searching for Historical Materials

> "Often not finding what you expected to find is far more interesting than finding what you expected to find."
> — Lisa Parcell, co-editor, *American Journalism: History, Principles, Practices*

be found in the Library of Congress. The placement of materials in an archive depends on the public or private "functional activity" that occurred and on whether they fall within the scope of interest of a particular archive.

In terms of the traditional distinction made between the two terms, a library is a "collecting agency," whereas an archive is a "receiving agency." The latter receives the records of groups, organizations, agencies, etc., and it arranges that material according to its source of origin (i.e., organization, agency, etc.). Such materials are cataloged by groups and series under the organization or agency, or some subdivision thereof, that created them. In terms of classification, therefore, it is well to bear in mind the explanation of one authority on the subject: "The librarian catalogs his material while the archivist describes his in guides, inventories, and lists. The librarian selects his materials, while the archivist appraises his; the librarian classifies his material in accordance with established classification schemes, while the archivist arranges his in relation to organic structure and function."[2]

Manuscript collections and archival materials are found in many places. The Manuscript Division of the Library of Congress is the main national manuscript repository for the United States.[3] In Britain the British Library of the British Museum holds a similar distinction. Yet in both countries many manuscript collections are found elsewhere. In this country, they may be in one of the presidential libraries, in state libraries and historical societies, in academic libraries, and in a variety of other repositories. The National Archives is, of course, the major federal archival repository in this country, as the Public Record Office in London is Britain's central repository for national records. But a great deal of diversity

archives was transferred to the newly created General Services Administration, and its name was changed to the National Archives and Records Service. In 1985 the National Archives became an independent agency, the National Archives and Records Administration. Today the National Archives occupies a large, imposing building in Washington, D.C., located halfway between the White House and the Capitol. There are now three additional Washington and suburban D.C. locations for United States government records; and, beyond that, the National Archives operates twenty-three other archives and records centers around the country. A catalog of the National Archives' holdings can be accessed online at http://www.archives.gov/index.html.

[2]T. R. Schellenberg, *Modern Archives: Principles and Techniques* (Chicago: University of Chicago Press, 1957), 23-24.

[3]Catalogs of the holdings of many libraries and archives may be accessed online. The Library of Congress catalog can be accessed at http://www.loc.gov.

characterizes archives in both countries. In this country, for instance, there are state and local archives, and even federal records are dispersed among the National Archives in Washington and various regional federal archives and record centers. There are, in fact, a variety of archives other than state, local, and national ones available to researchers. For instance, there are the National Film Archives in London, Vanderbilt University's Television News Archives, and the data Archive of the Inter-university Consortium for Political and Social Research in Ann Arbor, to name only a few of the types of archives that have appeared in recent decades.

> "Archival work can be dusty, dreary, expensive, and time-consuming. But it also can be fascinating, fun, and rewarding. Historical research is like opening a box of Cracker Jack. You know a prize is in there somewhere. So you can't wait to dig in and explore the contents. There is nothing better than opening that first box of folders, pulling out a file, and immersing oneself in a place and time far removed from the present." — *Kim Mangun, author, Making Utah History*

In fact, many types of repositories hold historical materials. Items might be found in special libraries such as the library of the American Newspaper Publishers' Association Foundation in Washington, D. C., or the Wisconsin State Historical Society Library. Special collections can be found in these and many other libraries. Perhaps your own university library holds some.

Regardless, whether you are dealing with manuscript materials, archival records, or published or produced items, the problem of identifying the materials you need from the multitude of those existing is formidable. To assist one in handling this problem, a number of bibliographic tools are available.

Bibliographic Sources and Reference Works: A Selected Listing

Where and how can researchers find all the items to examine in their inquiries? A library provides numerous tools to assist in this task. They include published guides, catalogs, bibliographies, indexes, abstracts, and many other such items. Most libraries have databases for many of these sources, particularly for the most used ones. However, each library selects the databases it wishes to put online according to its own needs. To see which databases a library has online, go to its computerized Home Page and then to its Database Page. For the remainder of this chapter we shall refer to the various reference works, for purposes of description, as "sources," meaning bibliographic sources, and we shall refer to the records of history themselves as "materials."

It is important to understand that it would take a separate volume of considerable length to describe all the bibliographic sources that one might use. The following listing is not exhaustive. It contains a selection of two types of sources. First, we chose many of the standard bibliographic sources to include. Most of them can be found in university libraries, although every library will exercise discrimination in purchasing sources that it considers unnecessary or repetitious. Leads to additional standard sources can be found in Francis Paul Prucha's *Handbook for Research in American History: A Guide to Bibliographies and Other Reference Works* (2nd ed., 1994). Second, we selected sources of particular interest to communication historians. Space does not permit inclusion of all sources for the many topical subdivisions of communication history. Researchers, therefore, also might wish to consult M. Gilbert Dunn and Douglas W. Cooper's "A Guide to Mass Communication Sources" (*Journalism Monographs,* No. 74, November 1981), which contains numerous listings of bibliographies and sources of historical material. Although now dated, it is an invaluable guide for communication historians. They should not, however, expect to find leads to material of interest to them only in sources designated as "Communication Sources." Many general historical bibliographic sources are rich in references to materials that are useful, indeed indispensable, in communication history.

In terms of geographical scope, we emphasize sources pertaining to the United States. Some British sources are also included for several reasons. Before 1783, American history was also British history and can be studied with profit either from the perspective of British history or British imperial history. Moreover, many trans-Atlantic connections and influences characterize the historical nature of mass communication in both countries.

Bibliographic sources and other reference works are so extensive that we have not in the following lists attempted to be exhaustive. The list does contain, though, the works that usually are considered most important. For more items related to specific research topics, a search using the online library catalog WorldCat can prove fruitful. Many of the works, originally published as books, are no longer printed, but updated versions can be found online as parts of databases.

1. *Bibliographies of Bibliographies*

All of the sources contained in this section are cited with titles placed first for the convenience of the researcher. Most bibliographic tools are known by title. In the interest of brevity, annotations have been kept to a minimum or have been omitted. For serial and continuing publication, only the beginning dates are given. For example, *Humanities Index* is cited simply as *Humanities Index* (1974-), indicating that it has appeared in regular intervals since 1974 and continues to date.

American History: A Bibliographic Review (1985-). Its articles, features, and reviews are devoted to "American historical bibliography" broadly interpreted.

Bibliographic Index (1937-). A valuable current index that now appears three times a year and examines about 2,800 periodical sources, in addition to books, annually. It includes bibliographies published either separately or as parts of books and articles. To be listed, a bibliography must have fifty or more citations.

Bibliographies and Indexes in American History (1989-).

Bibliographies in American History: 1942-1978: Guide to Materials for Research. Henry Putney Beers (1982).

A World Bibliography of Bibliographies, Theodore Besterman, comp., 4th ed. rev., 5 vols. (1971). Updated by Alice Toomey, 1977; 4th ed. rev., 1980. A massive compilation of separately published bibliographies covering more than 16,000 subjects. International in scope, it is the best known work of this type of bibliographic literature.

Comment. The number of bibliographies available for research is immense and seems to increase with each year. Researchers will find the above sources helpful in delineating bibliographies pertinent to their subjects. They might also wish to consult the section on bibliography in the current *Books in Print* catalog, which can be found in the Reference Room of most libraries. They should make a practice of consulting on a regular basis the book review and appropriate special feature sections in scholarly journals relating to their studies. The *American Historical Review,* for instance, includes a "Documents and Bibliographic" section in each issue. Communication journals such as *American Journalism, Journalism History,* and *Journalism and Mass Communication Quarterly* have extensive coverage of books and articles in the field, including bibliographic sources. Also, researchers should be aware that in 1978 a group of bibliographers, historians, and librarians organized the Association for the Bibliography of History. This group later established the National Registry for the Bibliography of History located at Georgetown University. Since its beginning in 1981, the Registry has recorded work in all fields of historical bibliography.

2. *Basic Bibliographies in United States History*

General United States History Sources:

The American Historical Association's Guide to Historical Literature, 3rd ed. Mary Beth Norton, gen. ed., 2 vols. (1995). This is an essential, comprehensive bibliography to consider.

Bibliographical Guide to the Study of the Literature of the U.S.A., 5th ed. Clarence Gohdes and Sanford E. Marovitz (1984). Directed mainly to American literary history, but it covers many other subjects of interest to communication historians.

Bibliographies of the Presidents of the United States: 1789-1989. Carol Bondhus Fitzgerald, ed. (1987-1991). This multi-volume collection of annotated bibliographies covers all the American presidents through Ronald Reagan.

Books on Early American History and Culture, 1971-1980: An Annotated Bibliography. Raymond Irwin (2004).

A Guide to the Study of the United States of America: Representative Books Reflecting the Development of American Life and Thought, Donald H. Mugridge and Blanche P. McCrum (1960); updated by Roy P. Basler, Donald H Mugridge, and Blanche Prichard McCrum (1977).

Harvard Guide to American History, rev. ed. Frank Freidel, Richard Showman, and Oscar Handlin, eds. (1980). Still one of the best comprehensive bibliographies for United States history.

History of the United States of America: A Guide to Information Sources, Ernest Cassara, ed., 3 vols. (1977).

Writings on American History: A Subject Bibliography of Articles, James J. Dougherty, et al, comp. and ed., 6 vols. (1976-1986). Should be used in conjunction with *Writings on American History: A Subject Bibliography of Books and Monographs 1962-73* (cited below). Together they represent a continuation of a series begun in 1902. Subsequent volumes in that series appeared at intervals up to 1990. Recent volumes in the series including those cited here are standard bibliographic sources in United States history.

Writings on American History: A Subject Bibliography of Books and Monographs 1962-73, James R. Masterson, comp., 10 vols. (1985).

Comment. There are two extensive bibliographical series for United States history that provide comprehensive up-to-date coverage of the field: the Gale Information Guide Library published by the Gale Research Company and the Goldentree Bibliographies in American History published by Harlan Davidson.

Autobiographical and Biographical Sources:

American Autobiography, 1945-1980: A Bibliography, Mary Louise Briscoe, et al, eds. (1982).
American Diaries: An Annotated Bibliography of American Diaries Prior to the Year 1861, William Matthews, comp. (1945). An older source than the following one but still deserving of mention.
American Diaries: An Annotated Bibliography of Published Diaries and Journals, Laura Arksey, Nancy Pries, and Marcia Reed (1987). This work supersedes Matthews' guide (next entry).
American Diaries in Manuscript, 1580-1954: A Descriptive Bibliography, William Matthews (1974).
A Bibliography of American Autobiographies, Louis Kaplan, comp. (1962). Should be used together with the newer work *American Autobiography, 1945-1980: A Bibliography* mentioned above.
Research Guide to American Historical Biography. Robert Muccigrosso, et al, eds., 5 vols. (1988-1991).

Comment. A number of online bibliographic systems are available, such as the Online Computer Library Center (OCLC) in Dublin, Ohio, and the Research Libraries Information Network (RLIN21), which has the catalog records of more than 100 member libraries, archives, and museums. The RLIN contains the *Eighteenth-Century Short Title Catalogue* database that cites British and Colonial publications in English printed throughout the world. Hundreds of American libraries are contributing to this British Library-created database that lists 500,000 items. An especially useful online catalog is the OCLC's WorldCat, which has the searchable records of libraries worldwide, totaling two billion items in their holdings.

3. *Bibliographies in Communication History*

Standard Sources:

African-American Newspapers and Periodicals: A National Bibliography. James P. Danky and Maureen E. Hady, eds. (1998).
"The American Jewish Press, 1823-1983; A Bibliographic Survey of Re-

search and Study." Robert Singerman (*American Jewish History*, 1986: 422-44).

American Journalism History: An Annotated Bibliography. Wm. David Sloan (1989).

"American Periodicals: A Selected Checklist of Scholarship and Criticism, 1985-1991." James T. F. Tanner, comp. (*American Periodicals*, 1991: 132-37).

An Annotated Journalism Bibliography 1958-1968. Warren C. Price and Calder M. Pickett (1970).

"Annual Review of Work in Newspaper and Periodical History 1996-1998." Diana Dixon, comp. (*Media History*, 1999: 201-21).

Basic Books in the Mass Media: An Annotated Selected Booklist Covering General Communication, Book Publishing, Broadcasting, Film, Editorial Journalism and Advertising, 2nd ed. Eleanor Blum (1980).

Bibliographies and Lists of New York State Newspapers: Annotated Guide. Paul Mercer, comp. (1984).

A Bibliography in the History and Backgrounds of Journalism. Robert X. Graham, comp. (1940).

A Bibliography of Literary Journalism in America. Edwin H. Ford (1937).

A Bibliography of the History of Printing in the Library of Congress. Published by Horace Hart (1987).

The Bibliography of Newspapers and the Writing of History. Stanley Morrison (1954).

"Bibliography: Scholarship on Women Working in Journalism." Catherine C. Mitchell (*American Journalism*, 1990: 33-38).

"The Black Press to 1968: A Bibliography." Armistead S. Pride, comp. (*Journalism History*, 1977: 148-53).

Blacks and Media: A Selected, Annotated Bibliography, 1962-1982. J. William Snorgrass and Gloria T. Woody, comps. (1985).

British Periodicals and Newspapers, 1789-1832: A Bibliography of Secondary Sources. William S. Ward (1972).

"Chicanos and the Media: A Bibliography of Select Materials." Felix Gutierrez and Jorge Reina Schement, comps. (*Journalism History*, 1977: 52-55).

Contributions to Bibliography in Journalism. Various authors (1948, 1959, 1960).

The Dutch Language Press in America: Two Centuries of Printing, Publishing and Bookselling. Hendrik Edelman (1986).

Early Periodical Indexes: Bibliographies and Indexes of Literature Published in Periodicals before 1900. Robert Balay (2000).

"English-Speaking Caribbean Media History: Bibliographic References and

Research Sources." John A. Lent (*Journalism History*, 1975: 58-60).

Freedom of the Press: An Annotated Bibliography. Ralph E. McCoy (1968). McCoy compiled two supplements in 1979 and 1993, updating the bibliography to 1992.

The German Language Press of the Americas, Vol. 1: History and Bibliography 1732-1968: United States of America, 3rd. rev. ed. Karl John Richard Arndt and May E. Olson (1976).

"A Guide to Mass Communication Sources." M. Gilbert Dunn and Douglas W. Cooper (*Journalism Monographs*, No. 74, 1981).

Hispanic Periodicals in the United States, Origins to 1960: A Brief History and Comprehensive Bibliography. Nicolas Kanellos and Helvetia Martell (2000).

Historical Bibliography of the Press. International Committee of Historical Sciences (1930-1935).

A History and Annotated Bibliography of American Religious Periodicals and Newspapers Established from 1730 through 1830. Gaylord P. Albaugh, 2 vols. (1994).

History and Bibliography of American Newspapers, 1690-1820. Clarence S. Brigham, 2 vols. (1947). Another work, *Additions and Corrections to History and Bibliography of American Newspapers, 1690-1820*, appeared in the *Proceedings of the American Antiquarian Society*, April 1961; and the entire source is continued in *American Newspapers, 1821-1936: A Union List of Files Available in the United States and Canada*, cited below.

History of Journalism in the United States, a Bibliography of Books and Annotated Articles. Edwin H. Ford (1938).

Immigrant Labor Press in North America, 1840's-1970's: An Annotated Bibliography. Dirk Hoerder and Christiane Harzig (1987).

Information Sources in Advertising History. Richard W. Pallay (1979).

Journalism: A Bibliography. Carl L. Cannon (1924).

"Journalism as Art: A Selective Annotated Bibliography." Fleda Brown Jackson, W. David Sloan, and James R. Bennett (*Style*, 1982: 466-87).

The Journalist's Bookshelf, 8th ed. Roland E. Wolseley and Isabel Wolseley (1986).

"Literature and Media Change: A Selective Multidisciplinary Bibliography." Joseph Donatelli and Geoffrey Winthrop-Young (*Mosaic*, 1995: 165-86).

The Literature of Journalism: An Annotated Bibliography. Warren C. Price (1959).

"The Literature of Women in Journalism History." Marion Marzolf, Ramona R. Rush, and Darlene Stern, comps. (*Journalism History*, 1974-1975: 117-28), and

"The Literature of Women in Journalism History: A Supplement." Marion Marzolf (*Journalism History*, 1976-1977: 116-23).

"Media Ethics: A Bibliographical Essay." Joseph P. McKerns (*Journalism History*, 1978: 50-53, 68).

New York City Newspapers, 1820-1850: A Bibliography. Louis H. Fox (1928; repr. 1978).

News Media and Public Policy: An Annotated Bibliography. Joseph McKerns (1985).

Newspapers: A Reference Guide. Richard Schwarzlose (1987).

The Newspapers of Nevada, 1858-1979; A History and Bibliography. Richard E. Lingenfelter and Karen Rix Gas (1984).

"A Preliminary Bibliography: Images of Women in the Media, 1971-1976." Virginia Elwood (*Journalism History*, 1976: 121-23).

Press Freedom and Development: A Research Guide and Selected Bibliography. Clement E. Asante (1997).

The Religious Press in the South Atlantic States, 1802-1865. An Annotated Bibliography with Historical Introduction and Notes. Henry Smith Stroupe (1956; repr., 1970).

Related Sources:

American Popular Culture: A Guide to Information Sources. Larry N. Landrum (1982).

Business Communications: An Annotated Bibliography. Ruth M. Walsh and Stanley J. Birkin (1980).

Communication: A Guide to Information Sources. A. George Gitter and Robert Grunin (1980).

Communication and Society: A Bibliography on Communication Technologies and Their Social Impact. Benjamin F. Shearer and Marilyn Huxford, comps. (1983).

Communication and the Mass Media: A Guide to the Reference Literature. Eleanor S. Block and James K. Bracken (1991).

Communication and the United States Congress: A Selectively Annotated Bibliography of Committee Hearings, 1870-1976. George D. Brightbill, comp. (1978).

Control of the Media in the United States: An Annotated Bibliography. James R. Bennett (1992).

Handbook of American Popular Culture, 3rd ed. M. Thomas Inge, 3 vols. (2002). A source rich in bibliographic references to many subjects of interest to communication historians.

Iconic Communication; An Annotated Bibliography. W. H. Huggins and Doris R. Entwistle (1974).

International Communication and Political Opinion; A Guide to the Literature. Bruce Lannes Smith and Chitra M. Smith (1972).

MLA *International Bibliography of Books and Articles on the Modern Languages and Literature.* (1921-). The most comprehensive of the literary bibliographies.

Poststructuralism and Communication: An Annotated Bibliography. Gerald S. Greenberg (2005).

Propaganda and Promotional Activities: An Annotated Bibliography. Bruce Lannes Smith, Harold D. Lasswell, and Ralph Casey, eds. (1939; reissued 2016).

Studies of British Newspapers and Periodicals From Their Beginning to 1800; A Bibliography. Katherine Kirtley Weed and Richmond Pugh Bond (1947).

The Wilderness, the Nation, and the Electronic Era: American Christianity and Religious Communication, 1620-2000: An Annotated Bibliography. Elmer J. O'Brien (2009).

Comment. Communication historians may have reason to consult sources relating to the creative arts or to critical commentary about them. If that is the case, one should consult a library's Online Catalog or its physical Card Catalog (subject card section) for bibliographic sources related to a particular branch of the creative arts.

4. *Sources for Periodical and Less-Than-Book-Length Publications*

Access: The Supplementary Index to Periodicals (1975-). This index ceased publication as a printed publication in 2004 but remains current as an online resource.

Alternative Press Index (1969-). A subject index to more than 300 publications.

America: History and Life (1964-). Originally an abstracting publication. In 1974 it expanded into four parts: Part A, *Article Abstracts and Citations;* Part B, *Index to Book Reviews;* Part C, *American History Bibliography (Books, Articles and Dissertations);* Part D, *Annual Index.* Its coverage is limited to the history of the United States and Canada.

American Humanities Index (1975-).

Arts and Humanities Citation Index (1977-). A permutern subject index derived from identifying key words in a title. It covers more than 6,000 journals.

Book Review Index (1965-). An index to current reviews from more than 455 publications.

British Humanities Index (1962-). Formerly titled *Subject Index to Periodicals*. It mainly indexes popular periodicals but includes a number of scholarly ones too.

Canadian Periodical Index (1948-). Indexes 137 major magazines in French and English. The print edition of this publication ceased in 2002.

Catholic Periodical and Literature Index (previously the *Catholic Periodical Index*) (1930-).

Combined Retrospective Index to Book Reviews in Humanities Journals, 1802-1974. Research Publications, 10 vols. (1982-1984).

Combined Retrospective Index to Book Reviews in Scholarly Journals, 1886-1974. Evan Ira Farber, exec. ed., 15 vols. (1979-1982).

Combined Retrospective Indexes to Journals in History 1838-1974. Annadel N. Wile, exec. ed., 11 vols. (1977-1978).

Current Contents: Arts and Humanities (1977-2006). A weekly publication that reproduces in each issue the tables of contents in about 200 journals. It covers many historical journals.

Essay and General Literature Index (1900/1933-). A subject index to essays and articles found in hundreds of anthologies, collections, and other miscellaneous publications.

Humanities Index (continues as *Humanities Index/Abstracts*) (1974-). A basic source for scholarly articles that, along with the *Social Sciences Index*, supersedes the *Social Sciences and Humanities Index* (1965/1966-1973/1974). The latter was formerly the *International Index* (1920/1923-1964/1965), which, in turn, originally appeared as the *Readers' Guide Supplement* (1907/1915-1916/1919).

Index to Black Periodicals (1960-1999).

Index to Book Reviews in Historical Periodicals (1972-1977).

Index to Book Reviews (1973).

An Index to Book Reviews in the Humanities Journals (1960-1990). Indexes about 375 periodicals.

Index to Critical Film Reviews in British and American Film Periodicals (1974-1975). Covers 1930-1972.

Index to Free Periodicals (1976-1993).

Index to Jewish Periodicals (1963-). This publication is now available as a database offered by EBSCO.

Index to Periodical Articles by and about Blacks (1950-1984). A retrospective index is also available for this subject, *Blacks in Selected Newspapers, Censuses and Other Sources: An Index to Names and Subjects.* 3 vols. (1977-1985).

Index to Southern Periodicals. Sam G. Riley, comp. (1986). This is a companion volume to the author's *Magazines of the American South* (1985). It contains references to nearly 7,000 non-newspaper publications and is part of the series Historical Guides to the World's Periodicals and Newspapers, published by Greenwood Press.

The Literary and Historical Index to American Magazines, 1800-1850. Daniel Wells and Jonathan Daniel Wells (2004).

The Literary Index to American Magazines, 1815-1865. Daniel Wells, comp. (1980).

The Literary Index to American Magazines, 1850-1900. Daniel Wells, comp. (1996).

Poole's Index to Periodical Literature, 1802-1906. 7 vols. (1882, 1893, 1901, 1963). Usually considered the most important index of its kind for nineteenth-century periodical literature. *The Nineteenth Century Readers' Guide to Periodical Literature 1890-1899, with Supplementary Indexing, 1900-1922* serves as a supplement for the years designated in the title.

Popular Periodical Index (1974). Indexes about forty periodicals not included in *Readers' Guide to Periodical Literature.*

Readers' Guide to Periodical Literature (1900/1904-). The standard index for popular periodical literature mainly published in the United States since the beginning of the twentieth century. Along with print editions, it is also available as an online database and on a CD-ROM.

Recently Published Articles (1976-1990). Published three times annually by the American Historical Association. A standard source for journal articles in all fields of history.

Religious Index One: Periodicals (1953-1993).

Social Sciences Citation Index (1969-).

Social Sciences Index (continued as *Social Sciences Index/Abstracts*) (1974/1975-). See the above citation for the *Humanities Index.*

Wellesley Index to Victorian Periodicals 1824-1900 (1966-1989). An index to major British quarterly and monthly publications.

Comment. Researchers can stay current through computerized searches of online versions of a number of the indexes cited above. The online database *19th Century Masterfile* provides an "index to nineteenth century literature." It "contains the noted indexes: *Poole's Index to Periodical Literature, New York Times Index, Palmers Index to The Times, Harper's Magazine Index, Descriptive Catalogue of the Government Publications*, and others." Researchers can also consult a number of electronic sources such as the *Academic Index* (1980-) and the *Periodicals Content Index* (dates vary depending on the title). Periodicals range from the late eighteenth century to the late twentieth century. Some of the electronic sources offer full text services. Since there are indexes covering a wide array of subjects that are too numerous to mention, one might wish to consult "Abstracts and Indexes," a listing in *Magazines for Libraries*, 26th ed. Cheryl LaGuardia and William Katz, eds. (2017).

5. *Sources for Audiovisual Materials, Film, Radio, and Television*

African American Films Through 1959: A Comprehensive Illustrated Filmography. Larry Richards (2005).
America on Film and Tape: A Topical Catalog of Audiovisual Resources for the Study of United States History, Society and Culture. Howard B. Hitchens, ed. (1985).
American Film: An A-Z Guide. Peter Krämer and Paul Willetts (2003).
American Film Institute Catalog of Motion Pictures Produced in the United States (1999).
American Film Institute Catalog of Motion Pictures Produced in the United States: Ethnicity in American Feature Films, 1911-1960. (1997).
American Film Institute Catalog of Motion Pictures Produced in the United States: Feature Films (1971-1999).
American Film Institute Catalog of Motion Pictures Produced in the United States: Film Beginnings, 1893-1910; a Work in Progress (1995).
Art Directors in Cinema: A Worldwide Biographical Dictionary, rev. ed. Michael L. Stephens (2008).
Blacks on Television. A Selectively Annotated Bibliography. George H. Hill (1985).
British Broadcasting, 1922-1982: A Selected and Annotated Bibliography. Gavin Higgens (1983).
The British Film Catalogue 1895-1994, 3rd ed. Dennis Gifford and Claire Chandler (2001; ebook, 2016).
The British National Film Catalogue (1963-1975).
British National Film & Video Catalogue (1985-1992).
Broadcasting and Mass Media: A Survey Bibliography. Christopher Sterling,

ed. (1980).

Cable Television: A Comprehensive Bibliography. Felix Chin (2012).

Cassell Companion to Cinema. Jonathan Law (1998).

Catalogue of Copyright Entries: Motion Pictures. Library of Congress, 5 vols. (1928-2016). Covers films copyrighted 1894-1969.

Child Welfare Films; An International Index of Films and Film Strips on the Health and Welfare of Children (UNESCO, 1950).

The Complete Film Dictionary, 2nd ed. Ira Konigsberg (1999).

The Complete Index to World Film Since 1895. Alan Goble (1998).

A Comprehensive Encyclopedia of Film Noir: The Essential Reference Guide. John Abner Grant (2013).

The Critical Index: A Bibliography of Articles on Film in English, 1946-1973, Arranged by Names and Topics. John C. Gerlach and Lana Gerlach (1974).

Early Motion Pictures: The Paper Print Collection in the Library of Congress. Kemp Niver and Bebe Bergsten (1985). An invaluable collection covering films from 1894-1915. It includes newsreels and "documentaries" (i.e., films of actual people and events) as well as drama and other film genres.

Effects and Functions of Television: A Bibliography of Selected Research Literature, 1970-1978. Manfred Meyer and Ursula Nissen, eds. (1981).

Encyclopedia of American Radio, 1920-1960. Luther F. Sies (2014).

The Encyclopedia of American Radio: An A-Z Guide to Radio from Jack Benny to Howard Stern. Ronald W. Lackmann (2000).

Encyclopedia of Film Directors in the United States and Europe. Alfred Krautz, Hille Krautz, and Joris Krautz (1993-1997).

Encyclopedia of Film Themes, Settings and Series. Richard B Armstrong and Mary Willems Armstrong (2010).

Encyclopedia of Novels into Film, 2nd ed. John C. Tibbetts and James M. Welsh (2005).

Encyclopedia of Radio, 3 vols. (2004).

Encyclopedia of Television, 2nd ed. Horace Newcomb, ed., 4 vols. (2004; e-book, 2014).

Feature Films, 1940-1949: A United States Filmography, rev. ed. Alan G. Fetrow (2009).

Feature Films, 1950-1959: A United States Filmography, rev. ed. Alan G. Fetrow (2009).

Film and Television: A Guide to the Reference Literature. Mark Emmons (2006).

The Film Audience: An International Bibliography of Research, With Annota-

tions and an Essay. Bruce A. Austin (1983).

The Film Book Bibliography, 1940-1975. Jack C. Ellis, Charles Derry, and Sharon Kern (1979).

Film Criticism: An Index to Critics' Anthologies. Richard Heinzkill (1975).

The Film Encyclopedia: The Complete Guide to Film and the Film Industry, 7th ed. Ephraim Katz and Ronald Dean Nolen (2012).

The Film Index, a Bibliography (1941-1988).

Film Index International (British Film Institute, 1996, 2003-).

Film Literature Index (1973-). This is the most comprehensive index to film literature. After 1988 it expanded to include television and video references.

Film Research: A Critical Bibliography with Annotation and Essay. Peter J. Bukalski, comp. (1972).

Film Researcher's Handbook: A Guide to Sources in North America, South America, Asia, Australasia and Africa. Jenny Morgan (1996, 2014).

Film Study: An Analytical Bibliography. Frank Manchel, 4 vols. (1990).

Film Study: A Resource Guide. Frank Manchel (1973).

Frame by Frame III: A Filmography of the African American Diasporan Image, 1994-2004. Phyllis R. Klotman, Gloria J. Gibson, and Audrey T. McCluskey (2007). See also *Frame by Frame I* (1979), which covers films prior to 1978, and *Frame by Frame II* (1997), which covers films of 1978-1994.

From Silents to Sound: A Biographical Encyclopedia of Performers Who Made the Transition to Talking Pictures. Roy Liebman (2008).

Guide to American Cinema, 1930-1965. Thomas R. Whissen (1998).

Guide to American Cinema, 1965-1995. Daniel Curran (1998).

A Guide to American Crime Films of the Forties and Fifties. Larry Langman and Daniel Finn (1995)

A Guide to American Film Directors: The Sound Era 1929-1979. Harry Langman (1981).

A Guide to Latin American, Caribbean, and U.S. Latino Made Film and Video. Karen Ranucci and Julie Feldman, eds. (1998).

Guide to the Silent Years of American Cinema. Donald W. McCaffrey and Christopher P. Jacobs (1999).

Halliwell's Who's Who in the Movies, 4th ed. John Walker, ed. (2006).

Hispanics in Hollywood: An Encyclopedia of Film and Television. Luis Reyes and Peter Rubie (2000).

Index to Motion Pictures Reviewed by "Variety," 1907-1980. Max Joseph Alvarez (1982). Covers foreign and American films and short subjects reviewed by *Variety,* which neither *Readers' Guide to Periodical Literature* nor any other continuing periodical index includes.

International Dictionary of Broadcasting and Film, 2nd ed. Desi K. Bognar (2000, 2017).

International Dictionary of Films and Filmmakers, 4th ed. Tom Pendergast and Sara Pendergast (2001).

International Film Guide. Peter Cowie, et al (1964-).

International Index to Film Periodicals (1972-).

Leonard Maltin's Movie Guide. Leonard Maltin, ed. (2019; published annually since 1988). This guide provides plot summaries, cast, and other information for about 17,000 films.

Library of Congress Motion Picture, Broadcasting, Recorded Sound: An Illustrated Guide (2002).

The Macmillan Film Bibliography: A Critical Guide to the Literature of the Motion Picture. George Rehrauer, 2 vols. (1982).

Magill's Survey of Cinema: English Language Films. Frank N. Magill, ed., 1st Series, 4 vols. (1980); 2nd Series (1981). This is the core set of Magill's survey of films past and present. Since its appearance, the author has added several more sets: *Magill's Survey of Cinema: Silent Films*, 3 vols. (1982); *Magill's American Film Guide,* 5 vols. (1983); and *Magill's Survey of Cinema: Foreign Language Films,* 8 vols. (1985). In 1982 MaGill also began an annual review, *Magill's Cinema Annual* (1982-2014). The various Magill series are compilations that provide critical essays as well as basic data about outstanding films. The *Annual* is now an online database offered by Gale/Cengage.

The Motion Picture Guide. Jay Robert Nash and Robert Connelly, 12 vols. (1985-1987). This work is more than a guide. It provides a synopsis of content and criticism for each of its 35,000 entries covering English-language and notable foreign films.

Moving Pictures: An Annotated Guide to Selected Film Literature with Suggestions for the Study of Film. Eileen Sheahan (1979).

The Museum of Broadcast Communications Encyclopedia of Radio. Christopher H. Sterling and Michael C. Keith (2004).

National Union Catalog: 1973-1977, Films and Other Materials for Projection. Library of Congress, 7 vols. (1978). In 1953 *Films* became a separate publication among the Library of Congress catalogs. This is the most recent of those separately published catalogs. The Library attempts to catalog all films, filmstrips, and slide-sets produced in the United States and Canada that have an educational value.

The New Biographical Dictionary of Film, 6th ed. David Thomson (2014).

The New Historical Dictionary of the American Film Industry. Anthony Slide (2001; rev. 2014).

On the Air: The Encyclopedia of Old-time Radio. John Dunning (1998).

Photographic Literature: An International Bibliographic Guide to General and Specialized Literature on Photographic and Processing Techniques, Theories.... Albert Boni, ed., 2 vols. (1962, 1972). Includes citations back to the nineteenth century but mostly technical ones.

Picture Sources Three: Collections of Prints and Photographs in the United States and Canada. Ann Novotny, ed. (1975).

Radio and Television: A Selected, Annotated Bibliography. Supplement Two, 1982-1986. Peter K. Pringle, et al (1989).

Radio and Television; A Selected Bibliography. Patricia Beall Hamill (1960).

Radio Broadcasting and Television: An Annotated Bibliography. Oscar Rose (1947).

Radio Broadcasts in the Library of Congress, 1924-1941: A Catalog of Recordings. James T. Smart, comp. (1982).

Radio's Golden Years: The Encyclopedia of Radio Programs, 1930-1960. Vincent Terrace (1981).

The Republic Pictures Checklist. Len D. Martin (1998; rev. ed., 2006).

A Research Guide to Film and Television Music in the United States. Jeannie G. Pool and H. Stephen Wright (2011).

Retrospective Index to Film Periodicals 1930-1971. Linda Batty (1975).

The Routledge Film Music Sourcebook. James Eugene Wierzbicki, Nathan Platte, and Colin Roust (2012).

Schirmer Encyclopedia of Film. Barry Keith Grant (2007).

Scholar's Guide to Washington, D. C., for Audio Resources: Sound Recordings in the Arts, Humanities, and Social, Physical, and Life Sciences. James R. Heintze (1985).

Silent Film Necrology, 2nd ed. Eugene Michael Vazzana (2002; rev. ed. 2011).

Television: A Guide to the Literature. Mary B. Cassata and Thomas D. Skill (1985).

Television: A Guide to the Reference Literature. Mark Emmons (2006).

Television and Film: An Annotated Bibliography of Research Materials. Frank W. Hoffmann and Michael R. Pitts (2000).

Television Violence: A Guide to the Literature. P. T. Kelly (1999).

Total Television: A Comprehensive Guide to Programming from 1948 to the Present, 4th ed. Alex McNeil (1997).

The Virgin Encyclopedia of Film. James Monaco and James Pallot (1991).

The Virgin Encyclopedia of the Movies. Derek Winnert (1995).
The Whole Film Sourcebook. Leonard Maltin, ed. (1983).
Who's Who of Victorian Cinema. Stephen Herbert and Luke McKernan (1996).

Comment. Researchers interested in film history will find these two compilations useful: *The New York Times Film Review* (1970-), which covers reviews from 1913 to the present, and *Variety's Film Reviews* (1983-1997), which covers reviews starting in 1907. Many additional references for film, radio, and television history can be found online. A search on the OCLC's WorldCat website at www.worldcat.org can discover numerous works. Other sites that are particularly helpful include the following. They list numerous bibliographies and other reference works.

Film Reviews and Film Criticism Resources. http://www.lib.berkeley.edu/MRC/filmstudies/reviewslist.html.

Monash University Library: Film and Screen Studies: Reference Works. https://guides.lib.monash.edu/film-screen-studies/reference.

University of Michigan Research Guides: Film & Video Studies / Screen Arts & Cultures. http://guides.lib.umich.edu/content.php?pid=29215&sid=216797.

6. Abstracts and Digests

Abstracts in Anthropology (1970-).
Abstracts of Popular Culture (1976-).
America: History and Life, Part A (1964-). This is the standard source of abstracts in United States and Canada history.
Book Review Digest (1905-). Provides excerpts from and citations to nearly 100 American, Canadian, and British periodicals.
Communication Abstracts (1978-).
"Communication History Abstracts." Susan J. Henry, comp. (*Journalism History,* 1977: 101-03; 1979: 26-27, 64; 1980: 34-37, 79-80; 1981: 34-36; 1981-1982: 112-14; 1982: 73-75; 1982-1983: 108-10; 1983: 35-6, 64-66; 1983-1984: 34-36; 1985-1986: 114-16; and afterwards).
Dissertation Abstracts (1952-). Compiles abstracts of doctoral dissertations microfilmed. It does not cover all dissertations written in the United States, only those from institutions listed in each issue.
Historical Abstracts (1955-). A standard source of historical abstracts that is international in scope. Since 1975 it has directed researchers interested in his-

torical abstracts for United States and Canadian history to consult *America: History and Life.*

International Political Science Abstracts (1951-).

Journalism Abstracts (1963-). Abstracts master's theses and doctoral dissertations written in departments and schools of journalism and communication in the United States.

Media Review Digest (1970-). Covers material in 150 periodicals about films, videotapes, slides, maps, etc. Formerly (1970-1972) called the *Multi Media Reviews Index.*

Sociology Abstracts (1953-).

Comment. Researchers might wish to consult a current news digest. *Facts on File: A Weekly World News Digest with Cumulative Index* (1940-) is the basic one published in this country. *Keesling's Contemporary Archives: Weekly Diary of World with Index Continually Kept Up-to-Date* (1931-) is its British counterpart. They might also wish to consult specialized digests such as the *African Recorder: A Fortnightly Record of African Events with Index* (1962-) and the *Asian Events with Index* (1955-).

7. *Statistical Sources*

Guides

American Statistics Index (1973-). Indexes unclassified statistical information of the federal government. It covers more than 800 federal periodicals and reports, and its second part abstracts most of the material indexed. This source should be used in conjunction with *Statistical Reference Index* (cited below).

Guide to Resources and Services. Inter-university Consortium for Political and Social Research (1962-). The ICPSR describes itself as a "nonprofit archive for machine-readable data in the United States." Its scope is international; and for the United States, it includes data back to 1789. The *Guide* is published annually and is updated by a quarterly bulletin. Both are available on its website <http://www.icpsr.umich.edu>. Most of its data sets are available only to paying members of the ICPSR, but there are some exceptions.

Guide to U. S. Government Statistics, 4th ed. John Androit, ed. (1973-1998).

Historical Statistics of Black America. Jessie Carney Smith and Carrell Peterson Horton, comps. and eds., 2 vols. (1995).

Historical Statistics of the States of the United States: Two Centuries of Census,

1790-1990. Donald B. Dodd., comp. (1993).

Historical Statistics of the United States, 1790-1970. Donald B. Dodd and Wynelle S. Dodd (1976).

Historical Statistics of the United States, 1790-1970: The Midwest. Donald B. Dodd and Wynelle S. Dodd (1976).

Historical Statistics of the United States, 1790-1970: The South. Donald B. Dodd and Wynelle S. Dodd (1973).

Historical Statistics of the United States: Colonial Times to 1970. Bureau of the Census, 2 vols. (1975, 1989). A source intended to supplement *Statistical Abstract of the United States* (cited below). It describes itself as a "collecting" and "referring" source. Researchers will find excellent references to expanded detail of subject in the introduction to its various chapters.

Historical Statistics of the United States: Earliest Times to the Present. Susan B. Carter, 2 vols. (2006).

Nations Within a Nation: Historical Statistics of American Indians. Paul Stuart (1987).

Population Information in Nineteenth Century Census Volumes. Suzanne Schulze (1983). The author has continued this index in *Population Information in Twentieth Century Census Volumes: 1900-1940* (1985) and *Population Information in Twentieth Century Census Volumes: 1950-1980* (1988).

Statistical Reference Index (1980-). An index to statistical data in non-governmental periodicals and reports, etc. It should be used in conjunction with the above cited *American Statistics Index*.

Statistical Sources: A Subject Guide to Data on Industrial, Business, Social, Educational, Financial, and Other Topics for the United States and Internationally. Steven K. Wasserman, et al, eds. (1965-). The standard comprehensive guide for American statistical materials.

Abstracts, Handbooks, and Yearbooks

America Votes: A Handbook of Contemporary American Election Statistics (1956-). A biennial publication that covers presidential election statistics for the years from 1948. Publisher varies. For earlier years see the *Presidential Vote* and *They Voted for Roosevelt* (cited below).

"An Annotated Statistical Abstract of Communications Media in the United States." Dan Brown and Jennings Bryant, 259-302, in J. S. Salvaggio and Jennings Bryant, eds., *Media Use in the Information Age: Patterns of Adoption and Consumer Use* (1989).

Demographic Yearbook (1949-). An annual publication of the United Nations Statistical Office.

The Presidential Vote, 1896-1932. Edgar E. Robinson (1947). Election returns for 1936-1944 are covered in *They Voted for Roosevelt,* Edgar E. Robinson (1947). For subsequent presidential election statistics see *America Votes* (cited above).

Statistical Abstract of the United States (1879-). An annual publication considered the standard statistical summary of the United States.

Comment. Most libraries have a number of statistical abstracts covering a variety of subjects and regions. Consult either the Card Catalog or the Online Catalog to learn which ones are available in your library. Researchers will also find back editions of almanacs and yearbooks useful sources for statistics.

8. *Guides to Newspaper and Magazine Sources* (directories, indexes, and union lists)

(Union lists are sources that contain bibliographical information and data about location.)

An Alphabetical Index to the Titles in "American Newspapers 1821-1936, a union list...." Avis G. Clarke and Winifred Gregory Gerould (1958).

American Indian and Alaska Native Newspapers and Periodicals 1971-1985. Daniel F. Littlefield, Jr., and James W. Parins, eds. (1986). This volume brings the work of the editors' two previous volumes up-to-date. The three volumes cover the subject from 1826-1985 and are part of the series "Historical Guides to the World's Periodicals and Newspapers," published by Greenwood Press.

American Indian Periodicals from the Princeton University Library: Guide to the Microfilm Collection. Princeton University Library (1995).

American Newspapers, 1821-1936: A Union List of Files Available in the United States and Canada. Winifred Gregory, ed. (1937, repr. 1967). The standard source. It should be used in conjunction with *History and Bibliography of American Newspapers, 1690-1820.* Clarence S. Brigham, 2 vols. (1947, repr. 1976).

American Newspapers, 1821-1936. An Alphabetical Index to the Titles. Avis Gertrude Clarke (1958).

American Periodicals, 1741-1900: An Index to the Microfilm Collections. Jean Hoornstra and Trudy Heath (1979).

Antebellum Black Newspapers: Indices to New York Freedom's Journal (1827-

1829), *The Rights of All (1829), The Weekly Advocate (1837), and The Colored American (1837-1841)*. Donald M. Jacobs (1976).

Antislavery Newspapers and Periodicals: Annotated Index of Letters. John W. Blassingame and Mae G. Henderson, eds., 5 vols. (1980-1984).

Arkansas Union List of Newspapers. Arkansas Newspaper Project (1993).

The Arts and Crafts in New York: Advertisements and News Items from New York City Newspapers. Rita Gottesman, 3 vols. (1938-1965).

Asian-American Periodicals and Newspapers: A Union List of Holdings in the Library of the State Historical Society of Wisconsin and the Libraries of the University of Wisconsin. Maureen E. Hady and James Philip Danky (1979).

The Black Newspaper in America: A Guide. Henry G. La Brie (1973).

Black Newspapers Index (1977 to the present). (1987).

Black Periodicals and Newspapers: A Union List of Holdings in Libraries of the University of Wisconsin and the Library of the State Historical Society of Wisconsin. Susan Bryl and Erwin K. Welsch (1975).

The Black Press in Mississippi, 1865-1985: A Directory. Julius Eric Thompson (1988).

The Black Press in the South, 1865-1979. Henry Lewis Suggs (1983).

Blacks in Selected Newspapers, Censuses and Other Sources: An Index to Names and Subjects. James de T. Abajian, comp. (1985).

British Newspapers and Periodicals, 1632-1800: A Descriptive Catalogue of a Collection at the University of Texas. Powell Stewart (1981).

British Newspapers and Periodicals, 1641-1700: A Short-title Catalogue of Serials Printed in England, Scotland, Ireland, and British America. Carolyn Nelson and Matthew Seccombe (1987).

California: Union List of Newspapers (1937).

Catalogue of the Pamphlets, Books, Newspapers, and Manuscripts Relating to the [British] Civil War, the Commonwealth, and Restoration, 1640-1661. George Thomason (1908; repr. 1977).

Catholic Serials in Minnesota, 1866-1962: A Descriptive Bibliography and Union List. James D. Kellen (1964).

A Census of British Newspapers and Periodicals, 1620-1800. F. B. Kaye, R. S. Crane, and M. E. Prior (1966; repr. 2008).

Checklist of American 18th Century Newspapers in the Library of Congress. Library of Congress (1997).

Chronological Tables of American Newspapers, 1690-1820: Being a Tabular Guide to Holdings of Newspapers Published in America Through the Year 1820. Edward Connery Lathem (1972).

Chapter 6: Searching for Historical Materials

Colorado Newspapers. Online Computer Library Center (1978-1991).

Directory of New Jersey Newspapers, 1765-1970. William C. Wright and Paul A. Stellhorn (1977).

Directory of Newspaper Indexes. Susan Janney (1989).

Directory of U.S. Negro Newspapers, Magazines & Periodicals in 42 States: The Negro Press; Past, Present & Future: A Documentary Research Report 1827-1967. Thelma Thurston Gorham (1967).

Editor and Publisher International Yearbook (1920-). Lists newspapers.

Extant Collections of Early Black Newspapers: a Research Guide to the Black Press, 1880-1915, with an Index to the Boston Guardian, 1902-1904. Georgetta Merritt Campbell (1981).

Gale Directory of Publications (formerly the *Ayer Directory of Publications*) (1869-). Since 1993 it has been titled *Gale Directory of Publications and Broadcast Media.* This is the basic directory for mass media in the United States, Canada, and Puerto Rico. Its title has changed over the years, but it has traditionally been associated with the name of its founder, N. W. Ayer.

A Guide to Newspapers and Newspaper Holdings in Maryland. Maryland Newspaper Project (1991).

Guide to the American Ethnic Press: Slavic and East European Newspapers and Periodicals. Lubomyr Roman Wynar (1986).

Hawaii Newspapers: A Union List. Sophia McMillen and Nancy Jane Morris (1987).

Index to Black Newspapers. Black Newspaper Indexing Project (1977).

Index to Early American Periodicals. Computer Indexed Systems (1999).

Iowa Union List of Newspapers. Online Computer Library Center (1994).

Kentucky Union List of Newspapers (1994).

Latin American Newspapers in United States Libraries: A Union List. Steven M. Charno (1968).

Louisiana Newspapers, 1794-1961: A Union List.... T. N. McMullan, et al (1965).

Mississippi Newspapers, 1805-1940: A Preliminary Union List.... Mississippi Historical Records Survey (1942).

Mississippiana: Union List of Newspapers. George Lewis (2009).

Missouri Newspaper Project Union List (1990).

Montana Historical Society Newspaper Project: A Union List of Montana Newspapers in Montana Repositories. Montana Historical Society (1986).

Native American Periodicals and Newspapers 1828-1982: A Bibliography, Publishing Records, and Holdings. James P. Danky, ed., and Maureen E. Hady, comp. (1984). The volume identifies and locates 1,164 publications by and about American Indians.

New Mexico Newspaper Project. University of New Mexico / Online Computer Library Center (n.d.).

New Mexico Newspapers: A Comprehensive Guide to Bibliographical Entries and Locations. Pearce S. Grove, Becky J. Barnett, and Sandra J. Hansen (1975).

> "Don't avoid original sources just because they're on microfilm. If you get crossed eyes and a headache the first day you look at microfilms, your eyes will adjust and microfilm won't actually hurt the second day."
> — Julie Williams, author, *The Significance of the Printed Word in Early America*

Newspaper Indexes: A Location and Subject Guide for Researchers. Anita C. Milner, 3 vols. (1977-1982).

Newspaper Press Directory and Advertisers' Guide (1846-). One of the two standard British directories. *Willing's Press Guide* (1874-) is the other.

Newspapers and Periodicals by and about Black People: Southeastern Library Holdings. North Carolina Central University (1978).

Newspapers in Libraries of Metropolitan Chicago, a Union List.... University of Chicago (1931).

Newspapers in Microform. Library of Congress (1978).

Newspapers in Microform. University Microfilms International (1995-)

Newspapers in Microform: United States, 1948-1983. Library of Congress, 2 vols. (1984). Identifies repository locations of newspapers.

Newspapers in Missouri, a Union List. Missouri Newspaper Project (1994).

Newspapers on Microfilm, 6th ed. George E. Schwegmann, Jr., comp. (1967). Succeeded by *Newspapers in Microform* (cited above).

Pacific Northwest Newspapers on Microfilm at the University of Washington. Glenda Pearson, Lea Ehrlich, and Cynthia Fugate (1983).

Pennsylvania Newspapers: A Bibliography and Union List. Glenora E. Rossell and Ruth Salisbury (1978).

A Preliminary Checklist of Connecticut Newspapers, 1795-1975. Don Gustafson, 2 vols. (1978).

"Preliminary Guide to Indexed Newspapers in the United States, 1850-1900." Herbert O. Brayer (*Mississippi Valley Historical Review,* 1946).

Rivington's New York Newspaper: Excerpts from a Loyalist Press, 1773-1783. Kenneth Scott, comp. (1973).

Serials in Microform. University Microfilms International (1993-2000).

Texas Newspapers, 1813-1939. A Union List.... Historical Records Survey (U.S.). Texas (1941).

Union List of Newspapers in Delaware. Delaware Newspaper Project (1990).

Union List of Newspapers in Pennsylvania. Pennsylvania State Library (1961).

Union List of Newspapers, New York, 1821-1936. New York State Library (1968).

A *Union List of Newspapers Published in Michigan.....* Elizabeth Read Brown (1954).

Union List of North Carolina Newspapers. North Carolina State Department of Archives and History (1963).

Union List of North Dakota Newspapers, 1864-1976. Carol Koehmstedt Kolar (1981).

Union List of Ohio Newspapers Available in Ohio. Arthur De Witt Mink (1946).

A Union List of Serials in Idaho Libraries. Paul C. Conditt (1969).

Union List of Serials in Libraries of the United States and Canada, 3rd ed. Edna B. Titus, ed., 5 vols. (1965).

A Union List of Vermont Newspapers. Vermont Newspaper Project (2000).

United States Newspaper Program National Union List. Compiled by the On-line Computer Library Center (OCLC), 4th ed., 8 vols. (1999). This list is a compilation based on the results of the United States Newspaper Program (USNP). Supported by the Organization of American Historians, the Library of Congress, the Council on Library Resources, and the National Endowment for the Humanities, the USNP was a cooperative effort by librarians, archivists, and historians to organize extant copies of newspapers in this country and its Trust Territories for purposes of research. Its work involved identifying existing newspapers, identifying newspaper holdings, and preserving through microfilming those papers deemed valuable for research. The USNP's work began in the mid-1970s and has been completed for most states. It has replaced some of the standard newspaper sources mentioned above.

A Union List of Newspapers Published in Michigan.... Elizabeth Read Brown (1954).

Washington State Union List of Newspapers On Microfilm. Gayle L. Palmer (1991).

West Virginia Newspapers, 1790-1990: A Union List. Harold M. Forbes (1989).

Women's Periodicals and Newspapers: from the 18th Century to 1981; a Union List of the Holdings of Madison, Wisconsin, Libraries. Maureen E. Hady, Barry Christopher Noonan, and Neil E. Strache (1982).

Writer's Market. Writer's Digest Books (1929-). Contains listings of magazines.

Comment. A number of published state and local listings of newspapers exist. See "Guides to Newspapers" in Prucha's *Handbook for Research in American History: A Guide to Bibliographies and Other Reference Works*, 2nd ed. (1994). For those in your library, consult the reference librarian.

9. *Sources for Government Publications and Documents* (directories, indexes, guides and catalogs)

Catalog of the Public Documents of Congress and of All Departments of the Government of the United States. U.S. Superintendent of Documents (1963). Database is available online. The last set in a sequence of sources that indexed United States government publications back to the Continental Congress. The previous titles in the sequence were *A Descriptive Catalogue of the Government Publications of the United States, September 5, 1774-March 4, 1881*, Benjamin Perley Poore, comp. (1885); *Comprehensive Index to the Publications of the United States Government 1881-1893*, John Griffith Ames, comp., 2 vols. (1905); and *Catalog of the Public Documents of Congress and of All Departments of the Government of the United States for the Period, March 4, 1893, to December 31, 1940.* U. S. Superintendent of Documents, 45 vols. (1896-1945). This series of sources has been replaced by the *Monthly Catalog of United States Government Publications* (cited below).

CIS/Index (the Congressional Information Service's Index to Publications of the United States Congress) (1970-). Database is available online. Issued monthly, this is the best index to Congressional documents. By using this index one can order a complete microfiche copy of a document from the CIS if it is not available in the library.

Guide to U. S. Government Publications. John L. Andriot, ed., 2 vols. (1980-1986). The Gale Group publishes a journal of the same name that updates the information periodically.

Index to U. S. Government Periodicals (1970-). Covers nearly 200 government-published periodicals. After 1988 this publication continues as the *U. S. Government Periodicals Index*, published by the Congressional Information Service, and since that date it also became available online by subscription as the ProQuest *Government Periodicals Index*.

Introduction to United States Government Information Sources, 6th ed. Joe Morehead (1999). An explanation of the location and use of public documents, mainly contemporary ones.

Monthly Catalog of the United States Government Publications. U. S. Super-

Chapter 6: Searching for Historical Materials

intendent of Documents (1895-). Title varies. Since 1940 this has been the standard index for government documents. This catalog is available as an online database under the name *Catalog of U. S. Government Publications*. The database is available online.

Subject Guide to U.S. Government Reference Sources. Gayle J. Hardy and Judith Schiek Robinson (1996).

United States Government Publications, 3rd. rev. ed. Rae Elizabeth Rips (1952). A revision of Anne Morris Boyd's 1931 standard compilation of publications. Rips' edition covers publications up to the post-World War II period.

Comment. Many of the traditional printed guides to government documents have been replaced by online databases. Historians can check online availability by doing an Internet search for the titles of publications listed above. Many university documents librarians consider MarciveWeb Docs their favorite index to documents provided by the Government Printing Office. (See http://home.marcive.com/marciveweb-docs.) Also, there are a number of checklists, catalogs, indexes, and breviates to particular government publications as well as a variety of general guides. Researchers should become familiar with those available in their libraries; and, particularly for published historical documents, they should check their library's Online Catalog or its physical Card Catalog under the subject headings "Documentary History," "Documents of," "Documents on," etc. In this section we have considered some of the standard sources for government publications and documents. For an expanded treatment, researchers might wish to consult Thomas Mann's *The Oxford Guide to Library Research*, 4th ed. (2015).

10. *Guides to Archival and Manuscript Materials and to Special Libraries and Special Collections*

Archival and Manuscript Sources

American Literary Manuscripts: A Checklist of Holdings in Academic, Historical, and Public Libraries, Museums, and Authors' Homes in the United States, 2nd ed. J. Albert Robbins, ed. (1977).

British Archives: A Guide to Archive Resources in the United Kingdom. Janet Foster (2014).

Directory of Archives and Manuscript Repositories in the United States, 2nd ed. National Historical Publications and Records Commission (1988). Should be used in conjunction with *A Guide to Archives and Manuscripts in the United States* and *National Union Catalog of Manuscript Collections* (cited below).

A Directory of Broadcast Archives. Donald G. Godfrey, comp. (1983). Covers the U.K. and Canada as well as the United States.

A Guide to Archives and Manuscripts in the United States. Philip M. Hamer, ed. (1961). For years this was the standard work in the field. It remains a useful and much consulted source.

A Guide to Manuscripts in the Presidential Libraries. Dennis A. Barton, et al (1985).

Guide to Sources in American Journalism History. Lucy Caswell, coordinator (1989). Sponsored by the American Journalism Historians Association, this volume offers an extensive list of sources (such as archival holdings of journalists' personal correspondence) regarding print and electronic news media throughout American history.

Guide to the Archives of the Government of the Confederate States of America. Henry Putney Beers (1998). A free digital copy is available online.

Guide to the Hoover Institution Archives. Charles G. Palm and Dale Reed (1980). A guide to materials in the Hoover Institute on War, Revolution, and Peace. This major repository of historical materials since the late nineteenth century contains numerous items and collections of interest to communication historians (e.g., on censorship, propaganda, public opinion, and twentieth-century wars).

Guide to the Manuscript Materials for the History of the United States to 1783: In the British Museum, in Minor London Archives, and in the Libraries of Oxford and Cambridge. Charles McLean Andrews and Frances G. Davenport (reprint ed., 2013).

Guide to the National Archives of the United States. National Archives and Records Service (1987). Database is available online. Along with this guide, there are similar guides for most regions of the United States.

Handbook: The Center for Research Libraries (1996). An inventory published by the Center describing its holdings. They include various newspapers, periodicals, press summaries, clipping files, radio broadcasts and scripts, and microforms of a variety of "underground press" titles. Since 1996, this publication has been available as an online resource. See http://crl.edu.

The National Inventory of Documentary Sources in the United States. Chadwyck-Healey, Inc., 4 parts: Part 1, *Federal Records;* part 2, *Manuscript Division, Library of Congress;* part 3, *State Archives, Libraries and Historical Societies;* part 4, *Academic Libraries and Other Repositories* (1983-). A microfiche source, it reports the location of collections and describes the material available within them. It is available as a fee-based database from ProQuest.

National Union Catalog of Manuscript Collections. Library of Congress (1962-1993). A standard and continuing source that begins where Hamer's *A Guide to Archives and Manuscripts in the United States* ended. In 1993 *NUCMC* ceased publishing the print version of its catalog, and records are now available through the OCLC's WorldCat database. See http://www.loc.gov/coll/nucmc/oclcsearch.html.

North American Film and Video Directory. Olga S. Weber (1976). Lists film archives but does not describe their holdings.

Researcher's Guide to Archives and Regional History Sources. John C. Larsen (1988).

Untapped Sources: America's Newspaper Archives and Histories. Jon Vanden Heuvel (1991). Along with providing a "bibliography in narrative form" of historical works about newspapers and journalists, this book describes the holdings of a number of major archives.

Comment. The Research Libraries Information Network maintains a database assessing the research collections of each member. Also, beyond the basic guides listed here, there are numerous ones published for specific state, local, and private repositories. A useful partial listing of those available is indexed in Prucha's *Handbook for Research in American History* (2nd ed., 1994) (cited above).

Directories for Special Libraries and Special Collections

(The term "Special Libraries" means libraries with a special focus and purpose such as the Library of the American Newspaper Publishers Association Foundation in Washington, D. C., or libraries devoted to particular studies, such as film or journalism libraries at various universities. "Special Collections" are particular holdings found in libraries large and small and elsewhere.)

Directory of Newspaper Libraries in the United States and Canada. Grace D. Parch, ed. (1976).

The International Directory of News Libraries. Special Libraries Association (1989).

Newspaper Libraries in the U. S. and Canada: An SLA Directory, 2nd ed. Elizabeth L. Anderson, ed. (1980). This volume supersedes the *Directory of Newspaper Libraries in the U. S. and Canada* mentioned previously.

Research Libraries and Collections in the United Kingdom: A Selective Inventory and Guide. Stephen Roberts, et al (1978).

Special Collections in College and University Libraries. Elizabeth A. Sudduth, et al (2005).

Subject Collections: A Guide to Special Book Collections and Subject Emphasis as Reported by University, College, Public, and Special Libraries in the United States and Canada, 6th ed. Lee Ash, ed., 2 vols. (1985).

Subject Directory of Special Libraries. Gale, Cengage Learning (2015).

Subject Directory of Special Libraries and Information Centers, 46th ed. Matthew Miskelly (2018).

Survey of Special Collections and Archives in the United Kingdom and Ireland. Jackie M. Dooley, et al (2013).

Comment. Special libraries and special collections offer a rich lode for researchers, but they are as varied as they are numerous. The above sources can help to narrow the field, as can online searches. Regarding the latter, start by searching for "special libraries manuscripts-manuscript collections" and "special libraries manuscripts-special collections." The presidential libraries represent an especially inviting resource for communication historians. Aside from the personal papers of the presidents and various related materials, they hold many sources relating to the persons associated with press relations and publicity during a particular presidency. There are presidential libraries for every president since Herbert Hoover. Earlier presidential papers are located at the Library of Congress. Information about the individual presidential libraries can be found online, and printed guides to the collections are available for each one.

11. *Indexes to Miscellaneous Historical Materials*

Author Biographies Master Index: A Consolidated index to More Than 1,140,000 Biographical Sketches.... Geri Speace (1997). A supplement by Barbara MacNeil contains an index to 658,000 more sketches.

Biography and Genealogy Master Index, 1981-1985: A Consolidated Index to More Than 3,200,000 Biographical Sketches, rev. 2nd ed. Miranda C. Herbert and Barbara McNeil, eds., 8 vols. (1980). An index to biographical indexes and directories, etc., with several subsequent supplements. This guide has been periodically updated since its first publication. Since 1997, it has been available as an online database.

Biography and Genealogy Master Index: 1996-2000 Cumulation: A Consoli-

dated *Index to More Than 2,870,000 Biographical Sketches in 416 Current and Retrospective Biographical Dictionaries*. Barbara McNeil (2000).

Biography and Genealogy Master Index 2009. 2 vols. (2009). This index provides 600,000 citations to articles appearing in 200 editions and volumes of 110 biographical dictionaries and who's whos.

Biography Index (1946-). A guide to articles and biographies and to obituaries, letters, collections, diaries, etc., appearing in more than 2,000 periodicals.

Catalog to the *Microbook Library of American Civilization (LAC)*. The *LAC* is a microfiche collection of thousands of books and materials relating to all aspects of American life and literature from its beginning to 1914. Communication historians will find the *LAC* an essential source for which the Catalog provides separate author, title, and subject indexes. There is also a corresponding *Microbook Library of English Literature*, complete with author and title but not subject indexes.

Columbia University Oral History Collection. Meckler Publ. (1985). This book provides a guide to the Columbia collection, which has more than 1,000 oral history interviews. An online guide to the collection, including descriptions of the interviews, is available. It can be found with an Internet search for "Home - Oral History Research Guide at Columbia."

Directory of Oral History Collections. Allen Smith (1988).

Directory of Oral History Programs in the United States. Produced by the Microfilming Corporation of America (1982).

Dissertations in History 1970-June 1980. Warren F. Kuehl (1985). An index by author and subject covering all universities that award doctoral degrees in history. It supplements two previous volumes by the same author: *Dissertations in History: An Index to Dissertations Completed in History Departments of United States and Canadian Universities 1873-1960,* vol. 1 (1965) and *Dissertations Completed in History Departments of United States and Canadian Universities 1961-June 1970,* vol. 2 (1972). Searchable databases of dissertations are available online. Some of them contain full texts. Listings may be found in Chapter 7, "Historical Research on the Internet," in this book.

A Guide to Microform Collections in the Humanities and Social Sciences Division of the Library of Congress. Patrick Frazier (1996).[4] A database containing the

---

[4] As Thomas Mann states, "There are hundreds of large, prepackaged research collections in a bewildering variety of subject areas, and there is likely to be one or more of interest to any scholar.... Most of these collections are commercially available sets that are duplicated in many ... research libraries." Thomas Mann, *The Oxford Guide to Library Research* (New York: Oxford University Press, 1998), 221. For a useful overview of the use of microforms and CD-ROM collections, see 220-44 of Mann's book.

information from the *Guide* is available in the online holdings of the Library of Congress.

Journalist Biographies Master Index. Alan E. Abrams, ed. (1979). Includes about 90,000 references to historical and contemporary journalists appearing in approximately 200 biographical directories and other such sources.

Microform Research Collections: A Guide. Suzanne Cates Dodson, 2nd ed. (1984).

National Inventory of Documentary Sources in the United States: [Part 1] Federal Records. (1984-1985). This collection, as well as the following three parts, is a microfiche document.

National Inventory of Documentary Sources in the United States: [Part 2] Manuscript Division, Library of Congress. (1983).

National Inventory of Documentary Sources in the United States: [Part 3] State Archives, Libraries and Historical Societies (1985).

National Inventory of Documentary Sources in the United States: [Part 4] Academic Libraries and Other Repositories (1985).

Oral History: A Reference Guide and Annotated Bibliography. Patricia Pate Havlice (1985).

The Oral History Collection of Columbia University. Elizabeth B. Mason and Louis M. Starr, eds. (1979). A catalog specifying the nearly 800 memoirs of the Columbia collection available in microform. See "Columbia University Oral History Collection" above for additional information about Columbia's collection.

Oral History Collections. Alan M. Meckler and Ruth McMullin (1975). International in scope and containing a subject index.

Reference Sources in History: An Introductory Guide, 2nd ed. Ronald H. Fritze, Brian E. Coutts, and Louis Andrew Vyhnanek (2004).

Mass Communication Sources

Various types of original and other primary sources are available to communication historians. Since historians often deal with the content of the mass media, they should know how to find items such as newspaper and magazine files and broadcast transcripts and tapes. There are a vast number of collections of such material, many more than we can list here, and of indexes to the material. M. Gilbert Dunn and Douglas W. Cooper's *Journalism Monograph*, No. 74, "A Guide to Mass Communication Sources" (November 1981), mentioned earlier, will prove invaluable in the historian's search for indexes and media files. Indexes to the media and their contents are available in most good university research libraries. In this section, we will concentrate on printed sources. Indexes and millions of pages of publications can be found in online databases. We'll discuss them in Chapter 7, "Historical Research on the Internet."

Many libraries and archives hold primary sources. For American newspaper holdings, no library surpasses the Library of Congress. The American Antiquarian Society's collection of newspapers published between 1690 and 1876 is the largest for that period. It includes some 18,000 newspaper titles, comprising more than 2,000,000 issues. Newspapers from all fifty states and from Great Britain, Central America, Canada, and the West Indies are represented. Many of the earlier ones are reproduced in a set of 70,000 microcards. The set is available in many libraries. The Wisconsin State Historical Society and Harvard University libraries also have substantial national collections. State, regional, and special newspaper collections can be found in various libraries. The United States Newspaper Program has located, catalogued, and preserved on microfilm extant newspapers published from the eighteenth century to the present. Directories to individual state projects are available online at https://www.neh.gov/us-newspaper-program. *Newspapers on Microfilm* (1967) and *Newspapers in Microform* (1984), both of which were discussed earlier in this chapter, catalog all American newspapers that are available in microform. Working with microforms can be tedious, and fortunately the National Digital Newspaper Program (the digital version of the United States Newspaper Program) has made available the contents of more than 2,600 newspapers. The free database is available at https://chroniclingamerica.loc.gov/newspapers/.

Once the researcher locates a newspaper, considerable effort remains to locate content relevant to the topic under study. One of the pieces of good news about the Internet is that millions of newspaper pages have been digitized and are word-searchable. That makes finding items of interest to a particular research project much easier and quicker. We'll list many of the sites in Chapter 7, "Historical Research on the Internet."

Fortunately, indexes to the contents of a number of papers are also available. Unfortunately, most have begun only recently and therefore do not include early newspaper issues. Indexing of the *Wall Street Journal,* for example, began in 1956 and of the *Christian Science Monitor* in 1954. The contents of some newspapers, however, have been indexed for long periods. The best known and most used index is that of the *New York Times,* dating from 1851. Thomas W. Jodziewicz's *Birth of America: the Year in Review, 1763-1783: A Chronological Guide and Index to the Contemporary Colonial Press* indexes fifty-two newspapers. A number of major newspaper indexes are available online. "Historical Newspapers and Indexes On The Internet — USA" <http://www.researchguides.net/newspapers.htm> and the Library of Congress' "Newspaper & Current Periodical Reading Room" <http://www.loc.gov/rr/news/oltitles.html> provide links to indexing and digitizing projects in more than half of the states. Indexes are also available in most libraries or through the inter-library loan system in either print or microprint. Anita C. Milner's three-volume work *Newspaper Indexes: A Location and Subject Guide for Researchers* (1977), though dated, provides a helpful guide. Some state and local historical societies index newspapers and maintain local card files.

Major projects are well underway and many completed to provide searchable full texts of newspapers through online services. ProQuest and Readex, for example, offer databases with millions of pages from more than 2,000 historic newspapers, including the *Atlanta Constitution, Boston Globe, Portland Oregonian*, and many other major publications. Such commercial services normally require the user to pay a fee. On the other hand, numerous digitized newspapers are available through the projects sponsored by such entities as the National Archives and can be a valuable source. The historian should bear in mind, however, that many newspapers have not been indexed and research in their pages will require considerable time searching for particular types of material.

Particular mention should be made of the index for the *New York Times* because many people consider it the major American newspaper of record. The index goes back to 1851 although its coverage is more complete after 1905, when it became an annually published index. Several other publications enhance access to the content of the *Times*, including the *New York Times Obituaries Index, 1858-1968* (1970), the *New York Times Obituaries Index II, 1969-1978* (1980), the *Personal Name Index to "The New York Times Index," 1851-1974*, 22 vols. (1976-1983), and supplements to the *Personal Name Index* that have brought it up to 2006.

Along with the *New York Times, Christian Science Monitor*, and *Wall Street Journal*, some of the major American newspapers that have indexes are the *Atlanta Constitution, Boston Globe, Chicago Sun-Times, Chicago Tribune, Detroit News, Houston Post, Los Angeles Times, New Orleans Times-Picayune, San Francisco Chronicle, USA Today*, and *Washington Post*. The indexed years are limited, however, and most of the papers are not indexed before 1972. Gale/Cengage offers a fee-based database, the National Newspaper Index, which indexes the *Christian Science Monitor, Los Angeles Times, New York Times, Wall Street Journal USA Today*, and *Washington Post* since 1977. For England, the index of the *Times* of London is available for issues since 1790.

Chapter 6: Searching for Historical Materials

The same thing that has been said about newspapers applies to other communication sources. Material is available in abundance, but the historian must know how to find it. A number of guides will help. Many university libraries hold large collections of bound volumes of magazines that offer a wealth of material. The American Antiquarian Society has extensive collections of magazines, books, and pamphlets published before 1900. Indexes of magazine content may be found in such references as *American Periodicals, 1741-1900; an Index to the Microfilm Collections* (1979), *Poole's Index to Periodical Literature, 1802-1906* (1882-1908), *Nineteenth Century Readers' Guide to Periodical Literature, 1890-1899, with Supplementary Indexing, 1900-1922* (1944), *The Readers' Guide to Periodical Literature* (1900-), *Popular Periodicals Index* (1973-1990), and a number of other publications and services. The online database *19th Century Masterfile* mentioned earlier provides a convenient means of searching for items. In advertising history, both newspapers and magazines include thousands of advertisements that may serve as the raw material for study. Pamphlets, likewise, may be found in various libraries and collections. The researcher will find valuable such bibliographical sources as Charles Evans, comp., *American Bibliography: A Chronological Dictionary of All Books, Pamphlets and Periodicals Printed in the United States of America (1639-1800)* (a fourteen-volume work published between 1903 and 1959) and Bernard Bailyn's *Pamphlets of the American Revolution* (1956). Of particular value is the digital version of Evans' work. It is available online and includes full-text versions of 36,000 printed works. Access to it is fee-based.

Finding historical material on film, radio, and television is more difficult. Much of the content of broadcasting never was recorded, and the high costs of recording and using broadcast material discourage preservation. Researchers will find some valuable primary sources from radio history in online sites such as the Internet Archive's audio section <http://www.archive.org/details/old timeradio>, although the site provides a highly selective set of materials representing only a tiny fraction of broadcast content. Chapter 7, "Historical Research on the Internet," in this book lists several online sources for research in broadcast history. Many silent films were photographed on combustible nitrate stock — and entire archival collections have exploded or burned, with the loss of numerous films. There have been efforts to transfer motion pictures to other types of film stock, but they come too little and too late, and much material has been lost permanently. Thus archives and library holdings for broadcasting and film are not as large as for print. Copyright regulations also have discouraged the duplication of material. The high costs of storing recordings sometimes have led to decisions by their owners to destroy them.

Despite the problems, substantial amounts of programming material may be found. Several publications provide guides to locating programs. Among the more thorough are *History in Sound: A Descriptive Listing of the KIRO-CBS Collection of the World War II Years and After* (1963), Alex McNeil's *Total Television: A Comprehensive Guide to Programming from 1948 to the Present* (1997), and Tim Brooks and Earle Marsh's *The Complete Directory of Prime Time Network Television, 1946-Present* (2007). Similar guides to motion picture films are also available. The Internet Movie Database <http://www.imdb.com> provides plot synopses, cast names, and other information about thousands of movies, as well as television programs and other video material. Some indexing to individual programs has been done, but it is not as voluminous as indexing for the print media. Vanderbilt University's Television News Archive has published *Television News Index and Abstracts* since 1972 covering evening news broadcasts on the national networks. Its website <http://tvnews.vanderbilt.edu> provides synopses of network news programs aired since 1968. As the permanent value of broadcast programming has gained heightened recognition in the last several years, such services have increased, and today broadcast and film historians have at their disposal a considerable store of guides.

In addition to the media content that may be found in files, a number of published sources of primary material are available. Anthologies of journalistic writing, editorial cartoons, newspaper front pages, magazine art, photographs, advertisements, and various other items have been published in large numbers. Works such as Louis Snyder and Richard Morris' *A Treasury of Great Reporting* (1962) and Allan Nevins' *Newspaper Press Opinion, Washington to Coolidge* (1928), for example, contain numerous articles as they originally appeared in newspapers. Most anthologies contain works in one genre (such as Sloan, Wray, and Sloan, *Great Editorials* [2nd ed., 1997], and Sloan and Wray, *Masterpieces of Reporting* [1997]) or works by a single author or publication. The *Diary of World Events* is an extensive 31-volume collection of reproductions of newspaper stories from 1938 to 1945 covering World War II. David A. Copeland edited two of the most comprehensive series dealing with the American media and war and with public issues as covered in the media. The eight-volume series "Greenwood Library of American War Reporting" contains more than 2,500 documents. The seven-volume series "Debating Historical Issues in the Media of the Time" covers the colonial era through World War I. Searches of Internet websites can sometimes turn up similar material. The historian also may find useful material in such works as journalists' and advertising executives' autobiographies and memoirs. They contain many personal recollections and much historical material based on first-hand observations. Trade journals such as *Editor and Publisher* (1901-), *Advertising Age* (1947-), *Broadcasting* (1931-), *Moving Picture World* (1907-1927), and *Variety* (1905-) also offer many articles written by historical figures in the mass media and other material based on primary research.

Computerized Bibliographic Systems

As one can see, the work of identifying, locating, and gathering materials can be long and time consuming. In this day when online sources have become commonplace, might not the Internet be substituted for a manual bibliographic search? At present the question must be answered with equivocation.

First of all, let us define our terms. In our brief discussion of this point, we shall use the term *database* to mean systematically collected and prepared information stored in a manner that facilitates searching and retrieval. *Database vendors* will be used to refer to companies that deal with the development of systems and services that allow users to access databases online. In some cases a database vendor also produces its own databases, such as Bell & Howell's ProQuest Direct, the Thomson Corporation's Expanded Academic ASAP (EAA), Northern Light, Corbis, Questia Media, HarpWeek, Lexis/Nexis, and EBSCO. It is the custom of universities to acquire the products of some but not all of these commercial database vendors. Both academic and public libraries usually provide their patrons free access to some databases or subsidize a portion of the charges for an individual search. It is also possible for researchers to buy their own subscriptions to database systems. In any case, vendors charge fees for access to their databases.

Internet searches, then, are possible. Moreover, the reasons to use them are compelling. They offer speed and convenience and might produce information difficult to find in a manual search. They can scan interdisciplinary sources and even locate institutions where there is a cluster of activity on a given subject. Since researchers in one discipline are not always familiar with the research and sources in another, the Internet can bridge that gap by providing cross-disciplinary access to activity and sources. Important items for communication historians already are in databases. Some of the databases are listed in Chapter 7 of this book. They include, among many others, such services as *Historical Abstracts, America: History and Life, Dissertation Abstracts,* and indexes to the *New York Times,* the *Wall Street Journal,* the *Washington Post,* and many other publications, as well as several news services. Indeed, many websites such as American Memory and Making of America and fee-based services such as Readex's Early American Imprints offer full texts of materials rather than a simple citation.

There are, however, mitigating arguments to consider. One is the potential cost. If a historian does not have access to the subscription databases of a university library, the costs for using databases may be prohibitive. A second consideration is that no database will have all the sources that a historian probably will want to consult. Various databases may have the texts of thousands of documents, but it is unlikely that any single database will have everything in need of investigation. Furthermore, databases tend to be less complete for older sources than for recent ones.

An Internet bibliographic search is of questionable value if done without adequate preparation. Only a well delineated topic would be feasible to search, and, as we have seen, narrowing down a topic can take time and experimentation. Consequently, a good deal of manual preparation normally is necessary before one is ready to conduct a computerized search. Time spent in preparing for a computerized search will be time well spent. The preparation can be a positive experience even if the search is not run. Preparing for a search sometimes helps one to identify major statements relating to a topic. It can also hone skills used in manual work with the bibliographic sources. Such skills will serve one well in the everyday work of research.

All things considered, it seems advisable to recommend that one not rely inordinately on an Internet search. It is most useful as a method to employ along with a manual search in an effort to determine the location of recently published materials on a well-defined topic. Because of the constantly changing nature of the information available on databases and sometimes because of the difficulty encountered in retrieving it, it is also recommended that researchers consult the appropriate librarians or information specialists at their institutions. As is so often the case, the best results will probably come from the collaboration of the researcher and the librarian.

The Library Physical Card Catalog

Most libraries in this country use the Library of Congress (LC) classification system. The system assigns a code, which is comprised of letters and numbers, to each book and every other item in a library. The code indicates the location of each item in a library's holdings. Armed with that code and a map of a library's physical shelving arrangement, a researcher can easily find any item.

The LC system divides subjects into twenty-one broad categories, each designated by a letter of the alphabet. Additional letters or numbers are added to specify subcategories. For example, books in history are classified under C, D, E, and F.

C = Auxiliary Sciences of History (History of Civilization, Archaeology, and a variety of other subtopics)

D = World History

E = History of the Americas (America and the United States)

F = History of the Americas (U. S. local and British, Dutch, French, Latin, and Spanish America)

Additional letters and numerals are assigned to separate these basic groups into classes and subdivisions. The letters DA, for instance, are used to designate Great Britain. Books in journalism are classified PN (a subcategory of P, which designates language and literature). The full list of fields and their letters can be found online at http://www.loc.gov/catdir/cpso/lcco. In order to browse through a section containing books of interest (in a library with open stacks), simply follow the instructions that libraries post to indicate the location of the various classifications. However, to make a systematic search for specific authors, books, and subjects, the library catalog should be consulted.

Libraries use two types of catalogs: the venerable assemblage of file drawers known as the Card Catalog and the newer Online Catalog. These catalogs index books and materials in the libraries in which they are located.

Although most searching today takes place through an Online Catalog, research at some libraries requires an understanding of the arrangement of the traditional catalog. Some libraries have not computerized 100 per cent of their holdings, and they still maintain Card Catalogs. In some cases, libraries distinguish between their older acquisitions (those up to a certain date), which remain catalogued in the Card Catalog, and their newer acquisitions, which are entered in their Online Catalog. Also, all of a library's specialized collections (including, for example, music) may or may not be included in the Online Catalog. At the Library of Congress, an important library for historians, many items from the special collections are listed only in the Card Catalog.

There are many similarities between the two types of catalogs, but let us begin by explaining some features of the Card Catalog. As we begin, though, we'll suggest that for the time being you simply scan the next few paragraphs describing the physical Card Catalog. Should you find at some point that you indeed do need to work with a Card Catalog, then you may wish to return to and read the following section more closely.

Each card in a Card Catalog provides basic bibliographic information about a book, and each includes a "call number" indicating where this book can be found in the library. Cards are arranged alphabetically in the drawers according to the author, title, and subject. Researchers may encounter two types of Card Catalogs. In one, called a "dictionary catalog," the author, title, and subject cards are filed together. In the other, called a "divided catalog," they are separated into two parts: the "author-title" catalog and the "subject" catalog.

When using the Card Catalog, it is necessary to understand several important filing rules. Regarding author and title cards or citations, remember:

1. Articles *a, an,* and *the,* and their foreign equivalents, if they appear first in the title, are not considered part of that title for filing purposes. They are, however, considered part of it when they appear internally in the title.

2. Abbreviations are treated as if they were spelled out in full. (Dr. is found as Doctor, St. as Saint, etc.)

3. *M', Mc,* and *Mac* are all filed as if they were *Mac.*

4. Numbers in a title are filed as if they were spelled out in full (50 is found as Fifty).

5. Prefixes such as *de* or *von* usually are not considered part of a person's surname according to the standard rules of filing.

One also should be aware that organizations and agencies are considered as authors when they issue publications. They may be public ones such as the United States Office of Censorship and the United States National Archives, or they may be private ones such as the Institute of Early American History and Culture or the Association for Education in Journalism and Mass Communication.

Since researchers may know neither the name nor the title of books pertaining to their topic, particularly in the early stages of a bibliographic search, they tend to find subject cards more useful. For purposes of discussion these subject cards will be referred to as the "subject catalog" with the understanding that in a library that has a "dictionary catalog" they would be interfiled alphabetically with the author and title cards.

The subject catalog has much to offer researchers. Yet at first its arrangement might appear illogical. Subject cards are filed alphabetically for the sake of convenience. Consequently, a sequence of subjects may be unrelated. To correct this incongruity, catalogers add "see also" cards and citations. The researcher should not confuse them with the "see" references that direct one to a proper subject heading in cases where the subject heading one has in mind is non-existent in the classification system. A "see also" reference serves a different function. It directs one to other existing subject headings related to the one under examination. This cross-reference system can be used to round out the extent of one's subject according to the possibilities that the system provides. For example, the "see also" reference for the subject "Journalism" would lead one to additional and related subject headings such as "College and School Journalism," "Press," and "Reporters and Reporting," which would not be filed in the subject catalog in proximity to the subject heading "Journalism." According to standard rules of cataloging, "see also" references are placed at the end of the first general division of a subject run. Subject headings are filed with the general subject category coming first, followed by the various subdivisions of that subject. For example, consider "the Press" as a subject heading. Entries in the subject catalog for that subject begin with a general category labeled "the Press." Directly after that there are various subdivisions into which catalogers separate the subject, "the Press," such as "Press — History," "Press — Argentine," etc. "See also" references appear at the end of the section "the Press." When justified, they also may be found at the end of any subdivision of the subject where there is an appropriate cross-reference to make. The subject catalog, however, only lists subjects for which a particular library has holdings. Most libraries that use the Library of Congress classification system have the five-volume set the *Library of Congress Subject Headings* (2001) near the catalog. This set is the authority for subjects in that library's catalog and can lead the user to other useful headings.

Subject headings can appear confusing at first. Using them calls for a little knowledge, imagination, and some patience, too, but the results can be rewarding. It helps to understand a few basic rules that govern the arrangement of the subject catalog. There are four basic types of subject headings:

1. A single noun without adjective modifiers and undivided (e.g., "History" or "Journalism").

2. A noun followed by subject divisions (e.g., "History — Bibliography" or "Journalism — U. S.").

3. A noun and an adjective modifier in either uninverted (e.g., "Political Cartoons") or inverted (e.g., "Journalism, Commercial") form.

4. A phrase composed of two nouns (with or without modifiers) linked by a conjunction or a preposition (e.g., "Press and Politics").

These basic divisions are often subdivided according to form, topic, geography, and chronology. Form and topical subdivisions are listed first, followed by geographical and chronological ones. Consider the following examples. (These headings and those that follow were chosen as examples of general order and are not consecutive runs. In a Card Catalog, one will find intervening entries.)

Propaganda

Propaganda — Addresses, Essays, Lectures

Propaganda — Bibliography
Propaganda — Collections
Propaganda — History
Propaganda, American
Propaganda, British
Propaganda, Chinese
and,
United States — History
United States — History — Addresses, Essays, Lectures
United States — History — Bibliography
United States — History — King Philip's War 1675-1676
United States — History — King George's War 1744-1748
United States — History — Revolution 1775-1783
United States — History — Constitutional Period 1789-1809

Beginning researchers should note that it is worthwhile to follow a subject heading division through all the levels of its divisions. In the following case of a run of subdivisions, someone interested in journalism and the Spanish-American War of 1898 would miss much of consequence to that topic by failing to consider the full listing of subdivided subject headings:

United States — History — War of 1898
United States — History — War of 1898 — Cartoons
United States — History — War of 1898 — Journalists
United States — History — War of 1898 — Personal Narrative

A little detective work combining knowledge of subject and thoroughness of approach will produce the greatest yield from the subject catalog.

The Library Online Catalog

Entries in a library's Online Catalog are arranged along lines similar to those of the Card Catalog. The main menu of a library's Online Public Access Computer (the station for the library's catalog) features these options:

Author
Title
Author/Title
Subject
Keywords

There may be other options, too, such as ones for Library Information, but the above ones are the essential guides to the library's holdings. If one is searching for a known item, the "Author," "Title," or "Author/Title" options can be used. Upon selecting an option and entering a query, the frame and supplementary frames that appear on the screen will show the call number and the basic bibliographical information about a book that the Card Catalog entries formerly did. If the "Subject" option is selected, the search will be constrained by the controlled vocabulary of the Library of Congress Subject Headings, which the Online Catalog also uses. If the "Keyword" option is used, the search can be focused on words and terms very specific to a research topic. It allows one to enter a query for a search term rather than a title.

The Historical Researcher and Bibliography

Although there is no single search tool or total bibliographic instrument for historians, the apparatus available to them is vast. As we have seen, it is as diverse as it is extensive. To a considerable degree, one's success in producing worthwhile history depends on mastering bibliographic sources. They can provide the necessary direction to the multitude of materials that provide the foundation for historical inquiry. Beginning researchers should become familiar with the essential bibliographic sources in their university libraries and employ them to make their own working bibliographies comprehensive and up to date.

Scholars today are encountering a bibliographic revolution. As a number of citations listed in this chapter prove, it is well underway. If it were possible for the young historians today to go back in time a mere forty years, they would appreciate how striking the bibliographic expansion has been for historical studies. The computer and Internet, of course, have been responsible for much of this expansion, but not for all. Technology of many types has enlarged the potential of bibliography, and for that potential to be realized the historian and the bibliographer must work together. No one, however, doubts that, as a consequence of technical advances influencing bibliography, the historian's mastery of available primary and secondary materials has grown and will continue to grow.

What will be the result of it all? It seems reasonable to suggest that with all of the benefits that the bibliographic revolution can and will bring, historians will continue to work with scarcity amid abundance. They will, consequently, be forced to contemplate once again the limitations of historical knowledge, vast though it may be and vaster yet it may become.

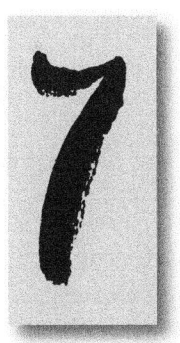

HISTORICAL RESEARCH ON THE INTERNET

Since the first edition of *Historical Methods in Mass Communication* was published in 1989, the most dramatic change in the research process has been the proliferation of information on the Internet. In 1989 the new technology that was of most interest to historians was online catalogs for libraries. In 2010, when the book's third edition was published, there were more than 190 million websites. Today, as this chapter is being written, there are more than 1.9 billion websites and more than 4.6 billion web pages. For practical purposes, though, the number of "stable" (that is, supposedly permanent) websites has been around 170 million for a few years, and about three-quarters of websites are not active. Still, for the last several years, the number of web pages has been increasing at a breakneck pace. The growth of the Internet has added greatly to the capacity of historians to identify and gather both primary and secondary sources.

The Internet offers several benefits for historical research, but it also has limitations. Historians should take advantage of the benefits but at the same time exercise a critical mind about the limitations.

Benefits of the Internet

The most obvious benefit of the Internet is that it can provide guides and access to some material without requiring historians ever to get up from their chairs. Although most material for historical research does not exist on the Web, the Internet can help with locating and accessing primary and secondary sources and conducting bibliographical searches. On the Internet, historians can find references to material and much digitized matter. Prior to the Internet, searches for such material required trips to libraries and archives. Those trips could be both time-consuming and expensive. Moreover, with today's ability for digitizing of documents, some libraries and archives have begun to discard their original documents. Today, historians can determine whether a library possesses a specific book or journal and if an archive has relevant primary documents in its holdings by accessing online catalogs remotely. One of the obvious values of such a capability is that the Internet can save historians enormous amounts of time, and, as anyone knows who has spent hours visiting archives or searching through library holdings, a historian's time is precious.

Almost as important as time saving is the fact that some Internet research can replace travel. The Internet probably will not, in the foreseeable future, provide files of all the primary or even secondary material that historians require. However, enormous amounts of material are now available on the Internet that at one time could be found only in archives. Primary material that can be found only in archives is so essential that professional historians invest large amounts of time and money to examine it. Historians who are professors still spend entire summers traveling to archives. Travel is still required for most archival material, but the Internet has reduced the amount of travel many historians have to do. That is of particular importance to students, who often have to complete a research project in the course of one semester and have neither the time nor the money to travel to distant archives.

Two main types of information are available on the Internet: (1) information you have to pay for and (2) freely available information. Most libraries maintain subscriptions to expensive scholarly databases that provide access to citations, abstracts, and even the full texts of popular periodicals and scholarly journals. Familiarizing oneself with the databases to which a particular library subscribes is time well spent. They can provide a wealth of material. Using them is one way to access costly online information without charge to the individual user. An advantage of these databases over the free information available on the Web is often the quality of content. Because databases are scholarly by nature, their content is usually more reliable than what one finds on free Internet sites.

On the free Internet sites, a variety of web pages contain secondary accounts of historical topics, and many of them provide bibliographies or links to other sites with bibliographies. Chat groups also can provide a source of ideas on topics, and often members of the groups will help inquirers identify history articles and books on specific topics. In the field of communication history, for example, the "Jhistory" site furnishes a forum for historians to exchange information. Its URL (Uniform Resource Locator, i.e., the address for an Internet site) is https://

Chapter 7: Historical Research on the Internet

networks.h-net.org/jhistory/. Of course, every statement that is posted on such sites is not authoritative, but often members of the group are able to provide useful references to both primary and secondary sources.

The most valuable material for historical research, of course, is primary documents. On most topics in communication history, the Internet will not be a complete source for primary material, but a growing body of primary documents is available there. Some sites are devoted to specific topics, and they sometimes provide large numbers of documents. Others provide registers (finding aids) for manuscript collections. Unfortunately, there are few such sites dedicated to the field of communication history, and most of those offer only a portion of the extant primary material that might be relevant to one's investigation.

Still, any document historians can find can be added to the body of research that must be done. So even if the relevant primary material available on the Internet is limited, it still may help to provide a more complete account than historians could write without it.

Despite some of its limitations, an immense advantage the Internet has over most archives is that much of its textual material is searchable by individual words. Paper documents in archives typically are only indexed or categorized. The benefits of searchable text are readily evident. For example, Cornell University's and the University of Michigan's "Making of America" collection has digitized more than 260 monograph volumes and approximately 100,000 journal articles from American magazines in the 1800s, and the entire collection is searchable.[1] Thus, if, for example, a historian were looking for references to the editor Sarah Josepha Hale in any of those articles, they could be found almost instantaneously. Prior to the Internet, such a search might have taken months.

Limitations of the Internet

Despite such attractive features of the Internet, it does present a number of limitations. The greatest shortcoming is that much of the primary material that exists in some form today has not been digitized and placed on the Internet. Despite the fact that some well publicized projects have put the contents of a number of magazines and newspapers on the Internet, the fact remains that many magazines, newspapers, and other forms of mass communication are not available there. The same is true of most other forms of primary material, from personal papers and private diaries to public reports. For example, the Manuscript

---

[1] The "Making of America" collections are at http://collections.library.cornell.edu/moa _new/index.html and http://quod.lib.umich.edu/m/moagrp/.

Division of the Library of Congress houses more than 11,000 separate manuscript collections containing more than 60,000,000 items, and only a fraction of them are on the Internet. A thorough historical research project will require primary sources, and the only place many of them may be found is in physical archives.

Furthermore, a substantial amount of the primary material on the Internet is found at for-profit sites that require a fee for access. In the field of communication history, for example, "HarpWeek" has digitized the contents of *Harper's Weekly* magazine from 1857 to 1912, but access is fee-based. A subscription costs approximately $84,000. In 2002, the National Newspaper Association and Cold North Wind Corporation announced plans to create "America's Chronicles SM," providing access to the digital archives of more than 3,000 community newspapers. Now operating under the name Paper of Record (at PaperofRecord.com), the project has digitized 20 million pages of both American and international newspapers. Researchers may purchase annual, limited access to the database (for a price of $71 to $240 per year). Higher-priced subscriptions are also available but are intended for institutions. Fortunately for poor students and historians, many libraries maintain subscriptions to databases, and some of the material available through the fee-based private services can be found on other free, public sites.

> "A historian I know tells his class, 'the Internet is not a resource, but a way to find resources.' Against this view, many students feel that the Internet is the only source they need. Our job as journalism historians is to dispel both views by simultaneously accepting the Internet as a wonderful new source, understanding its real limitations, and viewing its contents with a sharp skepticism." — David Mindich, founder of Jhistory

Several fee-based databases also provide access to the contents of secondary sources. Through those services, researchers can access searchable full texts of a wide range of journal articles. Some major vendors are EBSCO, First Search, ProQuest, and the Gale Group. Subscription fees are so expensive as to be prohibitive for individual historians, but many libraries subscribe to the services and make them available to patrons. Digitized books are not as readily available as journal articles. Some services offer online libraries, and their holdings have been increasing in number. For example, Questia Media, which at one time promoted itself as the "World's Largest Online Library," had only 7,000 books in 2009, and books in communication accounted for only about 7% of them. In 2018, however, it offered access to more than 78,000 books and more than 9 million periodicals articles.

On the other hand, Project Gutenberg, which has digitized books whose copyright has expired (those published more than ninety-five years ago), provides the texts of 60,000 or so books (double the number it had a decade earlier). Access is free. More modest collections may be found at such websites as Read Print at www.readprint.com and The Internet Classics Archive at http://classics.mit.edu.

Another limitation on Internet material is U. S. copyright law. As a result of the Sonny Bono Copyright Term Extension Act of 1998, copyrighted "works for hire" (such as newspaper articles) are now protected for ninety-five years. Thus, a work published in, for example, 1950 will not enter the public domain until the year 2045. Works by individuals, that is, those not done as an employee, are protected for seventy years after the death of the author. The cost to acquire the right to include such material on the Internet limits the number of works available. Google Books, however, has reached a legal agreement with numerous publishers and authors. It estimates that 130 million book titles have been published in print form, and it says it hopes to be able to provide all of them in digitized form on its website. As of 2018, its collection included 2 million books.

Another problem the researcher should be aware of is that errors, fabrications, incompleteness of the text, and related shortcomings are more likely to appear in Internet documents than in paper documents. Printed books, as one example of a paper document, usually have gone through an editing and proofreading process before being published. Virtually anyone, however, can put a text on the Internet without following rigorous safeguards. Errors can be made in the scanning or keyboarding process required in digitizing a text. Parts of a text may be omitted or altered for any variety of reasons. Texts may even be fictionalized. For example, a document called the "Willie Lynch speech of 1712" can be found on hundreds of websites without any indication that it was created in the twentieth century. The speech purports to be the remarks of a slave owner about how to control American slaves. Several groups have found the text on the Internet, apparently accepted it at face value, and used it to support their political agendas — despite the fact that a number of websites have exposed it as a hoax. Similarly, the researcher should be wary of material that members sometimes share on chat groups. Frequently, they are not based on evidence, are biased, are superficial, or suffer from other shortcomings.

The superficiality of much of the material on the Internet deserves particular attention. Much of it is of an introductory nature and lacks the depth needed for serious research. Wikipedia, the online encyclopedia, may provide useful information, but it should be used only as a reference source. Students would be well advised to study what *Britannica* Online has to offer about their topic in order to help them recognize the depth of the Internet material they find. Or they might compare it to how a recommended textbook covers their topic. In general, students should not assume that an Internet search provides dependable answers to significant questions. Though search engines like Google have made finding quick answers to some basic factual questions much quicker and easier, too much reliance on this method can lead students to false information and biased interpretations. Internet searches reveal what information people have chosen to put on websites, not necessarily what information scholars have agreed upon is authoritative.

Wikipedia, one of the more popular destinations on the Internet, embodies the promise and peril of Web-based research. On the one hand, it is a democratic forum to compile information about numerous subjects, many of which scholars have unduly neglected. Subjects that otherwise might have evaded public attention get some because an Internet search directs one to Wikipedia. On the other hand, Wikipedia's democratic nature is also its biggest flaw. Although Wikipedia has monitors of its content, incorrect information can easily make it onto the site, and there are no standards for peer review by scholars. This problem leads to entries of variable quality and reliability. In 2006 the *Chronicle of Higher Education* asked faculty experts to give letter grades to the Wikipedia entries for subjects in their fields. An engineering professor found the entry for "flow cytometry" worthy of an "A" grade, but two entries more relevant to historians, those for Aldous Huxley's novel *Brave New World* and the African-American Civil-Rights Movement, received grades of "B-" and "C," respectively.[2] Students should be cautious when relying on Wikipedia when conducting research and consider it at best a quick source of basic information that can later be checked in better sources. Wikipedia itself explains, "Wikipedia editors try their very hardest to maintain this site. Multiple measures ... are used to prevent vandalism of this site and maintain its credibility. But Wikipedia can be edited by anyone at any time. This means that any information it contains at any particular time could be vandalism, a work in progress, or just plain wrong."[3]

The easy accessibility of Internet material poses another trap for students. If they have used a number of Internet sources for a research project, what indication is there that they were the best sources? To address this problem, some professors limit the percentage of sources that may be taken from the Internet.

---

[2]Brock Read, "Can Wikipedia Make the Grade?" *Chronicle of Higher Education* (October 27, 2006), A31-A36.
[3]https://en.wikipedia.org/wiki/Wikipedia:Wikipedia_is_not_a_reliable_source

For example, if a research project uses ten sources from the Internet, then forty more might have to be taken from print sources.[4] Others require students to compare their Internet sources with traditional ones found in the library. Surfing the Web and quickly locating sources for a paper does not guarantee its quality.

One should also remember the difference between Internet sources one might find doing a general Web search and articles found online through paid library databases or online journals. Libraries pay thousands (and sometimes millions) of dollars for these online sources, which are just as reliable as print resources. One should not think that subscription online journals and articles are suspect because they are "from the Internet." The text in an online journal is identical to that of the same article in the print version of a journal.

Clearly, historians using the Internet for research must bring the same critical faculties to evaluating sources found there as one would with traditional sources. Those standards of evaluation are discussed in Chapter 5, "Historical Sources and Their Evaluation," of this book.

Types of Material on the Internet

Primary Documents

The ideal world for historical research might be one in which every record ever created existed in digitized, easily searchable form on the Internet. We are many years from such a situation, but a large body of primary material does exist on the Internet, and it is increasing all the time. The greatest amount of material is about general history, not specifically communication history. However, communication historians often will find that research into a variety of general-history material will give a fuller perspective on communication topics than communication research alone will do. Many collections that are not specifically about communication may contain pertinent documents that will help to shed light on the communication topic.

A list of helpful sites, along with their URL addresses, is provided later in this chapter.

One free site in particular, however, deserves special mention. It is "American Memory" (subtitled "Historical Collections for the National Digital Library").

---

[4]Steven R. Knowlton, "How Students Get Lost in Cyberspace," *New York Times Education Supplement*, 2 November 1997, sec. 4A, p.18, and Michael Richards, "Students and the Web: A Cautionary Tale," *European History Newsletter* of the European History Section, the Southern Historical Association (Fall 1998), 3-4.

It contains "collections of American culture and history, mostly derived from Library of Congress special collections. Photographic panoramas, sound files, movies, photos and documents can be found in abundance." It offers more than 9 million digitized items from more than 100 historical collections. The texts are searchable by individual words.

Two other excellent sites are the University of Michigan's and Cornell University Library's "Making of America" (MOA) collections, a part of the "American Memory" project. Each provides a "searchable digital library of primary sources in American social history from the antebellum period through Reconstruction, [and is] particularly strong in the subject areas of education, psychology, American history, sociology, religion, and science and technology."

A number of sites also have digitized texts and images that are specific to communication history. They run the gamut from advertising to magazines to newspapers to broadcasting. A few, especially those that are part of the "American Memory" project, contain substantial collections. Most, however, have only a small portion of the extant primary material on their topics, but even those can provide sources to serve as a starting point for research or as a part of a research project.

Bibliographies

Many websites include bibliographies of articles and books in communication history. Rob Rabe, for example, a professor at Marshall University, maintains a website that includes a bibliography of more than 4,000 articles and books in media history. "Historical Abstracts," a fee-based website, provides bibliographical references to more than 2,000 journals. Several other databases specialize in bibliographies covering a variety of fields that may be of interest to historians. The *Journal of American History* provides a keyword search of works that have been published in a large number of scholarly journals, although none of the publications are specific to communication history. Many articles about communication history have been published, however, in journals outside the field, and the *JAH* site provides a good means of creating a bibliography of those works. Google Scholar, likewise, provides Internet-wide searching capabilities similar to the online search function that libraries use for their local collections. It searches journals and books, and the researcher may search by such items as keywords, author names, and book and article titles.

Despite the proliferation of sites with bibliographies, the best way to identify pertinent articles and books is through the several bibliographies on communication history that have been published. They are much more complete than the bibliographies found on websites. Still, the Internet can be quite useful by helping to locate more recent works. Also, since published bibliographies tend to focus on journals in the communication field, the Internet can help the researcher locate articles that have been published in non-communication journals.

Secondary Sources

Many free websites include history essays. However, they tend to be short and superficial, often written by the individuals who maintain personal websites. Rarely does one find substantive pieces with thorough documentation. Most have never been subjected to a rigorous review process, and it is not unusual to find errors in them. For those reasons, the researcher should not rely on them as secondary literature. Published books and articles remain the best sources.

Though historians should take care in using secondary materials on the Internet, a large amount of reliable material is available. Numerous scholarly journals are available on fee-based databases. Starting in 2002, Google began partnering with some of the world's leading research libraries to scan their holdings and make them available for free on the Internet. Because of copyright law, the vast majority of recently published books and scholarly articles are not available in this manner, but the communication historian will find a rich and easily accessible collection of materials via Google Scholar at http://scholar.google.com. For example, historians may consult exact page images of such classic works as Robert Park's *The Immigrant Press and Its Control* and Walter Lippmann's *Public Opinion* without making a trip to a physical library. In addition, some scholarly journals have started to move or already have moved entirely online and do not exist in print. For example, *Media History Monographs* at https://blogs.elon.edu/mhm and the *Journal of Religion and Popular Culture* at https://www.utpjournals.press/loi/jrpc publish peer-reviewed scholarship on significant topics in communication history. Likewise, *Flow* at www.flowjournal.org is an online journal that features original essays on media history and culture.

Catalogs of Archives and Libraries

Nearly all research libraries and many archives have their holdings catalogued online. Thus, historians may sit at a home computer and check whether the local library has a particular book or journal. Of particular value is the online catalog of the Library of Congress, the repository of the vast majority of books ever published in the United States.

An even more important tool is WorldCat, a worldwide catalog of books and other materials. It contains 2.7 billion records (as of November 2018) from more than 70,000 libraries (including the Library of Congress). WorldCat, like the Library of Congress Catalog, has records for almost every book, CD, video, and journal ever published in the United States, as well as many published abroad. Researchers can search WorldCat (at https://www.worldcat.org) from anywhere they have Internet access, and an advantage it has over the Library of Congress Online Catalog is that one can quickly determine which libraries near the researcher have a desired item.

Similarly, catalogs of many archival holdings may be accessed online. The "Best of History Websites" and "History Matters" are good starting points for locating archival sites on the Internet. Much of their material is aimed at history teachers, but they also include links to numerous other sites that describe holdings of manuscripts, archives, rare books, historical photographs, and other primary sources. Among the better archives for research in communication history are the following, and online catalogs can help historians identify their holdings.

The Online National Union Catalog of Manuscript Collections contains reference material for a large body of records held by the Library of Congress.

The United States Newspaper Program, funded by the National Endowment for the Humanities, is a "cooperative national effort among the states and the federal government to locate, catalog, and preserve on microfilm newspapers published in the United States from the eighteenth century to the present." Its site provides references to the preservation projects in all the states. Links lead directly to the websites of the individual states, where the researcher can identify their holdings.

The American Antiquarian Society has an extensive collection of publications before 1877, and its online catalog "contains records for the Society's collections of books, pamphlets, manuscripts, newspapers, lithographs, and broadsides."

The Wisconsin Historical Society has extensive newspaper holdings and many other primary sources. It gives its Archives Mission Statement as this: "To identify, collect, organize, preserve, publicize, and provide public access to primary resources that document the history of Wisconsin and selected subjects of American history." The website provides detailed references to and descriptions of its holdings.

The News Media History site, which operates as part of the Briscoe Center

Chapter 7: Historical Research on the Internet

for American History at the University of Texas, has an extensive collection of "personal papers of media industry pioneers, research archives, [and] newspapers." The collection includes documents for both print and electronic media. Some of the significant collections include extensive runs of various newspapers; the news clipping and research morgues of the *New York Times*, the *New York Herald Tribune*, the *New York Journal-American,* and *Newsweek*; the archives of a number of photojournalists; and the papers of Walter Cronkite and other journalists. The website provides information about the collections of the center.

How To Find Material on the Internet

With the vast amount of material that exists on the Internet, one needs a way to conveniently locate relevant sources. Fortunately, the Internet makes such searches easy. There are four elementary ways to go about finding material.

The first way is to access specific websites that one assumes will have the material for which one is searching. We have listed later in this chapter a number of websites that historians will find useful, including brief descriptions of their content and their URL addresses. In accessing a website, it is crucial to get its address exactly correct. While the potential for a problem may seem great, addressing a website is similar to addressing a letter through the U. S. Postal System. If you mail a letter to a friend and get the street address or Zip Code wrong, there's a good chance the letter will be returned to you. If you wish to avoid the potential of making an error in typing an address, it is sometimes simpler to do a search just by typing the name of the website. Your search will give you a number of hits, but the site for which you are searching should be near the top.

The second way is to follow links from one website to another. Many websites have such links, and they can quickly lead the researcher to a whole host of relevant Internet sites. For example, the Historic Pages website at http://historicpages.com/nprhist.htm contains links to a number of other sites that provide material related to a variety of topics in history. The links are to these sites:

American Antiquarian Society
State of Wisconsin Historical Society (Archives Division)
Library of Congress Newspapers & Periodicals
Civil War Newspapers in GIF format
Documents of American History online
Index of Web Sites related to the Civil War
Internet Public Library

There are many Internet sites with such links. They provide excellent starting places for Internet research. Later in this chapter you will find a list of a number of sites providing helpful links.

The third way is through "electronic indexes," databases that provide information about publications. Virtually all libraries, both academic and public, subscribe to at least some of these databases. Databases contain full texts of or index journal articles, essays, books, magazine articles, and other materials. The following are examples of databases that focus on history.

Accessible Archives: Contains full texts of material from periodicals from the eighteenth through early twentieth century.

America: History and Life: Provides citations and abstracts of works in U. S. and Canadian history.

Historical Abstracts: Provides citations and abstracts of works in world history from 1450 to the present. (However, it excludes U. S. and Canadian history.)

JSTOR (Journal Storage): Contains full texts of hundreds of scholarly journals, some going back to the nineteenth century.

Many libraries are replacing their print versions of publications with such databases.

The fourth way is to use a search engine or directory. Search engines, such as Google or Dogpile, are built by electronic "spiders" that search the Web for sites to include in the search engine. Directories, such as Yahoo! and Ask.com, are built by human editors who decide what content to include in the directory. Therefore, directories generally index fewer pages than search engines, but the editors have identified those pages as being appropriate to their respective subject areas. (We should add that over time, as some companies acquired other ones, they sometimes became amalgams of search engines and directories, so that the functions are not distinct. So we'll use the term "search engines" generically.)

Search engines and databases allow researchers to locate items by keywords that appear in any material on most websites. Once one learns the procedure, finding material is not difficult. However, conducting effective searches takes some experience. Search engines and databases employ many similar search procedures. Each, however, has its own quirks. In general, though, search techniques can be applied across different interfaces.

Individual search engines have their own procedures for conducting searches. Google's and Dogpile's standard search, for example, will look for texts that contain all the terms the researcher provides. For example, if one typed in the words *newspaper editorial opinion during World War II*, Google and Dogpile

Chapter 7: Historical Research on the Internet

would locate items that contain any of the words in that phrase even though a particular text might not have all the words. In their "advanced search" mode, however, both Google and Dogpile allow the researcher to specify that a search look for the precise wording of a phrase.

For performing searches, most search engines and databases employ "Boolean" logic. Boolean "operators" are words that are used to specify the relationship of two or more search terms. Boolean logic uses words such as AND, OR, and NOT in order to locate topics, focus searches, and limit the scope of searches. Here's how they work. The term OR linking keywords will find every document with either the first keyword or the second keyword. The term AND will locate only documents that include both keywords — or many keywords as long as they are included in the search and separated with the word AND. The term NOT will locate documents that have the first keyword but not the second. (Some search engines require that AND, OR, and NOT be capitalized. Otherwise they will ignore the words.)

To illustrate the concepts in an engine search, let's use the topic "newspaper editorial opinion during World War II" as an example. We may ask the search engine to look for all items with one specific word, in this case, let us say, *editorial*. The search would probably result in millions of hits, including any site that had the word *editorial* in it.[5] Thus, the search would turn up such items as today's National Conference of Editorial Writers that are unrelated to the World War II topic. The search would be much too broad. If we searched for *editorial* OR *newspaper*, we would get even more results.

We would need to limit the search. One way to do that would be to search for a term such as *newspaper editorial opinion during World War II*. If we want to search for an exact phrase — that is, all words in the exact order that they are typed in — most search engines will provide a search mode that specifies the phrase verbatim or will allow the use of quotation marks to specify the phrase. One needs to be careful, though, about making such a search too limited. If we searched for *"newspaper editorial opinion during World War II"* (in quotation marks), the search would be limited to only those sources that contain the exact phrase *newspaper editorial opinion during World War II* (all seven words in the same order). It would not locate sites that did not have the complete phrase even though they might contain all the words *newspaper, editorial, opinion, during, World, War,* and *II*.

We can use the word AND to locate sites that contain more than one key-

---

[5]When the authors conducted a search for sites containing the word "editorial," Bing and Yahoo! each found 41 million, and Google found 1.2 billion.

word. Thus, we could search for *editorial* AND *newspaper* AND *World War II* and identify sites that contain all three of those terms. However, the search would not locate a site that had only two of them, e.g., *editorial* and *World War II*. By using parentheses, we can determine which words the search engine or database groups together. Our search might look like this: *newspaper AND editorial AND opinion AND (World War II)*.

With some search engines and databases, the word NOT can be used to limit the number of hits a search locates. (However, a Boolean NOT is not compatible with all search engines.) Let us say we want to locate sites that have newspaper editorial opinion but not magazine opinion about World War II. By using the word NOT before the word *magazine*, we could then conduct a search that looks for the words *newspaper, editorial, opinion,* and *World War II* but not *magazine*.

Using a combination of Boolean operators, quotation marks, and parentheses, a researcher can devise a powerful search. For example, to ensure results for all spellings of World War II, the following search would work well with most engines and databases: *newspapers AND ("World War II" OR "World War Two" OR "World War 2")*.

In conducting engine and database searches, the wise approach is to use a variety of ways to look for words and terms so that the search is narrow enough to be manageable without overlooking pertinent sites. The researcher should keep in mind that different sources use different search algorithms, so that what works in one search interface may not work in another.

List of Recommended Websites

The Internet has a multitude of sites that can be of value to the communication historian. In the list below, we have provided those that seem most helpful, along with brief descriptions of their content. They are listed by categories of content, such as "primary material" and "indexes." However, many, if not most, sites provide a variety of types of content. So you should not limit yourself to searching for specific material in only one category. Many of the sites are fee-based. Most university libraries probably subscribe to most of the sites. Since, however, access to those sites is available only through the member libraries' websites, we have provided URL addresses to web pages that describe the contents of the database sites and not necessarily to the sites themselves. We compiled this list in September 2018. Websites come and go, and some of the ones listed here may

Chapter 7: Historical Research on the Internet 207

disappear, but these sites are among the better established ones.[6]

Because Internet sources of use to historians are so numerous, we have not tried to include them all. Those in the following list are the ones that have the most extensive holdings. At the end of some sections we have included names and URLs, but not descriptions, of sites that have very focused content or have limited holdings. The historian can locate additional online sources by doing searches for specific types of documents and other content.

1. Sites with Links to Other Sites

http://www.loc.gov/rr/news/oltitles.html
Newspaper Archives/Indexes/Morgues. This Library of Congress site includes links to newspaper archive sources on the Internet, including full texts and indexes.

http://guides.library.cmu.edu/primarysources
History: Primary Sources: Archival Resources. Carnegie Mellon University Libraries has links to numerous sources in history, including archival databases, archival directories, audio/visual material, books, government and other documents, essays, dissertations, legal material, letters and diaries, magazines, journals, newspapers, and oral histories.

http://guides.library.cmu.edu/govdocs
Government Documents (United States). Carnegie Mellon University Libraries. This site is a sub-site of Carnegie Mellon's History: Primary Sources: Archival Resources listed above. This sub-site has links to numerous sites with documents from federal, state, and local entities.

http://guides.library.cmu.edu/newspapers
Newspapers: Directories. Carnegie Mellon University Libraries. This site is another sub-site of Carnegie Mellon's History: Primary Sources: Archival Resources listed above. This sub-site has links to numerous sites with sources for not only U.S. newspapers but those from around the world, ethnic and African-American newspapers, women's interest newspapers, and various other topics.

---

[6]The most complete descriptive listing of sites of interest to historians can be found in Dennis A. Trinkle and Scott A. Merriman, *The History Highway: A 21st century guide to Internet resources*, 4th ed. (Armonk, N. Y.: M. E. Sharpe, 2006), and their related book, *The American History Highway: A Guide to Internet Resources on U.S., Canadian, and Latin American History* (New York City: Routledge, 2007). Both books are, however, more than a decade old, and since then so much material has been added to the Internet that the two books are now dated.

https://sites.google.com/site/onlinenewspapersite/Home/usa
Google United States Online Historical Newspapers. Has links to all fifty states.

http://www.ibiblio.org/slanews/internet/archives.html
U.S. News Archives on the Web. "These pages provide links to United States news archives available on the Web." Sources are arranged by states and cities.

http://www.ibiblio.org/slanews/internet/intarchives.htm
International News Archives on the Web. "These pages provide links to non-US news archives available on the Web. Papers are arranged by region and country." Most of the papers are from the 1990s and later.

http://www.nationalarchives.gov.uk
The National Archives (United Kingdom) has links to the National Archives in the British Isles, other British and international archives, family history resources, online resources for the historian and social scientist, and digital archives. This site is a good starting place for research in British history. Access is limited to individuals who are registered and have a password.

http://www.otr.com/
Radio Days. Has links to 550 radio websites.

http://www.historicpages.com/nprhist.htm
Historic Pages. Has links to the following websites: American Antiquarian Society; State of Wisconsin Historical Society (Archives Division); Library of Congress Newspapers & Periodicals; American Journalism Review; Civil War Newspapers in GIF Format; Documents of American History Online; Index of Web Sites Related to the Civil War; and Internet Public Library.

http://blackpressresearchcollective.org
Black Press Research Collective. Has links, at its "Resources" tab, to newspaper archives and other online sources.

http://en.wikipedia.org/wiki/List_of_online_newspaper_archives
Wikipedia. Maintains a "list of online newspaper archives" with links to them.

https://www.library.illinois.edu/hpnl/guides/newspapers/
University of Illinois Library. History, Philosophy, and Newspaper Library. Has links to numerous collections and individual newspapers that are available online.

Chapter 7: Historical Research on the Internet

http://www.xooxleanswers.com/free-newspaper-archives/
Xooxle National, State & Local Newspaper Archives. Provides links to numerous digitized newspaper and magazine archives, many of which are free. Includes these categories: U.S. state and regional newspapers, college and student newspapers, magazines, European, and rest of the world.

http://icon.crl.edu/digitization.php
International Coalition on Newspapers: Newspaper Digitization Projects. "This page highlights and links to past, present, and prospective digitization projects of historic newspapers. The focus is primarily on digital conversion efforts, not full-text collections of current news sources."

http://www.digitalhistory.uh.edu
Digital History. Contains links to a variety of museum and archives websites and other sites that provide primary sources, teaching aids, and other material.

http://www.oah.org
Organization of American Historians. Has many links to other websites in the field of history.

http://explorehistory.ou.edu/1483-primary-source-collections/
Exploring U.S. History. This site maintained by the History Department at the University of Oklahoma has links to thirty-eight collections of primary sources.

https://aslh.net/resources-for-doing-legal-history/
Resources for Doing Legal History. This website of the American Society for Legal History has links to numerous online sites to aid historical research.

https://blogs.loc.gov/thesignal/2013/09/71-digital-portals-to-state-history/
71 Digital Portals to State History. Links to state "sites that bill themselves as general-interest portals to historical resources."

http://besthistorysites.net
Best of History Websites. Provides links to many other websites, such as the Library of Congress, Digital History, and Center for History and New Media. This is a good site to start a search for other websites with holdings of primary documents.

http://www.timepage.org/lnk/bhistory.html
Cycles in U.S. History: Documenting American History. Includes links to other sites that have primary documents.

https://guides.library.yale.edu/ushistory
U.S. History & American Studies Research Guide. Provides instruction on how to do historical research projects, along with links to sites with primary sources. Intended for students.

http://guides.lib.udel.edu/c.php?g=85352&p=548910
History: Websites for U.S. History. University of Delaware Library. Includes links to other sites about the United States that cover several subjects over long time periods. Some have secondary and some have primary material.

http://www.searchbeat.com/society/History/
History Timelines ... The History Beat. Provides links to many other history websites.

http://ncph.org/what-is-public-history/additional-resources/
National Council on Public History. Provides articles about the study of history and includes links to the websites of other history organizations.

http://www.periodicalresearch.org
Research Society for American Periodicals. This site provides links to websites with digitized contents of periodicals.

http://digital.library.upenn.edu/books/serials.html
On-Line Books Page: Serials (University of Pennsylvania). "This page lists freely accessible archives of serials (such as magazines, journals, newspapers, and other periodicals)." It includes links to the titles in the Making of America collections but contains other titles as well, including many periodicals.

http://www.educonnect.com/KeyUS/
The Key to U.S.: A Guide to Internet Resources for Social Studies. Provides links to many other websites, including a number that focus on history.

http://www.unc.edu/~haman
Harry Amana's Web Page. The website of a retired journalism professor has a "Minority, Diversity & Black Press Sites" page with more than "150 links to sites on the black press, minority journalism organizations, multicultural studies, and on the history and culture of African Americans, Arab Americans, Asian Americans, Latinas and Latinos, and Native Americans. These include links on Amistad, Amos 'n' Andy, Charlie Chan, The Cisco Kid, Tonto, and Zorro."

https://rrchnm.org/category/projects/content/digital-collection/#projects
Roy Rosenzweig Center for History and New Media. Contains links to a variety of sites that

deal with various aspects of research in history using new technological tools. The center "develops online teaching resources, digital collections and exhibits, open-source software, and training in digital literacy and skills."

http://historymatters.gmu.edu/browse/wwwhistory
History Matters provides a searchable and indexed database of numerous U.S. and world history sites. "Information is provided on the type of website ... and the type of resource (text, images, audio, and video).... The full search feature allows you to quickly locate WWW.History resources by topic, time period, keyword, or type." Many of the sites to which this one links contain primary material.

http://www.historyguide.org/resources.html
The History Guide. Resources for Historians. Although this site does not have primary material itself, it provides links to a number of sites that do, such as A Chronology of United States Historical Documents, The Digital Librarian: History, Documents of World War II, and Documenting the American South.

http://historymatters.gmu.edu/mse/oral/online.html
Oral History Online. History Matters. Provides links to "exemplary sites" for oral history.

http://www.oralhistory.org/centers-and-collections/
Oral History Association. Provides links to oral history centers and collections. Please note: A variety of websites have oral history collections. A good way to find them is to do an Internet search for terms such as "oral history collections online" and "oral history archives online."

https://ucsd.libguides.com/c.php?g=90745&p=983303
Guide to Online Primary Sources: African Americans. Provides links to other sites, including some historical ones with primary sources from publications.

2. Catalogs, Directories, and Guides to Library and Archival Collections

http://www.loc.gov
Library of Congress. The website has the LoC's catalog online and links to a variety of digital collections, such as the Chronicling America: Historic American Newspapers project.

http://lcweb.loc.gov/coll/nucmc/
National Union Catalog of Manuscript Collections. Catalogues manuscripts in the Library of Congress.

http://www.loc.gov/rr/program/bib/bibhome.html
Library of Congress Bibliographies, Research Guides and Finding Aids. This site contains descriptions of both printed materials and digital collections held at the Library of Congress.

http://www.loc.gov/rr/microform/guide/
A Guide to Microform Collections in the Humanities and Social Sciences Division of the Library of Congress

https://www.archives.gov/research/catalog
National Archives Catalog. The catalog provides access to 2 million electronic records.

https://catalog.gpo.gov/
Catalog of U.S. Government Publications. "The CGP is the finding tool for federal publications that includes descriptive information for historical and current publications as well as direct links to the full document, when available." Covers 1992-present. Its "Advanced Search" function allows searches of documents going back to the 1870s.

https://www.neh.gov/us-newspaper-program
United States Newspaper Program. "The USNP was a cooperative national effort among the states and the federal government to locate, catalog, and preserve on microfilm newspapers published in the United States from the eighteenth century to the present. With NEH funding and technical assistance from the Library of Congress, all state projects were successfully completed." This site provides references to the preservation projects in all the states.

http://archives.chadwyck.com/marketing/index.jsp
Archive Finder. Fee-based. "Archive Finder is a current directory which describes over 220,000 collections of primary source material housed in thousands of repositories across the United States, the United Kingdom and Ireland."

http://www.archivegrid.org/web/index.jsp
ArchiveGrid. Fee-based. Searches "through historical documents, personal papers, and family histories held in archives around the world." Provides online access to a million descriptions of archival collections owned by thousands of libraries, museums, historical societies, and archives worldwide.

http://www.cinema.ucla.edu
UCLA Film and Television Archive. This website has a catalog of the material at the archive, which contains more than 350,000 motion pictures, 160,000 television programs, and 27 million feet of newsreel footage.

Chapter 7: Historical Research on the Internet

http://catalog.mwa.org
American Antiquarian Society. This catalog "contains records for the Society's collections of books, pamphlets, manuscripts, newspapers, lithographs, and broadsides."

https://library.duke.edu/rubenstein/uarchives/collections-guides
Duke University Archives. Provides guides to digitized collections in the Duke archives.

https://www.wisconsinhistory.org/Records/Article/CS4002
http://digicoll.library.wisc.edu/wiarchives/
Wisconsin Historical Society. Archival Resources in Wisconsin: Descriptive Finding Aids. The Wisconsin Historical Society has extensive newspaper holdings and many other primary sources. The online catalog has "archival finding aids describing collections held at 24 repositories throughout Wisconsin." Archives holdings include manuscript collections, state government records, and local government records.

http://www.cah.utexas.edu/collections/news_media_history.php
Dolph Briscoe Center for American History: News Media History Collection. The main page provides information about the collections of the center. The media history collection is "home to one of the largest collections of archival materials related to the history of the news media." The center also has links to other websites, including some that have image and media collections.

http://icon.crl.edu
ICON: International Coalition on Newspapers. "The ICON database is the most comprehensive source of information about significant newspaper collections in print, digital and micro formats. The large and growing database is designed to inform library decisions on the development, management and preservation of newspaper collections. Current statistics: 47,540,219 issues from 171,612 publications dating from 1649–2015." Many of the full-text collections are fee-based.

https://oralhistoryportal.library.columbia.edu/project.php
Columbia Center for Oral History. This site provides descriptions of the thousand or so oral history interviews at the CCOH.

3. Indexes of Primary Material in Communication History

https://guides.library.harvard.edu/news/us
Guide to Newspapers and Newspaper Indexes. This website provides links to numerous free and fee-based online sites.

https://www.proquest.com/products-services/wellesley.html
Wellesley Index to Victorian Periodicals, 1824-1900. Fee-based. Includes indexes and abstracts. "Forty-five important monthly and quarterly titles are indexed, covering the period from the beginning of the *Westminster Review* in 1824 to the end of the century." The database is the electronic equivalent of the five-volume work of the same name.

https://www.ebsco.com/products/research-databases/readers-guide-retrospective-1890-1982
Reader's Guide Retrospective. Fee-based. Indexes general-interest periodicals published in the United States from 1890 to 1982. Includes book reviews, indexes, and abstracts.

https://history.paratext.com/ncm/landing/index.php
19th Century Masterfile: 1106-1930. Fee-based. A "scholarly database for finding published material from the 12th Century through 1930" that has more than 15 million citations. Contains *Poole's Index to Periodical Literature, New York Times Index, Palmers Index to The Times, Harper's Magazine Index, Descriptive Catalogue of the Government Publications*, and others. Indexes periodicals, newspapers, books, images, and U.S. and U.K. government documents.

https://www.proquest.com/products-services/periodicals_index.html
Periodicals Index Online. Fee-based. Covers 1665-1995. An index to 9 million articles published in the arts, humanities, and social sciences. "Three centuries of the arts, humanities, and social sciences indexed coverage, ... with access to a growing collection of over 18 million citations.... Over 6,000 journals are included, with around one million records from new journals added yearly. Complete runs of these titles are indexed."

https://www.ebscohost.com/archives/atla-monographs/humanities-social-sciences-index-retrospective
Humanities & Social Sciences Index Retrospective. Fee-based. Covers 1907-1984. Indexes 1,200 scholarly journals and specialized periodicals in the humanities and social sciences, with "more than 1,300,000 citations and over 240,000 book reviews."

https://www.ebsco.com/products/research-databases/humanities-international-index
Humanities International Index. Fee-based. Covers 1975-present. Has indexing and abstracts for more than 2,200 journals and contains more than 4 million "bibliographic records from a multitude of U.S. and international publications."

https://www.proquest.com/products-services/iimp_ft.html
International Index to Music Periodicals. Fee-based. Covers 1874-present. "[P]rovides indexing and abstracts for more than 600 international music periodicals, plus full text for 220 journals."

Chapter 7: Historical Research on the Internet   215

https://www.ebsco.com/products/research-databases/music-index
Music Index. Fee-based. Covers 1970-present. Indexes and abstracts more than 600 music periodicals. Covers "music, musicians and the music industry. In addition to journal articles, it provides citations for book reviews, obituaries and news articles."

https://www.ebsco.com/products/research-databases/rism-series-aii-music-manuscripts-after-1600
RISM Series A/II: Music Manuscripts after 1600. Fee-based. Covers 1600-1800. "This database is an annotated index of music manuscripts held in libraries, archives, monasteries, schools and private collections around the world." Provides a guide to more than 615,000 manuscripts by 22,500 composers found in 800 libraries and archives in thirty-two countries.

4. Primary Documents in Communication History

https://www.loc.gov/collections/
Library of Congress Digital Collections. This site "is a gateway to rich primary source materials relating to the history and culture of the United States." It has millions of digital items from nearly 330 historical collections." It is searchable by topic. This is an excellent site for research into primary documents throughout the whole course of American history. Its collections are topical and cover such areas related to communication history as daguerreotypes, photographs, films, sheet music, animation, graphic arts, posters, editorial cartoons, broadsides, and others.

Periodicals and journals

https://babel.hathitrust.org/cgi/mb?a=listis;c=1930843488;sz=100
Cornell Making of America. This free site contains millions of pages from thousands of primary sources, including the contents of twenty-three major magazines from the nineteenth century. Originally created as a collaborative effort between Cornell University and the University of Michigan, it "is a searchable digital library of primary sources in American social history from the antebellum period through Reconstruction."

http://quod.lib.umich.edu/m/moagrp/
University of Michigan Making of America (MOA) Collection. This searchable "collection is particularly strong in the subject areas of education, psychology, American history, sociology, religion, and science and technology." It has 3.8 million pages from more than 10,000 books and 50,000 journal articles.

http://www.accessible-archives.com/collections/
Accessible Archives — Magazines and Newspapers. Fee-based. Database contains articles

and other primary material from eighteenth- and nineteenth-century periodicals. Among its collections are America and World War I: American Military Camp Newspapers; The Civil War: A Newspaper Perspective; Women's Suffrage Collection [newspapers]; South Carolina Newspapers [1732-1780]; and the files of *Frank Leslie's Weekly, Godey's Lady's Book, The Liberator, National Anti-Slavery Standard, Pennsylvania Gazette*, and *Virginia Gazette*; and eight newspapers from Delaware County, Pa. (1825-1871). The collections are full-text and are searchable.

https://www.readex.com/content/early-american-imprints
Early American Imprints: An Archive of Americana Collection. Fee-based. Database "contains virtually every known book, pamphlet and broadside published in America between 1640 and the first two decades of the 19th century — more than 75,000 printed items in all." The site has four collections: Early American Imprints, Series I: Evans, 1639-1800; Early American Imprints, Series II: Shaw-Shoemaker, 1801-1819; Early American Imprints, Series I & II: Supplements from the Library Company of Philadelphia, 1670-1819; and Early American Imprints, Series I and II: Supplements from the American Antiquarian Society, 1652-1819.

https://www.proquest.com/products-services/aps.html
American Periodicals Series. Fee-based. Covers 1740-1940. Contains digitized images of more than 7 million pages from more than 1,000 titles, including American magazines, journals, and newspapers.

https://www.ebscohost.com/archives/aas-historical-periodicals-collection
American Antiquarian Society Historical Periodicals Collection. Fee-based. Covers 1684-1912. Full-text of several thousand magazines and journals.

https://www.proquest.com/products-services/periodicals_archive.html
Periodicals Archive Online. Fee-based. Covers 1802 to 2005. Contains more than 2 million digitized, full-image articles in the arts, humanities, and social sciences from 750 "respected" journals.

https://www.amdigital.co.uk/primary-sources/eighteenth-century-journals
Eighteenth Century Journals: A Portal to Newspapers and Periodicals, c1685-1835. Fee-based. British publications.

http://www.bodley.ox.ac.uk/ilej/
Internet Library of Early Journals (British): "A digital library of 18th and 19th Century journals." Magazines include *Annual Register* (1758-78), *Gentleman's Magazine* (1731-50), *Philosophical Transactions of the Royal Society* (1757-77), *Blackwood's Edinburgh Magazine* (1843-52), *Notes and Queries* (1849-69), and *The Builder* (1843-49).

Chapter 7: Historical Research on the Internet

https://www.proquest.com/products-services/british_periodicals.htmlcals.shtml
British Periodicals. Fee-based. Covers 1680s to 1960s. Offers more than 6 million searchable page images and full text for approximately 500 British publications.

http://www.harpweek.com
HarpWeek. Fee-based. Contains pdfs of the pages of *Harper's Weekly* and searchable digitized content from 1857 to 1912. The site offers free access to much of its graphic content, but access to most digitized content requires a fee.

Newspapers

https://chroniclingamerica.loc.gov
Chronicling America: Historic American Newspapers. Sponsored by the National Endowment for the Humanities and Library of Congress as part of the National Digital Newspaper Program, this collection is part of the Library of Congress Digital Collections. The collection, which includes more than 2,600 newspapers, has more than 13 million digitized newspaper pages from 1789-1963. A word-search function allows the researcher to narrow searches by state and date. A list of and links to the newspapers is at https://chroniclingamerica.loc.gov/newspapers/. More information about the collection is available at the National Digital Newspaper Program website at http://www.neh.gov/projects/ndnp.html.

https://news.google.com/newspapers
Google Newspaper Archives. Has searchable pdfs of thousands of newspapers from the United States and other countries, from the 1700s to 2009. The extent of content varies from newspaper to newspaper.

https://elephind.com
Elephind: Search the World's Historical Newspaper Archives. Has links to more than 3,500 newspapers, with more than 180 million items, in the United States and around the world. Allows advanced search and browsing.

http://www.researchguides.net/newspapers.htm
Historical Newspapers and Indexes On The Internet – USA. Includes searchable texts from selected newspapers in thirty-six states.

https://www.readex.com/content/americas-historical-newspapers
America's Historical Newspapers. Fee-based. This site has full-texts of 1,100 historic newspapers (starting in 1690) published in 50 states and the District of Columbia. It includes the following collections: Ethnic Newspapers, Early American Newspapers, 1690-1922; Agricultural Newspapers; Mercantile Newspapers; Newspapers of Record; Cam-

paign Newspapers; Religion: Denominational Newspapers; *Washington Evening Star* (1852-1981); and *Cleveland Leader* (1854-1913). See next entry.

https://www.readex.com/collections
Readex Collections. Fee-based. Along with "America's Historical Newspapers," Readex offers numerous collections of historical media content, including the following: African-American Newspapers, 1827-1998; African-American Periodicals, 1825-1995; Afro-Americana Imprints, 1535-1922: America's Historical Government Publications; America's Historical Imprints; American Broadsides and Ephemera (1749-1900); American Pamphlets, 1820-1922; American Underworld: The Flash Press; Black Authors, 1556-1922; Caribbean Newspapers, 1718-1876; Early American Imprints (1639-1819); Hispanic American Newspapers, 1808-1980; and World Newspaper Archive (1800-1925).

https://newspaperarchive.com
Newspaper Archive. Fee-based. Full-text covers 1753-present. Contains tens of millions of newspaper pages (along with various genealogical records), searchable by keyword, newspaper location, and date.

https://www.proquest.com/products-services/pq-hist-news.html
ProQuest Historical Newspapers. Fee-based. Covers 1791-2013. Includes more than 55 million newspaper pages. For most titles, the collection includes digital reproductions of every page from every issue in downloadable pdfs. Along with "mainstream" newspapers, the site includes a number of newspapers in the following special collections: International Newspapers, Black Newspapers, American Jewish Newspapers, Communist Historical Newspapers, and American Civil War Era Newspapers.

http://www.accessible-archives.com/collections/the-civil-war/a-newspaper-perspective/
Civil War 1860-1865: A Newspaper Perspective. Fee-based. Covers 1860-1865. This collection in the Accessible Archives database contains the full texts of articles about major events from 2,500 issues of the *New York Herald*, *Charleston Mercury*, and *Richmond Enquirer*.

https://www.proquest.com/libraries/academic/news-newspapers/Newspaperscom-Library-Edition.html
Newspapers.com Library Edition. Fee-based. Digital archive of more than 4,000 titles from the 1700s to the 2000s.

https://www.proquest.com/libraries/academic/news-newspapers/US-Major-Dailies.html
U.S. Major Dailies. Fee-based. Coverage varies, 1980-present. Provides full-text of the *New*

York Times, Wall Street Journal, Washington Post, Los Angeles Times, and Chicago Tribune.

https://www.ebsco.com/products/research-databases/newspaper-source
Newspaper Source. Fee-based. Covers 1995-present. Full-text of 60 national (U.S.) and international newspapers, including the *Christian Science Monitor, USA Today, Washington Post, Washington Times, The Times* (London), and *Toronto Star*, and of 320 regional (U.S.) newspapers. In addition, it has "complete television and radio news transcripts from CBS News, CNN, CNN International, FOX News, NPR and more."

https://www.ebsco.com/products/research-databases/newspaper-source-plus
Newspaper Source Plus. Fee-based. Covers late 1990s-present. Full-text for 1,200 newspapers, 40 news magazines, and 130 newswires. The site has 77 million articles and 1.8 million TV and radio news transcripts.

https://www.readex.com/content/world-newspaper-archive
World Newspaper Archive. Fee-based. Covers 1800-1925. Provides fully searchable digital replicas of historical newspapers from around the globe, including Africa, Latin America, Eastern Europe, and South Asia.

https://www.ebscohost.com/archives/magazine-archives/the-nation
The Nation Digital Archive. Fee-based. Full-text of the *Nation* weekly newspaper. Covers 1865-present. A "fully searchable electronic version of the [*Nation's*] complete backfile." Along with the *Nation's* archive, EBSCO has other fee-based websites that include the searchable contents of these magazines: *Architectural Digest, Bloomberg, Businessweek, Esquire, Forbes, Fortune, Life, Maclean's, National Review, The New Republic, New Scientist, People, Sports Illustrated, Time*, and *US News & World Report*.

https://www.gale.com/c/the-times-digital-archive/
The Times Digital Archive, 1785-2012. Fee-based. Includes searchable full-text of the contents of *The Times* (of London).

Miscellaneous publications

https://www.ebsco.com/products/research-databases/masterfile-complete
MasterFILE Complete. Fee-based. Covers 1995-present. Content includes "more than 2,300 full-text magazines and journals, more than 870 full-text reference books, more than 73,000 full-text primary source documents, more than 1.6 million photos, maps and flags, more than 70,000 videos from the Associated Press."

https://quod.lib.umich.edu/e/ecco/
Eighteenth Century Collections Online (ECCO) - TCP. This project of the Text Creation

Partnership of participating libraries contains the searchable texts of more than 2,400 titles (books, pamphlets, essays, broadsides, and other items). See next entry for information about a fee-based site for additional EECO titles.

https://www.gale.com/primary-sources/eighteenth-century-collections-online
Eighteenth Century Collections Online. Fee-based. Covers 1700s. A searchable collection of 32 million pages of text from more than 180,000 titles (200,000 volumes of books, pamphlets, essays, broadsides, and other items) published in Great Britain and the American colonies.

https://www.gale.com/c/litfinder
LitFinder. Fee-based. Covers antiquity to the present. "150,000 full-text poems and over 800,000 poetry citations, as well as short stories, speeches, and plays. Researchers can easily target the information they are looking for through various refine search and results limiter options. Biographies, work summaries, photographs, and a glossary are also included."

http://www.ripm.org/
RIPM: Retrospective Index to Music Periodicals (1760-1966). Fee-based. Contains more than a million full-text pages of periodicals, along with annotated citations to music articles, book reviews, and biographical information.

https://www.ebscohost.com/archives/aas-historical-periodicals-collection/applied-science-business-index-retrospective
Applied Science & Business Periodicals Retrospective: 1913-1983. Fee-based.

Advertising

https://library.duke.edu/digitalcollections/advertising/
Duke University Libraries Digital Advertising Collections. Has a variety of collections of advertising and commercials, including the following: AdViews: A Digital Archive of Vintage Television Commercials; John E. Brennan Outdoor Advertising Survey Reports, 1947-1980; Emergence of Advertising in America, 1850-1920; JWT Newsletters; Medicine and Madison Avenue; Outdoor Advertising Association of America Slide Library, 1891-1994; Outdoor Advertising Association of America (OAAA) Archives, 1885-1990s; John Paver Papers, 1920-1979; and R.C. Maxwell Company Records, 1904-1990s. This is a searchable database. The next three websites are part of the collection.

https://repository.duke.edu/dc/adaccess
Ad*Access. Covers 1911-1955. An image database of more than 7,000 advertisements printed in U. S. and Canadian newspapers and magazines.

https://repository.duke.edu/dc/eaa
"Emergence of Advertising in America: 1850-1920." "This collection presents over 3,300 items relating to the early history of advertising in the United States. The materials, drawn from the David M. Rubenstein Rare Book & Manuscript Library at Duke University, provide a significant and informative perspective on the early evolution of this most ubiquitous feature of modern American business and culture."

https://repository.duke.edu/dc/mma
"Medicine and Madison Avenue." This collection "presents images and information for approximately 600 health-related advertisements printed in newspapers and magazines. These ads illustrate the variety and evolution of marketing images from the 1910s through the 1950s. The collection represents a wide range of products such as cough and cold remedies, laxatives and indigestion aids, and vitamins and tonics, among others."

http://www.adflip.com/
Ad Flip. Has reproductions and details about ads, organized by categories, from 1940 through 2003.

https://www.luerzersarchive.com/en/search.html
Lurzer's Ads of the World Archive. Searchable database of more than 60,000 ads.

http://www.advertisingarchives.co.uk/en/page/show_home_page.html
The Advertising Archives. Database has more than 1 million British and American ads, 1850-present.

https://www.loc.gov/collections/broadsides-and-other-printed-ephemera/about-this-collection/
Printed Ephemera: Three Centuries of Broadsides and Other Printed Ephemera. More than 10,000 items from the 18th to the 20th century.

https://www.coloribus.com
Coloribus: Advertising Archive. Database has more than 2 million ads, 1990-present.

http://www.vintageadbrowser.com
Vintage Ad Browser. More than 100,000 ads (starting in 1800) organized by product and decade. Searchable by keyword.

http://www2.vcdh.virginia.edu/gos/
The Geography of Slavery in Virginia. More than 4,000 newspaper ads for runaway and captured slaves and servants. Covers 1736-1803.

http://www.pmadarchive.com
Philip Morris USA Inc. Advertising Archive. More than 50,000 images of tobacco ads, 1909-1990s.

http://www.loc.gov/pictures/collection/bbc/
Library of Congress Baseball Card Collection. More than 2,000 cards sponsored by cigarette companies from 1887 to 1914.

http://www.loc.gov/pictures/collection/pga/
Library of Congress Popular Graphic Arts Collection. "About 15,000 historical prints (ca. 1700-1900) created to document geographic locations or popular subjects and sometimes used for advertising and educational purposes." Keyword search can be done for specific ad topics or all ads.

http://www.loc.gov/teachers/classroommaterials/connections/cocacola-ads/
Fifty Years of Coca-Cola Television Advertisements. Covers 1950-2000.

Broadcast, sound recording, film, and images

https://tvnews.vanderbilt.edu
Vanderbilt Television News Archive. Covers 1968-present. Contains more than 1.1 million records, including regularly scheduled newscasts from ABC, CBS, NBC, CNN and Fox News, as well as "abstracts at the story level of regular evening newscasts and catalog records for each special news report." It also has thousands of hours of special news-related programming, including ABC's *Nightline* since 1989. "Special news broadcasts found in the Archive include political conventions, presidential speeches and press conferences, Watergate hearings, coverage of the Persian Gulf War, the events of September 11, 2001, the War in Afghanistan, and the War in Iraq."

http://www.museum.tv/debateweb/html/index.htm
History of Televised Presidential Debates. Contains photos, news stories, videotapes, and memoranda from the debates of 1960 to 2008.

https://www.lib.umd.edu/libraryofamericanbroadcasting
Library of American Broadcasting. "The LAB is the nation's most extensive collection of broadcast history, policy and tradition, including historic documents, professional papers, oral and video histories, books, scripts and photographs."

https://archive.org/details/oldtimeradio
Old Time Radio. This site is part of the Internet Archive, which has millions of pages, including 4 million audio recordings and 3 million videos. See https://archive.org/about/

Chapter 7: Historical Research on the Internet

for links.

https://archive.org/details/movies
Moving Image Archive. "This library contains [several million items] uploaded by Archive users which range from classic full-length films, to daily alternative news broadcasts, to cartoons and concerts."

https://alexanderstreet.com/products/world-newsreels-online-1929-1966
World Newsreels Online, 1929–1966. Fee-based. This collection of 8,000 newsreels focuses primarily on the World War II era.

https://www.ebsco.com/products/research-databases/ap-images-collection
AP Images Collection. Fee-based. Covers 1826-present. More than 12 million photographs, 36,000 audio sound bites, and 340,000 graphics.

http://cylinders.library.ucsb.edu
UCSB Cylinder Audio Archive. This site is hosted by the Department of Special Collections at the University of California, Santa Barbara, and contains digital copies of 8,000 cylinder recordings, the precursors to vinyl records. Audio files available include both music and recordings of speeches.

http://www.historicalvoices.org
Historical Voices. The National Gallery of the Spoken Word. "From Thomas Edison's first cylinder recordings and the voices of Babe Ruth and Florence Nightingale to Studs Terkel's timeless interviews and the oral arguments of the US Supreme Court, the collections of the NGSW digital library cover a variety of interests and topics."

Historic books

http://www.gutenberg.org
Project Gutenberg. Free. Includes the full texts of more than 57,000 books, along with other items, published before 1924. The website contains links to similar projects that offer almost 100,000 titles.

http://onlinebooks.library.upenn.edu
On-Line Books Page (University of Pennsylvania). Lists more than 2 million free books available online, along with links to sites with more than 15 million additional ones.

https://books.google.com/advanced_book_search
Google Books and Google Book Search. Free. Has readable page images of 2 million books. Searches can be done for both book titles and keywords within books.

https://archive.org/details/texts
Internet Archive eBooks and Texts. Free. Has more than 15 million books and other texts.

http://quod.lib.umich.edu/e/eebogroup/
Early English Books Online (EEBO) – TCP. Covers 1475-1700. The Text Creation Partnership (TCP) provides searchable text and pdfs for more than 60,000 titles. See next entry for information about a fee-based site for additional EEBO titles.

http://eebo.chadwyck.com/home
Early English Books Online (EEBO). Fee-based. Covers 1473-1800. Contains full-text digital facsimiles of 135,000 titles from "the first book printed in English by William Caxton, through the age of Spenser and Shakespeare and the tumult of the English Civil War."

Minority and gender sources

http://www.proquest.com/en-US/catalogs/databases/detail/genderwatch.shtml
Gender Watch. Fee-based. Covers 1970-present. A full-text database of 219,000 articles from 200 publications that focus on gender.

www.wpcf.org/women-in-journalism/
Women in Journalism. Washington Press Club Foundation Oral History Project. Provides information about a project that includes "comprehensive, full-life interviews with women journalists — from pioneers of early women's journalism, to champions of civil rights, to celebrities in the world of broadcast television — who have made significant contributions to society through careers in journalism since the 1920s." Some of the 60 interviews and transcripts are available online.

https://www.proquest.com/products-services/ethnic_newswatch.html
Ethnic NewsWatch. Fee-based. Covers 1990-present. A full-text database of newspapers, magazines, and journals of the ethnic, minority, and native press in the United States and other countries. The database also contains Ethnic NewsWatch: A History, which "provides historical coverage of Native American, African American, and Hispanic American periodicals from 1959-1989." The entire collection has 2.5 million articles, editorials, columns, reviews, etc., from 340 publications.

https://www.proquest.com/products-services/bsc.html
Black Studies Center. Fee-based. Full-text includes the *Chicago Defender*, 1909-1975; International Index to Black Periodicals—Full Text, 1902-present; Black Literature Index; and Schomburg Studies on the Black Experience.

Chapter 7: Historical Research on the Internet   225

5. Primary Documents in American History

Many online sites that we don't list in this section are available. To locate additional sites, do an Internet search using such terms as "American history digital archives" and "American history digital documents."

https://babel.hathitrust.org/cgi/mb?a=listis;c=1930843488;sz=100
Cornell Making of America (MOA) Collection. This site is Cornell University's contribution to the voluminous MOA collection. Access is free. We listed it in the previous section on primary sources in communication history. Along with all the publications listed there, it has many more documents pertinent to the study of American history from the colonial period through Reconstruction.

https://www.loc.gov/collections/
Digital Collections. This free site from the Library of Congress "provides one of the largest bodies of noncommercial high-quality content on the Internet" and "provides free and open access ... to written and spoken words, sound recordings, still and moving images, prints, maps, and sheet music that document the American experience. It is a digital record of American history and creativity...." Its 329 themed collections offer more than 7 million digitized items from the Library of Congress and other historical collections. The texts are searchable.

http://www.loc.gov/rr/mss/ammem.html
Online Collections from the Manuscript Division. The Library of Congress' Manuscript Division provides materials in 85 themed collections that are available as digital images or as searchable text. The collections include such titles as "African American Odyssey," "American Life Histories: Manuscripts from the Folklore Project, WPA Federal Writers' Project, 1936-1940," "American Women: A Gateway to Library of Congress Resources for the Study of Women's History and Culture in the United States," "The Frederick Douglass Papers at the Library of Congress," and "Samuel F. B. Morse Papers at the Library of Congress." It also has a number of collections related to mass communication subjects, such as photography, moving film, and broadcasting.

https://www.lexisnexis.com/help/CU/Serial_Set/Serial_Set_Digital.htm
U.S. Serial Set. Fee-based. Covers 1789-1969. Includes full-text Congressional reports and documents as well as executive agency and departmental reports ordered to be printed by Congress. Documents deal with a wide range of American life, such as westward expansion, scientific exploration, politics, international relations, business, and manufacturing.

https://www.gpo.gov/help/u.s._congressional_serial_set.htm
U.S. Congressional Serial Set. Free. Covers 1957-present. Contains searchable full-texts of U.S. Senate and House reports and documents. See next entry.

https://www.readex.com/content/us-congressional-serial-set-1817-1994
U.S. Congressional Serial Set, 1817-1994. Fee-based. "[P]rovides more than 370,000 individual publications originally bound in 14,000 volumes. This definitive digital edition contains a wealth of documents, illustrations, maps and charts on cultural, legislative, military, political, social and scientific history."

https://www.archives.gov
National Archives. Includes a catalog of U. S. National Archives and Records Administration holdings — documenting "the rights of American citizens, the actions of Federal officials, and the national experience" — along with some digitized material.

https://aad.archives.gov/aad/index.jsp
Access to Archival Databases (AAD). U.S. National Archives site provides access to records in selected historic databases, mainly from the 20th century.

http://www.archive.org/
Internet Archive. This site was "founded to build an 'Internet library,' with the purpose of offering permanent access for researchers, historians, and scholars to historical collections that exist in digital format...." It includes several million items, including texts, audio, music, and moving images.

https://www.loc.gov/collections/federal-writers-project
American Life Histories: Manuscripts from the Federal Writers' Project, 1936 to 1940. This "collection of life histories consists of approximately 2,900 documents, compiled and transcribed by more than 300 writers from 24 states."

https://sourcebooks.fordham.edu/mod/modsbook.asp
Internet Modern History Sourcebook. Free. Has full-texts of numerous documents from American history categorized by topic.

http://historymatters.gmu.edu
History Matters. This site has a limited number — 1,016 in September 2018 — of primary documents "in text, image, and audio about the experiences of ordinary Americans throughout U. S. history. All of the documents ... are accompanied by annotations that address their larger historical significance and context."

Chapter 7: Historical Research on the Internet

http://www.teacheroz.com/generalUS.htm#documents
General U.S.A. History has the digitized texts of documents on a variety of topics in American history.

https://www.gale.com/c/sabin-americana-1500-1926
Sabin America, 1500-1926. Fee-based. Based on Joseph Sabin's bibliography, this collection contains 65,000 volumes and several million pages of text covering "North, Central and South America and the West Indies." It offers "original accounts of exploration, pioneering, settlement, the western movement, military actions, Native Americans, slavery and abolition."

https://britannicalearn.com/product/annals-of-american-history/
Annals of American History Online. Fee-based. From *Encyclopedia Britannica*. Covers 1493-present. More than 2,000 documents include full-texts of speeches, essays, historical accounts, memoirs, poems, editorials, biographies, and images, as well as encyclopedia entries.

https://www.gale.com/primary-sources/archives-unbound
Archives Unbound. Fee-based. Has full-text collections on African-American studies, American studies, political history, law, and other topics.

https://docsouth.unc.edu/browse/collections.html
Documenting the American South. Free. Covers the colonial period through the first decades of the 20th century. The digital collection provides "access to texts, images, and audio files related to southern history, literature, and culture. DocSouth includes thirteen thematic collections of books, diaries, posters, artifacts, letters, oral history interviews, and songs." The 16 thematic collections include such subjects as "The Church in the Southern Black Community" and "First-Person Narratives of the American South."

https://cwld.alexanderstreet.com
Civil War Letters and Diaries. Fee-based. Has 100,000 pages of diaries, letters, and memoirs of 2,000 authors.

http://avalon.law.yale.edu
The Avalon Project: Documents in Law, History, and Diplomacy. This site from the Yale University Law School has documents from 400 B.C. to 2003 A.D.

https://alexanderstreet.com/products/north-american-womens-letters-and-diaries
North American Women's Letters and Diaries. Fee-based. Covers colonial times to 1950. Includes 150,000 indexed and searchable pages of diaries and letters of more than 1,500 women.

http://womhist.alexanderstreet.com
Women and Social Movements in the United States: 1600 to 2000. Fee-based. Includes "124 document projects or archives and 5,100 documents and 180,000 pages of additional full-text sources."

https://literature.proquest.com/marketing/index.jsp
Literature Online (LION). Fee-based. A searchable collection of 330,000 works (from 600 A.D. to the present) of English and American poetry, drama, and prose, as well as biographies, bibliographies, and key criticism and reference resources. Intended mainly for the study of literature.

http://www.letrs.indiana.edu/web/w/wright2/
Wright American Fiction, 1851-1875. Wright American Fiction provides the full-text of 2,900 novels by 1,450 authors published in the United States.

https://www.gale.com/c/making-of-the-modern-world
Making of the Modern World: The Goldsmiths-Kress Library of Economic Literature. Fee-based. Covers 1450-1945. Has more than 11 million pages.

https://www.ebsco.com/products/research-databases/regional-business-news-plus
Regional Business News Plus. Fee-based. Covers 1990-present. This database provides "full text for nearly 120 regional business publications, current news from more than 1,300 full-text newspapers and newswires, and more than 1.8 million full-text articles from newspaper columns and TV and radio news transcripts." Updated daily. EBSCO provides a similar but smaller collection at its site Regional Business News.

https://www.proquest.com/products-services/abi_inform_complete.html
ABI/INFORM Complete. Fee-based. Covers 1971-present. "The database features thousands of full-text journals, dissertations, working papers, key business and economics periodicals such as the *Economist*, country- and industry-focused reports, and downloadable data."

https://www.usa.gov
USA.gov. This site is the official U.S. gateway to all government information.

https://memory.loc.gov/ammem/amlaw/
A Century of Lawmaking for a New Nation. This Library of Congress site "brings together online the records and acts of Congress from the Continental Congress and Constitutional Convention through the 43rd Congress, including the first three volumes of the Congressional Record, 1873-75."

Chapter 7: Historical Research on the Internet

http://www.vcdh.virginia.edu/index.php?page=VCDH
Virginia Center for Digital History. Site includes 14 collections on topics from the American colonial era through the 1970s.

https://www.mtholyoke.edu/acad/intrel/ww1.htm
Documents of World War I. Mt. Holyoke College sites have thousands of digitized documents related to wars from World War I through the Vietnam War.

https://afterslavery.wordpress.com/about/
After Slavery Project. Site has links to numerous collections of primary documents dealing with "Race, Labor and Politics in the Post-Emancipation Carolinas."

http://www.civilwarhome.com/indexcivilwarinfo.htm
Civil War Home: Index of Civil War Information Available on the Internet. Site has texts of numerous documents.

6. Genealogical Research

Historians sometimes need to trace an individual's family history or check for basic biographical information. A good source is genealogical websites. Such sites are legion in number. The following list contains some of the most popular and is arranged by free and fee-based sites.

http://www.cyndislist.com/#N
Cyndi's List of Genealogy Sites on the Internet. Free. This site, which itself does not have genealogical documents, has thousands of links to genealogical records.

http://www.genealogytoday.com/genealogy/states/
Genealogy Today StateGenSites. Free. Offers a database of more than 20,000 genealogy websites, categorized by states.

http://www.familysearch.com
Family History Library of the Church of Jesus Christ of Latter-day Saints (Mormon). Free. Has extensive searchable genealogical records.

https://www.archives.gov/research/genealogy
Resources for Genealogists. Free. This National Archives site includes directories of "Census Records, Military Records, Immigration Records (Ship Passenger Lists), Naturalization Records, and Land Records," as well as numerous digitized documents.

http://www.usgenweb.org
USGenWeb Project. Free. With links to thousands of websites, USGenWeb "provides links to state sites, which, in turn, provide gateways to the counties."

https://www.findagrave.com
Find a Grave. Free. Database is searchable. Entries usually include biographical information.

https://billiongraves.com
Billion Graves. Free. Database is searchable. Provides limited information.

http://www.genealogy.com/index_n.html
Genealogy.com. Fee-based.

http://www.ancestry.com/
Ancestry.com. Fee-based.

http://www.archives.com/Genealogy
Fee-based.

http://www.myheritage.com/Genealogy
Fee-based.

https://www.genealogybank.com
GenealogyBank. Fee-based.

https://www.fold3.com
Fee-based. U.S. military records.

7. Bibliographies

http://mupfc.marshall.edu/~rabe/resources.htm
History of Mass Communication in America: An Internet Bibliography. This personal website of Robert A. Rabe, a journalism professor at Marshall University, lists approximately 4,500 books and articles, categorized by subject.

http://www.american-journalism.org
American Journalism Historians Association. On its "Archives" tab, the journal *American Journalism* indexes its articles and book reviews published since 1983.

Chapter 7: Historical Research on the Internet

http://www.museum.tv/archives/etv/index.html
Museum of Broadcast Communications: Encyclopedia of Television. Includes more than 1,000 original essays and bibliographical information.

https://www.jstor.org/journal/jamericanhistory
JSTOR: The Journal of American History. Provides a keyword search of items in a large number of scholarly journals (including more than 300 history journals).

https://scholar.google.com/intl/en/scholar/help.html
Google Scholar. This site "provides a simple way to broadly search for scholarly literature. From one place, you can search across many disciplines and sources: articles, theses, books, abstracts and court opinions, from academic publishers, professional societies, on-line repositories, universities and other web sites."

http://www.abc-clio.com/products/serials_ahl.aspx
America: History and Life. Fee-based. A bibliographical reference to the history of the United States and Canada from prehistory to the present, covering more than 2,000 journals.

http://www.oxfordbibliographies.com
Oxford Bibliographies. Fee-based. Bibliographies are arranged in 41 categories, including history and communication.

http://www.mla.org/bibliography
MLA International Bibliography. Fee-based. Covers 1880s-present. Produced by the Modern Language Association of America. Contains more than 2.7 million bibliographic records pertaining to literature, language, linguistics, and folklore. Provides access to scholarly research in 3,000 journals and series and covers relevant monographs, working papers, proceedings, bibliographies, and other formats. Annually indexes 70,000 books and articles. Includes dissertations and theses, indexes, abstracts, and scholarly journals.

8. *Full-Texts of Secondary Material: Books, Journal Articles, Encyclopedias, Biographies, Dissertations, Etc.*

https://www.ebsco.com/products/research-databases/history-reference-center
History Reference Center. Fee-based. Covers BC-present. Features full-text from 650,000 records, including biographies of historical figures, reference books, encyclopedias, non-fiction books, and history journals, as well as maps, historical photos, and primary source documents.

http://www.anb.org
American National Biography Online. Fee-based. Includes biographical articles on more than 19,000 people from all eras. Has search capabilities, internal cross-references, photographs, illustrations, and links to external web resources.

http://www.ndltd.org/about
Networked Digital Library of Theses and Dissertations. Free. Has texts of more than 1 million theses and dissertations, with links to other sites.

http://www.openthesis.org
OpenThesis. Free. Has texts of theses, dissertations, and other scholarly documents.

https://www.proquest.com/libraries/academic/dissertations-theses/pqdtglobal.html
Dissertations and Theses Global. Fee-based. Has full-text of more than 2 million titles and searchable records of 2 million more.

https://www.proquest.com/products-services/ProQuest-Research-Library.html
Research Library. Fee-based. Covers 1971-present. This general database includes content from more than 6,000 titles, including newspapers, magazines, scholarly journals, trade publications, dissertations, theses, and other sources.

https://help.oclc.org/Discovery_and_Reference/FirstSearch/FirstSearch_databases/ECO
Electronic Collections Online (OCLC). Fee-based. Covers 1995-present. A searchable database of abstracts and full-text articles in 5,000 journals in a variety of subject areas.

9. Citations, Indexes, and Abstracts of Secondary Literature

https://www.gale.com/c/biography-and-genealogy-master-index
Biography and Genealogy Master Index. Fee-based. Includes 17 million citations compiled from more than 2,000 publications. Covers 5 million contemporary and historical figures.

https://www.ebsco.com/products/research-databases/communication-mass-media-complete
Communication & Mass Media Complete. Fee-based. Covers 1915-present. Has indexing and abstracts for 670 journals and full-text for 430.

https://www.imdb.com
The Internet Movie Database. Free. Gives plot synopsis, lists actors and directors, and provides other information about thousands of motion pictures.

Chapter 7: Historical Research on the Internet

http://www.cios.org
ComAbstracts. Fee-based. Has "article and book abstracts from the scholarly literature of the communication field." Allows keyword searches of approximately 130 scholarly journals.

http://www.clcd.com/#/welcome
Children's Literature Comprehensive Database (CLCD). Fee-based. Covers 1993-present. Recent literature for children, books, reviews, awards, and teaching materials. Reviews 3,000 books annually. Has "more than 145,000 links to web pages featuring authors and illustrators." Includes book reviews, catalogs, indexes, abstracts, and reference sources and tools.

https://www.proquest.com/products-services/Books-in-Print.html
Books in Print. Fee-based. Contains bibliographical references and abstracts for more than 20 million books and other published material, including in-print, out-of-print, out-of-stock, and forthcoming titles.

https://help.oclc.org/Discovery_and_Reference/FirstSearch/FirstSearch_databases/ArticleFirst
ArticleFirst (OCLC). Fee-based. Covers 1990-present. Contains bibliographic citations that describe items listed on the table of contents pages of more than 16,000 journals in science, medicine, social science, technology, business, the humanities, and popular culture. Has more than 27 million records.

https://secure.historians.org/members/services/cgi-bin/memberdll.dll/info?wrp=dissertations.htm
Directory of History Dissertations. Has searchable index of 55,000 dissertations produced in university departments of history in the United States and Canada.

https://oatd.org
Open Access Theses and Dissertations. Has searchable index of more than 4 million theses and dissertations.

https://www.ebsco.com/products/research-databases/ebsco-open-dissertations
EBSCO Open Dissertations. Covers 1933-present. Has searchable records for more than 800,000 electronic theses and dissertations from around the world.

10. General Reference Works and Contemporary Sources

https://www.loc.gov/rr/askalib/virtualref.html#genref
Virtual Reference Shelf. Library of Congress site has links to numerous online reference

works such as encyclopedia, dictionaries, almanacs, and research guides.

http://assignmenteditor.com
Assignment Editor. Features resources and tools used in newspaper journalism, such as newspaper websites, records, directories, etc.

http://www.refdesk.com
Reference Desk. This website has links to a huge number of sites, including daily news, stock market information, weather forecasts, and many other topics.

http://www.drudgereport.com
Matt Drudge website gives links for access to news media and columnists throughout the world.

https://www.thepaperboy.com/index.cfm
Paperboy. Provides links for access to more than 16,000 contemporary newspapers from around the world.

https://www.lexisnexis.com/en-us/products/lexisnexis-academic.page
LexisNexis Academic. Fee-based. Provides access to full-text documents from 17,000 sources, including news, business, and legal publications.

EXPLANATION IN HISTORY

When historians practice their craft, they perform a number of overlapping tasks. They gather and evaluate information and consider ways to explain it. They might begin to compose preliminary drafts of the written product at an early stage of the investigation. There is no better way to stimulate thought about a subject. For the sake of illustrating the component elements involved in history, it is again necessary to make a somewhat artificial division of the process. What happens in historical inquiry after one gathers and evaluates all the germane evidence about a topic? At that juncture it is necessary to confront a mass of collected material and to decide how to explain it.

Clarification of Purpose

The task involves understanding of the subject, for the subject must be comprehended fully before a written account can be prepared. This comprehension entails clarification of purpose. From the start of the project, one has had ideas about the subject and why and how the investigation of it should proceed. At some early point in the inquiry, one delineated the topic and probably used a working hypothesis as a tool to lend purpose and direction to the study. Consequently, the matter of clarifying purpose has been interwoven with the investigation throughout its course. Now, however, it must be refined into final form before the writing of the narrative can occur.

"Historians can be remarkably clear about their intentions," the historian Leonard Ray Teel has declared. "Having settled on a subject, and committed to seeking the truth, they search out numerous routes to the past, starting on the main highways, diverging onto tributary roads and dusty lanes, alert for contexts, settings, milestones, memories, stories, documents, facts. From these sojourns, they return to piece together a narrative, attempting, as the Civil War historian Shelby Foote has said, 'to reconcile differences and bring order out of multiplicity.'"[1]

Definition of the purpose of inquiry, of course, varies from person to person and from topic to topic. For example, David Dary examined 204 newspapers for his study *Red Blood & Black Ink: Journalism in the Old West*. For what purpose? From the outset, he realized that many things could be derived from such a mass of material. Yet he also realized that even this abundant record of newspaper sources, plus the other numerous primary and secondary sources he used, was inadequate to produce a "definitive history of journalism in the Old West." Consequently, he narrowed his focus and decided to write a book that would "capture the social memory of newspaper journalism in the Old West," one that would also "capture and affirm the flavor, emotion, and color of newspaper journalism in a vast region stretching from the Canadian border southward to the Rio Grande, and westward from the Mississippi River to the Pacific Ocean." With that purpose in mind, Dary was able to show how the newspapers served as a social factor in that region while explaining the nature of Western journalism and what it was like to be a journalist working there while settled communities developed from the frontier.[2]

On the other hand, in his award-winning biography of the Georgia editor Ralph McGill, Prof. Teel was interested in knowing how McGill "became a model for a social reformer willing to risk hostility and isolation to break the 'spiral of silence' in public opinion about one particular taboo [racial segregation], often called the greatest moral issue in twentieth-century America."[3]

Consider another case, that of Harold Davis and his biography *Henry Grady's New South*. Davis offers an insightful explanation of his thinking process as he worked on the biography. He wrote, "Beginning the research, I had no preconceived notions of Grady beyond those shaped by Raymond B. Nixon's book, *Henry W. Grady: Spokesman of the New South*, published in 1943. That work, a model for accuracy and scholarly care, showed Grady as a relatively selfless man and certainly a courageous one, seeking to rejuvenate the South following the Civil

---

[1]Leonard Ray Teel, *Ralph Emerson McGill: Voice of the Southern Conscience* (Knoxville: University of Tennessee Press, 2001), ix.

[2]David Dary, *Red Blood & Black Ink: Journalism in the Old West* (New York: Alfred A. Knopf, 1998), xiii and 273.

[3]Teel, *Ralph Emerson McGill*, xv.

> "'Let the game come to you' — an adage used by sports journalists to help them understand and communicate what is truly happening — has merit for the historian, too. If you've been thorough with your sources, the themes will float up from the material and beg you to tell their story." — Lynne Flocke, author, 'False' Ideas and the First Amendment

War by creating a new regional economy.

"About a year into my studies, I began to perceive a different pattern in the evidence. My Grady would not be the Grady that Nixon described. There would still be much about him to admire, especially his quick intelligence, energy, and oratory, but he was not the selfless developer of the South. He was anything but that.... Except in a general and sentimental sense, Grady's heart belonged not to the whole South, but to Atlanta, proclaimed at the height of his powers as his 'first and only love.' It was for Atlanta that he used most of his instincts, intelligence, energy, and time. This book will explain that, somehow or other, he strove to make a difference for Atlanta, leaving the rest of the South to enjoy what the city could not garner for itself."[4]

In his study *Abolition and the Press*, Ford Risley provides another helpful explanation of the process by which historians develop the purposes for their works. Risley's intent was to provide a historical account that would explain an important subject that historians had overlooked. As he explains, "As I began studying the abolitionist period, it became clear that no published work had examined the role of the antislavery press as a whole. Although there are many noteworthy studies of various aspects of the abolitionist era — including several excellent biographies of antislavery editors — no work has tried to make sense of what these editors and their publications as a group tried and, in many cases, managed to accomplish."[5]

As another example, consider Stephen Koss and his biography of A. G. Gardiner, one of the best known British Liberal publicists of the first quarter of the twentieth century. Why should Gardiner's biography be written? Perhaps because he wrote no autobiography or perhaps because he was one of the most influential of British editors during a time historians tend to perceive as probably the last "golden era" of newspaper editors in England. Reason enough, it would seem. However, if Gardiner had failed to produce an autobiography, he had published, aside from his regular journalistic writing, a number of books,

---

[4]Harold E. Davis, *Henry Grady's New South: Atlanta, a Brave and Beautiful City*, (Tuscaloosa: The University of Alabama Press, 1990), ix-x, 18.

[5]Ford Risley, *Abolition and the Press: The Moral Struggle Against Slavery* (Evanston, Ill.: Northwestern University Press, 2008), xiv-xv.

essays, and pamphlets. Therefore, he had expressed himself on most of the subjects that would command historical attention, and the record of that expression existed for any historian to study. Koss' problem in deciding why this biography was necessary, in determining the purpose of the study, was made more difficult by the fact that Gardiner was himself no stranger to the craft of biography. He had several biographies to his credit. In fact, he was quite aware of the limitations of biography and once warned that "there are few more agreeable forms of impertinence than to sit in judgment upon other people." Gardiner knew that biography could never be a substitute for someone speaking for himself and that it could never reach a subject's deepest feelings. But he also said that biography could achieve things that autobiography could not. It could, for instance, transcend the life of its immediate subject by placing that person in the context of historical events. Thus Gardiner believed that biography could be informative about the values of men and women and about how they interact with the events of their day. By producing such studies, he claimed, biographies perform "a conspicuous public service."[6]

> "While the historian must beware losing focus by wandering too far down a tantalizing side path in the research, he or she must be open to going to any lengths to fully understand and contextualize a person or event historically. The 'what' can never be fully understood without explaining the 'why' of human action and is seldom as interesting." — *Frank Fee, University of North Carolina*

Koss' biography reflects Gardiner's thoughts on the subject. It is a well-tooled professional biography that is informative about the Liberal politics of Gardiner's day and also about the workings of the press and the social and intellectual currents of British life at that time. Just when he reached his decision about how to treat his subject in this instance, Koss did not say. Perhaps it occurred early in his work. Perhaps it grew as his knowledge of his subject matured. Regardless, at the point of contact with constructing the final version of the biography, Koss understood the particular nature of his study. His purpose in writing was clear, and that fact is present throughout his well-defined study of this major journalist.

Understanding the purpose behind an investigation is but one element in the refinement of thinking about an inquiry that has to occur for it to proceed. In fact, refinement of thinking about a topic involves a number of considerations and activities. As was the case in clarifying the purpose of a study, these ele-

[6]Quoted in Stephen Koss, *Fleet Street Radical: A.G. Gardiner and the "Daily News"* (Hamden, Conn.: Archon Books, 1973), 1-2.

ments of thought and design may have been present from the beginning of the inquiry, but they must be honed into precise form before the construction of the final narrative can be attempted. They include matters of *interpretation, causation,* and *theory.*

Interpretation in History

An interpretive element permeates all history. One begins research by selecting a particular topic to investigate. Why? As research proceeds, one refines the purpose of the inquiry. That is an interpretive act. One attempts to answer certain questions based on evidence discovered. Why those and not others? One evaluates evidence. That involves constant interpretation. Since all the material gathered cannot be used, some will be kept and some discarded. Again, that involves interpretation. We all hold values about life and society — and we know how different individual values can be. The merest consideration of current politics and public debate affords proof enough of that proposition. Individual as well as social and cultural values shape historical thought. People unfamiliar with the study of history are apt to say, "Historians say this" or "History proves this." The only thing such statements prove is those people's unfamiliarity with history. Historical explanations once advanced are not facts frozen in eternal correctness. They are interpretations based on interpretations. Nowhere is this issue more evident than in the way in which historians attempt to treat facts and handle generalization.

History involves the interpretation of facts. That statement is more complex than it seems. When historians discuss the interpretation of facts, they do not have in mind uncontroversial or conventional data about the past. Many things that happened in the past can be validated notwithstanding the possibilities of human error or deliberate falsification. They can be proven beyond reasonable doubt, and, indeed, they constitute much of our knowledge about the past. Article II, section 4 of the United States Constitution provides for the removal of a president from office by means of impeachment and conviction for "Treason, Bribery, or other high Crimes and Misdemeanors." The publisher Joseph Pulitzer was born on April 10, 1847, in Makó, Hungary. On August 15, 1896, William Allen White published the editorial "What's the Matter with Kansas?" These are all, of course, easily demonstrable statements.

In their discussion of facts, historians have another type of fact in mind — facts with extended meanings. We call these "historical facts." They may be a human action, an event, an idea, a social condition — anything of historical significance that existed in the past.

These facts, as E. H. Carr explained in his classic statement, *What Is History?*, cannot stand alone.[7] For instance, in 1896 Alfred Harmsworth inaugurated the *Daily Mail* in London. An immediate success as a half-penny newspaper, it became the core publication in his expanding press empire. He became, as Lord Northcliffe, Britain's, and probably the world's, greatest press baron, and the *Daily Mail* became Britain's most prosperous popular newspaper. Other papers and proprietors copied it. None could match it. Lord Salisbury's often quoted comment that it was a paper "written by office-boys for office-boys" was mere fiction — as erroneous as the idea that it was a cheap paper for cheap minds. In general, the *Daily Mail* contained trustworthy news, well-written features, and attractive human interest stories, plus advertisements in abundance. Northcliffe supervised it from a distance. He insisted it be clean and respectable as well as interesting; and, as it matured, he tried to increase its quality.

Nevertheless, the mere mention of Harmsworth's launching the *Daily Mail* in 1896 is a fact with an idea always attached to it. The paper is commonly known from its inception as the vanguard of irresponsible sensationalism in the British press. There were, of course, many examples of sensationalism in the British press before this time, and during his lifetime Northcliffe despaired of the "yellow journalism" then popular in the United States, the journalistic style his critics claimed he copied.

The extended fact in this case goes beyond the simple fact that Harmsworth launched the *Daily Mail* when and where he did. It includes ideas about how he changed the British press and influenced society. Accordingly, this extended fact deals with Harmsworth's ambition, power, and personality as well as his philosophy of journalism and his genius at implementing it. All of these matters are subjects of controversy. They were when Northcliffe was alive, and they remain so today. Consequently, they must be explained. Such explanation or interpretation gives meaning to the basic fact (i.e., Harmsworth started the *Daily Mail* in 1896). Consequently, one can say, "historical facts," facts with extended meanings, do not speak for themselves. Historians interpret them.

Ideas, as we can see, frequently attach themselves to facts. Consider the example of the tabloid newspapers that appeared in the United States in the 1920s. What were they? In terms of basic fact, they were small newspapers, with pages about one half the dimensions of a standard paper. But the mention of tabloid journalism conjures up certain images or ideas, not particularly inspiring

---

[7]Edward Hallett Carr, *What Is History?* (New York: Alfred A. Knopf, 1965), 15.

Chapter 8: Explanation in History

ones. Most often the idea of disreputable journalism springs to mind in connection with the tabloids of the 1920s. To understand the development of this variety of journalism as a historical fact, historians have many questions to ask about it. When did it first appear? Why did it appear and flourish at that time and place? Why did it have mass appeal? Why did "respectable" journalists hold it in disdain? Did it perform any social function? Did it represent a natural or abnormal development in journalism? Historians, of course, are not of one mind when responding to those questions, though they do not dispute the presence and growth of tabloid newspapers in the 1920s. It is the ideas attached to the basic fact that occasion disagreement — an act of interpretation.

Nowhere is the interpretive element in history more pronounced than in the efforts historians make to generalize about their material. It can be argued that history is present thought about particular things of the past, but it should now be obvious that these particular things might be large past occurrences. They may be a war, a revolution, or a movement. Or they may be a single human action. The range is great. It bears repeating that the concern for the particular is one of the distinguishing characteristics of history. But individual things, as we have seen in our discussion of historical facts, do not exist alone.

Consequently, historians not only attempt to understand a particular thing but also to comprehend it in its relationship to other things. The process involves, as G. R. Elton once explained, understanding how the pieces fit together. "Meaningful interconnections in the particular, illuminating generalization beyond the particular — these," he said, "are the marks that distinguish the inspired and inspiring historian from the hack."[8]

In relating a particular historical phenomenon to other associated ones, historians employ a variety of methodological techniques. They may use content analysis, or literary analysis, or perhaps a comparative approach. Frequently, they search their information for ideas to serve as bridges of explanation. Even those historians who speak with candor about how they shuffle and reshuffle their notes in search of an idea, in fact, describe a process of hunting for connections.[9] The goal is to understand relationships and patterns within and among historical phenomena. Every stage of the process (i.e., establishing the meaning of a historical fact, discovering its relationship with other facts, or perceiving a broad generalization or pattern to describe it) involves interpretation.

A consideration of these forms of interpretation delivers us to the core of

---

[8] G. R. Elton, *Political History: Principles and Practice* (New York: Basic Books, 1970), 98.
[9] See comments by Robert W. Palmer and John William Ward in L.P. Curtis, Jr., ed., *The Historian's Workshop* (New York: Alfred A. Knopf, 1970), 175 and 312.

historical reconstruction. Interpretation in history, however, is easy to mismanage. Since we know that it is influenced by selection, imperfect evidence, and the values of the interpreter, the suggestion of possible mismanagement does not surprise us.

Successful management of interpretation depends on five types of control. The first concerns *evidence*. It must be controlled by mastering the various methods used in evaluating sources. We discussed those methods in Chapter 5. Beyond that, the evidence must be selected by the use of logical criteria. This process is basically a task of finding the evidence that is germane to the subject and of adjusting one's "working hypothesis" to fit it. It bears repeating at this point that a "working hypothesis" must be broad enough in design to accommodate all the evidence, including that which can be called "contrary evidence." It must not be a rigid theoretical concept that restricts the potential selection, use, or explanation of the evidence.

> "The fun in historical research is the opportunity to also learn the context in which an event or issue occurred. Nothing happens in isolation. Thus, the researcher MUST place the issue or event into the times of what else is going on locally or nationally, such as society, culture, economics, geography and transportation." — Lucinda Davenport, Michigan State University

The second control relates to *context*. Knowledge of the context of a historical topic is one of the hallmarks of history, and it carries one beyond the evidence that directly relates to the topic. John Tosh stated what most historians know when he wrote, "Questions of historical explanation cannot ... be resolved solely by reference to evidence. Historians are also guided by their intuitive sense of what was possible in a given historical context, by their reading of human nature, and by claims of intellectual coherence."[10] They need, then, perspective, imagination, and a sense of historical time. How much? Enough to inform them about how the various influences on their topics developed, enough to allow them to understand the social, economic, political, and cultural realities that gave meaning to society at the time under consideration, and enough to allow them to grasp what it was like to live at that time.

The third control relates to the *status of historical writing* on the topic. As we have mentioned before, the researcher must take into account the opinions of others who possess a significant knowledge about the topic. In other words, the researcher must be familiar with what other historians have written on the topic. The historiographical element is essential, since historical writing changes

---

[10]John Tosh, *The Pursuit of History: Aims, Methods and New Directions in the Study of Modern History* (London: Longman, 1984), 117.

Chapter 8: Explanation in History

> "Journalism and mass communications history is most useful when put in total context of what was happening at the time, rather than treated as isolated history that is significant just because it is journalism and mass communications." — Kenneth Campbell, University of South Carolina

over time. In a sense, a topic acquires a historical life of its own. Historical interpretation of a particular topic might expand or change as new information is discovered or new preferences exercised. Or it might evolve in accordance with changing social outlooks. The researcher must know about the main currents of this changing historical commentary on the subject and be able to respond to it when necessary.

The fourth control deals with constructing *generalizations*. They should not be impaired by simplistic reduction or by overexpansion or by careless language. There is an art to generalizing in historical writing. General statements should be related to textual details and to specific examples. They must rest on evidence — or on a sound expansion of the meaning of that evidence. The reverse is also true. Specific material must be related to generalization to give writing focus, force, and direction. The interaction between the two, between the specific and the general, is an ongoing manifestation of the interplay that exists between historians and their material.

The final control concerns the need to develop a particular type of *self-discipline*. Opinion and judgment pervade all history. Bias can take many forms and needs to be controlled. It may be an unrestrained preference, a prejudice, an unexamined opinion, or even a well-intentioned theoretical predisposition. It may be a manifestation of a too enthusiastic commitment to a communication theory, a philosophy, a nation, an ideology, or a political system. It might be uncontrolled class, cultural, or occupational attachment. The best controls for bias are self-awareness and recognition of an objective standard. Regarding the former, it is important to develop an awareness of self — of your own values, commitments, and preferences. Then, for your history to have the integrity it deserves, you must attempt to transcend your own time and circumstances and to assume the status of an honest referee between past and present. Subjectivity there will be in history, but there also can be a recognition of an objective standard. It is a plausible corrective for bias.

Explaining Causation

Discussion of causation is an old element in history. It is also subjected to much abuse. In particular, people unfamiliar with the nature of history tend to reduce historical causation to levels of argument (or persuasion, conviction, or hunch) that have little lasting consequence. Think of the number of people in our own present society who claim to know what caused the Cold War or the American intervention in Vietnam or Iraq or the improvement or decline in the national economy under any recent U. S. president. Causation, in fact, is one of the main features of the way in which teachers present history. Consider the number of topics encountered in most surveys of United States communication history such as the causes of Yellow Journalism, the decline of mass magazines, the historic changes in radio formats, the growth of the media as big business, etc. Beyond such obvious examples of concentration on causation, it can be added that causal statements frequently appear in historical narration.

> "Historical research is all about understanding context. It is the realization that life does not take place in a vacuum, but is the product of many different forces influencing a person, an organization, an event, or a period in time." — Andrew Clark, University of Texas at Arlington

All of this is proof that historians as well as their audiences are as interested in the "why" as much as in the "who" and the "what" of history. That interest may be a reflection of the influence of science on modern life, or it may be an indication of belief in the idea that monolithic forces are at work on a grand scale. Perhaps it is a manifestation of humans' timeless curiosity. Regardless, it exists.

The matter of handling causation involves major problems. It is much more complex than many people, even beginning researchers, might suppose. Ascertaining causes in history is a precarious matter. For instance, what caused the New Journalism that became so important in the United States and England at the end of the nineteenth century? Perhaps the Pulitzers and Harmsworths caused it. Or, if they had never lived, perhaps other people like them might have appeared to do what they did. On the other hand, the New Journalism may have resulted from conditions of the time. Perhaps it occurred as the result of the "chance" convergence of many factors at that particular time. It is clear that problems of historical causation involve consideration of the full scope of possible explanations.

They also deal with an understanding of the relationship between causes and results. Do certain causes necessarily produce certain results in history? Did high literacy rates and newspaper reading, for example, help bring about the American Revolution? Can we reach a definitive answer? The concept of causal effect can be a problem for the historian. Thus, historians tend to be cautious when dealing with causes. "No historical cause ever *must have* a given known

Chapter 8: Explanation in History

> "Journalism historians surrender too much when they slip in functionalist explanations for historical outcomes. It's not enough to say interpretative reporting or broadcast news or anything else came about because there was a need for these innovations. Our job is to tell how real human beings sought to respond to their actual situations." — *Tim Vos, author, Gatekeeping in Transition*

effect, namely, the historical event to be explained," claimed G. R. Elton. "The best that historians can say is that it *did have* that effect."[11] The distinction he made must be grasped to understand the nature of historical causation, which differs from causal explanations advanced in the physical sciences and to a lesser extent in the social and behavioral sciences. Scientists sometimes posit that certain causes must produce certain results. It would be more accurate to describe the relationship between historical cause and result as one in which causes produced effects and consequences.

The problem of causation is complicated further by the understandable tendency to want to make distinctions between causes. Are some causes "antecedent" and others "immediate," and, if they are, can they be separated? The idea, for example, that the American colonial press was a vehicle for the spread of the revolutionary idea in the decade or so before the start of the American Revolutionary War is usually accepted as true. Very well, what made that press, or a particular part of it, a revolutionary weapon? What caused it to be what it was? Does the work of revolutionary publicists explain that cause, or should one search more deeply and widely? Perhaps the explanation lies beyond the seemingly immediate cause of publicists mobilizing the printed word to achieve revolutionary goals. An indispensable part of the explanation might lie in the gradual growth of a revolutionary mentality, or perhaps it was a byproduct of the development of the press in the American colonies. In fact, there probably were many causes that explain the presence of the revolutionary press at that time. Some causes appeared later than others, while some were concurrent. How far back should one go in pursuit of causes? How much should we deal with antecedent causes, and how immediate to the revolution should we attempt to be in our explanation? Could the immediate causes have occurred without the antecedent ones; and when, where, and why did the latter make their appearance? Furthermore, once these decisions are made, should one then affix weights to the various designated causes?

A number of historians claim that the distinctions between "paramount" and "contributory" causes are artificial. Jacques Barzun and Henry F. Graff warn

[11]Elton, *Political History*, 141.

that making exact distinctions leads to "self-stultification."[12] Some historians believe it is useful to discuss various causes of an event separately in order to explain them. This does not mean, however, that they are making a substantive distinction between them. Some causes may be incidental to an event, and common sense impels one to dismiss them from serious discussion in a causal explanation. But full and adequate explanation must be given of all the causes that can be discovered to have had a meaningful relationship to the event. Can quantitative distinctions be made between these causes? Most historians doubt that such measurements can be made. So they tend to avoid assigning priority to any one cause or ranking an order of causes.

In resolving these problems — and let us admit that no one can ever resolve them with complete satisfaction — there are a number of considerations to keep in mind. For instance, historical causes exist in time and are conditioned by it. They are products of things created by people — institutions, opinions, interests, and other manifestations of their existence. Consequently, we return once again to the matter of *context*. The historian's own mind must be searched for answers to the following questions: Does one know enough about the times under consideration and the forces acting upon them to probe into the causation of an event? Has one achieved sufficient detachment from present assumptions and presuppositions to allow that event and those people involved in it the benefit of being understood on their own grounds?

None of the recognized principles that historians employ when dealing with causation are devoid of the personal element. In many cases, for instance, causal explanations can run beyond what the evidence tells us. The motives of the people the historian is studying may be blurred. Inferences must be made. It is at this point that the historian's *intuition*, which is something different from a hunch or guess, comes into play. The historian's intuition involves advancing reasonable conjecture rather than hastily informed speculation. It involves making statements, suggesting elements of explanation, governed by a grasp of probability that, in turn, reflects available evidence plus wide knowledge of the subject. Or consider the historian's rejection of single causation. Rarely in human affairs is there a single cause of thinking or actions even at the level of the individual. Since there is no single cause for all occasions and since a number of causes can be associated with any important event, historians deal with *multiple causation*. Interrelationships and interactions among them often can be discovered only by the historian's intuition. Understanding, too, that the causes of

---

[12]Jacques Barzun and Henry Graff, *The Modern Researcher*, 5th ed. (New York: Harcourt Brace Jovanovich, 1992), 189.

important events and institutional changes can never be known in full, we can appreciate that there is no room in historical causal explanation for dogmatic thinking. Such causal discussion must have a certain degree of tentativeness, one that allows the debate about causes to remain open.

Finally, consider the matter of *evidence*. As the British classicist C. S. Lewis observed, "Anyone can be simple if he has no facts to bother about."[13] No one expects to encounter causal explanations that are not grounded in evidence. Surely, ones that can be refuted by evidence would be deemed unsatisfactory. Historians also must remember that it is they who select the evidence and attach a causal significance to it. Furthermore, even the most informed historian must allow for the imperfect nature of historical evidence.

We can conclude that any discussion of causation that the historian attempts must depend on available evidence and on the judgment of the historian. Neither is sufficient to produce 100% certainty. Whether we approach historical causal explanations with contextual knowledge, intuitive judgment, multiple causation, or evidence in mind, it is clear that the historian's professional competency is crucial in the equation.

Theory and Historical Explanation

The place of theory in history is a matter of continuing debate. Theory has various shades of meaning. There are theories *in* history and theories *of* history. When some scholars speak of "theory," they have a specific concept in mind. For social scientists, theory is a key element in the conceptual framework that characterizes their explanations. Sometimes the word "theory" may refer to conjecture, or it may refer to a scientifically accepted general principle or body of principles. In general, a theory might be considered as a device to organize and classify knowledge. Thus, in historical research, the words "idea," "hypothesis," and "theory" sometimes can be virtually interchangeable.

Historians disagree on the place of theory in history. Some explicitly adopt theories to explain history. Others treat theories as useful devices that can provide a means for describing, and possibly for understanding, human behavior. They might also use a theory to provide intelligible connections between related human actions. It is human nature to want to make sense of complex situations, and theory, some historians believe, helps accomplish that goal. "You have to have something," Lawrence W. Levine has argued, "that tells you what facts you

---

[13]C. S. Lewis, *Mere Christianity* (New York: Macmillan, 1943), 145.

want in and what you don't, what's significant and what is less significant, and what is insignificant. Something has to tell you. That filter is often, whether you know it or not, a kind of theory."[14] Seen in that way, a theory is simply an organizing principle, and there is little disagreement about its use.

It is the use of theory as a formal explanation that causes controversy. In the field of communication history it is not unusual to hear calls for the use of theory or of "new theories." In the broad academic area of mass communication, where social and behavioral science dominates, theory receives particular emphasis in university graduate programs. It is not surprising that historians who studied in those programs should be particularly aware of theory and the special reverence for it. So when they hear calls for the use of theory in historical study, they may be prone to think that proponents are arguing for the use of theories such as agenda setting or others associated with social and behavioral science.

> **Two Views about Theory:**
>
> "Theory is a lens through which evidence is viewed in order to see more clearly its meaning. It nudges historical scholarship beyond the straightforward narrative to a higher level of subtlety, sophistication and influence."
> — Barbara Friedman, University of North Carolina
>
> "Theory is to historical research what the lines in a coloring book are to art — useful until you outgrow it."
> — Jim McPherson, author, *Journalism at the End of the American Century*

Few advocates of making communication history more theoretical, however, have such theories in mind. In fact, to understand their concepts of theory, one needs to ignore the term "theory" as used in social and behavioral science. Theories in the sciences usually deal with direct cause-effect relationships and are required to be capable of precise formulation. Researchers in the sciences expect that studies need to be replicable. Social and behavioral sciences tend to reflect those principles. That is not the case with most theories used in communication history. To apply such notions to theory in history, argue proponents of theoretical history, unfairly attempts to hold their approaches to the standard notions of theory held in the social sciences. Instead, they think of theory in looser terms. "Theory" is closer to a general idea than a testable explanation.

Most proponents of theory in communication history work within a Cultural Studies school or with its cousin Critical Theory. The views among theorists in those schools can vary widely. To understand their concept of theory, though,

---

[14]Lawrence W. Levine and Ann Lage, "An Interview with Lawrence W. Levine," *Journal of American History* 93 (December 2006): 800.

Chapter 8: Explanation in History

> "The moment a person forms a theory, his imagination sees, in every object, only the traits which favor that theory." — *Thomas Jefferson, 1787*

one must go beyond a definition that regards it as simply a "general idea" and recognize that, at heart, it is an ideological perspective. Cultural and critical studies define "culture" as a shared set of social values, and researchers tend to believe that media messages serve as agents of social control by reinforcing social values. In historical studies of the mass media, for example, theorists argue that history can be explained as a process in which a small group of powerful owners used media content to maintain social control for their own benefit. "The roots of cultural and critical studies are diverse," explains one expert, "and stem from sociology, psychology, and political science, among other theoretical perspectives.... [Media] messages, according to critical theory, have tremendous impact on audiences." Cultural and critical studies researchers draw on such ideas as Marxist theory of elites' harmful control of the media, psychoanalysis (with claims that media messages represent unconscious desires), feminist research (with claims that communication oppresses women or can liberate them), and postmodernism (with claims that communication messages have no true meaning in the real world).[15]

Other historians reject completely the use of formal theory. They believe that it oversimplifies causes, improperly superimposes a structure on the human actions of the past, and thus misunderstands the distinctiveness of the people and events they are studying. Moreover, they see theory as a detriment to their own type of rigorous generalization that proceeds from the bottom up. They believe that imposing theory on history results in violation of the foundational principles for the study of history. In the study of communication history, some of the most prominent adherents of cultural studies and critical theory, for example, are not trained in historical research and fail to adhere to the normal standards. Their reliance on theory, without corresponding evidence from primary sources, illustrates the problems that can result when historians employ theoretical assumptions at the expense of evidence.

Of course, historians, like other scholars, theorize all the time about problems in their inquiries. The term "theory," however, when used specifically, means something more than theorizing in general. It is used to connote the application of a specific, coherent, structured explanation for a particular problem.

---

[15] Sean Baker, "Cultural and Critical Studies," Chapter 19 in Shuhua Zhou and Wm. David Sloan, *Research Methods in Communication*, 3rd (Northport, Ala.: Vision Press, 2015), 312.

One may speak, for instance, of a theory of social mobility, or of economic growth, or of social behavior, or of communication effects, etc.

Historians commonly use theories *in* history in a number of ways. Some casually adopt them from one of the social sciences. Some treat them as they would handle any interpretation, as an idea to be used or discounted. In *The Generation of 1914*, for instance, Robert Wohl studied generational theories and found "that no available model of generations was flexible enough to encompass the baffling variety of ways in which the term 'the generation of 1914' and its synonyms had been used in the discourse of early twentieth-century Europe." In the end he decided to "abandon theoretical and lexicographical consistency as standards and try to find out what people living in the early twentieth century meant by 'the generation of 1914.'"[16] His book is a superb example of a historian who refused to subordinate his evidence to theory.

Peter Gay, however, in *The Education of the Senses*, aimed "to integrate psychoanalysis with history." He claimed his intention was not to write psychohistory but rather "history informed by psychoanalysis." The "ways of psychoanalysis, its theories and its techniques," he maintained, might "build the very bridge between individual and collective experience that most historians, deeply uneasy with the Freudian dispensation, have persisted in treating as problematic."[17] By using that approach, he was able to overturn a number of stereotyped ideas about Victorian sexual attitudes and behavior.

It is difficult to deny the presence of theory in history. When most historians use theory, they do so by applying it to their study of a particular situation. Some work with theory in an explicit manner; others do not. But if you start with the idea that a simple hypothesis or explanatory concept is a theory, then it is clear that theory, whether used in an implicit or explicit way, is part of historical inquiry.[18]

Some historians make the distinction between "small scale theory," theory applied to specific problems, and "grand theory," a theory of a more general type

---

[16]Robert Wohl, *The Generation of 1914* (Cambridge, Mass.: Harvard University Press, 1979), 2.

[17]Peter Gay, *The Bourgeois Experience: Victoria to Freud, Vol. 1: Education of the Senses* (New York: Oxford University Press, 1984), 8 and 16.

[18]Some historians such as Lester Stephens prefer to make a distinction between a theory and a hypothesis and see the former as broader than the latter (Stephens, *Probing the Past: A Guide to the Study and Teaching of History* [Boston: Allyn and Bacon, 1974], 33). Some others choose to consider a hypothesis as a type of theory. See, for example, Tosh, *The Pursuit of History*, 115; and James West Davidson and Mark Hamilton Lytle, *After The Fact: The Art of Historical Detection*, 2nd ed. (New York: Alfred A. Knopf, 1986), 86.

such as Frederick Jackson Turner's frontier thesis or the agenda-setting theory of the mass media. The latter might be part of a historian's assumptions before he or she begins a particular inquiry.[19]

Theories *of* history also have attracted some historians. Since ancient times, numerous scholars have been fascinated by the idea that there is a force that determines history and establishes a pattern for human events. Because they ponder the question of the ultimate historical reality, they might be better called philosophers of history. They are the grand systematizers of history, detecting regularities and correlations in and among human actions. Some of their established patterns are cyclical in nature, others linear, and some merely ideological, but, since they impose a systematic meaning on history and explain that meaning by a pattern they believe all history follows, their type of metaphysical conceptualization of history is deterministic. They are interested in discovering the laws behind history. Karl Marx, Oswald Spengler, and Arnold Toynbee are among the better known philosophers of history in recent centuries. A more common type of determinism is that associated with the word "progress." The Whig interpretation of history, which has had numerous proponents in the English-speaking world, is a classic example of using the idea of democratic progress to interpret history. Historians who accept this interpretation view human events as a record of upward progress, and their ideas have influenced a great deal of historical perception. In communication history, such grand theories occasionally show up. The various interpretations discussed in Chapter 2 of this book are based on underlying assumptions about the fundamental causes behind history.

The majority of historians remain unconvinced by deterministic explanations of history. They are dubious about the existence of single causes and laws of history. Determinism, they believe, is a form of reductionism that forces historians to be too selective, even manipulative, in choosing supporting evidence and leads them to organize that evidence in a manner that fails to correspond to the great diversity of human reality. They have serious doubts about the idea that the key to humankind's experience lies in a mechanistic force that is beyond its control. By making other causal factors a manifestation of that force, they contend, determinists impose an inevitability on history that is not there.

Nevertheless, most historians find deterministic conceptualization of history and the grand patterns suggested by a Toynbee or a Marx to have some appeal. Theories can stimulate thought about history and can suggest possible explanations for particular chapters of history. One does not have to be a Marxist,

---

[19]Davidson and Lytle, ibid., 87.

for instance, to recognize that his philosophy of history can help one to understand the nature of capitalism. Or, to carry the example of capitalism a bit further, communication historians might well find substantial assistance in Marx's ideas if they wish to inquire into the relationship between business and the press.

It can be concluded that historians in general use theory in some way in their studies. For the most part, however, they use it in a different way than social scientists who shape their studies according to a strict theoretical framework as defined by their various disciplines. Simply stated, theory does not play the role in historical inquiry that it does in the social sciences. Historians use theories in a more elastic manner than social scientists do. In most cases, they employ theory as they would use any interpretation, as an explanation to be adapted, developed, or rejected. The philosophers of history excepted, their focus is on men and women in the past who lived in endless variety and along the way interacted with the forces that influenced their times.

Issues related to explanation are of crucial importance and require careful consideration, for how well you understand your subject will guide the writing of the final draft of your essay. The clarity of your understanding will help assure the coherence and significance of the words you choose to put on paper.

WRITING

To say that the narrative element is important to history is like observing that numbers are important to arithmetic. The beginning researcher, however, needs to contemplate the full meaning of that statement.

The use of narrative, however, is not without its critics. Criticism can be found even among historians. The critics charge that the narrative is an artificial creation that fails to connect to real life. Some postmodern critics claim that narratives contain hidden agendas.

Supporters of narrative respond that it resembles the flow of real life. They argue that it is a reflection of reality, not an artificial structure imposed on it. One of the things historians have in mind when they speak of being objective is that they develop the vision to see beyond their own cultural climate and to appreciate that of some past time. In the effort that historians make to understand some time other than their own — using all the conventions of their discipline — lies the reason for their narrative being termed *studied* rather than *created*. Historians do not create their subjects. They try to reconstruct them, to show what was interconnected in them, and to explain their significance. In the process, they dispel misconceptions, offer new interpretations based on the evidence, and establish the needed framework for discussing matters of continuity and change related to their subjects.

They have, moreover, found narration the best means to communicate with a broad audience. Consequently, while admitting there is some validity in the charges brought against narrative history, the authors of this book agree with the statement that narration is "a defining element of history-writing."[1] In the following discussion, we shall concentrate on the general elements that are most germane to historical writing, and we use the term "the historical narrative" to mean narrative accounts rather than the grand narratives that were popular in the nineteenth century.

> "Take care to write well. The root of history is 'story.'"
> — Mike Sweeney, author, *From the Front: The Story of War*

The Historical Narrative

One of the main objects of historical research is communication that normally takes the form of a composition. It may be a book-length composition or one of shorter variety. For most beginning researchers, it will be a seminar paper. Whatever the project, composition can be the most difficult task involved in historical inquiry — and for some historians the most satisfying.

When should writing begin? It would be misleading to suggest that it occurs only at the end of a research project. To the contrary, it should begin as early as possible, not only because it is an incentive to precise and serious thought about the subject but also because it is the surest means for discovering gaps and dead ends in the material collected. The final composition must be a polished version. Aside from incorporating all pertinent evidence and the previously discussed elements of historical thinking, it also must manifest the qualities that characterize the historical narrative.

History, as we have seen, differs from the social sciences, which are modeled on the natural sciences, in a number of ways. Consideration of composition underscores that difference. No one would deny that a strong analytical as well as a narrative element characterizes history, but without the narrative element history becomes something other than history. Moreover, many of the methodological techniques associated with newer areas of interest such as historical demography are, as Barbara Tuchman said, "methods of research, not of communication."[2] History communicates through narrative, which is perhaps its greatest cognitive instrument.

The historical narrative is not a simple linear creation. It is a narrative incorporating analysis and causal argument. It is a mixture of storytelling and expla-

---

[1] Joyce Appleby, Lynn Hunt, and Margaret Jacob, *Telling the Truth About History* (New York: W. W. Norton, 1994), 235.

[2] Barbara W. Tuchman, *Practicing History: Selected Essays by Barbara W. Tuchman* (New York: Alfred A. Knopf, 1981), 63.

Chapter 9: Writing

> "History should be a fun story, well told. A lot of good writers are attracted to historical studies because history is fun to write and to read." — Julie Williams, author, *The Significance of the Printed Word in Early America*

nation based on evidence and intuitive reasoning. It is one of the oldest forms of investigation that have characterized the study of humankind. History's commitment to narrative is as old as Western civilization. Many historians, including Allan Nevins, a journalism historian who was outspoken on the subject, have believed that, since the time of Herodotus, history has been at its greatest when considered a type of literature rather than a branch of science.[3] In fact, many of the founders of history as it emerged and grew in the modern world were concerned with its literary qualities. In the eighteenth century, renowned writers such as Voltaire and Gibbon even entertained thoughts of making history the modern successor of the epic.[4] Surely there was an epic character to a number of the great nineteenth-century masters of the craft such as Thomas Macaulay and Francis Parkman.

While it is true that a scientific school emerged among historians in the late nineteenth century and succeeded in placing a great stress on research and analysis as the discipline was coming into its own as a separate academic field of inquiry, interest in the narrative was never lost. It remains to this day an esteemed and irreplaceable quality of history. The social sciences do not claim any interest in narrative. It is true that a few scholars who write about communication history use a structure similar to that used in social and behavioral science. However, most of those trained in history employ narrative mixed with exposition. Among contemporary works in communication history, those that have received awards almost invariably have relied on a narrative structure.

The historical narrative has much in common with the fictional narrative. Both are stories about events and people, both strive to create a perceptive and lasting impression of life, and both involve essentially a chronological arrangement. The similarity is not surprising since history was a branch of literature until about 200 years ago and since both history and literature are custodians of the literary tradition. To write history, one must give serious thought to the narrative element and its implementation.

---

[3]Ray Allen Billington, comp., *Allan Nevins On History* (New York: Charles Scribner's Sons, 1975), 202.
[4]Lionel Gossman, "History and Literature: Reproduction or Signification," in Robert H. Canary and Henry Kozicki, eds., *The Writing of History: Literary Form and Historical Understanding* (Madison: University of Wisconsin Press, 1978), 13-14.

If this stress on narrative has been a distinguishing quality of history, it also has created problems. At times it has encouraged too great an emphasis on portraying individuals in history and too little on conditions affecting them, or too much stress on political history and too little on social. It also has led some writers to interject their own observations without restraint.

> "A biographer's job is to breathe life back into figures who have died, and that takes more than the recitation of facts." — Dale Cressman, author, Television News Pioneer Elmer W. Lower

Moreover, as the pull of sciences grew in modern society, a number of scholars came to question history's commitment to narrative. Historical study lacked analysis and precision and was too subjective, they charged. There was a degree of truth in those criticisms, depending on what history and whose history one has in mind, for there are flaws enough to be found in historical writing over the years. That hardly makes history different from any other major form of scholarship. The charges of the critics, however, frequently reflected the wishes of some scholars that history become more scientific, that it become a social science. That being the case, it should be remembered that the historical narrative always has contained an analytical element and, whether at times flawed or not, that it has as much soundness to its credit as any other field of study.

It also is worth remembering that the historical past, as its records show, is an imperfect object to study and that the results of such a study must bear the imperfection that its evidence imposes. History attempts to capture parts of the ever-expanding and diverse mosaic of the past in fullness and truthfulness. Its claim is not perfect certainty. In fact, historical writing, with its combination of narrative and exposition, is one of the most difficult of writing genres. It resembles fictional literature with its story-telling. Fiction writers, however, may create their details from the imagination, while historians must deal with facts. Historical writing with its use of exposition, on the other hand, resembles writing in the social sciences. Social scientists, however, are content with a formulaic presentation of their findings. Historians, on the other hand, try to place their findings in an interesting narrative account. The historical narrative, which remains the most widespread form of historical writing, has its limitations. They cannot be dismissed. Indeed, recognition of them explains why its major generalizations are seldom unqualified.

Of the problems integral to historical writing, none is more pervasive than that of the tension between its analytical and narrative elements. The analytical element, of course, has grown during the last hundred years. Are the ramifications of this growth detrimental, or even fatal, to history? G. R. Elton provided a point worth considering about that question. "The essential demand of all historical material," he wrote, "is that it be used to recreate life, which is movement. The whole difficulty of historical reconstruction and writing lies in this fundamental truth about history: it contains a multiple situation forever on the move."[5]

The analytical element poses a twofold problem in historical writing. First, it is difficult to accommodate it to the intrinsic movement in history to which Elton referred, and, second, there is the danger that it will fragment narrative — perhaps destroy it.

The problem of tension between these two elements in history is an old one that reflects the nineteenth-century conflict between scientific and literary history. Most historians, however, consider the problem as one of integration rather than conflict. Arthur M. Schlesinger, Jr., wrote that historical writing "should integrate narrative and analysis in a web rendered seamless by literary art."[6] Although it is possible to wonder if that web can ever become seamless, the goal of integration of analysis and narrative is laudable. It respects artistry, the concern for truth and evidence, and the demand for full and intelligible explanation.

> "Effective historical analyses offer strong narratives and arguments. Arguments become compelling not by shouting in tones of moral outrage, but by careful deployment of evidence." — Linda Steiner, University of Maryland

Despite its flexible format, the historical narrative has identifiable characteristics. Since it goes beyond simple narration and involves analysis, questioning, and generalization, it is, before all else, an interpretive narrative. It is also concerned with movement and with historical time. It has a beginning and an end and in between a unified development that is, to varying degrees, chronological.

Consequently, the historical narrative has a structure. For most historians, that structure is not based on theory, which, as Louis O. Mink explained, "makes possible the explanation of an occurrence only by explaining it in such a way that the description is logically related to a systematic set of generalizations or

---

[5]G. R. Elton, *Political History: Principles and Practice* (New York: Basic Books, 1970), 160.

[6]Carol Bondhus Fitzgerald, "Toward a Bibliography of the Writings of Arthur M. Schlesinger, Jr.: 1935-June 1984," with a Foreword by Arthur Schlesinger, Jr., *American History: A Bibliographic Review* 1 (1985): 37.

laws."[7] Rather than impose that type of theoretical structure on their writing, historians structure it to fit the particularity of their subject and their own grasp of it. The way they perceive the subject and mold it into an intelligible and truthful whole gives the historical narrative its unity. In the process, at least to some degree, they must indulge in pattern-making. Pattern in this case refers to the effort to see logical ways in which evidence fits together rather than to an overarching systematic explanation. For instance, Stephen Koss' *The Rise and Fall of the Political Press in Britain* (2 vols., 1981/1984), one of the most important contributions to communication history, is a superb example of a work by a historian who discovered the necessary pattern to make his abundant material comprehensible to his readers.

> "When writing the narrative, think *frosting*. Without it, a cake is dry, unappealing to look at, and the layers don't hold together. With it, the cake has form and consistency, it is beautiful to behold, and the ingredients remain a mystery until it is sliced into pieces." — Kim Mangun, author, Making Utah History

This concern for readers is another characteristic of the historical narrative. The audience is an imperative factor for historians to consider. History should be directed to a wide audience that might be described as generally educated. To reach that audience, historical writing should possess order, lucidity, and crispness. That means it should be free of jargon, that overused technical terminology characteristic of specialized activity. History's language, in other words, should be clear and interesting. At the same time, much "scholarly" history — such as that found in research papers and journal articles — often employs writing styles that are different from those one would use when writing for a general audience. Yet, even when the audience is an academic one, historical writing should be marked by such characteristics as clarity and smooth flow.

Far from being a mechanical creation, historical writing involves personal choices and preferences of many sorts. Style is among the foremost of the concerns. By simple definition, one can describe style as the manner, tone, or character of discourse. On one level, it depends on the use of words and phrases — on their selection, pairing, and rhythm — and on the connotations they convey. On another level, style reflects a writer's sense of proportion and his or her literary ability to create a mood. In either case, it reveals the creative spirit behind the composition. Although style in historical writing can be as varied as the writers themselves, it should reflect the basic attributes associated with this form of

[7]Louis O. Mink, "Narrative Form As a Cognitive Instrument," in Canary and Kozicki, eds. *The Writing of History*, 131-32.

inquiry. At its best it also has literary grace. Accordingly, the stress on style can be considered as another evidence of the importance of the narrative element in historical composition.

Unity of Composition

It is easy enough to understand that historical writing should have coherent unity. That principle, however, is easier to state than to achieve. A composition must have thematic unity. A narrative should be structured around one central idea, or theme. Without it, the work falls apart. If the composition is no more than a collection of historical data and details, or if it is an unintegrated assortment of pieces of information, it works poorly. It must do more than pull together a group of facts, details of how the historian conducted the research, quotations, places, names, and dates. All of its parts must work together as a unified whole knit around the central theme.

To achieve unity, historians should be attentive to the organization of material. To what degree should it be topical and to what degree should it be chronological? Too much of either could destroy the historical narrative. The topical arrangement represents a horizontal expansion of the subject that can destroy movement; and, if one uses a strict multi-topical approach, it can be repetitious beyond the limits of a reader's patience. On the other hand, excessive use of chronology would reduce narrative to a simple listing based on order of occurrence. Some mixture of the topical and the chronological is needed, and it must be capable of covering the evidence and unifying it into a coherent whole. There are other factors to consider in establishing continuity. Where does the narrative start and end, and why there? Once you provide logical answers for those questions, there remains the challenge of sustaining continuity.

A number of literary and rhetorical devices can assist one in that task, but sustained continuity is mainly the result of a historian's imagination. Only that imagination informed by evidence can reconstruct from the remaining record of the past the life that once was part of it. The process is one of providing a natural coherence for diverse evidence that can be found to explain your subject.

One other matter regarding unity deserves mentioning, particularly for the consideration of communication historians whose scholarly backgrounds are varied. It will deliver us again to differences between history and the social sciences. In this case, the difference is one of form. Historians attempt to reconstruct some segment of life in their presentations, and in their explanations they try to provide a coherent account that is true to that life. From start to finish their compositions are built around the reality of life that is their subject, and they tend to have continuous flow. Social scientists, to the contrary, tend to structure their compositions as if they are parts of a scientific problem. They divide them according to the perceived parts of that type of problem. Consider the following headings that one might encounter in a composition in one of the social sciences:

Introduction
Prior Published Research on the Topic
Hypothesis
Method
Discussion of findings
Conclusion

Such a division, of course, might have been made for sound pedagogical purposes. Nevertheless, it exemplifies the social science approach to a problem and sometimes appears in a modified form in historical papers presented at conferences of communication educators. Composition so divided bears obvious comparison with the arrangement associated with writing in the natural sciences.

Such an arrangement might serve the compositional needs of the social sciences, but it does not lend itself to the prerequisites of historical writing. It lacks narrative flow and, indeed, destroys the integration characteristic of historical composition. Its methodological divisions impose a systematic form of explanation on its subject. While it is true that a historical composition has an introduction, a body or main text, and a conclusion, it is also true that it has little or no textual delineation by rigid headings. When divisions of some form are used in historical writing, they indicate a change of focus in the ongoing narrative. They do not reflect parts of a scientific problem. Historical narrative is the art of communicating to a general audience what you know, what you do not know, and what the readers expect to discover about a particular subject. It is a type of discussion that explains as it proceeds.

Nevertheless, some communication historians imitate the structure of social science articles appearing in such journals as *Journalism and Mass Communication Quarterly* and fill their manuscripts with descriptions of their research methods and listings of their numerical findings. Those problems are the marks of researchers unfamiliar with historical methods, those who rely too exclusively on behavioral and social science methods that theorists and researchers have tried to adopt in communication studies. Such methods are, however, while sometimes useful, inadequate by themselves for historical research. Historical method has a long and solid tradition. Historians using it properly face no compulsion to provide minute descriptions of the methodology they employed. The quality of the research should be obvious from the narrative, from the properly documented sources, and from the soundness of historians' reasoning. Researchers who emphasize their methods tend to be the ones who also list in detail the findings of those methods. They pile percentage upon percentage and number upon number. When finished, their manuscripts sometimes have twenty pages of technique and numbers, and a half page of not quite meaningful narrative and discussion. In historical study, as in other research, the researcher should remember that techniques are important primarily because they are ways to discover something. Findings are important because of the understanding they can help provide. In historical writing, the emphasis should be on the discoveries and on understanding, not on descriptions of methodology.

Constructing an Effective Historical Composition

Historians are no exception to the rule that writers must pay attention to numerous practical aspects of composition. Although it is beyond the scope of this book to review all the elements of writing, it can be recommended that beginning researchers follow the old dictum: study the language. Make a habit of reviewing syntax and vocabulary. Though written many years ago, *The Elements of Style* by William Strunk, Jr., remains a fine source to consult for guidance about constructing effective language. Beginning researchers might wish to consider that classic brief introduction to plain English or some other selection of the same genre along with Savoie Lottinville's more recent *The Rhetoric of History*.[8]

Effective use of the language is a requirement of good history, and the following five aspects of scholarly writing deserve the attention of anyone who undertakes to write history. The points are (1) clarity and continuity, (2) development, (3) footnotes, (4) quotations, and (5) revision of the composition.

1. Clarity and Continuity

These twin qualities of proficient historical narrative depend, of course, on one's command of the basic mechanics of writing. Beyond that, they stem from three requirements of composition: plain words, effective sentences, and well-formed

---

[8]William Strunk, Jr., and Richard De A'Morelli, *The Elements of Style*, Classic Edition, 2018 Update (San Luis Obispo, Calif: Spectrum Ink, 2018); Savoie Lottinville, *The Rhetoric of History* (Norman: University of Oklahoma Press, 1976).

paragraphs.

Consider *plain words*. They need not be bland. Indeed, they can be eloquent. But they must be intelligible to the wide audience historians hope to reach. The key lies in selecting the words most capable of conveying the precise meaning you have in mind. Well-chosen words connote sharp meaning and can eliminate awkward phrasing. Be precise about what you want to say, find the appropriate words to express it, and eliminate careless language. William Strunk, Jr., the co-author of *The Elements of Style*, placed a premium on precision in writing. "Omit needless words," he advised. "Vigorous writing is concise. A sentence should contain no unnecessary words, a paragraph no unnecessary sentences, for the same reason that a drawing should have no unnecessary lines and a machine no unnecessary parts. This requires not that the writer make all his sentences short, or that he avoid all detail and treat his subjects only in outline, but that every word tell." Study the meanings of words, be curious about language, and make a habit of reaching for the dictionary.

Intended meaning can be obscured by awkward sentences and sentence pattern as well as by faulty word selection. *Sentences* reflect the literary artistry of the writer as much as any other component of writing. They establish rhythm and coordinate, subordinate, and emphasize ideas. Effective sentence structure depends on correct syntax, perception of logical relationships, placement of words, and stylistic preferences. Good sentences generally avoid too much complexity — such as multiple clauses. "A scrupulous writer," advised George Orwell, the English critic and commentator, "in every sentence that he writes, will ask himself at least four questions, thus: 1. What am I trying to say? 2. What words will express it? 3. What image or idiom will make it clearer? 4. Is this image fresh enough to have an effect?" Barbara Tuchman, who twice won the Pulitzer Prize for history, said of sentences and good writing, "Nothing is more satisfying than to write a good sentence. It is no fun to write lumpishly, dully, in prose the reader must plod through like wet sand. But it is a pleasure to achieve, if one can, a clear running prose that is simple yet full of surprises. This does not just happen. It requires skill, hard work, a good ear, and continued practice." Study each sentence you write, and rewrite it until you are convinced that it gives graceful expression to the idea that you wish it to convey.

Well-constructed paragraphs, the third requirement needed to establish clarity and continuity, are hallmarks of all effective writing. They are, of course, units, not mere collections of sentences. As such they must be thought through and developed. Unlike paragraphs in journalistic writing, they are not simply typographic blocks. In almost all cases, a common theme permeates a paragraph

Writing Tips from Masters

"Suppose you tell all the truths of science in a way that bores the reader. What is the good? The truths don't stay in the mind, and nobody thinks any better of you because you have told them the truth tediously." – Charles Dana, American newspaper editor (1819-1897)

"There should be two main objectives in ordinary prose writing: to convey a message and to include in it nothing that will distract the reader's attention or check his habitual pace of reading. He should feel that he is seated at ease in a taxi, not riding a temperamental horse through traffic." – Robert Graves, English poet and novelist (1895-1985)

"Clarity. Clarity. Clarity. When you become hopelessly mired in a sentence, it is best to start fresh." – Strunk & White, *The Elements of Style*

"To get the right word in the right place is a rare achievement. To condense the diffused light of a page of thought into the luminous flash of a single sentence, is worthy to rank as a prize composition just by itself.... Anybody can have ideas – the difficulty is to express them without squandering a quire of paper on an idea that ought to be reduced to one glittering paragraph." – Mark Twain, American novelist and humorist (1835-1910)

"The most valuable of talents is never using two words when one will do." – Thomas Jefferson, American President (1743-1826)

"I have made this letter long, because I have not had the time to make it shorter." – Blaise Pascal, French mathematician and philosopher (1623-1662)

"What is easy to read has been difficult to write. The labour of writing and rewriting, correcting and recorrecting, is the due exacted by every good book from its author.... A limpid style is invariably the result of hard labour, and the easily flowing connection of sentence with sentence and paragraph with paragraph has always been won by the sweat of the brow." – George Macaulay Trevelyan, English historian (1876-1962)

"Learn to write well, or not to write at all." – Charles Dickens, English novelist (1812-1870) and integrates the sentences within it. Those sentences should not only convey information but also interact with one another. Most paragraphs have a well-defined topic sentence that receives early and prominent display. By stating the subject of a paragraph, a topic sentence gives it focus and directs the reader to the sentences that follow. As the remainder of the paragraph unfolds, various transitional devices can be employed to smooth connections and sharpen movement. Thus a paragraph acquires internal clarity and continuity.

It is also necessary for a paragraph to have external continuity, a sequential relationship with the paragraphs preceding and following it. The way in which the paragraph relates to the whole composition helps to build its external continuity as does a writer's conscious effort to make the topic of one paragraph a continuation in some way of the subject and narrative flow of the preceding one. This sense of continuation may result either from creating a natural chronological or topical transition from one paragraph to another or from the use of a number of transitional devices. Regarding the latter method, the writer might refer to a word or idea at the end of the previous paragraph, or repeat a word from it, or perhaps use a transitional expression. In such instances, the transitional or connecting language usually appears at the beginning of the following paragraph. Paragraphs, like words and sentences, are rhetorical supports that sustain the structure of composition, and there is no substitute for the care a writer should take in constructing them.

2. *Development*

Since book-length compositions with their prefaces, introductions, and various types of concluding chapters allow more flexibility in handling these elements, we primarily consider here an article-length composition. The first page of a short composition is indeed, as several authorities on historical writing suggest, one of the "supreme tests of the art of composition."[9] That being the case, opening lines assume particular significance. Consider these two. William E. Smith wrote the first; Charles Levermore, the second.

> "Send it to Bla-ar!" exclaimed President Andrew Jackson when he and his friends were puzzled with a baffling problem.[10]

[9] Jacques Barzun and Henry F. Graff, *The Modern Researcher,* 5th ed. (New York: Harcourt Brace Javonovich, 1992), 218.
[10] William E. Smith, "Francis P. Blair, Pen-Executive of Andrew Jackson," *Mississippi Valley Historical Review* 17 (March 1931), 543.

> The mechanical evolution of the modern newspaper is due chiefly to the steam-engine and the telegraph, but the evolution of the modern journalistic spirit is due chiefly to an aggressive democracy.[11]

Both historians, as these examples show, understood the requirements of effective openings. As an initial sentence, neither could fail to capture one's imagination. They illustrate the first rule for opening lines: they must engage the reader's interest. They must also suggest the central idea of the composition. First lines cannot be duds. They connect the reader with the subject and set the narrative in motion. They must, therefore, encourage the reader to continue. The way is thus open for the remaining part of the initial paragraph and perhaps one or several of the following ones to establish the setting and purpose of the composition. That, in turn, should be done in a manner that complements the narrative.

Here is another example of a beginning, this one from a book. Notice how the historian Julie Williams, in the opening to her account of the importance of printed material in early America, starts with an interesting first sentence and follows it with a thematic introductory paragraph.

> From a vessel rocking gently in the Bay of the Mother of God, Spanish Father Juan Baptista de Segura did not realize he was about to embark on one of the earliest but most typical of American colonial acts.
>
> Instead, he was anticipating the divine opportunity before him in the thick forests of Ajacán. Here was a chance for the unadulterated word of God to unleash its almighty power. Here, in 1570, was his own sacred appointment to be God's sentinel to an ignorant and unconverted people, to introduce them to the Holy Gospel, and to transplant civilization as God intended into this new and untamed world, a world which the English called "Virginia." Typical of Americans to follow, Father Segura planned to use the printed word as a tool in his mission of instituting a different culture — a new church, a European form of civilization — among the Indians of Ajacán.[12]

That beginning, while it works as an effective way to get the reader into Prof.

---

[11]Charles H. Levermore, "The Rise of Metropolitan Journalism, 1800-1840," *American Historical Review* 6 (April 1901): 446.

[12]Julie Hedgepeth Williams, *The Significance of the Printed Word in Early America* (Westport, Conn.: Greenwood Press, 1999), 1.

Williams' book, would work equally well for a shorter article. It is a good model for anyone wishing to write engaging history.

Concentrate on beginnings. It is easy to err in constructing them. They should bear the same precision of thought and sense of narrative flow that characterize the body of the composition.

While much historical writing presents its account in a narrative, storytelling fashion, let's look briefly at *scholarly* historical writing. Such writing often is expected to give attention to certain forms. The reason is that the purpose of much scholarly writing is to provide understanding or add to knowledge rather than only to tell a story. Thus, one finds that academic conferences and history journals in the communication field often ask that manuscripts include specific points. Normally, those points include a statement of the study's theme, a literature review, and an explanation of how the study adds to existing knowledge. Historians handle such matters in different ways, but usually they include them in the introduction of their manuscript. Thus, a typical structure of a conference paper or article manuscript includes the parts illustrated by the following basic outline.

I. Introduction

The introduction has the following four parts:

1. Narrative paragraph or two about the subject
2. Statement of the theme of the study
3. Literature review

It is necessary to discuss only those works that deal specifically and directly with the study's topic and that focus in their entirety or in large part on the topic. In other words, the literature review need not include works that just happen to mention the topic in a small treatment on a larger subject. At the same time, the review does need to demonstrate that the researcher has a mastery of the broad scope of historical work and how her study fits within it. The literature review should be written as a literate, thoughtful historiographical essay rather than as an annotated bibliography. Ideally, it should be one pithy paragraph and not an extended, lengthy discussion. Much of the detail may be placed in the notes. The most important historical works may be named in the paragraph and must be included in a footnote or footnotes.

4. Statement of the importance of the research to historical study

This statement should explain how the present study adds to the existing

Copyright

Although dealing with copyright regulations is a complicated matter for researchers, it is not an insurmountable one. Published matter and material appearing on the Internet can be copied according to the rules of fair use. Although the doctrine of fair use fails to define precisely the limits about the use of copyrighted works, it does afford scholars considerable leeway. It allows authors to quote small amounts of text and to use small amounts of graphic and pictorial material from copyrighted works for scholarly purposes (e. g., to support points in a researcher's own writing). Of course, the material used must be kept in context, reproduced accurately, and acknowledged by proper citation.

In determining how much material may be copied in this manner, it can be assumed that it would be improper for a researcher to reproduce a large portion of an article, essay, or chapter of a book. "Substantiality" is a key concept in determining how much is acceptable. Reproduced material should be kept short, and it should not comprise a substantial part of either the original or the new composition. As an authority on the topic explains, even though "no specific formula exists regarding the amount of an original work" that may be used, "[i]f a large amount of the original copyrighted work or the most significant part of it is taken, the fair use defense may not protect the secondary use."[1]

Federal law has established varying numbers of years for copyright protection, but the protection can run for longer than 100 years. For example, works created after January 1, 1978, are protected for seventy years after the author's death. On the other hand, material published before 1923 already is in the public domain. A good textbook, such as W. Wat Hopkins' *Communication and the Law*, can answer most questions historians will have about copyright law.

---

[1] W. Wat Hopkins, ed., *Communication and the Law, 2010 Edition* (Northport, Ala.: Vision Press, 2010), 138.

knowledge that earlier historians have produced about the subject. It should be a natural outgrowth of the literature review.

II. Body

The body of the manuscript uses either a chronological or a topical structure. That is, it is arranged to cover various parts of the subject in temporal order, or each section discusses a particular thematic aspect of the subject. For purposes of illustration, let us consider a manuscript with the title "The First Party Press, 1789-1816." In the *chronological* arrangement, the sections might be something such as these:

1. The Genesis of the Party Press, 1789-1795
2. The Press and the Formation of Party Organizations, 1795-1798
3. The Press and the Sedition Act, 1798-1800
4. The Press and the Election of 1800
5. The Press and the Republican Ascendancy, 1800-1808
6. The Press and the Twilight of Federalism, 1808-1816

For the *topical* arrangement, the sections might be these:

1. Politics, the Press, and Public Opinion
2. Party Support of the Press
3. Party-Press Relationships
4. The Purposes of the Press
5. Newspaper Methods
6. The Party Press and Freedom of the Press

III. Conclusion

This part of the manuscript offers the author the opportunity to provide a mature, reasoned, thoughtful, insightful assessment of the subject he has studied. What explanation has he brought to this subject? What new insight have we learned about the nature of the topic from this study of it?

The final paragraph or paragraphs of the manuscript should contain the author's concluding thoughts about the subject rather than a mere summary of material covered. Summaries are unnecessary. In forming concluding comments for a composition, it can be helpful to keep in mind the definition of a conclusion as "reasoned judgment." Accordingly, one can expect to find meaningful reflections about the subject in concluding comments. Care should be taken not to allow conclusions to over-run either the evidence presented or the limits of logical reflection based upon that evidence.

3. Footnotes

Nothing more characterizes scholarly writing than the presence of footnotes and quotations. Both are used for specific purposes. Footnotes may be either of a citation or supplementary type. Sometimes the two types are combined. Citation footnotes supply the necessary reference for both direct and indirect quotations, paraphrased material, statistical data, material taken from a specific source, references to distinct ideas and interpretations not your own, and essential facts that are not part of general knowledge. They acknowledge sources used and validate the composition.

Supplementary footnotes elaborate matters of record referred to in the text. You can also use them to comment on a point introduced in the composition, perhaps a controversial point, and to reflect on the commentary of another historian on a particular question. Employ them in a judicious manner and keep them brief. They should not become repositories for all other knowledge about material covered in the text.

Following is a list of standard footnote forms for frequently used types of sources.

I. Basic Forms

Primary item in a manuscript collection

[1]Carl W. Ackerman to C. V. Van Anda, 30 August 1918, Carl William Ackerman Papers, Manuscript Division, Library of Congress, Washington, D. C., box 122.

Primary item in a published collection of primary material

[2]E. L. Godkin to Henry Villard, 13 October 1887, Rollo Ogden, ed., *Life and Letters of Edwin Lawrence Godkin* (New York: Macmillan, 1907), 447.

Primary item in a secondary source

³Thomas Jefferson to Archibald Stuart, 14 May 1799, quoted in Wm. David Sloan, *The Media in America*, 10th ed. (Northport, Ala.: Vision Press, 2017), 75.

(For primary references in secondary sources, use "quoted in" for direct quotations and "cited in" for references to indirect quotations.)

> "A footnote should appear at the end of material from any one source that you cite, or at the end of the paragraph, whichever comes first. Never leave someone guessing about where the material came from. It's better to footnote too much than too little." — Julie Williams, author, *The Significance of the Printed Word in Early America*

Magazine article

⁴Edward P. Mitchell, "Mr. Dana of 'The Sun,'" *McClure's Magazine*, October 1894, 374.

Newspaper

⁵*New York Times*, 15 March 1880, 15.

(In the case of American newspapers, add and italicize the city even if it is not part of the newspaper's proper name. At the beginning of the footnote, add the author and title for a signed article.)

Non-American newspaper without location in title

⁶*The Times* (London), 15 April 1870, 6.

Book

⁷Bernell Tripp, *Origins of the Black Press: New York, 1827-1847* (Northport, Ala.: Vision Press, 1992), 61.

Volume in a multivolume series with the same title

⁸Elizabeth Bisland, *The Life and Letters of Lafcadio Hearn*, 2 vols. (Boston: Houghton Mifflin, 1906), 1: 2.

Separately titled volume in a multivolume series

⁹Carol Sue Humphrey, *The Press of the Early Republic, 1783-1833*, vol. 2, History of American Journalism (Westport, Conn.: Greenwood Press, 1996), 44.

Paperback edition

¹⁰Joseph F. Wall, *Henry Watterson: Reconstructed Rebel* (New York: Oxford University Press, 1956; Bantam Books, 1960), 80.

Later edition of a book

¹¹Wm. David Sloan, ed., *The Age of Mass Communication*, 2nd ed. (Northport, Ala.: Vision Press, 2008), 158.

Reprint edition of a book

¹²James C. Austin, *Petroleum V. Nasby* (1948; reprint ed., New York: Twayne, 1965), 91.

Component by one author in a work by another

¹³Bruce Evensen, "Progressivism, Muckraking and Objectivity," in Steven R. Knowlton and Karen L. Freeman, eds., *Fair & Balanced: A History of Journalistic Objectivity* (Northport, Ala.: Vision Press, 2005), 143.

Journal article

¹⁴Bonnie Brennan, "From Religiosity to Consumerism: Press Coverage of Thanksgiving, 1905-2005," *Journalism Studies* 9:1 (2008): 24.

Dissertation

¹⁵Aimee Edmondson, "In Sullivan's Shadow: The Use and Abuse of Libel Law During the Civil Rights Movement," Ph.D. dissertation, University of Missouri, 2008, 47.

Plagiarism

Plagiarism is the of act taking another's material and presenting it as one's own. It is an offense. One should never do it.

Plagiarism, in its most elementary form, is using words verbatim from a source without acknowledging the source. For example, failure to place quotation marks around verbatim material or to give credit to the source constitutes plagiarism. The "source" may be either primary or secondary material. The rule of practice is this: Always place in quotation marks any material used verbatim from a source, and always acknowledge the source.

The historian may commit plagiarism, however, by less blatant means. Taking a distinctive idea from another and presenting it as one's own original idea is a violation of the most basic principles of scholarship. That rule applies even if the historian casts the idea in his or her own words. Among other forms of plagiarism is borrowing extensively from another scholar's research material or writing, even if the source is acknowledged. It must not be done.

Plagiarism is so serious an offense that professional colleagues denounce historians who commit it, professors lose their jobs, and students are expelled from school.

It is also a grave offense to the whole scholarly pursuit. As the American

Conference Paper

[16] Debra van Tuyll, "The Transnational Paradigm as a Method of Analyzing Early Colonial American Journalism" (paper presented at the annual meeting of the American Journalism Historians Association, Salt Lake City, Utah, October 7, 2018), 5-6.

Reference Book

[17] *Encyclopaedia Britannica*, 15th ed., s. v. "Suffragists."
(When citing well-known reference sources, it is customary to omit the facts of publication and page numbers. Simply cite the title and edition of the source, followed by "s.v." and title of the article. [s.v.= *sub verbo* or "under the word"].)

Historical Association's "Statement of Plagiarism" puts it, plagiarism "is a serious violation of the ethics of scholarship. It undermines the credibility of historical inquiry."

Even though the Internet has raised concerns about the ease with which students may plagiarize research papers, actually students who were intent on doing so always could find ways to cheat even before the appearance of the Internet. The Internet has, in fact, made it easier to detect instances of plagiarism. Search engines such as Google <www.google.com>, Yahoo! <www.yahoo.com/>, and Dogpile <www.dogpile.com> make it easy for professors and editors to check instances of suspicious writing. Furthermore, a number of sites are dedicated specifically to identifying plagiarism in research papers. They include <www.plagiarism.org>, <www.turnitin.com>, and <www.grammarly.com>, among many. Using the Internet has become a common practice to catch plagiarism that a couple of decades ago might have gone undetected.

Besides the fact that plagiarism constitutes intellectual theft, students have another good reason not to engage in it. Two of the prime purposes of research are to increase one's knowledge and to improve research skills. Simply taking the work of another robs the student of the great benefits that historical research has to offer the researcher. So, stealing from another is actually cheating oneself.

No one has anything to gain through plagiarism, but everyone has much to lose. So always follow the basic rule about plagiarism: Don't do it.

Internet Sources

For material gathered on the Internet, footnote forms should be the same as those above but with added details about the location of the material on the Internet. Footnotes are expected to include the following elements: (1) the name of the Internet site, (2) its address, and (3) the date on which the researcher accessed the material.

[18]Horace Greeley to Abraham Lincoln, 18 November 1862, The Abraham Lincoln Papers at the Library of Congress, https://www.loc.gov/item/mal1958200/ (accessed February 8, 2019).

II. General Rules

1. Ibid. is used for a reference to the work in the preceding footnote. Do not underline or italicize Ibid. or put it in quotation marks.
2. Ibid. should not be used if the preceding note has more than one citation.
3. When two or more sources are cited in a note, they should be separated by a semicolon.
4. For later references, use the author's last name and the title of the work or, if the title is lengthy or has a subtitle, a shortened title (e.g., Tripp, *Origins of the Black Press*, 106).
5. The author's name should appear in a note even if it is mentioned near the citation in the text.
6. If it is necessary to quote from a passage that itself is quoted in a secondary source, cite it as such. The footnote reference should contain the identity and location of the quotation plus a citation of the secondary source in which you found it. Usually, "quoted in" or some similar phrase follows the reference to the quotation and introduces the secondary source that contains it.
7. There is no need to cite references for general knowledge, such as information readily found in encyclopedias or, in a routine manner, in a variety of secondary sources. Nor is it necessary to cite conventional facts or well-known remarks.
8. For additional guidelines, consult a generally accepted manual (such as *The Chicago Manual of Style* or Kate L. Turabian's *Manual for Writers of Research Papers, Theses, and Dissertations*) and consistently follow the forms of that specific manual.

4. Quotations

Quotations, like footnotes, should be used with care. They might be utilized to illustrate a point, to provide a sample of your evidence, to increase the forcefulness of your argument, to give life to a character in the narrative, or to provide readers with a particular point of record or with someone's original language. Barzun and Graff, who make a habit of offering sage advice on historical writing, suggest the following as the first principle of the art of using quotations: "*Quotations are illustrations, not proofs*. The proof of what you say is the whole body of facts and ideas to which you refer, that is, to which you point. From time to time you give a sample of this evidence to clinch your argument or to avail your-

Chapter 9: Writing

self of a characteristic or felicitous utterance."[13] That principle merits particular attention, for it is frequently misunderstood.

When using quotations in historical writing, adhere to the following guidelines:

> "You know when you see long block quotations in a research article and you just skip over them? Yeah, so do the rest of us. Save quotations for truly memorable wording, and paraphrase the rest." — Lisa Parcell, co-editor, *American Journalism: History, Principles, Practices*

- Keep their use to a minimum. (Dorothy Sayers, the English novelist, cautioned: "A facility for quotation covers the absence of original thought.")
- Keep them short.
- Keep them in the context of their original meaning.
- Consult a primary source, rather than a secondary one, for a quotation whenever possible.
- Integrate them into your own narrative.
- Introduce quotations with attributions (e.g., H. V. Kaltenborn commented...).
- Comment on uncustomary language and ideas contained in a quotation.
- Avoid quoting from textbooks or general reference sources unless the quoted words are themselves the subject you wish to examine.

5. *Revision of the Composition*

Good writing emerges in stages, one of which is that of revision. "The best history is the product of revision almost as much as it is of vision," wrote Arthur M. Schlesinger, Jr.[14] His comment elicits the consent of anyone who has ever attempted to write a serious piece of history. Early drafts of compositions afford one the opportunity to experiment with language, arrangement, and explanation. Revision provides the opportunity to refine all matters of composition from syntax to interpretation. Revision gives you the chance to sharpen language, to smooth transitions, to tone up or down the particular phrases, and to make any modification that might be in order when the individual parts of the composition are viewed in the perspective of the full draft.

At this stage of writing, careless language should be purged from the narra-

---

[13]Jacques Barzun and Henry F. Graff, *The Modern Researcher*, 5th ed. (New York: Harcourt Brace Jovanovich, 1992), 275.

[14]Schlesinger, Foreword to Fitzgerald's "Toward a Bibliography of the Writings of Arthur M. Schlesinger, Jr.," 37.

tive as well as all contractions, archaic words, and examples of tautology. Revision should include a close, critical reading of every word in the composition. Be sure the meaning of every word, phrase, sentence, and idea will be clear to your audience on a first reading. Christopher Morley (1890-1957), an American journalist and novelist, advised writers to place a premium on clarity. "[T]he rule of clearness," he said, "is not to write so that the reader can understand, but so that he cannot possibly misunderstand." Weed out any pedantic or euphemistic expressions that slipped in. Remember too that history should be written in the past tense and in the active voice. Although it is permissible to take some liberty with the latter, minimize using passive verbs. Excessive use of the passive voice can hinder effective writing by blurring subjects in sentence constructions. It caters to indirect and imprecise expression. Consequently, be conscious of the use you make of it and employ it only when reflection convinces you of its propriety. Examine the composition for matters of connection, continuity, and clarity.

> "Write, rewrite, and rewrite again, always remembering the fundamentals you learned in junior high: strong topic sentences, brevity, and clarity. Only through revision can you accomplish polished writing." — David Davies, author, The Postwar Decline of American Newspapers, 1945-1965

Revision also should go beyond matters of syntax and rhetoric and include substantive considerations. In terms of explanations, does the composition say, in its various parts and in whole, what you intended for it to say? Can you prove by a convincing amount of evidence or by reasonable argument what you have stated in writing? Does it conform to the dictates of common sense?

Revision, we can conclude, is valuable beyond question in the construction of composition. It is a creative and imaginative act in the art of writing.

Checklist for Proofreading

After completing the final copy of the composition, there is still one more exercise to perform. You are responsible for everything in the composition, from correctness of fact to correctness of language. That means you also assume responsibility for any typing mistakes that appear in the final version of the composition. Consequently, a careful proofreading of your work is a necessary final act of composition to rid it of mechanical mistakes. The following list enumerates items that always merit checking.

- Accuracy of quotations
- Agreement of verb tense
- Proper spelling
- Subject-verb agreement
- Proper punctuation (Pay particular attention to the use of commas. They are the most commonly misused punctuation mark. If you think proper use of commas is of no importance, consider what difference it would make if Melville had begun *Moby Dick* not with "Call me Ishmael" but with "Call me, Ishmael.")
- Clear antecedents for pronouns
- Consistency (You should create a checklist to use in order to establish consistency of usage. Hyphenated words, names, titles, tricky spellings, capitalizations, matters of syntax — anything that a computerized check might not catch — can be included.)
- Capitalization (Capitalize names of deities, races of mankind, historical periods, etc.)
- Hyphenated words and phrases (Check for proper and consistent usage.)
- Formation of plural nouns
- Titles of offices
- Titles of sources
- Footnotes (Double-check the form for every footnote, and be sure the bibliography includes an entry for every footnote source.)
- Pagination (Check for order and omissions.)

Proofreading your own writing necessitates a great deal of concentration and patience. It can be done in several ways, of which a line by line ruler check is one. Hardly anything distracts the reader more than mechanical errors. Regardless of the time and effort proofreading requires, it can make a difference in the appearance and quality of your work, and it can help keep your reader absorbed in your account.

PRESENTATION AND PUBLICATION

Historians have a duty to share their findings with others. They do not study for self-gratification alone. Even though the knowledge historians gain in their search for the past may be satisfying in itself, the true historian has an obligation to contribute that knowledge to others. The biblical declaration that "you are the light of the world" applies in a modern sense to historians. They may not hide their light under a basket. The necessity of sharing knowledge goes beyond the cliché "publish or perish" known to untenured professors. Only by publication or public presentation can historians fulfill their role of keeping alive knowledge of the past and expanding the understanding of present and future generations.

But few historians think of publication as only a duty. Most relish the thought. To see one's work presented to the public is one of the things that dreams are made of. How dreary would be the profession if historians thought of presentation and publication only as obligations. There would be little joy then, only the drudgery of working in the mines. While the true historian gets excited over each nugget discovered during research, few can put out of mind the anticipation of seeing those nuggets displayed.

Perhaps it is that anticipation — combined with the fear of failure for professors whose jobs, tenure, and salary frequently depend on publication — that makes the attempt to have a paper accepted for conference presentation or an article or book for publication a cause for anxiety. All types of worries run through the mind: Where should I submit my article? What if it's rejected? Why haven't I heard from the publisher yet? Do I dare open this email from the publisher? These worries are natural, and the historian must accept the fact that they come with the profession. But the worries never should be a cause for not attempting publication or presentation. No historian, no writer of any sort, ever published anything without trying. The first attempt, moreover, is always the most difficult. There are keys to writing publishable history. Familiarity with the topic, adequate research, and competent composition are the main ones, but to these should be added one other: experience. The more one attempts to publish, the more experience one gains. Experience improves the likelihood of publication, and success in publication can encourage additional attempts.

> "Be open to criticism, and upon receiving suggestions for revision, take them to heart — follow up on them, and do not let them discourage you. The process of publishing is a craft — you cannot master it overnight. It takes time, but with patience, you will see results." — Greg Borchard, editor, Journalism History

How should one proceed in pursuit of that goal? With a focus on the practical aspects of getting historical works accepted for presentation and publication, the following advice is not intended as a lofty discussion of historical ideas and practices. Rather, it is offered as a body of pragmatic suggestions that deal with the basic subject of turning historical writings into print. It covers various topics ranging from the basic practices of locating a paper competition to preparing a journal manuscript to finding a book publisher. Much of the chapter is intended to aid the historian who has never published or made a conference presentation. Some of it will benefit historians who wish to expand their production.

Conference Presentations

It is easier to have a paper accepted for presentation at a conference than to have an article accepted for publication. Consequently, historians sometimes let their research and writing quality slip when preparing a submission for a paper competition. Such a practice should be avoided. Ease of acceptance should not reduce the rigor of historical study. Once a historian accepts slipshod work, subsequent shoddiness becomes more readily acceptable. No matter what the final form of public display — whether it is a book, a journal article, or a conference paper — the historian should be satisfied with no less than the best work possible.

Conferences, conventions, and symposia abound for the presentation of papers on communication history. Some are national; many more are regional. A small number are devoted solely to communication history, while most accept

Chapter 10: Presentation and Publication

> "Though I have enjoyed my publication of journal articles and book chapters, I like conferences best for a simple reason: the interaction with other scholars. I feed off of their energy and am able to share ideas. I believe any historian who avoids conferences is missing out on a great resource." — *Nancy Dupont, University of Mississippi*

papers on communication history along with papers on other topics. Some are listed at the end of this chapter as an indication of the number and variety of conferences offering outlets for work in communication history. Since dates and locations for most conferences change from year to year, the historian considering submitting a paper should check with the sponsoring organization for details on the conference and competition. Addresses of scholarly, academic, and historical organizations are listed in the *Encyclopedia of Associations* (2016, updated periodically), which can be found in the reference section of most good libraries. Many organizations have websites that provide information on forthcoming conferences.

Three national conferences deal solely with communication history. They are the American Journalism Historians Association, the Joint Journalism and Communication History Conference (sponsored by the AJHA and the AEJMC History Division; held each spring in New York City), and the Symposium on the 19th Century Press, Civil War and Free Expression (held each November in Chattanooga, Tenn.). Since the AJHA's process for accepting papers is typical for others that use a competitive procedure, familiarity with its details will provide the historian with an awareness of such competitions in general. We'll use it for purposes of illustration.

The AJHA holds its annual conventions during the early part of October in different cities each year. The deadline for the paper submission normally is in the spring. Research papers are selected on a competitive basis. Papers submitted to the AJHA should not exceed twenty-five double-spaced pages, not including notes. A paper must be submitted by email, accompanied by a one-page abstract. The text of the email (but not the paper itself) must include the author's name, email address, telephone number, institutional affiliation, and student or faculty status. On the first page of the manuscript, only the paper's title should appear. Omitting the author's name is intended to assure anonymity in the evaluation process so that the name or position of the author does not influence judges' decisions. The AJHA competition requires that papers not be submitted simultaneously to other competitions. That restriction is intended to eliminate the possibility that an author might send the same paper to two competitions at the same time, requiring a duplication of judging effort. You may read the AJHA's

Manuscript Review
AJHA Annual Convention

Instructions to reviewers:
1. Fill in Manuscript Number, Reviewer Number, and Title below.
2. Please review the paper as it was written, not as the paper you would have written.
3. When writing comments in the comments section, please provide constructive suggestions for how the manuscript may be improved. Please identify strengths as well as weaknesses to encourage authors to keep working on the manuscript.
4. In the comments section, please identify strengths as well as weaknesses.

Manuscript No.:   Your Reviewer No.:
Title of Paper:

I. Please indicate your evaluation of the following dimensions of this manuscript:

Importance of the Scholarship to the Discipline and to AJHA members:
Minimal   1   2   3   4   5   6   7   8   Substantial   SCORE:

Methodological Clarity and Rigor:
Minimal   1   2   3   4   5   6   7   8   Substantial   SCORE:

Grounding in Appropriate Literature:
Minimal   1   2   3   4   5   6   7   8   Substantial   SCORE:

Writing Style:
Awkward   1   2   3   4   5   6   7   8   Elegant   SCORE:

II. My recommendation for this manuscript is as follows:
____ Present as submitted.
____ Accept with minor revisions. In your comments to the author (see below), please explain the specific changes that are necessary.
____ Reject.

III. This paper should be considered for:
____ J. William Snorgrass Award for outstanding minority-journalism research paper
____ Maurine Beasley Award for outstanding women's history research paper
____ Honors for top paper in the competition

IV. On a separate page, please provide detailed comments for the author(s). (These comments WILL be shared with the author.)

> "Along with sharing our research, conferences provide us with a forum to establish collaborative relationships with nationally known scholars and to form partnerships with other students and professors." — *Vanessa Murphree, author, The Selling of Civil Rights*

rules at its website at https://ajha.wildapricot.org.

Some conferences vary from these typical procedures. Not all conference papers are accepted on the basis of competition. Some conferences proceed along other lines and simply ask for proposals. On the other hand, some ask for papers long in advance of the conference.

Some principles of the mechanics of preparing a paper for submission apply almost universally. Papers should be typed double-spaced, and the manuscript should be as clean and neat as possible. They should be well researched, themes should be readily apparent, the writing should be readable, and conclusions should flow naturally from the evidence. Details on specific requirements should be obtained from the sponsoring organization.[1]

Three readers "blind" judge each AJHA submission. Blind judging assures that paper evaluators do not know who the authors are. Each judge completes an evaluation form on each paper and gives a brief statement of the basis for the evaluation. (A sample judging form from the AJHA is on the opposite page.) Decisions on papers, along with judges' comments, normally are given to authors approximately two months after the submission deadline.

Among the other conferences that hold competitions specifically for papers in communication history are the national convention of the Association for Education in Journalism and Mass Communication; the Broadcast Education Association; the AJHA Southeast Symposium; the Midwest Journalism History Conference; the AEJMC Southeastern Regional Colloquium in Newspapers, History, and Law; the Society for the History of Authorship, Reading and Publishing; and the Research Society for Victorian Periodicals.

Journal Articles

Outlets for articles on communication history are more numerous than many historians realize. Along with several journals that deal exclusively with communication history, scores of scholarly journals publish articles on the subject.

---

[1] For those few conferences that still accept printed papers, multiple copies normally should be submitted. Papers, unfolded, should be mailed in a large manila envelope. A self-addressed envelope or postcard should be included if the author wants to be assured of being notified that the addressee received the paper.

Among those devoted solely to communication history are *American Journalism, Journalism History, Victorian Periodicals Review, Film & History, Film History, Historical Journal of Film, Radio and Television,* and the online journals *Media History Monographs* and *Historiography in Mass Communication.* Other journals in the various fields of communication — such as the *Journal of Broadcasting and Electronic Media, Journalism and Mass Communication Quarterly, Journal of Advertising, Journal of Communication,* and *Journalism and Mass Communication Monographs* — publish history articles, while numerous historical journals outside those fields publish articles on communication. A list of representative journals that publish studies on communication history is provided at the end of this chapter.

> "Be sure to carefully read the articles in a journal to make sure it's the right place to submit your manuscript. If you're unsure, contact the editor." — Ford Risley, editor, *American Journalism*

Journals vary in their requirements, and authors should familiarize themselves with any journal to which they plan to submit an article. "Journals, even those within the field of media history," explains David Copeland, editor of the online journal *Media History Monographs*, "often have specific guidelines that differ from one publication to another. Knowing the parameters that a journal requires is essential to getting your work published in that journal. If you aren't sure, contact the journal's editor. He or she will be glad to tell you if your research is appropriate for the publication." *American Heritage,* for example, although publishing well-researched articles, attempts to appeal to a popular readership and, as one illustration of its editorial approach, omits footnotes, while *American Journalism* accepts only articles based on well-documented research in primary sources and requires footnotes.

One of the most common problems that editors lament is that authors have not familiarized themselves with the journals to which they submit manuscripts. "I'm amazed at the number of times we get submissions from people who I don't think have ever read the journal," Prof. Ford Risley, the editor of *American Journalism*, told the authors of this book, "— or if they have, they have just ignored what we are about. We get literary studies, manuscripts that are only 4,000-5,000 words, etc. (and sometimes from scholars who should know better). Of course, they are automatically rejected."

In preparing a manuscript, the author should adhere to scholarly standards and neat, professional practices. While some journals have their own rules, stylistic usage normally should adhere to that of a standard guide such as the Uni-

Chapter 10: Presentation and Publication

> "Most journals publish submission guidelines in each issue or on their websites. Make sure you follow those guidelines if you expect your article to be published." — Jim Martin, former editor, *American Journalism*

versity of Chicago Press' *A Manual of Style* or *The MLA Style Sheet* of the Modern Language Association. Some journals require their own, unique stylistic usages and citation formats. Manuscripts prepared specifically for those journals should abide by their guidelines. If the historian has a particular journal in mind, she should consult its style guide early on in the project.

For whatever journal the historian is writing, though, the guiding principle is that manuscripts should be consistent with normal, acceptable scholarly practices. Footnotes, no matter what the format used, should be consistent, providing the information necessary to show the reader clearly the source of the information, so that any reader who should wish to do so can find the source. An essential point to be remembered by the author who might have been trained in the writing style of advertising, broadcasting, journalism, or some other communication field is that historical articles must follow the mechanical requirements of normal English usage and style rather than the peculiar styles of professional fields in communication. No article submitted to a scholarly journal, for example, should use Associated Press style.

Here are some practices that normally should be followed:

• On the title page, include the author's name, mailing address, and email address, along with the study's title. Journals that accept submissions as email attachments usually require that the author information appear in the text of the email and not on a cover page of the manuscript.

• At the beginning of the first content page of the manuscript, only the title should appear, with the author information omitted.

• Type all material double-spaced, including footnotes and legends for illustrations and diagrams. Quotations also should be double-spaced, including long quoted passages. The latter (known as "block quotations") should be set off from the text by indenting them about one-half inch from the left-hand margin. Do not use quotation marks around block quotations.

• Do not hyphenate words at the end of lines.

• Leave margins around the page at least one-inch wide.

• Number pages consecutively, with the title of the study or distinctive word or phrase from the title appearing at the top of each page.

• Type footnotes (endnotes) on a separate page or pages at the end of the manuscript, rather than at the bottom of the content pages. Number them consecutively throughout the manuscript. They should be indicated in the text by Arabic numbers, raised slightly above the line. If the numbers occur at the end of sentences or at any other punctuation point, they are placed outside all marks of punctuation (other than colons and semicolons).

Many academic journals — and virtually all journals underwritten by publishing companies — use an online submission process. *American Journalism*, for example, uses ScholarOne. "The process," explains Prof. Risley, the journal's editor, "while it may seem to be impersonal, ensures that submissions are handled efficiently."

> "While we are accustomed to publishing our research in traditional printed journals, the Internet has made it possible to publish, even in media history, online. Online journals are not constrained by page limits, and you can include numerous visuals and audio with your research, something that is often cost prohibitive or impossible with traditional print journals." — David Copeland, editor, *Media History Monographs* (online journal)

If a journal requires that manuscripts be submitted as print copies, note the following practices:

• Use only a good grade of $8 1/2$ X 11-inch white typing or printing paper. Avoid onion-skin or some other type of erasable paper.

• Print (or type) on only one side of the paper.

• Most journals require multiple copies of the manuscript. Be sure that photocopies are legible.

What happens to a manuscript once its author has mailed it? Although hundreds of journals exist, what goes on in the inner sanctum of a journal's editorial office is, to many authors, mysterious. What historian has not wondered how those forces work that hold seemingly supernatural power over publication decisions? Not all journals operate in the same fashion, but most follow several standard practices. A look at how one journal, *American Journalism*, functions may serve to illustrate the general principles.

For every manuscript, the editor of *American Journalism* chooses three reviewers from its list of about 100 communication historians or from members of the journal's Editorial Board. The selection of reviewers is based on their areas of specialization, assuring that all three reviewers possess expertise in the topic the manuscript covers. Along with a copy of the manuscript (with any clue to authorship removed), each reviewer is asked to judge the manuscript according to five criteria and give a recommendation on whether the manuscript should be published. We've included the reviewing form on page 287. (The jour-

AMERICAN JOURNALISM
Manuscript Criteria

Please consider the following criteria as you review the manuscript and be specific about any revisions you suggest. These comments will be anonymously shared with the author.

A. Argument or Theme:
The purpose of the study is stated clearly. The manuscript is conceptual rather than simply descriptive. The main theme or argument is laid out plainly at the beginning, and a focus on that argument or theme is sustained throughout the manuscript.

B. Importance of the Scholarship to the Field:
The manuscript deepens historical understanding or advances historical knowledge about a significant problem, issue, or set of issues about the past. The author clearly explains the significance of the study and adequately answers the "so what" question.

C. Use of Literature:
The manuscript demonstrates familiarity with relevant scholarship. The author has explained how his/her work fits into the context of existing scholarship. While the manuscript might not have a discrete literature review section, it must cite relevant literature in establishing historical context, theoretical perspective, etc.

D. Evidence and Interpretation:
The author has selected the best available primary and secondary sources and makes appropriate use of them. The manuscript demonstrates a sophisticated level of historical analysis. The manuscript pays attention to historical process, with attention to matters such as cause, change, continuity, and consequence when relevant. The evidence supports the conclusions.

E. Quality of Writing:
The manuscript is well written and organized logically. The argument is clear. The writing successfully blends historical narrative or description with historical analysis. Contents and notes adhere to the style requirements of the *Chicago Manual of Style*, 16th ed.

Recommendation (check one)

___ Accept
___ Minor Revision
___ Major Revision
___ Reject

JOURNALISM HISTORY

Reviewer:

Manuscript No:

Title of Manuscript:

Journalism History seeks well-researched and well-written articles on topics of significance to journalism historians, with journalism defined in its broadest sense. In evaluating this manuscript, please make any comments that you think will help the author and/or editor. You do not have to concern yourself with stylistic and typographical problems unless you think they reflect deeper problems within the manuscript. In assessing the intellectual quality of the manuscript, please pay careful attention to its conceptualization, the research on which it is based, and its overall contribution to the field. Please consider the following.

Significance of Topic: The topic should be more than interesting. It should make a contribution to our knowledge and understanding. A purely descriptive article may be valuable because it breaks new ground, but articles are expected to go beyond descriptive documentation to address *why* things occurred.

Appropriateness for *Journalism History*: The journal cannot be all things to all people. Therefore, does this manuscript fit its mission? A manuscript on how the media covered some topic must ultimately tell something about the media, not just about the subject the media covered.

Quality of Research: The manuscript must be grounded basically in primary sources although secondary sources also may be used. The sources used must be appropriate to the topic, and the information presented in the manuscript must be accurate.

Quality of Conceptualization: Has the author decided what this manuscript is about, organized it accordingly, and supported the focus with appropriate source material? Are the conclusions appropriate to the thrust of it? Are the author's approach and methodology appropriate to the question or questions raised?

Quality of Writing: Flat prose can be edited; muddy, disorganized prose needs rethinking.

RECOMMENDATION

"X" before the selection:

_____ Accept

_____ Reconsider after revision

_____ Do not accept

If you recommended revision, how much is needed? (Type/write an X on the line)

Complete rewrite ———————————————————————— Little or none

Please explain your recommendation on the following pages. and make helpful comments to forward to the author. Please note that a sentence or a paragraph is not considered adequate feedback. If you want to make separate comments to the editor, please feel free to do so.

nal *Journalism History*, on the other hand, uses a more traditional reviewing form. Manuscript reviewers receive a rating sheet covering various aspects of its research, topical significance, and presentation and an open form for the reviewers to make written critiques that will help the author improve the manuscript or that indicate clearly why it was rejected. We've included *Journalism History's* form on page 288.) All reviewers are required to indicate whether they think the manuscript should be accepted, rejected, or returned to the author for revision. A manuscript may be published even if the reviewers do not unanimously recommend acceptance. However, *American Journalism* requires that at least two do so. On the other hand, the editor may require changes in the manuscript or reject it even though all three reviewers recommend it for publication.

Reviewers are encouraged to return their evaluations promptly, but the normal length of time for all three evaluations to be returned and the author notified is eight to twelve weeks. (Authors should be aware, however, that many journals take six months or longer to complete the evaluation process.) When a reviewer is tardy, the editor sends him or her a request for an immediate evaluation. (Some reviewers stick manuscripts in piles of "things to do next week," and not all journal editors energetically encourage reviewers to complete reviews. An author who has not received a decision within a reasonable time should not be reluctant to inquire of an editor about the status of the evaluation process.)

Rarely does *American Journalism* accept a manuscript exactly as first submitted. Manuscripts that are not appropriate for the journal — for example, because the subject is not historical — are automatically rejected. Once a manuscript has gone through the initial evaluation by reviewers, the author normally is asked to revise the manuscript in accordance with their suggestions and to resubmit it. The revised manuscript is then sent back to the same reviewers. Once the reviewers evaluate the revision, the editor evaluates it and then makes a decision on publication. Four decisions can be made: (a) if the manuscript remains clearly inferior, it is rejected, (b) if the revised manuscript, although still unpublishable, has potential for eventual publication, it is sent back to the author for further revision and another resubmission, based on the suggestions of the reviewers and the editor, (c) the manuscript is tentatively accepted, pending satisfactory revision, or (d) the manuscript is accepted with only minor changes required before publication. In all four instances, the editor's comments and those of reviewers are given to authors, with the intent being to make unpublishable manuscripts acceptable for publication upon revision or to improve acceptable manuscripts before publication.

Beginning historians should not be discouraged if a journal rejects a manuscript. One editor of a historical journal commented that he is "absolutely certain that everyone in our discipline who has published work in a journal has also had work rejected by a journal." He also urged authors to take advantage of the attention that reviewers pay to their work. "Referee reports," he advised, "are not judgments handed down from on high — they are collegial input — indicators of how a manuscript can be ... improved to better an author's chances of successful revision and eventual publication."[2]

> "It is amazing how many authors are sent reviewers' comments encouraging them to revise and resubmit their manuscripts to a journal, and they never follow through. A request to resubmit is an invitation to possible success and should never be ignored." — Patrick Washburn, former editor, *Journalism History*

American Journalism accepts about one in four submissions, making its acceptance rate a little lower than average in the field of communication. The normal acceptance rate for most communication journals is about one in three, although it is lower for some and higher for others. Some journals, primarily general historical ones such as the *American Historical Review* and the *Journal of American History*, receive more than 300 manuscripts each year and accept fewer than 10 per cent of submissions. The more demanding journals frequently have multi-tiered reviewing procedures in which a top-echelon editorial board evaluates manuscripts that reviewers have recommended for acceptance. At the other end of the spectrum are a few journals that claim to be refereed but that occasionally accept manuscripts without sending them through their normal evaluation process.

To improve one's chances of publication, beginning historians often are well advised to send their manuscripts to journals that have a regional, topical, or time period focus compatible with the subject of their work.

Book Publishing

Papers and articles can be satisfying, but for many historians they are not enough. Books are the goal. They allow the historian to develop an idea more fully, they normally are more prestigious than articles, and some even make money. But how does one publish a book in communication history?

---

[2]Christopher Tomlins, "Your Name in This Space: The Mysteries of Scholarly Publishing," *Perspectives* (The Newsmagazine of the American Historical Association), May 2002, 34-35. Tomlins was the editor of *Law and History Review*.

Chapter 10: Presentation and Publication

There are no sure-fire schemes for publication, but a number of practices will increase the possibilities. Along with conducting solid historical scholarship — knowledge of the topic, exhaustive research, competent writing — would-be authors should be familiar with various procedures in book publishing. Here is a checklist, but by no means exhaustive encyclopedia, of pertinent points.[3]

- Be knowledgeable about the scholarly field. Is the idea large enough to be made into a book? What other books have been published about the topic? Is the proposed book a significant addition to the field? Would other historians be interested in the book?
- Determine which publishers, if any, might be interested in the book. Which firms have published books on communication history? Study the websites and catalogs of publishers. (Catalogs can be found online.) Before querying the first publisher, compile a list of all potential publishers. Since a number of publishers reject most proposals, knowing that there are others that might be interested can help the author from becoming dejected.
- Consider whether a market exists for the book. The minimum number of potential sales before a publisher will accept a book varies from publisher to publisher, from about 300 to 7,000. Although some historians may feel that pure historical study cannot consider salability, it is incumbent on the would-be author to recognize that most firms are in book publishing as a business. Even non-profit university presses must break even.
- Write a polished, complete, but concise query. It should state clearly the following items: (a) the book's theme, (b) the book's significance, (c) the topics to be covered and special features, (d) the projected word length, (e) the perceived audience (other historians, libraries, university classes, and so forth), (f) competing books and the proposed book's advantages, and (g) the author's credentials (academic position, education, and related publications, for example). Include an annotated topical, chapter outline of the book. While much of the material — the outline, for instance — may be photocopied, the cover letter should be an original.
- Identify a specific editor to contact about your manuscript and write directly to that editor. If an editor cannot be identified by visiting a publisher's website, through a directory such as *Writer's Market*, or by another means, a telephone call or an email to the publishing firm would be in order. Some commer-

---

[3]Authors intending to submit book manuscripts to a university press might wish to consult Elaine Maisner, "Getting Published by a University Press," *Perspectives*, ibid., 28-31. Maisner is executive editor at the University of North Carolina Press.

cial publishers prefer to receive manuscripts from book agents rather than directly from authors. General information about publishers (such as website, email and mailing addresses, and telephone numbers) can be found in several standard sources normally held in the reference division of most libraries. The best known of these sources are *Literary Market Place* and *Writer's Market*, both of which are updated annually. They contain substantial information about literary agents, and the latter includes data from many publishers about the number of books they publish and the percentage of manuscripts they receive through agents or from unagented authors.

• Indicate whether the manuscript can be provided as a digital file. Digital files reduce the publishers' production costs. For some proposals, the form in which the author can provide the manuscript can be a critical factor.

Responses from publishers take many forms. The most common is rejection. Although publishers rarely give a contract on the sole basis of the original query, some do if they are confident that a market for the book exists and that the author has the credentials and track record to assure a quality work. More commonly, publishers with a tentative interest in the proposal ask for sample chapters or the entire manuscript before committing themselves to a contract.

Scholarly Paper Conferences

Listed here are conferences representative of those that include papers on communication history. Details and arrangements may change from year to year, and the historian considering submitting a paper should get the most recent information from the sponsoring organization.

Agricultural History Society
American Antiquarian Society
American Historical Association
American Journalism Historians Association
AJHA Southeast Symposium
American Printing History Association
American Society of Church History
American Studies Association
Association for Education in Journalism and Mass Communication
AEJMC-AJHA Northeast Regional History Conference
AEJMC, Southeast Regional Colloquium
Association for the Study of Afro-American Life and History
Broadcast Education Association
Business History Conference
Duquesne University's History Forum
Economic History Association
Great Lakes History Conference
The Historical Society
International Communication Association
Joint Journalism and Communication History Conference
Mid-America Conference on History
Mid-Continental American Studies Association

Military History Symposium
Missouri Valley History Conference
National Communication Association
New England Historical Association
New York Historical Society Conference
Northern Great Plains History Conference
Ohio Valley History Conference
Oral History Association
Organization of American Historians
Popular Culture Association
Research Society for Victorian Periodicals
Society for Historians of the Early American Republic
Society for the History of Authorship, Reading and Publishing
Society for Military History
Southern Historical Association
Southwest Education Council for Journalism & Mass Communication
Symposium on the 19th Century Press, Civil War and Free Expression
Western History Association

Journals Publishing Articles on Communication History

Following is a partial list of journals intended simply to illustrate some of those that publish articles on communication history. It includes not only journals specializing in communication history, but those also in general history, in various areas of communication study, in regional and state studies, and in related fields. Wm. David Sloan's *American Journalism History: An Annotated Bibliography* (1989) includes approximately 200 publications that have printed articles on the topic. Many journals besides those in the following list also publish occasional articles on communication history. We have included a few state journals as examples, but historians with manuscripts of specific geographic focus should inquire if there are regional journals that would be appropriate for publication. The historian considering submitting a manuscript to any journal should study it to determine requirements. If a particular journal cannot be found in a nearby library, the historian should consult *Magazines for Libraries*, Cheryl LaGuardia and William A. Katz, eds. (26th ed., 2017). It is a standard bibliographic source in most libraries, and it describes the bulk of the history journals currently in publication in this country. For a fuller list of journals covering many other subject areas, the American Historical Association website offers a "Directory of History Journals" with links to their websites. The AHA URL is https://www.historians.org/publications-and-directories/directories.

American Bar Association Journal
American Heritage
American Historical Review
American History
American Jewish History
American Journal of Economics and
Sociology
American Journal of Legal History
American Journalism
American Political Science Review
American Quarterly
American Studies

Annals of the American Academy of
  Political Science
Biography
Business History
Business History Review
California History
Civil War History
Diplomatic History
Ethnohistory
Film & History
Film History
Gender and History
Georgetown Law Journal
Georgia Historical Quarterly
Historian
The Historical Journal
History Today
Historical Journal of Film, Radio and
  Television
Huntington Library Quarterly
Indiana Magazine of History
Journal of Advertising
Journal of African American History
Journal of American Culture
Journal of American Ethnic History
Journal of American History
Journal of American Studies
Journal of Black Studies
Journal of Broadcasting and Electronic
  Media
Journal of Communication
Journal of Communication Inquiry
Journal of Contemporary History
Journal of the Early Republic
Journal of Politics
Journal of Popular Culture
Journal of Southern History
Journal of the Southwest
Journal of the West
Journal of Women's History
Journalism and Mass Communication
  Monographs
Journalism and Mass Communication
  Quarterly
Journalism History
Labor History
Maryland Historical Magazine
Mass Communication & Society
Media History Monographs (electronic)
Michigan Law Journal
Negro History Bulletin
New England Quarterly
New Jersey History
New Mexico Historical Review
New York History
New-York Journal of American History
Newspaper Research Journal
Nineteenth Century Studies
North Carolina Historical Review
Ohio History
Pacific Historical Review
Papers of the Bibliographical Society of
  America
Pennsylvania Magazine of History and
  Biography
Political Quarterly
Politics
Presidential Studies Quarterly
Public Opinion Quarterly
Review of Politics
Rhode Island History
Social Forces
South Atlantic Quarterly
Southwestern Historical Quarterly
Syracuse Law Review
Tennessee Historical Quarterly
Victorian Periodicals Review
Virginia Magazine of History and
  Biography
William and Mary Quarterly
Women's History Review

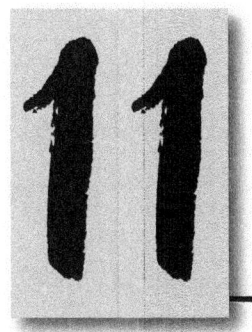

BIBLIOGRAPHY

Historians can find innumerable reference works, research manuals, and other works pertinent to their craft. Because of the volume of work, the following bibliography is necessarily abbreviated. It attempts to point the researcher to only the most useful writings. In instances where works are abundant, a decision has been made to include only recent ones and, with a few exceptions, only those of book length. For guidance in most general matters of historical study and for direction to additional guides and reference works, historians will find Jacques Barzun and Henry F. Graff's *The Modern Researcher* continually useful. Despite its general title, it emphasizes historical research. The works in the following bibliography comprise two broad categories: writings about historical study and research guides useful to the communication historian. The works cited in Chapter 6 of this manual also should be consulted for guidance in these areas.

The Study of History

Adelson, Roger, ed. *Speaking of History: Conversations with Historians*. East Lansing: Michigan State University Press, 1997.

Appleby, Joyce, Lynn Hunt, and Margaret Jacob. *Telling the Truth About History*. New York: W. W. Norton, 1994.

Bonnell, Victoria, and Lynn Hunt, eds., *Beyond the Cultural Turn: New Directions in the Study of Society and Culture*. Berkeley: University of California Press, 1999.

Boris, Eileen, and Nupur Chaudhuri, eds. *Voices of Women Historians: The Per-*

sonal, the Political, the Professional. Bloomington: Indiana University Press, 1999.

Bunzl, Martin. *Real History: Reflections on Historical Practice.* New York: Routledge, 1997.

Butterfield, Herbert. *The Origins of History.* New York: Basic Books, 1981 (reprint).

Carr, David, et al. *The Ethics of History.* Evanston, Ill.: Northwestern University Press, 2004.

Carr, Edward Hallett. *What is History?* 2nd ed., with an introduction by Richard J. Evans. Basingstoke, Hampshire, U.K.: Palgrave, 2001 (reprint, 2017).

Chartier, Roger. *Cultural History: Between Practices and Representations.* Ithaca, N.Y.: Cornell University Press, 1988.

Collingwood, R.G. *The Idea of History*, rev. ed. Mansfield Centre, Conn.: Martino Publishing, 2014.

Davidson, James West, and Mark Hamilton Lytle. *After the Fact: The Art of Historical Detection,* 6th ed. New York: McGraw-Hill, 2010.

Elton, G.R. *The Practice of History,* 2nd ed. Malden, Mass.: Blackwell, 2002.

Evans, Richard J. *In Defense of History.* New York: W. W. Norton, 1999.

Fellman, Susanna, and Marjatta Rahikainen. *Historical Knowledge: In Quest of Theory, Method and Evidence.* Newcastle upon Tyne, U.K.: Cambridge Scholars Pub., 2012.

Gaddis, John Lewis. *The Landscape of History: How Historians Map the Past.* New York: Oxford University Press, 2002.

Gustavson, Carl G. *The Mansion of History.* New York: McGraw-Hill Book Company, 1976.

Hexter, Jack H. *Doing History.* Bloomington: Indiana University Press, 1971.

Hobsbawn, Eric. *On History.* New York: The New Press, 1997.

Hunt, Lynn. *History: Why It Matters.* Boston, Mass.: Polity Press, 2018.

Le Goff, Jacques. *History and Memory.* New York: Columbia University Press, 1992.

Lewis, Bernard. *History Remembered, Recovered, Invented.* New York: Simon & Schuster, 1987 (reprint).

Lukacs, John. *At the End of an Age.* New Haven, Conn.: Yale University Press, 2002.

MacMillan, Margaret. *Dangerous Games: The Uses and Abuses of History.* New York: Random House, 2008; Modern Library Chronicles edition, 2010.

Marwick, Arthur. *The New Nature of History: Knowledge, Evidence, Language.* Chicago: Lyceum, 2001.

Chapter 11: Bibliography

Maza, Sara. *Thinking About History.* Chicago: University of Chicago Press, 2018.

Novick, Peter. *That Noble Dream: The "Objectivity Question" and the American Historical Profession.* Cambridge: Cambridge University Press, 2009 (reprint).

Palmer, Bryan. *Descent into Discourse: The Reification of Language and the Writing of Social History.* Philadelphia: Temple University Press, 1990.

Plumb, J.H. *The Death of the Past,* 2nd ed. New York: Palgrave Macmillan, 2004.

Scott, Joan Wallach. *Gender and the Politics of History*, rev. ed. New York: Columbia University Press, 1999.

Smith, Page. *The Historian and History.* New York: Alfred A. Knopf, 1964.

Stephens, Lester D. *Probing the Past: A Guide to the Study and Teaching of History.* Boston: Allyn & Bacon, 1974.

Thomas, Brook. *The New Historicism and Other Old-Fashioned Topics.* Princeton, N.J.: Princeton University Press, 1991.

Vaughn, Stephen. *The Vital Past: Writings on the Uses of History.* Athens: University of Georgia Press, 1985.

Veeser, H. Aram, ed. *The New Historicism.* New York: Routledge, 1989.

White, Deborah G. *Telling Histories: Black Women Historians in the Ivory Tower.* Chapel Hill: University of North Carolina Press, 2008.

Windschuttle, Keith. *The Killing of History: How a Discipline Is Being Murdered by Literary Critics and Social Theorists.* Paddington, U.K.: Macleay, 1996.

Conducting Historical Research

Aydelotte, William O., Allan G. Bogue, and Robert W. Fogel, eds. *The Dimensions of Quantitative Research in History.* Princeton, N.J.: Princeton University Press, 2016 (reprint).

Barzun, Jacques. *Clio and the Doctors: Psycho-History, Quanto-History & History.* Chicago: University of Chicago Press, 1976.

Barzun, Jacques, and Henry F. Graff. *The Modern Researcher*, 6th ed. Belmont, Calif: Wadsworth Cengage, 2012.

Benson, Lee. *Toward the Scientific Study of History.* Philadelphia: Lippincott, 1972.

Block, Jack. *Understanding Historical Research: A Search for Truth.* Glen Rock, N.J.: Research Publications, 1971.

Brundage, Anthony. *Going to the Sources: A Guide to Historical Research and Writing.* Hoboken, N.J.: John Wiley & Sons, 2018.

Clark, G. Kitson. *The Critical Historian.* New York: Garland, 1985 (reprint).

Danto, Elizabeth Ann. *Historical Research.* New York: Oxford University Press,

2008.

Dollar, Charles M., and Richard J. Jensen. *Historian's Guide to Statistics: Quantitative Analysis and Historical Research.* New York: Holt, Rinehart and Winston, 1971.

Elton, G.R. *Political History: Principles and Practice.* New York: Basic Books, 1970.

Fischer, David Hackett. *Historians' Fallacies: Toward a Logic of Historical Thought.* New York: Harper & Row, 1996 (reprint).

Gottschalk, Louis. *Understanding History: A Primer of Historical Method,* 2nd ed. New York: Alfred A. Knopf, 1969.

Heilig, Christoph, et al. *Historical Methodology.* Tübingen, Germany: Mohr Siebeck, 2016.

Hester, Richard. *Historical Research.* London: ETP, 2018.

Hexter, Jack H. *The History Primer.* New York: Basic Books, 1971.

Howell, Martha, and Walter Prevenier. *From Reliable Sources: An Introduction to Historical Methods.* Ithaca, N.Y.: Cornell University Press, 2001.

Isenberg, Michael T. *Puzzles of the Past: An Introduction to Thinking About History.* College Station: Texas A&M University Press, 1985.

Kammen, Carol. *On Doing Local History.* Lanham, Md.: Rowman & Littlefield, 2014.

Lewis, M. J., and Roger Lloyd-Jones. *Using Computers in History: A Practical Guide.* 2nd ed. London: Routledge, 2004.

McClelland, Peter D. *Causal Explanation and Model Building in History, Economics, and the New Economic History.* Ithaca, N.Y.: Cornell University Press, 1975.

McDowell, Bill. *Historical Research: A Guide for Writers of Dissertations, Theses, Articles and Books.* Hoboken, H.J.: Taylor and Francis, 2013.

Ritchie, Donald A. *Doing Oral History: A Practical Guide*, 3rd ed. Oxford: Oxford University Press, 2015.

Shafer, Robert J., et. al., eds. *A Guide to Historical Method,* 3rd ed. Homewood, Ill.: Dorsey Press, 1980.

Simonton, Dean Keith. *Psychology, Science, and History: An Introduction to Historiometry.* New Haven, Conn.: Yale University Press, 1990.

Stoffle, Carla J., and Simon Carter. *Materials and Methods for History Research*, rev. ed. New York: Libraryworks, 1982.

Taylor, Robert M. Jr., and Ralph J. Crandall, eds. *Generations and Change: Genealogical Perspectives in Social History.* Macon, Ga.: Mercer University Press, 1986.

Thompson, Paul. *The Voice of the Past: Oral History,* 4th ed. New York: Oxford University Press, 2017.

Vansina, Jan. *Oral Tradition: A Study in Historical Methodology.* Trans. H.M. Wright, ebook ed. London: Routledge, Taylor & Francis Group, 2017.

Williams, Michael A. *Researching Local History: The Human Journey.* New York: Routledge, 2015.

Winks, Robin W., ed. *The Historian as Detective: Essays on Evidence.* New York: Harper and Row, 1969.

Communication History Research

Altschull, J. Herbert. "The Journalist and Instant History: An Example of the Jackal Syndrome." *Journalism Quarterly* 50 (1973): 389-96.

Bates, Denise. *Historical Research Using British Newspapers.* Barnsley, England: Pen & Sword History, 2016.

Boyce, D. G. "Public Opinion and Historians." *History, the Journal of the Historical Association* (June 1978): 214-28.

Copeland, David A. "It's Primary: The importance of primary documents in conducting research." *Journalism Studies* 7:3 (2006): 463-66.

Dahl, Folke. "On Quoting Newspapers: A Problem and a Solution." *Journalism Quarterly* 25 (1984): 331-38.

Godfrey, Donald G., ed. *Methods of Historical Analysis in Electronic Media.* Mahwah, N.J.: Lawrence Erlbaum Associates, 2006.

Henry, Susan J. "Private Lives: An Added Dimension for Understanding Journalism History." *Journalism History* 6 (1979): 98-102.

Housman, Robert T. "Journalism Research in Relation to Regional History." *Journalism Quarterly* 13 (1936): 402-06.

Mott, Frank Luther. "Evidence of Reliability in Newspapers and Periodicals in Historical Studies." *Journalism Quarterly* 21 (1944): 304-10.

Rapport, Leonard. "Fakes and Facsimiles: Problems of Identification." *American Antiquarian* 42 (January 1979): 13-58.

Robertson, Craig. *Media History and the Archive.* London: Routledge, 2014.

Salmon, Lucy Maynard. *The Newspaper and the Historian.* New York: Oxford University Press, 1923. (An eBook version is available from Octagon Books.)

Smith, Paul. *The Historian and Film.* Cambridge: Cambridge University Press, 1976.

Taft, William H. *Newspapers as Tools for Historians.* Columbia, Mo.: Lucas Brothers, 1970.

Conducting Historical Research on the Internet

Browne, M. Neil. *History on the Internet 2001: Evaluating Online Sources.* Upper Saddle River, N.J.: Prentice Hall, 2000.

Craver, Kathleen W. *Using Internet Primary Sources To Teach Critical Thinking Skills in History.* Westport, Conn.: Greenwood Press, 1999 (rev. ed. 2005 by Roxanne M. Kent-Drury) .

Donnelly, David F., and Kristina Ross. "The Internet: Historical Media Research on the Virtual Archives." *Historical Journal of Film, Radio & Television* 17:1 (1997): 129-37.

Griffin, Roger A. "Using the Internet as a Resource for Historical Research and Writing" (website). http://www.austincc.edu/history/inres00title.html

Mann, Chris, and Fiona Stewart. *Internet Communication and Qualitative Research: A Handbook for Researching Online.* Thousand Oaks, Calif.: Sage, 2000.

Mindich, David T.Z. "Searching for Journalism History in Cyberspace." *American Journalism* 15:1 (1998): 103-08.

Mindich, David T.Z., Elliot King, Barbara Straus Reed, and David Abrahamson. "The Jhistorian Online." *American Journalism* 14:2 (1997): 209-22.

Ranganathan, Maya. "The Internet and history: An exploration of the transmission of history by political websites." *Journal of South Asian Studies* 29:2 (2006): 279-92.

Reagan, Patrick D. *History and the Internet: A Guide.* Boston: McGraw-Hill, 2002.

Reference and User Services Association. "Using Primary Sources on the Web" (website). http://www.ala.org/rusa/sections/history/resources/primary sources

Rosenzweig, Roy. "The Road to Xanadu: Public and Private Pathways on the History Web." *Journal of American History* 88:2 (2001): 548-79.

Ross, Kristina. "The Uses of History: The Media History Project." *American Journalism* 13:2 (1996): 225-32.

Spencer, David. "History and the Age of Cyberspace." *American Journalism* 15:1 (1998): 109-15.

Trinkle, Dennis A., and Scott A. Merriman. *The History Highway: A 21st Century Guide to Internet Resources*, 4th ed. Armonk, N.Y.: M. E. Sharpe, 2006. (A fee-based digital version by Trinkle, Auchter, and Larson, updated to 2016, is available through ProQuest.)

"User's Guide to the Internet" (U.S. National Archives website). https://www.archives.gov/research/alic/reference/internet-users-guide.html

Communication Research Methods

Beatty, Michael J., James McCroskey, and Kory Floyd. *Biological Dimensions of Communication: Perspectives, Methods, and Research*. Cresskill, N.J.: Hampton Press, 2009.

Brennen, Bonnie. *Qualitative Research Methods for Media Studies*. New York: Routledge, 2017.

Bucy, Erik P., and R. Lance Holbert. *Sourcebook for Political Communication Research: Methods, Measures, and Analytical Techniques*. New York: Routledge 2009. (A 2014 updated eBook version is available.)

Daymon, Christine, and Immy Holloway. *Qualitative Research Methods in Public Relations and Marketing Communications*. New York: Routledge, 2011.

Dochartaigh, Niall Ó. *Internet Research Skills*. London: SAGE, 2012.

Dominick, J. R., and J. E. Fletcher. *Broadcasting Research Methods*. Boston: Allyn & Bacon, 1985.

Fowler, Floyd J. *Survey Research Methods*, 5th ed. Thousand Oaks, Calif.: Sage, 2014.

Hayes, Andrew F., Michael Slater, and Leslie B. Snyder. *The SAGE Sourcebook of Advanced Data Analysis Methods for Communication Research*. Thousand Oaks, Calif.: Sage, 2008.

Jugenheimer, Donald W. *Advertising and Public Relations Research*, 2nd ed. London and New York: Routledge, 2015.

Kenney, Keith. *Visual Communication Research Designs*. New York: Routledge, 2009.

Krippendorff, Klaus. *Content Analysis: An Introduction to Its Methodology*, 4th ed. Thousand Oaks: Sage, 2019.

Parthasarathy, G. K. *Electronic Media and Communication Research Methods*. Delhi, India: GNOSIS, 2006.

Sloan, Luke, and Anabel Quan-Haase. *The SAGE Handbook of Social Media Research Methods*. Los Angeles and London: Sage, 2017.

Stacks, Donald W. *Primer of Public Relations Research*, 3rd ed. New York: Guilford Press, 2017.

Thompson, Paul. *Narrative and Genre: Contexts and Types of Communication*. New York: Routledge, 2017.

Webster, James G., Patricia F. Phalen, and Lawrence W. Lichty. *Ratings Analysis. The Theory and Practice of Audience Research*, 4th ed. New York: Routledge, 2014.

Wrench, Jason S. *Quantitative Research Methods for Communication: A Hands-on*

Approach. New York: Oxford University Press, 2019.

Zhou, Shuhua, and Wm. David Sloan, eds. *Research Methods in Communication*, 3rd ed. Northport, Ala.: Vision Press, 2015.

Research in Related Disciplines

Archer, Steven, and Kevin M. Bartoy. *Between Dirt and Discussion: Methods, Methodology, and Interpretation in Historical Archaeology.* New York: Springer, 2010.

Babbie, Earl. *The Practice of Social Research*, 14th ed. Boston: Cengage, 2016.

Baker, Alan R. H., and Mark Billinge. *Period and Place: Research Methods in Historical Geography.* New York: Cambridge University Press, 2010.

Barker, Chris, and Emma A. Jane. *Cultural Studies: Theory and Practice.* Thousand Oaks, Calif.: Sage, 2016.

Bast, Carol M., and Margie A. Hawkins. *Foundations of Legal Research and Writing*, 4th ed. Clifton Park, N.Y.: Cengage Learning, 2016.

Beins, Bernard C. *Research Methods and Statistics.* New York: Cambridge University Press, 2018.

Berg, Bruce L., and Howard Lune. *Qualitative Research Methods for the Social Sciences.* Harlow, U.K.: Pearson, 2017.

Bernard, H. Russell. *Research Methods in Anthropology: Qualitative and Quantitative Approaches*, 6th ed. Lanham, Md.: Rowman & Littlefield, 2018.

Bowen, Catharine Drinker. *Biography: The Craft and the Calling.* Westport, Conn.: Greenwood Press, 1978 (reprint).

Bradley, James E., and Richard A. Muller. *Church History: An Introduction to Research Methods and Resources.* Grand Rapids, Mich.: Wm. B. Eerdmans, 2016.

Burnett, Roger. *Research Methods in Library and Information Science.* Valley Cottage, N.Y.: Scitus Academics, 2017.

Clifford, Nick, et al. *Key Methods in Geography.* Thousand Oaks, Calif.: Sage, 2016.

Cohen, Louis, Lawrence Manion, and Keith Morrison. *Research Methods in Education.* New York: Routledge, 2018.

Cohen, Morris, and Kent C. Olson. *Legal Research in a Nutshell,* 12th ed. St. Paul, Minn.: West Publishing Co., 2016.

Coolican, Hugh. *Research Methods and Statistics in Psychology.* London and New York: Psychology Press, 2014.

da Sousa Correa, Delia, and W. R. Owens. *The Handbook to Literary Research*, 2nd ed. London: Routledge, 2009.

Chapter 11: Bibliography

Dean, Mitchell. *Critical and Effective Histories: Foucault's Methods and Historical Sociology.* New York and London: Routledge, 2016.

Denzin, Norman K., and Yvonna S. Lincoln. *The Sage Handbook of Qualitative Research*, 5th ed. Los Angeles: Sage, 2018.

East, W. Gordon. *The Geography Behind History*, rev. ed. New York: W.W. Norton, 1999.

Elias, Stephen. *Legal Research: How to Find and Understand the Law*, 18th ed. Berkeley, Calif.: Nolo, 2018.

Eller, Jack David. *Social Science and Historical Perspectives: Society, Science, and Ways of Knowing.* London: Routledge 2017.

Fitzgerald, Maureen F., and Susan Barker. *Legal Problem Solving: Analysis, Research and Writing*, 7th ed. Toronto, Ontario: LexisNexis, 2016.

Fong, Timothy P. *Ethnic Studies Research: Approaches and Perspectives.* Lanham, Md.: AltaMira Press, 2008.

Fowler, Floyd J. *Survey Research Methods.* Los Angeles: Sage, 2014.

Gergen, Kenneth J., and Mary M. Gergen, eds. *Historical Social Psychology.* Hillsdale, N.J.: Lawrence Erlbaum Associates, 1984. (A 2014 eBook version is available.)

Hall, John A., and Joseph M. Bryant. *Historical Methods in the Social Sciences.* London: Sage, 2005.

Hay, Iain. *Qualitative Research Methods in Human Geography*, 4th ed. Don Mills, Ontario, Canada: Oxford University Press, 2016.

Holt-Jensen, Arild. *Geography: Its History and Concepts*, 3rd ed. London: Sage, 2006. (A 2018 eBook version is available.)

Johnson, Janet Buttolph, and Henry T. Reynolds. *Political Science Research Methods*, 6th ed. Washington, D. C.: CQ Press, 2016.

Jucker, Andreas H., and Irma Taavitsainen. *English Historical Pragmatics.* Edinburgh, Scotland: Edinburgh University Press, 2013.

Kee, Howard Clark. *Miracle in the Early Christian World: A Study in Sociohistorical Method.* New Haven, Conn.: Yale University Press, 1983.

Langness, L. L., and Gelya Frank. *Lives: An Anthropological Approach to Biography* (7th printing). Novato, Calif.: Chandler & Sharp, 2001.

Mahoney, James, and Dietrich Rueschemeyer. *Comparative Historical Analysis in the Social Sciences.* Cambridge, U.K.: Cambridge University Press, 2014.

Marshall, Catherine, and Gretchen B. Rossman. *Designing Qualitative Research.* Los Angeles: SAGE, 2016.

Maas, Harro. *Economic Methodology: An Historical Introduction.* New York: Rout-

ledge, 2014.
McCollum, Jonathan, and David G. Hebert. *Theory and Method in Historical Ethnomusicology.* Lanham, Md.: Lexington Books, 2014.
Miller, Robert L. *Biographical Research Methods.* Thousand Oaks, Calif.: Sage, 2005.
Nestor, Paul, and Russell K. Schutt. *Research Methods in Psychology: Investigating Human Behavior,* 3rd ed. Los Angeles: Sage Publications, 2019.
Nicholas, R. M., and A. E. Standley. *Basic Bibliography Book: A Brief Guide to Compiling Bibliographies.* Kings Ripton, Cambridgeshire, England: Elm, 1984.
Nola, Robert, and Howard Sankey. *Theories of Scientific Method: An Introduction.* Hoboken, N.J.: Taylor and Francis, 2014.
Northey, Margot, et al. *Making Sense in Religious Studies: A Student's Guide to Research and Writing.* Don Mills, Ontario, Canada: Oxford University Press, 2015.
Parke, Catherine Neal. *Biography: Writing Lives.* New York: Routledge, 2002.
Patten, Mildred L., and Randall R. Bruce. *Understanding Research Methods: An Overview of Essentials.* 10th ed. New York: Routledge, 2018.
Pelto, Pertti J. *Mixed Methods in Ethnographic Research: Historical Perspectives.* New York and London: Routledge 2017.
Pitt, David C. *Using Historical Sources in Anthropology and Sociology.* New York: Holt, Rinehart and Winston, 1983.
Powell, Jason L. *From Historical Social Theory to Foucault.* Hauppauge, N.Y.: Nova Science Publishers, Inc., 2013.
Putman, William H., et al. *Legal Research.* Boston: Cengage Learning, 2016.
Ramsey, Alexis E. *Working in the Archives: Practical Research Methods for Rhetoric and Composition.* Carbondale: Southern Illinois University Press, 2010.
Reynolds, Amy, and Brooke Barnett, eds. *Communication and Law: Multidisciplinary Approaches to Research.* Mahwah, N.J.: Lawrence Erlbaum Associates, 2006.
Rose, Gerry. *Deciphering Sociological Research.* Beverly Hills, Calif: Sage, 1983.
Samuels, Warren J., ed. *The Craft of the Historian of Economic Thought.* Greenwich, Conn.: JAI Press, 1983.
Sanders, Chauncey. *An Introduction to Research in English Literary History.* New York: Macmillan, 1952.
Sharrock, Wes. *Ethnomethodology.* Los Angeles: Sage Publications, 2012.
Simonsen, Craig B., and Christian R. Andersen. *Computer-aided Legal Research (CALR) on the Internet.* Upper Saddle River, N.J.: Pearson/Prentice Hall, 2006.
Snooks, G. D. *Historical Analysis in Economics.* London: Routledge, 2014.

Spencer, Steve. *Visual Research Methods*. London: Routledge, 2010.
Stausberg, Michael, and Steven Engler. *The Routledge Handbook of Research Methods in the Study of Religion*. London and New York: Routledge, 2014.
Tilly, Charles. *As Sociology Meets History*. New York: Academic Press, 1981.
Watkins Dawn Elizabeth, and Mandy Burton. *Research Methods in Law*. New York: Routledge, 2018.
Wilson, Janie H., and Shauna W. Joye. *Research Methods and Statistics: An Integrated Approach*. Los Angeles: Sage, 2017.
Wilson, John F., and Thomas P. Slavens. *Research Guide to Religious Studies*. Chicago: American Library Association, 1982.

Approaches to History

Barker, John. *The Superhistorians: Makers of Our Past*. New York: Charles Scribner's Sons, 1982.
Barreyre, Nicolas, et al. *Historians Across Borders: Writing American History in a Global Age*. Berkeley: University of California Press, 2014.
Bartlett, Kenneth R. *The Experience of History*. Malden, Mass: Wiley-Blackwell, 2017.
Billington, Ray Allen, comp. *Allan Nevins on History*. New York: Scribner, 1975.
Boldt, Andreas Dieter. *Historical Mechanisms: An Experimental Approach to Applying Scientific Theories to the Study of History*. New York: Routledge, 2017.
Burckhardt, Jacob. *Judgments on History and Historians*. New York: Routledge, 2007 (reprint). (A 2012 eBook version is available.)
Burke, Peter, ed. *New Perspectives on Historical Writing*, 2nd ed. University Park: Pennsylvania State University, 2011 (reprint).
Burns, R. M. *Historiography: Critical Concepts in Historical Studies*, 5 vols. London: Routledge, 2011.
Butterfield, Herbert. *Writings on Christianity and History*. New York: Oxford University Press, 1979 (reprint).
Butterfield, Herbert. *Man on His Past: The Study of the History of Historical Scholarship*. Boston: Beacon Press, 1960 (reprint).
Butterfield, Herbert. *The Whig Interpretation of History*. New York: Norton, 1965 (reprint).
Carter, Shannon, et al. *History and Theory*. New York: Facts on File, 2012.
Cheng, Eileen K. *Historiography: An Introductory Guide*. London: Continuum, 2012.
Collingwood, R. G., et al. *The Principles of History and Other Writings in Phi-

losophy of History. Oxford: Oxford University Press, 2003.

Commager, Henry Steele. *The Search for a Usable Past.* New York: Alfred A. Knopf, 1967.

Conkin, Paul K., and John Higham, eds. *New Directions in American Intellectual History.* Baltimore: Johns Hopkins University Press, 1991 (reprint).

Couvares, Francis G. *Interpretations of American History: Patterns and Perspectives*, 8th ed. Boston: Bedford/St. Martins, 2009.

Cronin, Joseph. *Foucault's Antihumanist Historiography.* Lewiston, N.Y.: E. Mellen Press, 2001.

Cunliffe, Marcus, and Robin Winks. *Pastmasters: Some Essays on American Historians.* New York: Harper and Row, 1969.

Degler, Carl N. *Pivotal Interpretations of American History.* New York: Harper & Row, 1966.

Donovan, Timothy Paul. *Historical Thought in America: Postwar Patterns.* Norman: University of Oklahoma Press, 1973.

Elton, G. R. *Return to Essentials: Some Reflections on the Present State of Historical Study.* New York: Cambridge University Press, 2002 (reprint).

Fogel, Robert William, and G. R. Elton. *Which Road to the Past? Two Views of History.* New Haven: Yale University Press, 1983.

Gay, Peter. *A Loss of Mastery: Puritan Historians in Colonial America.* Berkeley: University of California Press, 1966.

Grob, Gerald N., and George Athan Billias. *Interpretations of American History: Patterns and Perspectives*, 6th ed. 2 vols. New York: Free Press, 2010. (A 2014 eBook version is available.)

Guinsburg, Thomas N. *The Dimensions of History: Readings on the Nature of History and the Problems of Historical Interpretation.* Chicago: Rand McNally, 1971.

Harlan, David. *The Degradation of American History.* Chicago: University of Chicago Press, 1997. (A 2009 eBook version is available.)

Hexter, Jack H. *On Historians: Reappraisals of Some of the Makers of Modern History.* Cambridge, Mass.: Harvard University Press, 1979.

Higham, John. *The Reconstruction of American History.* London: Hutchinson University Press, 1963.

Higham, John. *Writing American History: Essays on Modern Scholarship.* Bloomington: University of Indiana Press, 1970.

Hoffer, Peter Charles. *The Historians' Paradox: The Study of History in Our Time.* York: New York University Press, 2010.

Hofstadter, Richard. *The Progressive Historians: Turner, Beard, Parrington.* New

Chapter 11: Bibliography

New York: Alfred A. Knopf, 1968. (A 2012 eBook version is available.)

Hughes, H. Stuart. *History As Art and As Science.* New York: Garland, 1985 (reprint).

Iggers, Georg G. *Historiography in the Twentieth Century: From Scientific Objectivity to the Postmodern Challenge.* Middletown, Conn.: Wesleyan University Press, 2012.

Jameson, J. Franklin. *The History of Historical Writing in America.* Whitefish, Mont.: Kessinger Pub., 2011.

Kozicki, Henry, ed. *Developments in Modern Historiography.* London: Palgrave Macmillan, 2014.

Kraus, Michael, and Davis D. Joyce. *The Writing of American History*, rev. ed. Norman: University of Oklahoma Press, 1990.

Levin, David. *History as Romantic Art: Bancroft, Prescott, Motley, and Parkman.* Stanford, Calif.: Stanford University Press, 1959.

Levine, Lawrence W. *The Unpredictable Past: Explorations in American Cultural History.* New York: Oxford University Press, 1993.

Lowery, Zoe. *Historiography.* New York: Britannica Educational Publishing, 2016.

Nevins, Allan. *The Gateway to History*, rev. ed. Garden City, N.Y.: Anchor Books, 1962. (A 2016 eBook version is available.)

Patrides, C. A. *The Grand Design of God: The Literary Form of the Christian View of History.* London: Routledge and Kegan Paul, 1972. (A 2016 eBook version is available.)

Powicke, F. M. *Modern Historians and the Study of History: Essays and Papers.* Westport, Conn.: Greenwood Press, 1976.

Rabasa, Jose, et al. *The Oxford History of Historical Writing*, 5 vols. Oxford, U.K.: Oxford University Press, 2018.

Seligman, Edwin R. *The Economic Interpretation of History*, 2nd ed., rev. New York: Columbia University Press, 1970.

Skotheim, Robert Allen, ed. *The Historian and the Climate of Opinion.* Reading, Mass.: Addison-Wesley, 1969; London: Routledge, 2018 (reprint).

Startt, James D. "The Historiographical Tradition in 20th-Century America." *American Journalism* 15 (1999): 105-31.

Stern, Fritz, ed. *The Varieties of History: From Voltaire to the Present.* New York: Random House, 1973.

Stone, Lawrence. *The Past and the Present Revisited.* Boston: Routledge & Kegan Paul, 1987. (A 2005 eBook version is available.)

Thompson, James W., and Bernard J. Holm. *A History of Historical Writing*, 2 vols.

Gloucester, Mass.: Peter Smith, 1967.

Tillinghast, Pardon E. *The Specious Past: Historians and Others.* Reading, Mass.: Addison-Wesley, 1972.

Tosh, John. *Historians on History: Readings*, 3rd ed. New York: Routledge, 2018.

Tosh, John, with Sean Lang. *The Pursuit of History*, 4th ed. Harlow, England: Pearson Education Limited, 2006. (A 2015 eBook version is available.)

Trevelyan, George Macaulay. *Clio, A Muse and Other Essays.* Folcroft, Pa.: Folcroft, 1973. (A 2011 eBook version is available.)

Vaughan, Alden T., and George A. Billias. *Perspectives on Early American History: Essays in Honor of Richard B. Morris.* New York: Harper and Row, 1973.

Von Mises, Ludwig. *Theory and History.* New Haven, Conn.: Yale University Press, 1957.

Wagner, Anthony. *Pedigree and Progress: Essays in the Genealogical Interpretation of History.* Chichester: Phillimore, 1976.

Walsh, William H. *An Introduction to Philosophy of History*, rev. ed. Atlantic Highlands, N.J.: Humanities Press, 1976.

Wells, Ronald. *History and the Christian Historian.* Grand Rapids, Mich.: W.B. Eerdmans Pub. Co., 1998.

Wilson, Norman James. *History in Crisis?: Recent Directions in Historiography.* Boston: Pearson, 2014.

Wise, Gene. *American Historical Explanations*, 2nd ed., rev. Minneapolis: University of Minnesota Press, 1980.

Wish, Harvey. *American Historians.* New York: Oxford University Press, 1962.

Zammeto, John H. "Are We Being Theoretical Yet? The New Historicism, the New Philosophy of History, and Practicing Historians." *Journal of Modern History* 65 (1993): 783-814.

Approaches to Communication History

Comment: Writing on perspectives and interpretations in communication history has increased dramatically in the last forty years, although the only book-length work remains Wm. David Sloan's *Perspectives on Mass Communication History* (1991). It analyzes the various interpretive schools and their explanations of the major periods and topics related to mass communication in the United States. The student should be aware of the following articles and book chapters while recognizing that some are based primarily on the historian's intuition rather than on substantive research.

Arceneaux, Noah. "Reflections on Radio History, Preservation, and Relevance." *American Journalism* 33:3 (2016): 340-7.

Atwood, Roy. "New Directions for Journalism Historiography." *Journal of Communication Inquiry* 4:1 (1978): 3-14.

Beasley, Maurine. "A Conversation with Sidney Kobre." *Journalism History* 1 (1981): 18-24.

Carey, James. "The Problem of Journalism History." *Journalism History* 1 (1974): 3-5, 27.

Cloud, Barbara. "The Variety of Journalism History: 26 Years of Scholarship." *Journalism History* 26 (Winter 2000-01): 141-6.

"A Conversation with Alfred McClung Lee. " *Journalism History* 4 (1977): 2-7.

"A Conversation with Edwin Emery." *Journalism History* 7 (1980): 20-23.

"A Conversation with Harold L. Nelson." *Journalism History* 6 (1979): 66-69.

Conway, Michael. "The Ghost of Television News in Media History Scholarship." *American Journalism* 34:2 (2017).

Covert, Catherine L. "Journalism History and Women's Experience: A Problem in Conceptual Change." *Journalism History* 8 (1981): 2-6.

Daly, Chris. "The Historiography of Journalism History." *American Journalism* 26:1 (2009).

Dicken-Garcia, Hazel. "'What a Buzzel is This ... about Kentuck?' New Approaches and an Application." *Journalism History* 3 (1976): 11-15, 19.

Ekstrand, Victoria Smith. "The Presentist Media Landscape and the Practice of Doing History." *American Journalism* 30:3 (2013): 441-9.

Emery, Michael. "A Conversation with Robert W. Desmond." *Journalism History* 11 (1984): 11-17.

Feldstein, Mark. "The Journalistic Biography: Methodology, Analysis and Writing." *Journalism Studies* 7:3 (2006): 469-88.

Gleason, Timothy W. "Historians and Freedom of the Press Since 1800." *American Journalism* 5:4 (1988): 230-47.

Historiography in Mass Communication (online journal). http://history-jmc.com

Huntzicker, William. "Historians and the American Frontier Press." *American Journalism* 5 (1988): 28-47.

Hynes, Terry. "A Conversation with Leonard Levy." *Journalism History* 7 (1980): 96-103.

"An Interview with James Startt." *American Journalism* 39:4 (2012): 129-36.

"An Interview with Maurine Beasley." Conducted by Ford Risley and Reed Smith. *American Journalism* 25:4 (2008): 102-15.

"An Interview with Michael Murray." Conducted by Reed Smith. *American Jour-*

nalism 27:3 (2010): 158-73.

"An Interview with Patrick Washburn." Conducted by Reed Smith. *American Journalism* 26:3 (2009): 128-40.

"An Interview with Wm. David Sloan." Conducted by Ford Risley and Reed Smith. *American Journalism* 25:1 (2008): 125-35.

Kitch, Carolyn. "Rethinking Objectivity in Journalism and History: What Can We Learn from Feminist Theory and Practice?" *American Journalism* 16:2 (1999): 113-20.

Kobre, Sidney. "The Sociological Approach in Journalism History." *Journalism Quarterly* 22 (1945): 12-22.

McKerns, Joseph P. "The Limits of Progressive History." *Journalism History* 4 (1977): 88-92.

Mitchell, Catherine C. "The Place of Biography in the History of News Women." *American Journalism* 7:1 (1990): 23-32.

Nevins, Allan. "American Journalism and Its Historical Treatment." *Journalism Quarterly* 36 (1959): 411-22.

Nord, David Paul. "Intellectual History, Social History, Cultural History, and Our History." *Journalism Quarterly* 67 (1990): 645-48.

Olasky, Marvin. "Journalism Historians and Religion." *American Journalism* 6:1 (1989): 41-53.

Palmegiano, Eugenia. "Re-Constructing Media History." *American Journalism* 22:1 (2005): 133-36.

Park, Robert E. "The Natural History of the Newspaper," pp. 80-98 in Park, Ernest W. Burgess, and Robert D. McKenzie, *The City*. Chicago: University of Chicago Press, 1925.

Roessner, Amber, et al. "A Measure of Theory?: Considering the Role of Theory in Media History." *American Journalism* 30:2 (2013): 260–78.

Schwarzlose, Richard A. "A Conversation with Frederick S. Siebert." *Journalism History* 5 (1978): 106-09, 123.

Schwoch, James. "Origins, Paradigms, and Topographies: Methodological Considerations Regarding Area Studies and Broadcast Histories." *American Journalism* 9:3-4 (1992): 111-30.

Sloan, Wm. David. "Examining the 'Dark Ages' Concept: The Federalist-Republican Press as a Model." *Journal of Communication Inquiry* 7 (1982): 105-19.

Sloan, Wm. David. "Historians and the American Press, 1900-1945: Working Profession or Big Business?" *American Journalism* 3 (1986): 150-62.

Sloan, Wm. David. "Introduction." 1-9 in *American Journalism History: An Annotated Bibliography*, Wm. David Sloan, comp. Westport, Conn.: Greenwood

Press, 1989.
Sloan, Wm. David. "The Historians." 59-116 in *Makers of the Media Mind*, Wm. David Sloan, ed. Hillsdale, N.J.: Lawrence Erlbaum Associates, 1990.
Sloan, Wm. David. *Perspectives on Mass Communication History*. Hillsdale, N.J.: Lawrence Erlbaum Associates, 1991.
Sloan, Wm. David. "Why Study Media History?" *American Journalism* 10:3-4 (1993): 6-10.
Sloan, Wm. David, and Thomas A. Schwartz. "Historians and Freedom of the Press, 1690-1801: Libertarian or Limited?" *American Journalism* 5 (1988): 159-78.
Small, Melvin, ed. *Public Opinion and Historians: Interdisciplinary Perspectives*. Detroit: Wayne State University Press, 1970.
Smith, Carol, and Carolyn Stewart Dyer. "Taking Stock, Placing Orders: A Historiographic Essay on the Business History of the Newspaper." *Journalism Monographs* 132 (April 1992).
Spencer, David R. "To Theorize or Not To Theorize." *American Journalism* 22:1 (2005): 141-45.
Startt, James. "Historiography and the Media Historian." *American Journalism* 10:3-4 (1993): 17-25.
Steiner, Linda, Michael Robertson, Thomas Connery, and Rodger Streitmatter. "Sex, Lies, and Autobiography: Contributions of Life Study to Journalism History." *American Journalism* 13:2 (1996): 206-24.
Sterling, Christopher H. "Erik Barnouw (1908–2001): Broadcasting's Premier Historian." *Journal of Broadcasting & Electronic Media* 49:3 (2005): 354-61.
Sterling, Christopher H., and Michael C. Keith, "Where Have All the Historians Gone? A Challenge to Researchers." *Journal of Broadcasting & Electronic Media* 50:2 (2006): 345-57.
Stevens, John D., and Hazel Dicken Garcia. *Communication History*. Beverly Hills, Calif.: Sage, 1980.
Sweeney, Michael S. "Everyman His Own Historian — Not! A Defense of Our Profession — And a Plea for Its Future." *American Journalism* 23:1 (2006): 143-48.

Writing and Forms

American Psychological Association. *Publication Manual of the American Psychological Association*, 6th ed. Washington, D.C.: American Psychological Association, 2017 (reprint).
Barzun, Jacques. *Simple and Direct: A Rhetoric for Writers*, rev. ed. New York:

Quill, 2001.

Canary, Robert H., and Henry Kozicki, eds. *The Writing of History: Literary Form and Historical Understanding*. Madison: University of Wisconsin Press, 1978.

Carpenter, Ronald H. *History as Rhetoric: Style, Narrative, and Persuasion*. Columbia: University of South Carolina Press, 1995.

The Chicago Manual of Style, 17th ed. Chicago: University of Chicago Press, 2017.

Curthoys, Ann, and Ann McGrath. *How To Write History That People Want To Read*, 2nd ed. New York: Palgrave Macmillan, 2011.

Follett, Wilson, and Erik Wensberg. *Modern American Usage*, rev. ed. New York: Hill and Wang, 1998.

Prince, Mary Miles. *The Bluebook: A Uniform System of Citation*, 20th ed. Cambridge, Mass.: Harvard Law Review Association, 2016.

Lottinville, Savoie. *The Rhetoric of History*, rev. ed. Norman: University of Oklahoma Press, 1990.

Modern Language Association of America. *The MLA Style Manual and Guide to Scholarly Publishing*, 3rd ed. New York: MLA, 2008.

Rampolla, Mary Lynn. *A Pocket Guide to Writing in History*, 9th ed. New York: Bedford/St. Martin's, 2018.

Strunk, William, and E.B. White. *The Elements of Style*, 4th ed. New York: Longman, 1999.

Turabian, Kate L., et. al. *A Manual for Writers of Term Papers, Theses, and Dissertations*, 9th ed. Chicago: University of Chicago Press, 2018.

INDEX

Abajian, James de T., 170
ABI/INFORM Complete, 228
Abolition, 227
Abolition and the Press, 237
Abrahamson, David, 300
Abrams, Alan, 180
Abstracts in Anthropology, 166
Abstracts of Popular CultureBook Review Digest, 166
Abstracts of secondary literature, 232
Academic Index, 161
Academic Libraries and Other Repositories, 180
Access: The Supplementary Index to Periodicals, 158
Access to Archival Databases, 226
Accessible Archives, 204, 218
Accessible Archives — Magazines and Newspapers, 215-6
Accuracy, 53-4, 140
Ad Flip, 221
Ad*Access. Covers 1911-1955, 220
Additions and Corrections to History and Bibliography of American Newspapers, 1690-1820, 156
Adelson, Roger, 295
Advertisements, 170
Advertising Age, 185
Advertising and Public Relations Research, 301
Advertising Archives, 221
Advertising online sources, 220-2
AdViews: A Digital Archive of Vintage Television Commercials, 220
AEJMC-AJHA Northeast Regional History Conference, 292
African American Films Through 1959: A Comprehensive Illustrated Filmography, 161
African-American Newspapers, 1827-1998, 218
African-American newspapers and periodicals, 169-70, 171, 172
African-American Newspapers and Periodicals: A National Bibliography, 154
African-American newspapers online, 207

African-American periodicals, 224
African-American Periodicals, 1825-1995, 218
African American Odyssey, 225
African-American studies, 227
African Americans, 48-9, 160, 210, 211
African Recorder: A Fortnightly Record of African Events with Index, 167
Afro-Americana Imprints, 1535-1922, 218
After Slavery Project, 229
After The Fact: The Art of Historical Detection, 250n, 296
Age of Reform, The, 67, 108
Agenda setting, 251
Agricultural History Society, 292
Agricultural Newspapers, 217
Alaska newspapers, 169
Albaugh, Gaylord, 156
Allan Nevins On History, 255n, 305
Almanac sources online, 99
Alphabetical Index to the Titles in "American Newspapers 1821-1936, a union list," 169
Alternative Press Index, 158
Altschull, J. Herbert, 299
Alvarez, Max Joseph, 163
America: A Narrative History, 84
America and World War I. American Military Camp Newspapers, 216
America: History and Life, 158, 166, 167, 204, 231
America on Film and Tape: A Topical Catalog of Audiovisual Resources for the Study of United States History, Society and Culture, 161
America Votes: A Handbook of Contemporary American Election Statistics, 168
America's Chronicles SM, 196
America's Historical Government Publications, 218
America's Historical Imprints, 218
America's Historical Newspapers, 217-8
America's House of Lords, 37
American Antiquarian Society, 181, 183, 202, 203,

313

208, 213, 292
Historical Periodicals Collection, 216
American Autobiography, 1945-1980: A Bibliography, 154
American Bar Association Journal, 293
American Bibliography: A Chronological Dictionary of All Books, Pamphlets and Periodicals Printed in the United States of America (1639-1800), 183
American Broadsides and Ephemera (1749-1900), 218
American Civil War Era Newspapers, 218
American Diaries: An Annotated Bibliography of American Diaries Prior to the Year 1861, 154
American Diaries: An Annotated Bibliography of Published Diaries and Journals, 154
American Diaries in Manuscript, 1580-1954: A Descriptive Bibliography, 154
American Film: An A-Z Guide, 161
American Film Institute Catalog of Motion Pictures Produced in the United States, 161
American Film Institute Catalog of Motion Pictures Produced in the United States: Ethnicity in American Feature Films, 1911-1960, 161
American Film Institute Catalog of Motion Pictures Produced in the United States: Feature Films, 161
American Film Institute Catalog of Motion Pictures Produced in the United States: Film Beginnings, 1893-1910, 161
American Heritage, 284, 293
American Historians, 308
American Historical Association, 12, 292, 293
American Historical Association's Guide to Historical Literature, 153
American Historical Explanations, 308
American Historical Review, 152, 290, 293
American History (journal), 293
American History: A Bibliographic Review, 152
American History Bibliography (Books, Articles and Dissertations), 158
American History Highway, The: A Guide to Internet Resources on U.S., Canadian, and Latin American History, 207n
American history, primary documents online, 225-8
American Humanities Index, 158
American Indian and Alaska Native Newspapers and Periodicals 1971-1985, 169
"American Indians and the Media: Neglect and Stereotype," 48n
American Indian Periodicals from the Princeton University Library: Guide to the Microfilm Collection, 169
American Jewish History, 155, 293
American Jewish Newspapers, 218
"American Jewish Press, *1823-1983*, The; A Bibliographic Survey of Research and Study," 154-5
American Journal of Economics and Sociology, 293
American Journal of Legal History, 293
American Journalism (journal), 152, 155, 230, 284, 286-7, 289, 290, 293
American Journalism: A History of Newspapers in the United States Through 150 Years: 1690 to 1940, 33-4, 108

"American Journalism and Its Historical Treatment," 51n, 129n, 310
American Journalism Historians Association, 176, 230, 281-3, 292
Southeast Symposium, 281, 292
American Journalism History: An Annotated Bibliography, 94, 155, 293, 310
American Journalism Review online, 208
American Life Histories: Manuscripts from the Federal Writers' Project, 1936 to 1940, 132, 225, 226
American Literary Journalists, 1945-1995, 95
American Literary Manuscripts: A Checklist of Holdings in Academic, Historical, and Public Libraries, Museums, and Authors' Homes in the United States, 175
American Magazine Journalists, 95
American Memory, 199-200
American National Biography, 94
American National Biography Online, 232
American Newspaper Journalists, 95
American Newspaper Publishers' Association Foundation, 150
American Newspapers, 1821-1936: A Union List of Files Available in the United States and Canada, 156, 169
American Newspapers, 1821-1936. An Alphabetical Index to the Titles, 169
American Newsreel, The: A Complete History, 1911-1967, 143
American Pamphlets, 1820-1922, 218
American Periodicals, 155
American Periodicals, 1741-1900; an Index to the Microfilm Collections, 169, 183
"American Periodicals: A Selected Checklist of Scholarship and Criticism, *1985-1991*," 155
American Periodicals Series, 216
American Political Science Review, 293
American Popular Culture: A Guide to Information Sources, 157
American Printing History Association, 292
American Psychological Association, 311
American Quarterly, 293
American Society for Legal History, 209
American Society of Church History, 292
American Statistics Index, 167
American studies, 227
American Studies, 293, 294
American Studies Association, 292
American Underworld: The Flash Press, 218
American Women: A Gateway to Library of Congress Resources for the Study of Women's History and Culture in the United States, 225
Ames, John Griffith, 174
Ancestry.com, 230
Andersen, Christian, 304
Anderson, Benedict, 64
Anderson, Elizabeth, 177
Andrews, Charles McLean, 176
Andrews, Linton, 8n, 22
Andriot, John, 174
Annals of American History Online, 227
Annals of the American Academy of Political Science,

Chapter 12: Index

294
Annotated Journalism Bibliography 1958-1968, 155
"Annotated Statistical Abstract of Communications Media in the United States," 168
Annual Index, 158
Annual Register (1758-78), 216
"Annual Review of Work in Newspaper and Periodical History 1996-1998," 155
Antebellum Black Newspapers: Indices to New York Freedom's Journal (1827-1829), The Rights of All (1829), The Weekly Advocate (1837), and The Colored American (1837-1841), 169-170
Anthologies of journalism, 184
Anthropology, 64
Antislavery Newspapers and Periodicals: Annotated Index of Letters, 170
AP Images Collection, 223
Appleby, Joyce, 14n, 76n, 77n, 78n, 254n, 295
Applied Science & Business Periodicals Retrospective: 1913-1983, 220
Aptheker, Herbert, 16
Arab Americans, 210
Arceneaux, Noah, 309
Archer, Steven, 302
Architectural Digest, 219
Archival and Manuscript Sources, guides to, 175-7
Archival databases, 207
Archival directories, 207
Archival Resources in Wisconsin, 213
Archive Finder, 212
ArchiveGrid, 212
Archives
  definition of, 147-9
  library, 148-9
  preparations for research in, 100-1
Archives, libraries and historical societies (U.S.), 176
Archives Unbound, 227
"Are We Being Theoretical Yet? The New Historicism, the New Philosophy of History, and Practicing Historians," 308
Arkansas Union List of Newspapers, 170
Arksey, Laura, 154
Armstrong, Richard, 162
Arndt, Karl John Richard, 156
Art Directors in Cinema: A Worldwide Biographical Dictionary, 161
Article Abstracts and Citations, 158
ArticleFirst, 233
Arts and Crafts in New York: Advertisements and News Items from New York City Newspapers, 170
Arts and Humanities Citation Index, 158
As Sociology Meets History, 305
Asante, Clement, 157
Ash, Lee, 178
Ashley, Perry, 95
Asian-American Periodicals and Newspapers: A Union List of Holdings in the Library of the State Historical Society of Wisconsin and the Libraries of the University of Wisconsin, 170
Asian Americans, 210
Asian Events with Index, 167
"Assessment of Research Doctorate Programs: Testimony delivered to NRC," 12n
Assignment Editor, 234
Associated Press, 219
Association for Education in Journalism and Mass Communication, 292
  Southeastern Regional Colloquium, 281, 292
Association for the Bibliography of History, 152
Association for the Study of Afro-American Life and History, 292
At Dawn We Slept, 132
At the End of an Age, 14n, 296
Atlanta Constitution, 182
Atwood, Roy, 309
Audience of mass communication, 44-6, 81
Audio sources, evaluation of, 133
Audio/visual material
  online, 207, 226
  sources for, 161-6
Auerbach, Jerold, 117-8
Austin, Bruce, 163
Auteur analysis, 80
Author Biographies Master Index: A Consolidated index to More Than 1,140,000 Biographical Sketches, 178
Authorship of media content, 140
Autobiographical sources, 154
Avalon Project: Documents in Law, History, and Diplomacy, 227
Aydelotte, William, 71, 76n, 297
Ayer Directory of Publications, 171

B
Babbie, Earl, 302
Bailyn, Bernard, 38-9, 183
Bainton, Roland, 67n
Baker, Alan R. H., 302
Baker, Sean, 80, 81n, 249n
Balay, Robert, 96, 155
Barker, Chris, 302
Barker, John, 305
Barker, Susan, 303
Barnett, Becky, 172
Barnett, Brooke, 304
Barnouw, Erik, 94, 311
Barreyre, Nicolas, 305
Bartlett, Kenneth, 305
Barton, Dennis, 176
Bartoy, Kevin, 302
Barzun, Jacques, 68, 100n, 245-6, 264n, 274, 275n, 295, 297, 311
Baseball Card Collection online, 222
Basic Bibliography Book: A Brief Guide to Compiling Bibliographies, 304
Basic Books in the Mass Media: An Annotated Selected Booklist Covering General Communication, Book Publishing, Broadcasting, Film, Editorial Journalism and Advertising, 155
Basler, Roy, 153
Bast, Carol, 302
Bates, Denise, 299
Batty, Linda, 165
Beard, Charles, 35
Beasley, Maurine, 2, 309, 310

Beatty, Michael, 301
Beers, Henry Putney, 176
Behavioral sciences, 2, 3, 15-6, 20
Beins, Bernard, 302
Bennett, James, 156, 157
Benson, Lee, 297
Berg, Bruce, 302
Berger, Arthur, 302
Bergsten, Bebe, 162
Beringer, Richard, 72n
Bernard, H. Russell, 302
Best of History Websites, 202, 209
Besterman, Theodore, 152
Between Dirt and Discussion: Methods, Methodology, and Interpretation in Historical Archaeology, 302
Beyond the Cultural Turn: New Directions in the Study of Society and Culture, 295
Bias, 60-1, 62, 79-80, 81
Bibliographic computerized systems, 185-6
Bibliographic databases, 196-7
Bibliographic Index, 152
Bibliographic soundness, 53
Bibliographic sources, 151-84, 191
Bibliographical Guide to the Study of the Literature of the U.S.A., 153
Bibliographies, 230-1
  in communication history, 154-8
  Internet searches, 185-6
  of bibliographies, 151-2
  of United States History, 153
  online, 200-1
Bibliographies and Indexes in American History, 152
Bibliographies and Lists of New York State Newspapers: Annotated Guide, 155
Bibliographies in American History: 1942-1978: Guide to Materials for Research. Henry Putney Beers, 152
Bibliographies of the Presidents of the United States: 1789-1989, 153
Bibliographies, Research Guides and Finding Aids, 212
Bibliography in the History and Backgrounds of Journalism, 155
Bibliography of American Autobiographies, 154
Bibliography of History, 152
Bibliography of Literary Journalism in America, 155
Bibliography of Newspapers and the Writing of History, 155
Bibliography of the History of Printing in the Library of Congress, 155
"Bibliography: Scholarship on Women Working in Journalism, 155
Billias, George A., 306, 308
Billinge, Mark, 302
Billington, Ray Allen, 255n, 305
Billion Graves, 230
Biographical Dictionary, 99
Biographical Dictionary of American Journalism, 95
Biographical Dictionary of American Newspaper Columnists, 95
Biographical Research Methods, 304
Biographical sources, 95-6, 99, 154
Biographies, 231
  online, 227
Biography (journal), 294
Biography and Genealogy Master Index, 232
Biography and Genealogy Master Index, 1981-1985: A Consolidated Index to More Than 3,200,000 Biographical Sketches, 178
Biography and Genealogy Master Index: 1996-2000 Cumulation: A Consolidated Index to More Than 2,870,000 Biographical Sketches in 416 Current and Retrospective Biographical Dictionaries, 178
Biography and Genealogy Master Index 2009, 178-9
Biography Index, 179
Biography Online, 99
Biography: The Craft and the Calling, 302
Biography: Writing Lives, 304
Biological Dimensions of Communication: Perspectives, Methods, and Research, 301
Birkin, Stanley, 157
Birth of America: the Year in Review, 1763-1783: A Chronological Guide and Index to the Contemporary Colonial Press, 181
Black Authors, 1556-1922, 218
Black Literature Index, 224
"Black Media, The, 1865-Present: Liberal Crusaders or Defenders of Tradition?" 47n
Black Newspaper in America, The: A Guide. Henry La Brie, 170
Black Newspaper Indexing Project, 171
Black Newspapers, 218
Black Newspapers Index (1977 to the present), 170
Black Periodicals and Newspapers: A Union List of Holdings in Libraries of the University of Wisconsin and the Library of the State Historical Society of Wisconsin, 170
Black Press in Mississippi, The, 1865-1985: A Directory, 170
Black Press in the South, The, 1865-1979, 170
Black Press Research Collective, 208
"Black Press to 1968, The: A Bibliography," 155
Black Studies Center, 224
Blacks and Media: A Selected, Annotated Bibliography, 1962-1982, 155
Blacks in Selected Newspapers, Censuses and Other Sources: An Index to Names and Subjects, 160, 170
Blacks on Television. A Selectively Annotated Bibliography, 161
Blackwood's Edinburgh Magazine (1843-52), 216
Blanchard, Margaret, 94
Blassingame, John, 170
Bleyer, Willard, 33
"Blind" judging, 283
Block, Eleanor, 96, 157
Block, Jack, 297
Block quotations, 275, 285
Bloomberg magazine, 219
Bluebook, The: A Uniform System of Citation, 312
Blum, Eleanor, 155
Bognar, Desi, 164
Bogue, Allan, 76n, 297
Boldt, Andreas Dieter, 305
Bond, Richmond Pugh, 158
Boni, Albert, 165

Chapter 12: Index

Bonnell, Victoria, 295
Book publishing, 290-2
Book Review Index, 159
Books in Print, 152
Books in Print, 233
Books on Early American History and Culture, 1971-1980: An Annotated Bibliography, 153
Books online, 207, 223-4
Boolean searches, 205-6
Borchard, Greg, 17, 280
Boris, Eileen, 295
"Born in Slavery: Slave Narratives," 132
Boston Courier, 30
Boston Globe, 182
Boston Guardian, 171
Boston News-Letter, 33, 34
Bourgeois Experience, The: Victoria to Freud, 250
Bowen, Catharine Drinker, 302
Bowers, Claude, 35
Boyce, D. G., 299
Boyd, Anne Morris, 175
Bracken, James, 96, 157
Bradley, James E., 302
Brayer, Herbert, 172
Brennen, Bonnie, 301
Bridenbaugh, Carl, 72n, 74
Brigham, Clarence, 156, 169
Brightbill, George, 157
Briscoe Center for American History, 202-3
Briscoe, Mary Louise, 154
British Archives: A Guide to Archive Resources in the United Kingdom, 175
British Broadcasting, 1922-1982: A Selected and Annotated Bibliography, 161
British directories of newspapers, 172
British Film Catalogue 1895-1994, 161
British Film Institute, 163
British history online, 208
British Humanities Index, 159
British Library, 149
British National Archives, 208
British National Film & Video Catalogue, 161
British National Film Catalogue, 161
British Newspapers and Periodicals, 1632-1800: A Descriptive Catalogue of a Collection at the University of Texas, 170
British Newspapers and Periodicals, 1641-1700: A Short-title Catalogue of Serials Printed in England, Scotland, Ireland, and British America, 170
British Periodicals, 217
British Periodicals and Newspapers, 1789-1832: A Bibliography of Secondary Sources, 155
British publications, 154, 170, 216
British sources, 151
Broadcast Education Association, 292
Broadcast media, directories, 171
Broadcast programs, guides to, 184
Broadcasting, 142
 authenticity, 142
Broadcasting, 185
Broadcasting and Mass Media: A Survey Bibliography, 161
Broadcasting Research Methods, 301

Broadcasts online, 222-3, 225
Brooks, Philip, 148
Brooks, Tim, 184
Brown, Dan, 168
Brown, Elizabeth Read, 173
Browne, M. Neil, 300
Bruce, Randall, 304
Brundage, Anthony, 297
Bryant, Jennings, 168
Bryant, Joseph, 303
Bryl, Susan, 170
Buckingham, Joseph, 30
Bucy, Erik, 301
Builder, The, magazine (1843-49), 216
Bukalski, Peter, 163
Bullitt, William, 67
Bunzl, Martin, 296
Burckhardt, Jacob, 305
Burke, Peter, 305
Burnett, Roger, 302
Burns, R. M., 305
Burton, Mandy, 305
Bush, George W., 117
Business Communications: An Annotated Bibliography, 157
Business History (journal), 294
Business History Conference, 292
Business History Review, 294
Business information online, 228
Businessweek, 219
Butterfield, Herbert, 296, 305

C

Cable Television: A Comprehensive Bibliography, 162
Cain, Butler, 3
California History (journal), 294
California: Union List of Newspapers, 170
Campaign Newspapers, 217-8
Campbell, Georgetta Merritt, 171
Campbell, Kenneth, 18
Campbell, W. Joseph, 118-9
"Can Wikipedia Make the Grade?" 198n
Canadian Periodical Index, 159
Canary, Robert, 255n, 258n, 312
Cannon, Carl, 156
Capra, Frank, 134
Carey, James, 44-6, 309
Caribbean Newspapers, 1718-1876, 218
Carnes, Mark, 135n
Carpenter, Ronald, 312
Carr, David, 296
Carr, Edward Hallett, 14n, 91, 240, 296
Carter, Shannon, 305
Carter, Simon, 298
Carter, Susan, 168
Casey, Ralph, 158
Cassara, Catherine, 86
Cassara, Ernest, 153
Cassata, Mary, 165
Cassell Companion to Cinema, 162
Caswell, Lucy, 176
Catalog of the Public Documents of Congress and of All Departments of the Government of the United

States, 174
Catalog of U. S. Government Publications, 175, 212
Catalogs of archival holding, 202
Catalogs of Archives and Libraries, 201-2
Catalogue of Copyright Entries: Motion Pictures, 162
Catalogue of the Pamphlets, Books, Newspapers, and Manuscripts Relating to the [British] Civil War, the Commonwealth, and Restoration, 1640-1661, 170
Catholic Periodical and Literature Index, 159
Catholic Periodical Index, 159
Catholic Serials in Minnesota, 1866-1962: A Descriptive Bibliography and Union List, 170
Caudill, Ed, 74
Causal Explanation and Model Building in History, Economics and the New Economic History, 298
Causation, 243-7
  single factor, 246
Causes
  antecedent, 245
  immediate, 245
  multiple, 246
  paramount vs. contributory, 245-6
CBS Evening News, 117
CBS News, 219
Censorship: A World Encyclopedia, 94
Census Bureau (U.S.), 168
Census of British Newspapers and Periodicals, 1620-1800, 170
Census records, 229
Center for History and New Media, 209
Center for Research Libraries, 176
Century of Lawmaking for a New Nation, A, 228
Chandler, Claire, 161
Charleston Courier, 20-1
Charleston Mercury, 20-1, 218
Charno, Steven, 171
Chartier, Roger, 296
Charts online, 226
Chaudhuri, Nupur, 295
Checklist of American 18th Century Newspapers in the Library of Congress, 170
Cheng, Eileen, 305
Chicago Defender, 1909-1975, 224
Chicago Manual of Style, 274, 285, 312
Chicago newspapers, 174
Chicago Sun-Times, 182
Chicago Tribune, 182, 219
"Chicanos and the Media: A Bibliography of Select Materials," 155
Chief, The: The Life of William Randolph Hearst, 129
Child Welfare Films; An International Index of Films and Film Strips on the Health and Welfare of Children, 162
Children's Literature Comprehensive Database, 233
Chin, Felix, 162
Christian Science Monitor, 182, 219
Chronicling America: Historic American Newspapers, 217
Chronological structure in writing, 268
Chronological Tables of American Newspapers, 1690-1820, 170
Chronology of United States Historical Documents, 211

Church History: An Introduction to Research Methods and Resources, 302
Church in the Southern Black Community, 227
Church, Francis, 113
Churchill, Winston, 60
CIA World Factbook, 99
CIS/Index (the Congressional Information Service's Index to Publications of the United States Congress), 174
"Citation and Methodological Analysis of Media History," 70n, 106n
Civil War 1860-1865: A Newspaper Perspective, 218
Civil War History, 294
Civil War Home: Index of Civil War Information Available on the Internet, 229
Civil War Letters and Diaries, 227
Civil War Newspapers in GIF format, 203, 208
Civil War, The: A Newspaper Perspective, 216
Clarity in writing, 261-4
Clark, Andrew, 244
Clark, G. Kitson, 297
Clarke, Avis Gertrude, 169
Claussen, Dane, 138
Cleveland Leader (1854-1913), 218
Clifford, Nick, 302
Clio, A Muse and Other Essays, 308
Clio and the Doctors: Psycho-History, Quanto-History and History, 68n, 297
Cloud, Barbara, 309
CNN, 219
CNN International, 219
Cobb, Frank, 117-8
Cobb of The World, 118
Cohen, Louis, 302
Cohen, Morris, 302
Collingwood, R. G., 15, 296, 305
Colorado Newspapers, 171
Colored American (1837-1841), 170
Coloribus: Advertising Archive, 221
Columbia Center for Oral History, 213
Columbia University Oral History Collection, 179
ComAbstracts, 233
Combined Retrospective Index to Book Reviews in Humanities Journals, 1802-1974, 159
Combined Retrospective Index to Book Reviews in Scholarly Journals, 1886-1974, 159
Combined Retrospective Indexes to Journals in History 1838-1974, 159
Commager, Henry Steele, 306
Communication & Mass Media Complete, 232
Communication Abstracts, 166
Communication and Law: Multidisciplinary Approaches to Research, 304
Communication and Society: A Bibliography on Communication Technologies and Their Social Impact, 157
Communication and the Law, 267
Communication and the Mass Media: A Guide to the Reference Literature, 96, 157
Communication and the United States Congress: A Selectively Annotated Bibliography of Committee Hearings, 1870-1976, 157

Communication as Culture: Essays on Media and Society, 45n
Communication History, 311
Communication history, 19-23
  nature of, 10-1
  value of, 21-2
"Communication History Abstracts," 166
Communication research methods, 15-6
Communication studies, 79
Communication: A Guide to Information Sources, 157
Communist Historical Newspapers, 218
Comparative Historical Analysis in the Social Sciences, 303
Complete Directory of Prime Time Network Television, 1946-Present, 184
Complete Film Dictionary, 162
Complete Index to World Film Since 1895, 162
Comprehensive Encyclopedia of Film Noir: The Essential Reference Guide, 162
Comprehensive Index to the Publications of the United States Government 1881-1893, 174
Computer-aided Legal Research (CALR) on the Internet, 304-5
Computers, limitations of in historical research, 100
Conclusion in writing, 268-9
Conditt, Paul, 173
Confederate States of America, guide to archives, 176
Conferences, presentation of papers, 280-3, 292-3
Confidential nature of record, 122
Conflict interpretation of history, 35
Congressional Record, 106
Congressional Record, 1873-75, 228
Congressional Serial Set, 1789-1969, 225-6
Congressional Serial Set, 1817-1994, 226
Conkin, Paul, 306
Connelly, Robert, 164
Connery, Thomas, 311
Consciousness, relationship to mass communication, 44-6
Consensus School of interpretation, 37-40
Constitutional Convention, 228
Content analysis, 73-4, 75, 80
  inability to explain "why," 74-5
  limitations of, 74-5
Content Analysis: An Introduction to Its Methodology, 301
Context, 242, 246
Continental Congress, 228
Continuity in writing, 261-4
Contrary evidence, 242
Contributions to Bibliography in Journalism, 155
Control of the Media in the United States: An Annotated Bibliography, 157
"Conversation Between Eric Foner and John Sayles, A," 135n
"Conversation with Alfred McClung Lee, A," 309
"Conversation with Edwin Emery, A," 309
"Conversation with Frederick S. Siebert, A," 310
"Conversation with Harold L. Nelson, A," 309
"Conversation with Leonard Levy, A," 309
"Conversation with Robert W. Desmond, A," 309
"Conversation with Sidney Kobre, A," 309

Conway, Michael, 309
Coolican, Hugh, 302
Cooper, Douglas, 151, 156, 180
Copeland, David, 184, 284, 285, 286, 299
Copyright, 197, 267
  and film sources, 162, 183
  and Internet material, 197
  and secondary sources, 201
Cornell Making of America Collection, 215, 225
Coutts, Brian, 180
Couvares, Francis, 306
Covert, Catherine, 309
Cowie, Peter, 164
Craft of the Historian of Economic Thought, The, 304
Crandall, Ralph, 298
Crane, R. S., 170
Craver, Kathleen, 300
Credibility of source, 120
Creelman, James, 118
Cressman, Dale, 96, 125, 148, 256
Critical and Effective Histories: Foucault's Methods and Historical Sociology, 303
Critical Historian, The, 297
Critical Index, The: A Bibliography of Articles on Film in English, 1946-1973, Arranged by Names and Topics, 162
Critical theory, 28, 45
Critical Theory, 248-9
Cronin, Joseph, 306
Cronkite, Walter, 203
Cross on Evidence, 121
Cross, Rupert, 121
Crusaders, Scoundrels, Journalists: The Newseum's Most Intriguing Newspeople, 95
Cuban revolution, 108, 118-9
Cultural and Critical Studies, 60, 79-82
  ideological bias, 79-80
  methods, 80
"Cultural and Critical Studies," 80n, 81n, 249n
Cultural History: Between Practices and Representations, 296
Cultural School of interpretation, 41-4, 47
Cultural studies, 81
Cultural Studies School of interpretation, 44-6, 81, 240-9
  reliance on secondary sources, 45, 47
Cultural Studies: Theory and Practice, 302
Culture, definition of, 79
Cunliffe, Marcus, 306
Curran, Daniel, 163
Current Biography, 95
Current Contents: Arts and Humanities, 159
Current, Richard, 16-7
Curthoys, Ann, 312
Curtis, L.P., Jr., 241n
Cycles in U.S. History: Documenting American History, 209
Cyclical concept of history, 5
Cyndi's List of Genealogy Sites on the Internet, 229

D

da Sousa Correa, Delia, 302
Dahl, Folke, 299

Daigle, Lisa, 70n, 106n
Daly, Chris, 309
Dana, Charles, 263
Dangerous Games: The Uses and Abuses of History, 296
Danky, James, 154, 170, 171
Danto, Elizabeth Ann, 297
Dary, David, 236
Database vendors, defined, 185
Databases, 199
    defined, 185
Davenport, Frances, 176
Davenport, Lucinda, 56, 69, 242
Davidson, James West, 250n, 251n, 297
Davies, David, 71, 93, 276
Davis, Harold, 236-7
Davis, Richard Harding, 108, 118-9
Daymon, Christine, 301
De A'Morelli, Richard, 261n
Dean, Mitchell, 303
Death of the Past, The, 297
"Debating Historical Issues in the Media of the Time," 184
Deciphering Sociological Research, 304
Deconstruction, 76, 77, 82
"Deconstruction," 76n
Degler, Carl, 306
Degradation of American History, The, 306
Delaware County, Pa., newspapers (1825-1871), 216
Delaware Newspaper Project, 173
Demographic Yearbook, 169
Denzin, Norman, 303
Derrida, Jacques, 76, 77
Derry, Charles, 163
Descent into Discourse: The Reification of Language and the Writing of Social History, 297
Descriptive Catalogue of the Government Publications of the United States, September 5, 1774-March 4, 1881, 174
Descriptive Catalogue of the Government Publications, 161, 214
Designing Qualitative Research, 303
Desmond, Robert, 11, 85, 309
Determinism, 249, 251
Detroit News, 182
Development of American Journalism, The, 43
Development of narrative in writing, 264-9
Development of the Colonial Newspaper, The, 43
Developmental School of interpretation, 31-5, 47, 56-7
Developments in Modern Historiography, 307
Diaries online, 207
Diary of World Events, 184
Dicken-Garcia, Hazel, 309, 311
Dickens, Charles, 263
Dictionary of American Biography, 95
Dictionary of American Negro Biography, 95
Dictionary of Literary Biography, 95
Digital Collections from the Library of Congress, 225
Digital History, 209
Digital Librarian: History, 211
Dimensions of History, The: Readings on the Nature of History and the Problems of Historical Interpretation, The, 306
Dimensions of Quantitative Research in History, The, 76n, 297
Diplomatic History (journal), 294
Directories for special libraries and collections, 177-8
Directory of Archives and Manuscript Repositories in the United States, 175
Directory of Broadcast Archives, 176
Directory of History Dissertations, 233
Directory of History Journals, 293
Directory of New Jersey Newspapers, 1765-1970, 171
Directory of Newspaper Indexes, 171
Directory of Newspaper Libraries in the U. S. and Canada, 177
Directory of Newspaper Libraries in the United States and Canada, 177
Directory of Oral History Collections, 179
Directory of Oral History Programs in the United States, 179
Directory of U.S. Negro Newspapers, Magazines & Periodicals in 42 States: The Negro Press; Past, Present & Future: A Documentary Research Report 1827-1967, 171
Directory of World Museums & Living Displays, 136
Disappearing Daily, The, 36
Disciplines (academic), 9-10
Discourse analysis, 80
Discovering the News, 107-8
Dissertation Abstracts, 166
Dissertations, 167, 207, 231, 233
Dissertations and Theses Global, 232
Dissertations Completed in History Departments of United States and Canadian Universities 1961-June 1970, 179
Dissertations in History 1970-June 1980, 179
Dissertations in History: An Index to Dissertations Completed in History Departments of United States and Canadian Universities 1873-1960, 179
Dixon, Diana, 155
Dochartaigh, Niall, 301
Documentary sources (U.S.), guides to
    archives, libraries and historical societies, 176
    federal records, 176
    libraries and other repositories, 176-7
Documenting the American South, 211, 227
Documents of American History Online, 203, 208
Documents of World War I, 229
Documents of World War II, 211
Dodd, Donald, 168
Dodd, Wynelle, 168
Dodson, Suzanne Cates, 180
Doing History, 296
Doing Oral History: A Practical Guide, 132, 298
Dollar, Charles, 298
Dominick, J. R., 301
Donatelli, Joseph, 156
Donnelly, David, 300
Donovan, Timothy Paul, 306
Dooley, Jackie, 178
Dougherty, James, 153
Douglass, Frederick, Papers, 225

Chapter 12: Index

Doyle, Arthur Conan, 89n
Drudge, Matt, 234
Duke University Archives, 213
Duke University Libraries Digital Advertising Collections, 220
Dunn, Gilbert, 151, 156, 180
Dunning, John, 165
Dupont, Nancy, 281
Duquesne University's History Forum, 292
Duranty, Walter, 139
Dutch Language Press in America, The: Two Centuries of Printing, Publishing and Bookselling, 155
Dyer, Carolyn Stewart, 311

E

Early American Imprints (1639-1819), 218
Early American Imprints: An Archive of Americana Collection, 216
Early American Imprints, Series I & II: Library Company of Philadelphia, 1670-1819, 216
Early American Imprints, Series I and II: American Antiquarian Society, 1652-1819, 216
Early American Imprints, Series I: Evans, 1639-1800, 216
Early American Imprints, Series II: Shaw-Shoemaker, 1801-1819, 216
Early American Newspapers, 1690-1922, 217
Early English Books Online (EEBO), 1473-1800, 224
Early English Books Online (EEBO), 1475-1700, 224
Early Motion Pictures: The Paper Print Collection in the Library of Congress, 162
Early Periodical Indexes: Bibliographies and Indexes of Literature Published in Periodicals before 1900, 155
East, W. Gordon, 63, 303
Easton, David, 13
EBSCO Open Dissertations, 233
Economic History Association, 292
Economic Interpretation of History, The, 307
Economic Literature, 228
Economic Methodology: An Historical Introduction, 303
Economist, 228
Edelman, Hendrik, 155
Editor and Publisher, 185
Editor and Publisher International Yearbook, 171
Editor for Justice: The Life of Louis I. Jaffe, 132
Education of a Correspondent, The, 61n
Education of the Senses, The, 250
Effects and Functions of Television: A Bibliography of Selected Research Literature, 1970-1978, 162
Ehrlich, Lea, 172
Eighteenth Century Collections Online, 219, 220
Eighteenth Century Journals: A Portal to Newspapers and Periodicals, c1685-1835, 216
Eighteenth-Century Short Title Catalogue, 154
Ekstrand, Victoria Smith, 309
Election returns, 169
Electronic Collections Online, 232
Electronic indexes, 204
Electronic Media and Communication Research Methods, 301

Elements of Style, The, 261, 262, 312
Elephind: Search the World's Historical Newspaper Archives, 217
Elias, Stephen, 303
Eller, Jack David, 303
Ellis, Jack, 163
Elton, G. R., 9, 14n, 241n, 242, 245, 257n, 296, 298, 306
Elwood, Virginia, 157
Emergence of Advertising in America, 1850-1920, 220, 221
"Emergence of American Nationalism, The: A Quantitative Approach," 71n
Emery, Edwin, 106
Emery, Michael, 309
Emmons, Mark, 162, 165
"Emotionology: Clarifying the History and Emotions of Emotional Standards," 69n
Encyclopedia Britannica, 227
Encyclopedia Britannica Online, 99
Encyclopedia of American Journalism, 94
Encyclopedia of American Radio, 1920-1960, 162
Encyclopedia of American Radio: An A-Z Guide..., 162
Encyclopedia of Associations, 281
Encyclopedia of Film Directors in the United States and Europe, 162
Encyclopedia of Film Themes, Settings and Series, 162
Encyclopedia of Novels into Film, 162
Encyclopedia of Radio, 162
Encyclopedia of Television, 162, 231
Encyclopedia of Television News, 94
Encyclopedia of Twentieth-Century Journalists, 95
Encyclopedia of World Biography, 99
Encyclopedia sources, 99
Encyclopedia.com, 99
Encyclopedias on Internet, 227, 231
Endres, Kathleen, 94
Engler, Steven, 305
English Historical Pragmatics, 303
"English-Speaking Caribbean Media History: Bibliographic References and Research Sources," 155
Enlightenment, the, 28
Entwistle, Doris, 158
"Erik Barnouw (1908–2001): Broadcasting's Premier Historian," 311
Erikson, Erik, 67
Esquire magazine, 219
Essay and General Literature Index, 159
Essays online, 207
Ethics of History, The, 296
Ethnic newspapers, 171
Ethnic Newspapers, 217
Ethnic NewsWatch, 224
Ethnic NewsWatch: A History, 224
Ethnic studies, 45
Ethnic Studies Research: Approaches and Perspectives, 303
Ethnohistory, 294
Ethnomethodology, 304
"Evaluating Online Resources," 136n
Evaluation of sources, principles, 121-2

Evans, Charles, 183
Evans, Richard, 14n, 77n, 79, 296
"Everyman His Own Historian — Not! A Defense of Our Profession — And a Plea for Its Future," 311
Evidence, 5-6, 8, 13, 18, 19, 45-6, 53, 58-9, 78, 85-6, 88, 89, 90-1, 100, 103-6, 118, 120, 121, 128, 130, 139, 144, 239, 296, 299
  as basis of historical study, 103, 145
  conclusions and, 269, 283
  explaining causation, and, 243, 246, 247
  interpretation and, 242
  psychohistory and, 67, 68
  theory and, 249, 251
  writing and, 254, 255, 258, 259, 276
"Evidence of Reliability in Newspapers and Periodicals in Historical Studies," 140n, 299
"Examining the 'Dark Ages' Concept: The Federalist-Republican Press as a Model," 310
Experience of History, The, 305
Expertness of author of record, 122
Explanation in history, 25, 26-7, 49, 54, 235-52
Exploration, 227
Exploring U.S. History, 209
Extant Collections of Early Black Newspapers: a Research Guide to the Black Press, 1880-1915, with an Index to the Boston Guardian, 1902-1904, 171
Extended facts, 239-41
External criticism of records, 110-9
  collation, 110
  identification, 110
  textual verification, 110

F

Facts, 4, 8, 239-41
Facts on File: A Weekly World News Digest with Cumulative Index, 167
"Fakes and Facsimiles: Problems of Identification," 299
Family History Library of the Church of Jesus Christ of Latter-day Saints (Mormon), 229
Family history resources, 208
Farber, Evan Ira, 159
Feature Films, 1940-1949: A United States Filmography, 162
Feature Films, 1950-1959: A United States Filmography, 162
Federal Records, 180
Federal records (U.S.), 176
Federal Writers' Project, 132
Fedler, Fred, 115
Fee, Frank, 46, 59, 238
Feldman, Julie, 163
Feldstein, Mark, 309
Fellman, Susanna, 297
Fellow, Anthony, 89
Feminist history, 47-8
Feminist theory, 45
Fetrow, Alan, 162
"Fiction as History: A Review Essay," 17n
Fielding, Raymond, 98, 143
Fifty Years of Coca-Cola Television Advertisements, 1950-2000, 222

Film, 142-3, 155, 159, 167, 299
  authenticity, 142
  authorship, 142
  online, 215, 222-3, 225
  sources for, 133-5, 150, 161-6, 177, 183-4
Film & History (journal), 284, 294
Film and Television: A Guide to the Reference Literature, 162
Film Audience, The: An International Bibliography of Research, With Annotations and an Essay, 162-3
Film Book Bibliography, 1940-1975, 163
Film Criticism: An Index to Critics' Anthologies, 163
Film Encyclopedia, The: The Complete Guide to Film and the Film Industry, 163
Film History (journal), 284, 294
Film Index, a Bibliography, 163
Film Index International, 163
Film Literature Index, 163
Film Research: A Critical Bibliography with Annotation and Essay, 163
Film Researcher's Handbook: A Guide to Sources in North America, South America, Asia, Australasia and Africa, 163
Film Reviews and Film Criticism Resources, 166
Film Study: A Resource Guide, 163
Film Study: An Analytical Bibliography, 163
Find a Grave, 230
Finn, Daniel, 163
First-Person Narratives of the American South, 227
Fischer, David Hackett, 60, 298
Fitzgerald, Carol Bondhus, 153, 257n, 275n
Fitzgerald, Maureen, 303
Flash Press, 218
Fleet Street Radical: A.G. Gardiner and the "Daily News," 238n
Fletcher, J. E., 301
Flocke, Lynne, 57, 237
Flow online journal, 201
Floyd, Kory, 301
Fogel, Robert, 67, 76n, 297, 306
Follett, Wilson, 312
Fong, Timothy, 303
Footnotes, 269-74
Forbes, Harold, 173
Forbes magazine, 219
Ford, Edwin, 155, 156
Forgeries, 115-7
Fortune magazine, 219
Foster, Janet, 175
Foucault, Michael, 76, 77, 304, 306
Foucault's Antihumanist Historiography, 306
Foundations of American Journalism, 43
Foundations of Legal Research and Writing, 302
Fowler, Floyd, 301, 303
Fox, Louis, 157
FOX News, 219
Frame by Frame I, 163
Frame by Frame II, 163
Frame by Frame III: A Filmography of the African American Diasporan Image, 1994-2004, 163
Framework for Political Analysis, A, 13n
"Francis P. Blair, Pen-Executive of Andrew Jackson," 264n

Chapter 12: Index

Frank Leslie's Weekly, 216
Frank, Gelya, 303
Franklin, Benjamin, 121-2
Franklin, James, 121-2
Frauds, 115-9
Frazier, Patrick, 179
Frederick Douglass Papers, 225
Freedom of the Press, 36
Freedom of the press, 57
Freedom of the Press: An Annotated Bibliography, 156
Freedom's Journal (1827-1829), 169
Freidel, Frank, 153
Freud, Sigmund, 67
Friedman, Barbara, 248
Fritze, Ronald, 180
From Colony to Superpower: U.S. Foreign Relations Since 1776, 85
From Formalism to Poststructuralism, 76n
From Historical Social Theory to Foucault, 304
From Reliable Sources: An Introduction to Historical Methods, 298
From Silents to Sound: A Biographical Encyclopedia of Performers Who Made the Transition to Talking Pictures, 163
Frontier newspapers, history of, 42
Frontier thesis, 251
Fugate, Cynthia, 172

G

Gaddis, John Lewis, 296
Gale Directory of Publications and Broadcast Media, 171
Gale Information Guide Library, 153
Gardiner, A. G., 237-8
Gas, Karen Rix, 157
Gateway to History, The, 103n, 307
Gay, Peter, 250, 306
Geertz, Clifford, 64
Gender and History (journal), 294
Gender and the Politics of History, 297
Gender School of interpretation, 46-8
Gender Watch, 224
Genealogical Research, 229-30
Genealogy Today StateGenSites, 229
Genealogy.com, 230
GenealogyBank, 230
General U.S.A. History, 227
Generalizations, 241, 243
Generation of 1914, The, 250
Generations and Change: Genealogical Perspectives in Social History, 298
Gentleman's Magazine (1731-50), 216
Geography, 64-5
Geography Behind History, The, 53, 63, 303
Geography: Its History and Concepts, 303
Geography of Slavery in Virginia, 221
Georgetown Law Journal, 294
Georgia Historical Quarterly, 294
Gergen, Kenneth, 303
Gergen, Mary, 303
Gerlach, John, 162
Gerlach, Lana, 162

German Language Press of the Americas, Vol. 1: History and Bibliography 1732-1968: United States of America, 156
"Getting Published by a University Press," 291n
"Ghost of Television News in Media History Scholarship, The" 309
Gibson, Gloria, 163
Gifford, Dennis, 161
Gilje, Paul, 65n
Gitter, A. George, 157
Gleason, Timothy W., 309
Goble, Alan, 162
Godey's Lady's Book, 216
Godfrey, Donald, 176, 299
Gohdes, Clarence, 153
Going to the Sources: A Guide to Historical Research and Writing, 297
Goldentree Bibliographies in American History, 154
Goldsmiths-Kress Library of Economic Literature, 228
Google Book Search, 223
Google Books, 197, 223
Google Newspaper Archives. 1700s to 2009, 217
Google Scholar, 200-1, 231
Google United States Online Historical Newspapers, 208
Gorham, Thelma Thurston, 171
Gossman, Lionel, 255n
Gottesman, Rita, 170
Gottschalk, Louis, 298
Government documents
  evaluation of, 126-8
  online, 207
Government Documents (United States), 207
Government information, U.S., 228
Government Periodicals Index, 174
Government publications, U.S., 174, 175, 212
Government publications and documents (directories, indexes, guides and catalogs), 174-5
Government statistics, 167
Graff, Henry, 100n, 236-7, 245-6, 264n, 274, 275n, 295, 297
Graham, Robert, 155
Grand Design of God, The. The Literary Form of the Christian View of History, 307
Grand theory, 250-2
Grant, Barry Keith, 165
Grant, John Abner, 162
Graves, Robert, 263
Great Cases of Sherlock, 89n
Great Editorials, 184
Great Lakes History Conference, 292
"Great man" interpretation of history, 42
"Great Mutation, The," 72n, 74n
Great North American Indians: Profiles in Life and Leadership, 95
Greenberg, Gerald, 158
"Greenwood Library of American War Reporting," 184
Gregory, Winifred, 169
Griffin, Roger, 300
Grob, Gerald, 306
Grunin, Robert, 157

Guide to American Cinema, 1930-1965, 163
Guide to American Cinema, 1965-1995, 163
Guide to American Crime Films of the Forties and Fifties, 163
Guide to American Film Directors: The Sound Era 1929-1979, 163
Guide to Archives and Manuscripts in the United States, 175, 176, 177
Guide to Historical Method, A, 298
Guide to Latin American, Caribbean, and U.S. Latino Made Film and Video, 163
Guide to Manuscripts in the Presidential Libraries, 176
"Guide to Mass Communication Sources," 151, 156, 180
Guide to Microform Collections in the Humanities and Social Sciences Division of the Library of Congress, 179, 195-6
Guide to Newspapers and Newspaper Holdings in Maryland, 171
Guide to Newspapers and Newspaper Indexes, 213
Guide to Online Primary Sources: African Americans, 211
Guide to Reference Books, 96
Guide to Resources and Services, 167
Guide to Sources in American Journalism History, 176
Guide to the American Ethnic Press: Slavic and East European Newspapers and Periodicals, 171
Guide to the Archives of the Government of the Confederate States of America, 176
Guide to the Hoover Institution Archives, 176
Guide to the Manuscript Materials for the History of the United States to 1783: In the British Museum, in Minor London Archives, and in the Libraries of Oxford and Cambridge, 176
Guide to the National Archives of the United States, 176
Guide to the Silent Years of American Cinema, 163
Guide to the Study of the United States of America: Representative Books Reflecting the Development of American Life and Thought, 153
Guide to U. S. Government Publications, 174
Guide to U. S. Government Statistics, 167
Guinsburg, Thomas, 306
Gustafson, Don, 172
Gustavson, Carl, 63n, 82, 296
Gutierrez, Felix, 155

H

Hady, Maureen, 154, 170, 171, 173
Haley, Alex, 131
Hall, John A., 303
Halliwell's Who's Who in the Movies, 163
Hamer, Philip, 176, 177
Hamill, Patricia Beall, 165
Handbook for Research in American History, 177
Handbook for Research in American History: A Guide to Bibliographies and Other Reference Works, 96, 151, 174
Handbook of American Popular Culture, 157
Handbook: The Center for Research Libraries, 176
Handbook to Literary Research, The, 302
Handlin, Oscar, 98, 153

Hansen, Sandra, 172
Hard Times: An Oral History of the Great, 133
Hardy, Gayle, 175
Harlan, David, 306
Harmsworth, Alfred, 240
Harper's Magazine Index, 161, 214
Harper's Weekly, 196, 217
HarpWeek, 196, 217
Harry Amana's Web Page, 210
Hart, Horace, 155
Harvard Graduate School of Business Administration. 40
Harvard Guide to American History, 153
Harvard University libraries, 181
Harzig, Christiane, 156
Hatcher, Anthony, 132
Hathitrust.org, 215, 225
Havlice, Patricia Pate, 180
Hawaii Newspapers: A Union List, 171
Hawkin, Margie, 302
Hay, Iain, 303
Hayden, Joe, 124
Hayes, Andrew, 301
Hearst, William Randolph, 108, 118-9
Heath, Trudy, 169
Hebert, David, 304
Hebrews, 5
Hedgepeth, Julie, 47n
Hegemony, 79, 80
Heilig, Christoph, 298
Heintze, James, 165
Heinzkill, Richard, 163
Henderson, Mae, 170
Henry Grady's New South, 236-7
Henry W. Grady: Spokesman of the New South, 236-7
Henry, Susan, 166, 299
Herbert, Miranda, 178
Herbert, Stephen, 166
Herodotus, 5, 6, 8, 11, 15
Herring, George, 85
Hester, Richard, 298
Heuvel, Jon Vanden, 177
Hexter, Jack, 296, 298, 306
Higgens, Gavin, 161
Higham, John, 306
Hill, George, 161
Hilmes, Michele, 7
Hispanic American Newspapers, 1808-1980, 218
Hispanic American periodicals from 1959-1989, 224
Hispanic Periodicals in the United States, Origins to 1960: A Brief History and Comprehensive Bibliography, 156
Hispanics in Hollywood: An Encyclopedia of Film and Television, 163
Historian (journal), 294
Historian and Film, The, 299
Historian and History, The, 4n, 297
Historian and the Climate of Opinion, The, 307
Historian and the Film, The, 135
Historian as Detective, The: Essays on Evidence, The, 299
Historian's Guide to Statistics: Quantitative Analysis

Chapter 12: Index

and *Historical Research*, 298
"Historian's Opportunity, The," 62n
Historian's Workshop, The, 241n
"Historians, The," 311
Historians Across Borders: Writing American History in a Global Age, 305
"Historians and Freedom of the Press, 1690-1801: Libertarian or Limited?" 311
"Historians and Freedom of the Press Since 1800," 309
"Historians and the American Frontier Press," 309
"Historians and the American Press, 1900-1945: Working Profession or Big Business?" 310
Historians on History: Readings, 308
Historians' Fallacies: Toward a Logic of Historical Thought, 60n, 298
Historians' Paradox, The: The Study of History in Our Time, 306
Historic Pages, 203, 208
Historical Abstracts, 166, 200, 204
Historical Analysis: Contemporary Approaches to Clio's Craft, 72n
Historical Analysis in Economics, 304
Historical Bibliography of the Press, 156
Historical Essays (Rhodes), 21n
"Historical facts," 239-40
Historical Guides to the World's Periodicals and Newspapers, 94, 160, 169
Historical Journal, The, 294
Historical Journal of Film, Radio and Television, 284n, 294
Historical Knowledge: In Quest of Theory, Method and Evidence, 296
Historical Mechanisms: An Experimental Approach to Applying Scientific Theories to the Study of History, 305
Historical Methodology, 298
Historical Methods in the Social Sciences, 303
Historical Newspapers and Indexes On The Internet – USA, 181-2, 217
Historical newspapers online, 208
Historical research
  advantages over other methods, 15-6
  requirements of, 3-4
  value of, 2-3, 21
Historical Research, 297, 298
Historical Research: A Guide for Writers of Dissertations, Theses, Articles and Books, 298
Historical Research Using British Newspapers, 299
Historical Social Psychology, 303
Historical Society, The, 292
Historical Statistics of Black America, 167
Historical Statistics of the States of the United States: Two Centuries of Census, 1790-1990, 167-8
Historical Statistics of the United States, 1790-1970, 168
Historical Statistics of the United States, 1790-1970: The Midwest, 168
Historical Statistics of the United States, 1790-1970: The South, 168
Historical Statistics of the United States: Colonial Times to 1970, 99, 168
Historical Statistics of the United States: Earliest Times to the Present, 168
Historical study
  evidence, 6
  humanistic nature of, 6
  interpretation, 6-89
  origins of, 5
  purpose of, 17-8, 19
Historical Thinking: An Introduction, 55n
Historical Thought in America: Postwar Patterns, 306
Historical understanding, 55
Historical Voices. The National Gallery of the Spoken Word, 223
"Historiographical Tradition in 20th-Century America, The," 307
Historiography, 242-3
  defined, 97n
Historiography, 307
Historiography: An Introductory Guide, 305
"Historiography and the Media Historian," 311
Historiography: Critical Concepts in Historical Studies, 305
Historiography in Mass Communication (online journal), 284, 309
Historiography in the Twentieth Century: From Scientific Objectivity to the Postmodern Challenge, 307
"Historiography of Journalism History, The," 309
History
  as a form of knowledge, 4-9
  purpose of, 16-9
  value of, 1-2, 18-9
History & American Studies Research Guide, 210
History and Annotated Bibliography of American Religious Periodicals and Newspapers Established from 1730 through 1830, 156
History and Bibliography of American Newspapers, 1690-1820, 156, 169
"History and Literature: Reproduction or Signification," 255n
History and Memory, 296
"History and the Age of Cyberspace," 300
History and the Christian Historian, 308
History and the Internet: A Guide, 300
History and Theory, 305
History As Art and As Science, 14n, 307
History as Rhetoric: Style, Narrative, and Persuasion, 312
History as Romantic Art: Bancroft, Prescott, Motley, and Parkman, 307
History Highway, The: A 21st Century Guide to Internet Resources, 98n, 136n, 207n, 300
History in Crisis? Recent Directions in Historiography, 308
History in Sound: A Descriptive Listing of the KIRO-CBS Collection of the World War II Years and After, 184
History Matters, 132, 202, 226
History Matters History Guide. Resources for Historians, 211
History of American Journalism, 33
"History of American Journalism," 84
History of Historical Writing, A, 307
History of Historical Writing in America, The, 307

History of Journalism in the United States, a Bibliography of Books and Annotated Articles, 156
History of Mass Communication in America: An Internet Bibliography, 230
History of Printing in America, 29
History of Televised Presidential Debates, 222
History of the Mass Media in the United States: An Encyclopedia, 94
History of the United States of America: A Guide to Information Sources, 153
History on the Internet 2001: Evaluating Online Sources, 300
History, Philosophy, and Newspaper Library, 208
History: Primary Sources: Archival Resources. Carnegie Mellon University Libraries, 207
History Primer, The, 298
History Reference Center, 231
History Remembered, Recovered, Invented, 296
History Timelines ... The History Beat, 210
History Today (journal), 294
History: Websites for U.S. History. University of Delaware Library, 210
History: Why It Matters, 296
Hitchens, Howard, 161
Hitler, Adolf, diaries, 116
Hoaxes, 115
Hoaxes, 115-7
Hobsbawn, Eric, 14n, 296
Hoerder, Dirk, 156
Hoffer, Peter Charles, 306
Hoffmann, Frank, 165
Hofstadter, Richard, 67, 108, 306
Holbert, R. Lance, 301
Holloway, Immy, 301
Holm, Bernard, 307
Holt-Jensen, Arild, 303
Honorable Titan, An, 42-3
Hoopes, James, 132
Hoornstra, Jean, 169
Hoover Institute on War, Revolution, and Peace, guide to, 176
Hopkins, W. Wat, 267
Horton, Carrell Peterson, 167
Housman, Robert, 299
Houston Post, 182
"How Students Get Lost in Cyberspace," 199n
How To Write History That People Want To Read, 312
Howell, Martha, 298
Hudson, Frederic, 31-2
Hudson, Robert, 94
Huggins, W. H., 158
Hughes, H. Stuart, 14n, 307
Hughes, Howard, 115-6
"Humanist Looks at Empirical Social Research, The," 72n
Humanities & Social Sciences Index Retrospective, 1907-1984, 214
Humanities Index, 159, 160
Humanities Index/Abstracts, 159
Humanities International Index, 214
Humanities, 9, 10, 11-2, 14
Hunt, Lynn, 14n, 76n, 77n, 78n, 254n, 295, 296
Huntington Library Quarterly, 294

Huntzicker, William, 309
Huxford, Marilyn, 157
Hynes, Terry, 309
Hypotheses, 89-91, 235, 242, 247, 250

I
Ickes, Harold, 37
Iconic Communication; An Annotated Bibliography, 158
Idaho periodicals, 173
Idea of a University, The, 52
Idea of History, The, 15n, 296
Identity politics, 77
Ideological bias, 45, 79-80, 81
Ideological Origins of the American Revolution, The, 38
Iggers, Georg, 307
Illustrations online, 226
Imagined Communities: Reflections on the Origin and Spread of Nationalism, 64n
Immigrant Labor Press in North America, 1840's-1970's: An Annotated Bibliography, 156
Immigration records, 229
In Defense of History, 77n, 79n, 296
Index of Web Sites related to the Civil War, 203, 208
Index to Black Newspapers, 171
Index to Black Periodicals, 159
Index to Book Reviews, 158, 159
Index to Book Reviews in Historical Periodicals, 159
Index to Book Reviews in the Humanities Journals, 159
Index to Critical Film Reviews in British and American Film Periodicals, 159
Index to Early American Periodicals, 171
Index to Free Periodicals, 159
Index to Jewish Periodicals, 159
Index to Motion Pictures Reviewed by "Variety," 1907-1980, 163
Index to Periodical Articles by and about Blacks, 160
Index to Southern Periodical, 160
Index to U. S. Government Periodicals, 174
Indexes of primary material online, 213-5
Indexes to historical materials, 178-80
Indiana Magazine of History, 294
Individuals, role in history, 66-7
Infoplease, 99
Information literacy, 136-7
Information Process, The, 11-2
Information Sources in Advertising History, 156
Inge, Thomas, 157
"Intellectual History, Social History, Cultural History, and Our History," 310
Internal criticism of records, 110, 120-1
International Bibliography of Books and Articles on the Modern Languages and Literature, 158
International Coalition on Newspapers, 213
International Coalition on Newspapers: Newspaper Digitization Projects, 209
International Committee of Historical Sciences, 156
International Communication and Political Opinion; A Guide to the Literature, 158
International Communication Association, 292
International Dictionary of Broadcasting and Film,

164
International Dictionary of Films and Filmmakers, 164
International Directory of News Libraries, 177
International Encyclopedia of Communications, 94
International Film Guide, 164
International Index, 159
International Index to Black Periodicals—Full Text, 1902-present, 224
International Index to Film Periodicals, 164
International Index to Music Periodicals, 214
International News Archives on the Web, 208
International Newspapers, 218
International Political Science Abstracts, 167
Internet, 193-234
    benefits of, 193-5
    conducting historical research on, bibliography 300
    errors and fabrications on, 197
    limitations of, 195-9
    sources, 99-100
    superficiality of material, 197-8
"Internet, The: Historical Media Research on the Virtual Archives," 300
"Internet and history, The: An exploration of the transmission of history by political websites," 300
Internet Archive, 226
    audio section, 183
Internet Archive eBooks and Texts, 224
Internet Classics Archive, 197
Internet Communication and Qualitative Research: A Handbook for Researching Online, 300
Internet Library of Early Journals (British), 216
Internet Modern History Sourcebook, 226
Internet Movie Database, 184, 232
Internet Public Library, 203, 208
Internet Research Skills, 301
Internet sources, evaluation of, 136-7
Interpretation, 6-7, 25-49, 239-43
    conflict interpretation, 35
    Consensus School, 37-40
    critical theory, 45
    Cultural School, 41-4
    Cultural Studies School, 44-6
    Developmental School, 31-5
    ethnic studies, 45
    feminist theory, 45
    feminist, 47-8
    Gender School, 46-8
    "great man," 42
    liberation theory, 45
    Marxist theory, 45
    Minority School, 46, 48-9
    Nationalist School, 28-9
    necessity of, 49
    Neo-Conservative School, 40-1
    postmodernism, 45
    Progressive School, 35-7
    reasons for, 26-7
    ritual view of communication, 44
    Romantic School, 29-31
    should not be predetermined, 26

    sociological, 42
    symbolic meaning, 44
Interpretation of Cultures, The, 64n
Interpretations of American History: Patterns and Perspectives, 306
Inter-university Consortium for Political and Social Research, 150, 167
"Interview with James Startt, An," 310
"Interview with Lawrence W. Levine," 249n
"Interview with Michael Murray, An," 309
"Interview with Patrick Washburn, An," 310
"Interview with Wm. David Sloan, An," 310
Introduction, in writing, 266, 268
Introduction to Evidence, An, 121
Introduction to Philosophy of History, An, 308
Introduction to Research in English Literary History, An, 304
Introduction to United States Government Information Sources, 174
Intuition, 246
Iowa Union List of Newspapers, 171
Irving, Clifford, 115-6
Irwin, Raymond, 153
"Is There a Santa Claus?" 113
Isenberg, Michael, 298
Issues and Trends in Afro-American Journalism, 48-9
"It's Primary: The importance of primary documents in conducting research," 299

J
Jackson, Fleda Brown, 156
Jacob, Margaret, 14n, 76n, 77n, 78n, 254n, 295
Jacob of Ancona, 116
Jacobs, Christopher, 163
Jacobs, Donald, 170
Jameson, J. Franklin, 307
Jane, Emma A., 302
Janney, Susan, 171
Jefferson, Thomas, 249, 263
Jensen, Richard, 298
Jewish Newspapers, 218
"Jhistorian Online, The," 300
Jodziewicz, Thomas, 181
John Adams, 4
John E. Brennan Outdoor Advertising Survey Reports, 1947-1980, 220
Johnson, Gerald, 40-1
Johnson, Janet Buttolph, 303
Johnson, Roger, 67n
Johnson, Tom, 87
Joint Journalism and Communication History Conference, 281, 292
Jones, Derek, 94
Journal of Advertising, 284, 294
Journal of African American History, 294
Journal of American Culture, 294
Journal of American Ethnic History, 294
Journal of American History, 200, 290, 294
Journal of American Studies, 294
Journal of Black Studies, 294
Journal of Broadcasting and Electronic Media, 284, 294
Journal of Communication, 284, 294

Journal of Contemporary History, 294
Journal of Politics, 294
Journal of Popular Culture, 294
Journal of Religion and Popular Culture online journal, 201
Journal of Southern History, 294
Journal of the Early Republic, 294
Journal of the Southwest, 294
Journal of the West, 294
Journal of Women's History, 294
Journalism: A Bibliography, 156
Journalism Abstracts, 167
Journalism and Mass Communication Monographs, 284, 294
Journalism and Mass Communication Quarterly, 152, 284, 294
"Journalism as Art: A Selective Annotated Bibliography," 156
"Journalism Historians and Religion," 310
Journalism History (journal), 44, 152, 155, 156, 157, 284, 288, 289, 294
"Journalism History and Women's Experience: A Problem in Conceptual Change," 309
Journalism in the United States, from 1690 to 1872, 31-2
Journalism Monographs, 151, 156, 180
"Journalism Research in Relation to Regional History," 299
"Journalist and Instant History, The: An Example of the Jackal Syndrome," 299
Journalist Biographies Master Index, 180
"Journalistic Biography, The: Methodology, Analysis and Writing," 309
Journalist's Bookshelf, The, 156
Journals online, 201, 207
Joyce, Davis, 307
Joye, Shauna, 305
JSTOR: The Journal of American History, 204, 231
Jucker, Andreas, 303
Judgments on History and Historians, 305
Juergens, George, 8
Jugenheimer, Donald, 301
JWT Newsletters, 220

K
Kammen, Carol, 298
Kanellos, Nicolas, 156
Kaplan, Louis, 154
Katz, Ephraim, 163
Katz, William, 161, 293
Kaul, Arthur, 95
Kaye, F. B., 170
Kee, Howard Clark, 303
Keesling's Contemporary Archives: Weekly Diary of World with Index Continually Kept Up-to-Date, 167
Keith, Michael, 164, 311
Kellen, James, 170
Kelly, P. T., 165
Kenneth, Campbell, 243
Kenney, Keith, 301
Kentucky Union List of Newspapers, 171
Kern, Sharon, 163

Key Methods in Geography, 302
Key to U.S.: A Guide to Internet Resources for Social Studies, 210
Killing of History, The: How a discipline Is Being Murdered by Literary Critics and Social Theorists, 297
King, Elliot, 300
King Lists, 5
Kingdom and the Power, The, 129
Kitch, Carolyn, 310
Klibanoff, Hank, 82
Klotman, Phyllis, 163
Knowlton, Steven, 199n
Kobre, Sidney, 42-4, 309, 310
Kohut, Thomas, 67-8
Kolar, Carol Koehmstedt, 173
Konigsberg, Ira, 162
Koss, Stephen, 237-8
Kozicki, Henry, 255n, 258n, 307, 312
Kramer, Peter, 161
Kraus, Michael, 307
Krautz, Alfred, 162
Krautz, Hille, 162
Krautz, Joris, 162
Krippendorff, Klaus, 301
Kuehl, Warren, 179

L
Labor History (journal), 294
Lacher-Feldman, Jessica, 136n
Lackmann, Ronald, 162
Lage, Ann, 248n
LaGuardia, Cheryl, 161, 293
Lamme, Meg, 90
Land records, 229
Landrum, Larry, 157
Landscape of History: How Historians Map the Past, 296
Lang, Sean, 308
Langer, William, 66
Langman, Larry, 163
Langness, L.L., 303
Larsen, John, 177
Laslett, Peter, 74, 75
Lasswell, Harold, 158
Lathem, Edward Connery, 170
Latin American Newspapers in United States Libraries: A Union List, 171
Latinas and Latinos, 210
Law, Jonathan, 162
Le Goff, Jacques, 296
Lee, Alfred M., 309
Lee, James Melvin, 33
Legal documents online, 227
Legal History, 209
Legal material online, 207
Legal Problem Solving: Analysis, Research and Writing, 303
Legal Research, 304
Legal Research: How to Find and Understand the Law, 303
Legal Research in a Nutshell, 302
Legislative history online, 226

Chapter 12: Index

Leidholdt, Alexander, 132
Lent, John, 155
Leonard Maltin's Movie Guide, 164
Let My People Know: American Indian Journalism, 48
Letters online, 207
Levermore, Charles, 265n
Levin, David, 307
Levine, Lawrence, 247-8, 249n, 307
Levy, Leonard, 309
Lewis, Bernard, 296
Lewis, C. S., 247
Lewis, George, 171
Lewis, M. J., 298
LexisNexis Academic, 234
Liberal historians, 35-6
Liberation theory, 45
Liberator, The, 216
Libraries
    definition of, 147-9
    vs. archives, 148-9
Libraries and other repositories of records (U.S.), 176-7
Library Card Catalog, 186-90
    call numbers, 188
    dictionary catalog, 188
    filing rules, 188
    subject card catalog, 188-9
Library of American Broadcasting, 222
Library of American Civilization, 179
Library of Congress, 132, 149, 155, 162, 164, 165, 170, 172, 177, 181, 182, 195-6, 199-200, 202, 203, 207, 208, 209, 211, 212, 215, 217, 222, 225, 228, 234
    Baseball Card Collection, 222
    Bibliographies, Research Guides and Finding Aids, 212
    classification system, 166-7, 189-90
    digital collections, 215, 217
    Manuscript Division, 149, 195-6
    Newspapers & Periodicals, 203
    online catalog, 190-1, 201-2
    Popular Graphic Arts Collection, 222
    special collections, 199-200
    Subject Headings, 189
Library of Congress Motion Picture, Broadcasting, Recorded Sound: An Illustrated Guide, 164
Library reference room, 94, 98-9
Lichty, Lawrence, 301
Liebman, Roy, 163
Life and Times of Benjamin Franklin, 30-1
Life magazine, 219
"Limits of Progressive History, The," 310
Lincoln, Yvonna, 303
Lingenfelter, Richard, 157
Literary and Historical Index to American Magazines, 1800-1850, 160
Literary determinism, 77
Literary Index to American Magazines, 1815-1865, 160
Literary Index to American Magazines, 1850-1900, 160
Literary Market Place, 292
"Literature and Media Change: A Selective Multidisciplinary Bibliography," 156
Literature of Journalism, The: An Annotated Bibliography, 156
"Literature of Women in Journalism History," 156
"Literature of Women in Journalism History: A Supplement,"156
Literature Online, 228
Literature review, in writing, 266
LitFinder, 220
Littlefield Jr., Daniel, 169
Lives: An Anthropological Approach to Biography, 303
Lloyd-Jones, Roger, 298
London Daily Mail, 240
Long, Huey, 132
Lords and Laborers of the Press: Men Who Fashioned the Modern British Newspaper, 8n
Lords of the Press, 37
Los Angeles Times, 182, 219
Loss of Mastery, A: Puritan Historians in Colonial America, 306
Lottinville, Savoie, 126, 261, 312
Louisiana Newspapers, 1794-1961: A Union List, 171
Louisville Courier-Journal, 54
Lowery, Zoe, 307
Lucht, Tracy, 81
Ludgate, Georgia, 96
Lueck, Theresa, 94
Lukacs, John, 14, 296
Lune, Howard, 302
Lurzer's Ads of the World Archive, 221
Lytle, Mark Hamilton, 250n, 251n, 296

M

Maas, Harro, 303
Macaulay, Thomas Babington, 11
MacDougall, Curtis, 115
Maclean's magazine, 219
Macmillan Film Bibliography: A Critical Guide to the Literature of the Motion Picture, 164
MacMillan, Margaret, 296
Magazine sources, 183
    guides to, directories, indexes, and union lists, 169-74
Magazines for Libraries, 161, 293
Magazines of the American South, 160
Magazines online, 207, 216
Magill, Frank, 164
Magill's American Film Guide, 164
Magill's Cinema Annual, 164
Magill's Survey of Cinema: English Language Films, 164
Magill's Survey of Cinema: Silent Films, 164
Mahoney, James, 303
Main Currents in the History of American Journalism, 33
Maisner, Elaine, 291n
Makers of the Media Mind, 311
Making of America Collection, 195, 199-200, 215
Making of the Modern World, 228
Making Sense in Religious Studies: A Student's Guide to Research and Writing, 304
Maltin, Leonard, 164, 166

Man on His Past: The Study of the History of Historical Scholarship, 305
Manchel, Frank, 163
Mangun, Kim, 53, 150, 258
Manion, Lawrence, 302
Mann, Chris, 300
Mann, Thomas, 96, 148, 175, 179n
Mansion of History, The, 63n, 82, 296
Manual for Writers of Research Papers, Theses, and Dissertations, 274, 312
Manual of Style, 285
Manuscript Collections, 211
Manuscript Division, Library of Congress, 176, 180, 195-6
Manuscripts from the Federal Writers' Project, 1936 to 1940, 226
Maps online, 226
MarciveWeb Docs, 175
Marovitz, Sanford, 153
Marsh, Earle, 184
Marshall, Catherine, 303
Martell, Helvetia, 156
Martin, Jim 289
Martin, Len, 165
Marwick, Arthur, 14n, 60n, 296
Marx, Karl, 251-2
Marxist historians, 16, 17
Marxist theory, 28, 45, 249
Maryland Historical Magazine, 294
Maryland Newspaper Project, 171
Marzolf, Marion, 47-8, 156
Mason, Elizabeth, 180
Mass Communication: A Guide to Reference Sources, 96
Mass Communication & Society (journal), 294
Mass communication sources, 137-43, 180-5
Mass Media: A Chronological Encyclopedia of Television, Radio, Motion Pictures, Magazines, Newspapers, and Books in the United States, 94
MasterFILE Complete, 219
Masterpieces of Reporting, 184
Masterson, James, 153
Materials and Methods for History Research, 298
Matthews, Herbert, 61
Matthews, William, 154
Maza, Sara, 297
McCaffrey, Donald, 163
McClelland, Peter, 298
McCluskey, Audrey, 163
McCollum, Jonathan, 304
McCoy, Ralph, 156
McCroskey, James, 301
McCrum, Blanche, 153
McDowell, Bill, 298
McGill, Ralph, 236
McGrath, Ann, 312
McKernan, Luke, 166
McKerns, Joe, 95, 157, 310
McMillen, Sophia, 171
McMullan, T. N., 171
McMullin, Ruth, 180
McNeil, Alex, 165, 184
McNeil, Barbara, 178

McPherson, Jim, 248
"Measure of Theory, A?: Considering the Role of Theory in Media History, 310
Meckler, Alan, 180
Media and Communication Research Methods: An Introduction to Qualitative and Quantitative Approaches, 302
"Media Ethics: A Bibliographical Essay," 157
Media History (journal), 155
Media History and the Archive, 299
Media History Monographs (electronic journal), 201, 284, 294
Media Hoaxes, 115
Media in America, The: A History, 84
Media Review Digest, 167
Media Use in the Information Age: Patterns of Adoption and Consumer Use, 168
Medicine and Madison Avenue, 220, 221
Memoirs, 227
Memoirs of an Editor, 113
Mercantile Newspapers, 217
Mercer, Paul, 155
Mere Christianity, 247n
Merriman, Scott, 98n, 207n, 300
Merritt, Richard, 71
Methods of Historical Analysis in Electronic Media, 299
Meyer, Manfred, 162
Michigan Law Journal, 294
Michigan newspapers, 173
Microbook Library of American Civilization, 179
Microbook Library of English Literature, 179
Microform collections, 212
Microform Research Collections: A Guide, 180
Mid-America Conference on History, 292
Mid-Continental American Studies Association, 292
Midwest Journalism History Conference, 281
Midwest, and Progressive historians, 42
Military actions, 227
Military history online, 226
Military History Symposium, 293
Military records, 229, 230
Miller, Robert, 304
Milner, Anita, 172, 182
Mindich, David, 196, 300
Mink, Armistead, 155
Mink, Arthur De Witt, 173
Mink, Louis, 258n
Minnesota newspapers, 170
Minority and gender sources online, 224
Minority, Diversity & Black Press Sites, 210
Minority School of interpretation, 46, 48-9
Miracle in the Early Christian World: A Study in Sociohistorical Method, 303
Miskelly, Matthew, 178
Mississippi newspapers, 170
Mississippi Newspapers, 1805-1940: A Preliminary Union List, 171
Mississippiana: Union List of Newspapers, 171
Missouri Newspaper Project, 172
Missouri Newspaper Project Union List, 171
Missouri Valley History Conference, 293
Mitchell, Catherine, 155, 310

Chapter 12: Index

Mitchell, Edward, 113-4
Mixed Methods in Ethnographic Research: Historical Perspectives, 304
MLA International Bibliography, 231
MLA Style Manual and Guide to Scholarly Publishing, 312
MLA Style Sheet, 285
"'mob begin to think and reason, The': Recent Trends in Studies of American Popular Disorder, 1700-1850," 65n
Modern American Journalism, 43
Modern American Usage, 312
Modern Archives: Principles and Techniques, 149n
Modern Historians and the Study of History: Essays and Papers, 307
Modern Language Association, 285, 312
Modern Researcher, The, 100n, 246n, 264n, 275n, 295, 297
Monaco, James, 165
Monash University Library: Film and Screen Studies: Reference Works, 166
Montana Historical Society Newspaper Project: A Union List of Montana Newspapers in Montana Repositories, 171
Monthly Catalog of the United States Government Publications, 174
Moral judgments, 62
Morehead, Joe, 174
Morgan, Jenny, 163
Morris, Nancy Jane, 171
Morris, Richard, 184
Morrison, Keith, 302
Morrison, Stanley, 155
Morse, Samuel F. B., Papers, 225
Motion Picture, Broadcasting and Recorded Sound Division, 132
Motion Picture Guide, 164
Motion pictures, 212
Mott, Frank Luther, 33-4, 108, 140, 299
Moving film/images online, 225, 226
Moving Image Archive, 223
Moving Pictures: An Annotated Guide to Selected Film Literature with Suggestions for the Study of Film, 164
Moving Picture World, 185
Muccigrosso, Robert, 154
Muckrakers, 67
Mugridge, Donald, 153
Muller, Richard, 302
Multi Media Reviews Index, 167
Multiculturalism, 76, 77
Murphree, Vanessa, 283
Murphy, Sharon, 48
Murray, Michael, 94, 309
Museum of Broadcast Communications, 231
Museum of Broadcast Communications Encyclopedia of Radio, 164
Museum Of Broadcast Communications Encyclopedia of Television, 94
Music Index, 1970-present, 215
Music manuscripts online, 215
Music online, 226
Music periodicals, 214

Music Periodicals (1760-1966), 220

N

Narrative and Genre: Contexts and Types of Communication, 301
"Narrative Form As a Cognitive Instrument," 258n
Narrative, in historical writing, 8-9, 14, 55, 254-9
Nasaw, David, 129
Nash, Jay Robert, 164
Nation Digital Archive, 219
National Anti-Slavery Standard, 216
National Archives (United Kingdom), 208
National Archives (U.S.), 150, 226, 229
  guide to, 176
National Archives and Records Administration, 226
National Archives Catalog, 212
National Communication Association, 293
National Council on Public History, 210
National Cyclopedia of American Biography, 95
National Digital Newspaper Program, 181, 217
National Film Archives (London), 150
National Historical Information System, 99
National Historical Publications and Records Commission, 175
National Inventory of Documentary Sources in the United States, 176, 180
National Newspaper Index, 182
National Public Radio, 219
National Registry for the Bibliography of History, 152
National Review, 219
National Union Catalog: 1973-1977, Films and Other Materials for Projection, 164
National Union Catalog of Manuscript Collections, 176, 177, 211
Nationalist School of interpretation, 28-9
Nations Within a Nation: Historical Statistics of American Indians, 168
Native American periodicals, 224
Native American Periodicals and Newspapers 1828-1982: A Bibliography, Publishing Records, and Holdings, 171
Native Americans, 48, 210, 227
"Natural History of the Newspaper, The," 41, 310
Naturalization records, 229
Nature of History, The, 14n, 60n
"Neglected Pioneers: 19th Century Native American Newspapers," 48n
Negro History Bulletin, 294
Nelson, Carolyn, 170
Nelson, Harold, 309
Neo-Conservative School of interpretation, 40-1
Nestor, Paul, 304
Networked Digital Library of Theses and Dissertations, 232
Nevada newspapers, 157
Nevins, Allan, 51, 103, 129, 184, 305, 307, 310
New Biographical Dictionary of Film, 164
New Cambridge Modern History, 94
"New Directions for Journalism Historiography," 309
New Directions in American Intellectual History, 306
New England Historical Association, 293

New England Quarterly, 294
New Historical Dictionary of the American Film Industry, 165
New Historicism, The, 297
New Historicism and Other Old-Fashioned Topics, The, 297
New Jersey History (journal), 294
New Jersey newspapers, 171
New Left historians, 16, 17
New Mexico Historical Review, 294
New Mexico Newspaper Project, 172
New Mexico Newspapers: A Comprehensive Guide to Bibliographical Entries and Locations, 172
New Nature of History, The: Knowledge, Evidence, Language, 296
New Orleans Times-Picayune, 182
New Perspectives on Historical Writing, 305
New Republic, 219
New Scientist, 219
New York City Newspapers, 1820-1850: A Bibliography, 157
New York Herald, 31-2, 218
New York Herald Tribune, 203
New York Historical Society Conference, 293
New York History (journal), 294
New York Journal, 118-9
New York Journal-American, 203
New York newspapers, 172, 173
New York Sun, 31, 111, 113-5
New York Times, 36, 37, 42-3, 81, 139, 182, 203, 218-9
New York Times Film Review, 166
New York Times Index, 161, 214
New York Times Obituaries Index II, 1969-1978, 182
New York Times Obituaries Index, 1858-1968, 182
New York World, 117
New-England Courant, 30-1, 33, 121-2
New-York Journal of American History, 294
Newcomb, Horace, 94, 162
News Archives on the Web, 208
News Media and Public Policy: An Annotated Bibliography, 157
News Media History Collection, 202-3, 213
"Newspaper & Current Periodical Reading Room," 182
Newspaper and the Historian, The, 299
Newspaper Archive, 1753-present, 218
Newspaper archives, 208
Newspaper Archives/Indexes/Morgues, 207
Newspaper Digitization Projects, 209
Newspaper Indexes: A Location and Subject Guide for Researchers, 172, 182
Newspaper Libraries in the U. S. and Canada: An SLA Directory, 177
Newspaper Press Directory and Advertisers' Guide, 172
Newspaper Press Opinion, Washington to Coolidge, 184
Newspaper Research Journal, 294
Newspaper Source, 219
Newspaper Source Plus, 219
Newspaper sources (directories, indexes, and union lists), guides to, 169-74

Newspapers: A Reference Guide, 94, 157
Newspapers and Periodicals by and about Black People: Southeastern Library Holdings, 172
Newspapers & Periodicals online, Library of Congress, 208
Newspapers as sources, 181-3
indexes of, 181-3
Newspapers as Tools for Historians, 299
Newspapers: Directories, 207
Newspapers, guides to, 174
Newspapers in Libraries of Metropolitan Chicago, a Union List, 172
Newspapers in Microform, 172, 181
Newspapers in Microform: United States, 1948-1983, 172
Newspapers in Missouri, a Union List, 172
Newspapers of Nevada, 1858-1979; A History and Bibliography, 157
Newspapers of Record, 217
Newspapers on Microfilm, 172, 181
Newspapers online, 207, 217-9
Newspapers.com Library Edition, 218
Newsreels, 98, 134, 143, 212, 223
Newsweek, 203
Newton, Eric, 95
"Next Assignment, The," 66n
Nicholas, R. M., 304
Nightline, 222
19th Century Masterfile, 161-2, 183
19th Century Masterfile: 1106-1930, 214
Nineteenth Century Readers' Guide to Periodical Literature 1890-1899, with Supplementary Indexing, 1900-1922, 160, 183
Nineteenth Century Studies (journal), 294
Nissen, Ursula, 162
Niver, Kemp, 162
Nixon, Raymond, 236
Nokes, G. D., 121
Nola, Robert, 304
Nolen, Ronald Dean, 163
Noonan, Barry Christopher, 173
Nord, David Paul, 310
North American Film and Video Directory, 177
North American Women's Letters and Diaries, 227
North Carolina Historical Review, 294
North Carolina newspapers, 173
North Dakota newspapers, 1864-1976, 173
Northern Great Plains History Conference, 293
Northey, Margot, 304
Norton, Mary Beth, 153
Notable American Women 1607-1950: A Biographical Dictionary, 95
Notable Black American Men, 95
Notable Black American Women, 95
Notes and Queries (1849-69), 216
Notetaking, 92-3
Novels as historic sources, 128
Novels online, 228
Novick, Peter, 297
Novotny, Ann Milner, 165

O

O'Brien, Elmer, 158

Official documents, evaluation of, 126-8
Official Museum Directory, 136
Ohio History (journal), 294
Ohio newspapers, 173
Ohio Valley History Conference, 293
Olasky, Marvin, 310
Old Time Radio, 223
"Oldest Living Graduate, The," 111-4
Olson, Kent, 302
Olson, May, 156
On Doing Local History, 298
On Historians: Reappraisals of Some of the Makers of Modern History, 306
On History, 14n, 296
"On Quoting Newspapers: A Problem and a Solution," 299
On the Air: The Encyclopedia of Old-time Radio, 165
On the Great Highway: The Wanderings and Adventures of a Special Correspondent, 118
On-Line Books Page, 223
On-Line Books Page: Serials, 210
Online Collections from the Manuscript Division, 225
Online journals, 199
Online library searches, 145-7
Online National Union Catalog of Manuscript Collections, 202
"Online Reference Desk," 98n
Open Access Theses and Dissertations, 233
OpenThesis, 232
Opinion in media content, 140
Oral history, 131-23, 207, 213
Oral History: A Reference Guide and Annotated Bibliography, 180
Oral History: An Introduction For Students, 132
Oral History Association, 211, 293
Oral History Collection of Columbia University, 180
Oral history collections, 179
Oral History Collections, 180
Oral history interviews and songs, 227
"Oral History Online," 132
Oral History Online. History Matters, 211
"Oral History Research Guide at Columbia," 179
Oral sources, evaluation of, 131-3
Oral tradition, 131
Oral Tradition: A Study in Historical Methodology, 131, 299
Organization of American Historians, 209, 293
Original written records, 123-5
Origins of History, The, 296
"Origins, Paradigms, and Topographies: Methodological Considerations Regarding Area Studies and Broadcast Histories," 310
Outdoor Advertising Association of America (OAAA) Archives, 1885-1990s, 220
Outdoor Advertising Association of America Slide Library, 1891-1994, 220
Outlines, 88
Owens, W. R., 303
Oxford Bibliographies, 231
Oxford Guide to Library Research, 148, 175
Oxford Guide to Library Research: How To Find Reliable Information Online and Offline, 96

Oxford History of Historical Writing, The, 307

P
Pacific Historical Review, 294
Pacific Northwest Newspapers on Microfilm, 172
Pallay, Richard, 156
Pallot, James, 165
Palm, Charles, 176
Palmegiano, Eugenia, 310
Palmer, Bryan, 297
Palmer, Gayle, 173
Palmer, Robert, 241n
Palmers Index to The Times, 161, 214
Pamphlets, 128, 170, 183, 202, 213, 216, 220, 270
Pamphlets of the American Revolution, 38-9, 183
Paneth, Donald, 94
Paper of Record, 196
Paperboy, 234
Papers of the Bibliographical Society of America (journal), 294
Paragraphs in writing, 262, 263
Parcell, Lisa, 4, 149, 275
Parch, Grace, 177
Parins, James, 169
Park, Robert, 41, 310
Parke, Catherine Neal, 304
Parkman, Francis, 11
Parrington, Vernon, 35
Parthasarathy, G. K., 301
Parton, James, 30-1
Pascal, Blaise, 263
Past and the Present Revisited, The, 307
Past Imperfect: History According to the Movies, 135n
Pastmasters: Some Essays on American Historians, 306
Patrides, C.A., 307
Patten, Mildred, 304
Paver, John, Papers, 1920-1979, 220
Pearson, Glenda, 172
Pedigree and Progress: Essays in the Genealogical Interpretation of History, 308
Peloponnesian War, The, 5-6
Pelto, Pertti, 304
Pendergast, Sara, 164
Pendergast, Tom, 164
Pennsylvania Gazette, 30, 216
Pennsylvania Magazine of History and Biography, 294
Pennsylvania newspapers, 173
Pennsylvania Newspapers: A Bibliography and Union List, 172
People magazine, 219
Period and Place: Research Methods in Historical Geography, 302
Periodicals and journals, 215-7
 sources for, 158-6
Periodicals Archive Online, 1802-2005, 216
Periodicals Content Index, 161
Periodicals Index Online, 214
Persian Wars, The, 5
Personal element in historian's work, 61-2
Personal Name Index to "The New York Times Index,"

182
Personal records, 125-6, 141
  evaluation of, 125-6
Perspectives on Early American History: Essays in Honor of Richard B. Morris, 308
Perspectives on Mass Communication History, 28n, 47n, 308, 311
Phalen, Patricia, 301
Philip Morris USA Inc. Advertising Archive, 222
Philosophical Transactions of the Royal Society (1757-77), 216
Photographic Literature: An International Bibliographic Guide to General and Specialized Literature on Photographic and Processing Techniques, Theories..., 165
Photography online, 225
Physical remains, 135-6
Pickett, Calder, 155
Pictorial sources, evaluation of, 133-5
Picture Sources Three: Collections of Prints and Photographs in the United States and Canada, 165
Pitt, David, 304
Pitts, Michael, 165
Pivotal Interpretations of American History, 306
"Place of Biography in the History of News Women, The" 310
Plagiarism, 272-3
Platte, Nathan, 165
Plumb, J.H., 297
Pocket Guide to Writing in History, 312
Poetry citations, 220
Political Diaries of C. P. Scott 1911-1928, 126
Political history, 226, 227
Political History: Principles and Practice, 9n, 241n, 245n, 257n, 298
Political Quarterly, 294
Political science, 9, 10, 12
Political Science Research Methods, 303
Politics (journal), 294
Pollard, James, 8
Polo, Marco, 116
Ponder, Steve, 84
Pool, Jeannie, 165
Poole's Index to Periodical Literature, 160, 161, 183, 214
Poore, Benjamin Perley, 174
Popular culture, 156, 157
Popular Culture Association, 293
Popular Graphic Arts Collection, 222
Popular Periodical Index, 160, 183
Population Information in Nineteenth Century Census Volumes, 168
Population Information in Twentieth Century Census Volumes, 168
Portland Oregonian, 182
Postmodernism, 45, 76-9, 80, 249
  evidence and, 78
  historical narrative and, 78
  literary determinism, 77
  understanding of language, 77
  understanding of truth, 77
Poststructuralism, 77, 80
Poststructuralism and Communication: An Annotated Bibliography, 158
Potter, Vilma Raskin, 94
Powell, Jason, 304
Powicke, F.M., 307
Practice of History, The, 14n, 296
Practice of Social Research, The, 302
Practicing History: Selected Essays, 254n
Prange, Gordon. 132
"Preliminary Bibliography, A: Images of Women in the Media, *1971-1976*," 157
Preliminary Checklist of Connecticut Newspapers, 1795-1975, 172
"Preliminary Guide to Indexed Newspapers in the United States, *1850-1900*," 172
Preliminary reading, 83-5
Present-mindedness, 55, 56-8, 60-1
  how to avoid it, 57-8
"Presentist Media Landscape and the Practice of Doing History, The" 309
Presidential Debates, 222
Presidential libraries, 178
Presidential Studies Quarterly, 294
Presidential Vote, The, 1896-1932, 169
Press and America, The, 106
Press Freedom and Development: A Research Guide and Selected Bibliography, 157
Press, Politics, and Patronage: The American Government's Use of Newspapers 1789-1875, 104
Prevenier, Walter, 298
Price, Warren, 156
Pries, Nancy, 154
Primary sources, 104-37, 121-2, 148, 207, 211, 213-5, 225-8, 299, 300
  definition of, 104-5
  importance of, 104, 106-7
  vs. secondary sources, 104-6
Primer of Public Relations Research, 301
Prince, Mary Miles, 312
Principles of History and Other Writings in Philosophy of History, The, 305-6
Pringle, Peter, 165
Printed Ephemera: Three Centuries of Broadsides and Other Printed Ephemera, 221
Prior, M. E., 170
"Private Lives: An Added Dimension for Understanding Journalism History," 299
Probing the Past: A Guide to the Study and Teaching of History, 56n, 76n, 89n, 250n, 297
"Problem of Journalism History, The," 44, 309
Proceedings of the American Antiquarian Society, 156
Professional historians, 35, 39
Progressive Historians, The: Turner, Beard, Parrington, 306
Progressive School of interpretation, 35-7, 43
Project Gutenberg, 197, 223
Proofreading, 276-7
Propaganda and Promotional Activities: An Annotated Bibliography, 158
ProQuest Historical Newspapers, 218
Protocols of the Learned Elders of Zion, 115
Prucha, Francis Paul, 96, 151, 174, 177
"Psychiatry and History: An Examination of

Chapter 12: Index

Erikson's Young Man Luther," 67n
Psychoanalysis, 66-70, 80, 249, 250
  benefits of, 69-70
  inadequate to explain humans in the past, 68-9
Psychohistory, 66-9
  preconceptions of, 67-8
  problems with, 67-9
"Psychohistory and History: The Case of Young Man Luther," 67n
Psychohistory and Religion: The Case of Young Man Luther, 67n
"Psychohistory as History," 68n
Psychology, 65, 66-9
  causation and, 68
Psychology, Science, and History: An Introduction to Historiometry, 298
Public documents, 105-6, 139
"Public Opinion and Historians," 299
Public Opinion and Historians: Interdisciplinary Perspectives, 311
Public Opinion Quarterly, 294
Public Press, The, 1900-1945, 84
Public Record Office in (London), 149
Publication Manual of the American Psychological Association, 311
Publick Occurrences Both Forreign and Domestick, 33
Publishing
  books, 292-2
  journal articles, 283-90, 293-4
Purpose of primary record, 122
Purpose of research, as part of explanation, 235-9
Pursuit of History, The, 131, 242n, 250n, 308
Putman, William, 304
Puzzles of the Past: An Introduction to Thinking About History, 298

Q

Qualitative Research Methods for Media Studies, 301
Qualitative Research Methods for the Social Sciences, 302
Qualitative Research Methods in Human Geography, 303
Qualitative Research Methods in Public Relations and Marketing Communications, 301
Quan-Haase, Anabel, 301
Quantification, 70-6
  definition, 73-4
  inability to explain "why," 74-5
  limitations of, 72-6
  narrative writing and, 74-5
  usefulness, 71
Quantitative Research Methods for Communication: A Hands-on Approach, 301-2
Questia Media, 196
Quotations, use of in writing, 274-5

R

Rabasa, Jose, 307
Rabe, Robert, 200, 230
Race Beat, The: The Press, the Civil Rights Struggle, and the Awakening of a Nation, 82
Racism, 48-9

Radio, 7, 94, 309
  sources for, 133, 161-6, 176, 183
  websites, 132, 208, 219, 222, 228
Radio and Television: A Selected, Annotated Bibliography. Supplement Two, 1982-1986, 165
Radio and Television: A Selected Bibliography, 165
Radio Broadcasting and Television: An Annotated Bibliography, 165
Radio Broadcasts in the Library of Congress, 1924-1941: A Catalog of Recordings, 165
Radio Days, 208
Radio Voices: American Broadcasting, 1922-1952, 7n
Radio's Golden Years: The Encyclopedia of Radio Programs, 1930-1960, 165
Rahikainen, Marjatta, 296
Ralph Emerson McGill: Voice of the Southern Conscience, 236n
Rampolla, Mary Lynn, 312
Ramsey, Alexis, 304
Ranganathan, Maya, 300
Ranucci, Karen, 163
Rapport, Leonard, 299
Rather, Dan, 117
Ratings Analysis. The Theory and Practice of Audience Research, 301
R.C. Maxwell Company Records, 1904-1990s, 220
"Re-Constructing Media History," 310
Read, Brock, 198n
Read Print, 197
Reader's Guide Retrospective, 1890-1982, 214
Readers' Guide Supplement, 159
Readers' Guide to Periodical Literature, 160, 183
Readex Collections, 218
Reagan, Patrick, 300
Real History: Reflections on Historical Practice, 296
Recently Published Articles, 160
Reconstruction of American History, The, 306
Recorded Sound Reference Center, 132
Rector, Justine J., 49-50
Red Blood & Black Ink: Journalism in the Old West, 236
Reductionism, 68, 251
Reed, Barbara Straus, 300
Reed, Dale, 176
Reed, Marcia, 154
Reference Desk, 234
Reference Guide to Afro-American Publications and Editors, A, 1827-1946, 94
Reference room, 94, 98-9
Reference Sources in History: An Introductory Guide, 180
Reference tools, 98-9
Reference works, 96, 151-84
Reference Works, 233
"Reflections on Radio History, Preservation, and Relevance," 309
Regional Business News Plus, 228
Rehrauer, George, 164
Relativism, 77
Religion: Denominational Newspapers, 218
Religious Index One: Periodicals, 160
Religious Press in the South Atlantic States, The, 1802-1865. An Annotated Bibliography, 157

Remington, Frederic, 108, 118-9
Republic Pictures Checklist, 165
Research
  as a criterion for good history, 53
  how much is enough, 143-4
Research Guide to American Historical Biography, 154
Research Guide to Film and Television Music in the United States, 165
Research Guide to Religious Studies, 305
Research in Archives: The Use of Unpublished Primary Sources, 148
Research Libraries and Collections in the United Kingdom: A Selective Inventory and Guide, 178
Research Libraries Information Network, 177
Research Library, 232
Research Methods and Statistics, 302
Research Methods and Statistics: An Integrated Approach, 305
Research Methods and Statistics in Psychology, 302
Research Methods in Anthropology: Qualitative and Quantitative Approaches, 302
Research methods in communication, 301-2
Research Methods in Communication, 80n, 249n, 302
Research Methods in Education, 302
Research Methods in Law, 305
Research Methods in Library and Information Science, 302
Research Methods in Psychology: Investigating Human Behavior, 304
Research Society for American Periodicals, 210
Research Society for Victorian Periodicals, 281, 293
Researcher's Guide to Archives and Regional History Sources, 177
Researching Local History: The Human Journey, 299
Resources for Doing Legal History, 209
Resources for Genealogists, 229
"Rethinking Objectivity in Journalism and History: What Can We Learn from Feminist Theory and Practice?" 310
Retrospective Index to Film Periodicals 1930-1971, 165
Return to Essentials: Some Reflections on the Present State of Historical Study, 306
Review of Politics (journal), 294
Reviewing process
  by academic conferences, 281-3
  by journals, 286-9
Revision in writing, 275-6
Reyes, Luis, 163
Reynolds, Amy, 304
Reynolds, Henry, 303
Rhetoric of History, The, 126, 261, 312
Rhode Island History (journal), 294
Rhodes, James Ford, 20-1
Richards, Larry, 161
Richards, Michael, 199n
Richmond Enquirer, 218
Rights of All, 170
Riley, Sam, 72, 95, 160
RIPM: Retrospective Index to Music Periodicals (1760-1966), 220
Rips, Rae Elizabeth, 175
Rise and Fall of the Political Press in Britain, The, 258
"Rise of Metropolitan Journalism, 1800-1840, The" 264n
Risley, Ford, 237, 284, 286, 310
RISM Series A/II: Music Manuscripts after 1600, 215
Ritchie, Donald, 132, 298
Ritual view of communication, 44, 45
Rivington's New York Newspaper: Excerpts from a Loyalist Press, 1773-1783, 172
"Road to Xanadu, The: Public and Private Pathways on the History Web," 300
Robbins, J. Albert, 175
Roberts, Gene, 82
Roberts, Stephen, 178
Robertson, Craig, 299
Robertson, Michael, 311
Robinson, Edgar, 169
Robinson, Judith Schiek, 175
Roessner, Amber, 310
Romantic School of interpretation, 29-31
Romanticism, 29
Roots, 131
Rorty, Richard, 76n
Rose, Gerry, 304
Rose, Oscar, 165
Rosenzweig, Roy, 300
Ross, Kristina, 300
Ross, Robert, 7
Rossell, Glenora, 172
Rossman, Gretchen, 303
Rothfield, Anne, 98n
Roust, Colin, 165
Routledge Film Music Sourcebook, 165
Routledge Handbook of Research Methods in the Study of Religion, The, 305
Roy Rosenzweig Center for History and New Media, 210-11
Rubie, Peter, 163
Rueschemeyer, Dietrich, 303
Rush, Ramona, 156
Russell, Karen Miller, 91, 120

S

Sabin America, 1500-1926, 227
Sage Handbook of Qualitative Research, The, 303
SAGE Handbook of Social Media Research Methods, The, 301
SAGE Sourcebook of Advanced Data Analysis Methods for Communication Research, The, 301
Salisbury, Ruth, 172
Salmon, Lucy Maynard, 299
Salvaggio, J. S., 168
Samuels, Warren, 304
San Francisco Chronicle, 182
Sanders, Chauncey, 304
Sankey, Howard, 304
Schellenberg, T. R., 149n
Schement, Jorge Reina, 155
Schirmer Encyclopedia of Film, 165
Schlesinger, Arthur, Jr., 72, 257n, 275n
ScholarOne, 286
Scholar's Guide to Washington, D. C., for Audio

Chapter 12: Index

Resources: Sound Recordings in the Arts, Humanities, Social, Physical, and Life Sciences, 165
Schomburg Studies on the Black Experience, 224
Schools of journalism, 42
Schudson, Michael, 107-8
Schulze, Suzanne, 168
Schutt, Russell, 304
Schwartz, Thomas, 311
Schwarzlose, Richard, 94, 157, 310
Schwegmann, Jr., George, 172
Schwoch, James, 310
Science, 9, 10, 13-5
Scientific history online, 226
Scott, C. P., 8
Scott, Joan Wallach, 297
Scott, Kenneth, 172
Search engines, 204-5
Search for a Usable Past, The, 306
"Searching for Journalism History in Cyberspace," 300
Seccombe, Matthew, 170
Secondary sources, 46, 53, 104-9, 136, 196, 231-3
  definition of, 104-5
  evaluation of, 128-9
  online, 201
Selbourne, David, 116
Selden, Raman, 76n
Seldes, George, 36-7
Self-discipline, 243
Seligman, Edwin, 307
Sense of the Past, The: Thirteen Studies in the Theory and Practice of History, 62n
Sentences in writing, 262
Serials in Microform, 172
71 Digital Portals to State History, 209
"Sex, Lies, and Autobiography: Contributions of Life Study to Journalism History," 311
Shafer, Robert, 298
Sharrock, Wes, 304
Sheahan, Eileen, 164
Shearer, Benjamin, 157
Sheehy, Eugene, 96
Ship passenger lists, 229
Showman, Richard, 153
Siebert, Frederick, 310
Sies, Luther, 162
Significance of the Printed Word in Early America, The, 265n
Silent Film Necrology, 165
Silent films, 183
"Silliness in Excelsis," 67n
Simonsen, Craig, 304
Simonton, Dean Keith, 298
Simple and Direct: A Rhetoric for Writers, 311
Singerman, Robert, 155
60 Minutes Wednesday, 117
Skill, Thomas, 165
Skotheim, Robert Allen, 307
Slater, Michael, 301
Slavens, Thomas, 305
Slavery, 227
Slavery in Virginia, 221

Slide, Anthony, 165
Sloan, C. Joanne, 184
Sloan, Luke, 301
Sloan, Wm. David, 28n, 47n, 80n, 94, 155, 156, 184, 249n, 293, 302, 308, 310-11
Small, Melvin, 311
Smart, James, 165
Smith, Allen, 179
Smith, Bruce Lannes, 158
Smith, Carol, 311
Smith, Chitra, 158
Smith, Culver, 104
Smith, Henry Justin, 128
Smith, Jessie Carney, 167
Smith, Page, 4, 297
Smith, Paul, 135, 299
Smith, Reed, 309
Smith, William E., 264n
Snooks, G. D, 304
Snorgrass, J. William, 155
Snyder, Leslie, 301
Snyder, Louis, 184
So It Was True: The American Protestant Press and the Nazi Persecution of the Jews, 7
Social Explorer, 99
Social Forces (journal), 294
Social influence on media, 42-3
Social Science and Historical Perspectives: Society, Science, and Ways of Knowing, 303
Social sciences, 2, 3, 9, 10, 11, 12-4, 15-6, 20, 63-5
Social Sciences and Humanities Index, 159
Social Sciences Citation Index, 160
Social Sciences Index, 159, 160
Social Sciences Index/Abstracts, 160
Society for Historians of the Early American Republic, 293
Society for Military History, 293
Society for the History of Authorship, Reading and Publishing, 281, 293
"Sociological Approach in Research in Newspaper History, The," 42, 310
Sociological interpretation of history, 42
Sociology, 64-5
Sociology Abstracts, 167
Some Newspapers and Newspapermen, 36
Sonny Bono Copyright Term Extension Act of 1998, 197
Sound recordings online, 222-3
Sourcebook for Political Communication Research: Methods, Measures, and Analytical Techniques, 301
Sources
  audio, 133
  evaluation of, 103-44
  Internet, 136-7
  mass communication sources, 137-43
  official documents, 126-8
  oral, 131-3
  original written records, 123-5
  personal records, 125-6
  physical remains, 135-6
  pictorial, 133-5
  primary, 104-37, 121-2, 148, 207, 211, 213-5,

225-8, 299, 300
secondary, 46, 53, 104-9, 128-9, 136, 196, 201, 231-3
statistical, 129-31
types, 122-43
South America, 227
South Atlantic Quarterly, 294
South Carolina Newspapers [1732-1780], 216
Southern Historical Association, 293
Southern history, literature, and culture online, 227
Southern press, 157
Southern publications, 160
Southwest Education Council for Journalism & Mass Communication, 293
Southwestern Historical Quarterly, 294
Spanish-American War, 21
Speace, Geri, 178
Speaking of History: Conversations with Historians, 295
Special collections, 178
  defined, 177
Special Collections in College and University Libraries, 178
Special libraries, 178
  defined, 177
Specimens of Newspaper Literature: With Personal Memoirs, Anecdotes, and Reminiscences, 30
Specious Past, The: Historians and Others, 308
Spencer, David, 300, 311
Spencer, Steve, 305
Spengler, Oswald, 251
Spitz, Lewis, 67n
Sports Illustrated, 219
Stacks, Donald, 301
Standard authorities, 97-8
Standards of "good" history, 52-6
Standley, A. E., 304
Starr, Louis, 180
Startt, James D., 307, 310, 311
State & Local Newspaper Archives, 209
State Archives, Libraries and Historical Societies, 180
State of Wisconsin Historical Society (Archives Division), 203
Statistical Abstract of the United States, 169
Statistical and demographic data sources, 99
Statistical Reference Index, 168
Statistical sources, 167-9
  evaluation of, 129-31
Statistical Sources: A Subject Guide to Data on Industrial, Business, Social, Educational, Financial, and Other Topics for the United States and Internationally, 168
Status anxiety, 67
Stausberg, Michael, 305
Stearns, Carol, 69
Stearns, Peter, 69
Steiner, Linda, 257, 311
Stellhorn, Paul, 171
Stephens, Lester, 55-6, 76, 89, 250n, 297
Stephens, Michael, 161
Sterling, Christopher, 161, 164, 311
Stern, Darlene, 156
Stern, Fritz, 307

Stevens, John, 311
Stewart, Fiona, 300
Stewart, Powell, 170
Stoffle, Carla, 298
Stone, Lawrence, 307
Strache, Neil, 173
Streitmatter, Rodger, 311
Stroupe, Henry Smith, 157
Strunk, William, 261n, 262, 312
Stuart, Paul, 168
"Students and the Web: A Cautionary Tale," 199n
Studies of British Newspapers and Periodicals From Their Beginning to 1800; A Bibliography, 158
Style, 156
Subject Collections: A Guide to Special Book Collections and Subject Emphasis as Reported by University, College, Public, and Special Libraries in the United States and Canada, 178
Subject Directory of Special Libraries, 178
Subject Directory of Special Libraries and Information Centers, 178
Subject Guide to U.S. Government Reference Sources, 175
Subject Index to Periodicals, 159
Subjectivity, 76-7
Sudduth, Elizabeth, 178
Suggs, Henry Lewis, 170
Superhistorians, The: Makers of Our Past, 305
Survey of Special Collections and Archives in the United Kingdom and Ireland, 178
Survey Research Methods, 301, 303
Sweeney, Michael, 98, 122, 254, 311
Symbolic meaning of communication, 44, 45, 81
Symposium on the 19th Century Press, Civil War and Free Expression, 281, 293
Syracuse Law Review, 294

T
Taavitsainen, Irma, 303
Taft, William, 95, 299
"Taking Stock, Placing Orders: A Historiographic Essay on the Business History of the Newspaper," 311
Talese, Gay, 129
Tanner, James, 155
Taylor, A. J. P., 67n
Taylor, H. A., 8n
Taylor, Robert M., Jr., 298
"Technology and Ideology: The Case of the Telegraph," 45n
Teel, Leonard, 6, 84, 235-6
Television, 94, 138, 142, 212
  sources for, 150, 161-6, 183-4
  websites, 212, 219, 220, 222, 224, 231
Television: A Guide to the Literature, 165
Television: A Guide to the Reference Literature, 165
Television and Film: An Annotated Bibliography of Research Materials, 165
Television News Index and Abstracts, 184
Television Violence: A Guide to the Literature, 165
Telling Histories: Black Women Historians in the Ivory Tower, 297
Telling the Truth About History, 14n, 76n, 77n, 78n,

Chapter 12: Index

254n, 295
Tennessee Historical Quarterly, 294
Terkel, Studs, 133
Terrace, Vincent, 165
Texas Newspapers, 1813-1939. A Union List, 172
Text Creation Partnership, 219, 224
Textbooks, 84
Textual analysis, 80-1
Textual verification110
That Noble Dream: The "Objectivity Question" and the American Historical Profession, 297
Thematic statement, in writing, 266
Theories of history, 247, 251-2
Theories of Scientific Method: An Introduction, 304
Theory, 14, 26, 68, 89, 247-52, 296, 302, 304, 305, 308, 310
   Critical Theory, 45, 248-9
   Cultural Studies, 248-9
   definition of, 247, 248, 249-50
   deterministic, 251
   feminist theory, 45, 310
   grand theory, 250-2
   problems with, 54, 72, 243, 249
   psychoanalytical theory, 67-8, 70
   small scale theory, 250-1
   vs. hypothesis, 250n
Theory and History, 308
Theory and Method in Historical Ethnomusicology, 304
They Voted for Roosevelt, 169
"Thick Description: Toward an Interpretive Theory of Culture," 64n
Thinking About History, 297
Tholfsen, Trygve, 55
Thomas Woodrow Wilson: A Psychological Study, 67
Thomas, Brook, 297
Thomas, Isaiah, 29
Thomason, George, 170
Thompson, James W., 307
Thompson, Julius Eric, 170
Thompson, Paul, 298, 301
Thomson, David, 164
Thucydides, 5-6, 15
Tibbetts, John, 162
Tillinghast, Pardon, 308
Tilly, Charles, 305
Time
   as an aspect of historical study, 5, 20
   awareness of, 55
Time lapse, as criterion in evaluation of primary record, 121-2
Time magazine, 219
Timelines, 88
Times Digital Archive, 1785-2012, 219
Times (London), 182, 219
Tindall, George Brown, 84
Tinney, James S., 49-50
Titus, Edna, 173
"To Theorize or Not To Theorize," 311
Tomlins, Christopher, 290n
Toomey, Alice, 152
Topic definition, 52-3, 235-8
Topic selection, 85-7

big topics, 87
focusing study, 88-91
formulating questions, 90-1
historian's ability, 85
hypotheses, 89-91
significance, 86, 87
who, what, where, and when, 86
workability, 85-6
Topical structure in writing, 268
Toronto Star, 219
Tosh, John, 131, 242, 250n, 308
Total Television: A Comprehensive Guide to Programming from 1948 to the Present, 165, 184
"Toward a Bibliography of the Writings of Arthur M. Schlesinger, Jr.," 257n, 275n
Toward the Scientific Study of History, 297
Townsend, Robert, 12n
Toynbee, Arnold, 251
Trade journals, 185
Treasury of Great Reporting, 184
Trevelyan, George Macaulay, 263, 308
Trinkle, Dennis, 98n, 136n, 207n, 300
Tripp, Bernell, 5, 21, 47n, 60, 118
Truth in history, 3, 4, 8, 13, 17, 18, 54, 58, 59
Tuchman, Barbara, 62, 254n
Turabian, Kate, 274, 312
Turner, Frederick Jackson, 35, 251
Twain, Mark, 263

U

U.S. Congressional Serial Set, 1789-1969, 225-6
U.S. Congressional Serial Set, 1817-1994, 226
U.S. government publications (U.S.)
   catalogs of, 174, 175
   guides to, 174, 175
U.S. government statistics, 167
U.S. History & American Studies Research Guide, 210
U.S. Major Dailies, 218-9
U.S. National Archives and Records Administration 226
U.S. National Historical Information System, 99
U.S. News Archives on the Web, 208
UCLA Film and Television Archive, 212
UCSB Cylinder Audio Archive, 223
Understanding Historical Research: A Search for Truth, 297
Understanding History: A Primer of Historical Method, 298
Understanding Research Methods: An Overview of Essentials, 304
Union List of Newspapers in Delaware, 173
Union List of Newspapers in Pennsylvania, 173
Union List of Newspapers, New York, 1821-1936, 173
Union List of Newspapers Published in Michigan, 173
Union List of North Carolina Newspapers, 173
Union List of North Dakota Newspapers, 1864-1976, 173
Union List of Ohio Newspapers Available in Ohio, 173
Union List of Serials in Idaho Libraries, 173
Union List of Serials in Libraries of the United States and Canada, 173
Union List of Vermont Newspapers, 173

Union lists, 169-73
  defined, 169
United Nations Statistical Office, 169
United States Government Publications, 175
United States Newspaper Program, 173, 181, 202, 212
United States Newspaper Program National Union List, 173
Unity of composition in writing, 259-61
University of Chicago Department of Sociology, 41
University of Illinois Library. History, Philosophy, and Newspaper Library, 208
University of Michigan Making of America Collection, 215
University of Michigan Research Guides: Film & Video Studies / Screen Arts & Cultures, 166
Unpredictable Past, The: Explorations in American Cultural History, 307
Untapped Sources: America's Newspaper Archives and Histories, 177
Up From the Footnote: A History of Women Journalists, 47-8
US News & World Report, 219
USA Today, 182, 219
USA.gov, 228
"User's Guide to the Internet," 300
"Uses of History, The: The Media History Project," 300
USGenWeb Project, 230
Using Computers in History: A Practical Guide, 298
Using Historical Sources in Anthropology and Sociology, 304
Using Internet Primary Sources to Teach Critical Thinking Skills in History, 300
"Using Primary Sources on the Web," 300
"Using the Internet as a Resource for Historical Research and Writing," 300

V

van Tuyll, Debra, 26
Vanderbilt University Television News Archive, 150, 184, 222
Vansina, Jan, 131, 299
Varieties of History, The: From Voltaire to the Present, 307
"Variety of Journalism History, The: 26 Years of Scholarship," 309
Variety, 185
Variety's Film Reviews, 166
Vaughan, Alden, 308
Vaughn, Stephen, 297
Vazzana, Eugene Michael, 165
Veeser, H. Aram, 297
Vergobbi, David, 54
Vermont Newspaper Project, 173
Victorian Periodicals, 1824-1900, 214
Victorian Periodicals Review, 284, 294
Villard, Oswald Garrison, 36
Vintage Ad Browser, 221
Virgin Encyclopedia of Film, The, 165
Virgin Encyclopedia of the Movies, The, 166
Virginia Center for Digital History, 229
Virginia Gazette, 216
Virginia Magazine of History and Biography, 294
Virtual Reference Shelf, 233
Visual Communication Research Designs, 301
Visual images online, 222-3
Visual Research Methods, 305
Vital Past, The: Writings on the Uses of History, 297
Voice of the Past, The: Oral History, 298
Voices of Women Historians: The Personal, the Political, the Professional, 295-6
Von Mises, Ludwig, 308
Vos, Tim, 245
Vyhnanek, Louis Andrew, 180

W

Wagner, Anthony, 308
Walker, John, 163
Wall Street Journal, 182, 219
Walsh, Ruth, 157
Walsh, William, 308
Ward, John William, 241n
Ward, William, 155
Washburn, Patrick, 290, 310
Washington Evening Star (1852-1981), 218
Washington Post, 182, 219
Washington Press Club Foundation Oral History Project, 224
Washington State newspapers, 172
Washington State Union List of Newspapers On Microfilm, 173
Washington Times, 219
Wasserman, Steven, 168
Watkins, Dawn Elizabeth, 305
Weber, Olga, 177
Webster, James, 301
Wedgwood, C. V., 62, 82
Weed, Katherine Kirtley, 158
Weekly Advocate, 170
Wellesley Index to Victorian Periodicals 1824-1900, 160, 214
Wells, Daniel, 160
Wells, Jonathan, 160
Wells, Ronald, 308
Welsch, Erwin, 170
Welsh, James, 162
Wensberg, Erik, 312
West Indies, 227
West Virginia Newspapers, 1790-1990: A Union List, 173
Western History Association, 293
Westminster Review, 214
"'What a Buzzel is This ... about Kentucky?' New Approaches and an Application," 309
What Is History? 14n, 91n, 240, 297
"Where Have All the Historians Gone? A Challenge to Researchers," 311
Which Road to the Past? Two Views of History, 306
Whig interpretation, 44n, 251
Whig Interpretation of History, The, 305
Whissen, Thomas, 163
White, Deborah, 297
White, E.B., 312
Who Was Who in America, 95
Who's Who in America, 95

Chapter 12: Index

Who's Who of Victorian Cinema, 166
Whole Film Sourcebook, The, 166
"Why Study Media History?" 311
Wierzbicki, James, 165
Wikipedia, 99, 197, 208
Wikipedia Biography Portal, 99
Wilderness, The, the Nation, and the Electronic Era: American Christianity and Religious Communication, 1620-2000: An Annotated Bibliography, 158
Wile, Annadel, 159
Willems, Mary, 162
Willetts, Paul, 161
William and Mary Quarterly, 294
Williams, Julie, 172, 255, 265-6, 270
Williams, Michael, 299
Williams, T. Harry, 132
"Willie Lynch speech of 1712," 197
Willing's Press Guide, 172
Wilson, Janie, 305
Wilson, John, 305
Wilson, Norman James, 308
Wilson, Trevor, 126
Wilson, Woodrow, 117-8
Windows on the World: World News Reporting 1900-1920, 85
Windschuttle, Keith, 297
Winks, Robin, 299, 306
Winnert, Derek, 166
Winthrop-Young, Geoffrey, 156
Wisconsin Historical Society, 150, 181, 202, 213
 Archives Division, 208
Wise, Gene, 308
Wish, Harvey, 308
Wohl, Robert, 250
Wolseley, Isabel, 156
Wolseley, Roland, 156
Women, 47-8
Women and Social Movements in the United States: 1600 to 2000, 228
Women in Journalism. Washington Press Club Foundation Oral History Project, 224
"Women in Media, 1700-Present: Victims or Equals?" 47n
Women's History Review, 294
Women's-interest newspapers, 207
Women's Letters and Diaries, 227
Women's Periodicals and Newspapers: from the 18th Century to 1981; a Union List of the Holdings of Madison, Wisconsin, Libraries, 173
Women's Periodicals in the United States, 94
Women's Suffrage Collection [newspapers], 216
Woody, Gloria, 155
Word choice in writing, 262
Working bibliography, 97
Working hypotheses, 235, 242
Working in the Archives: Practical Research Methods for Rhetoric and Composition, 304
World Bibliography of Bibliographies, 152
World Newspaper Archive, 219
World Newspaper Archive (1800-1925), 218
World Newsreels Online, 1929–1966, 223
World War II, 211
World We Have Lost, The, 74
WorldCat, 145-6, 202
Wray, Cheryl, 184
Wrench, Jason, 301
Wright American Fiction, 1851-1875, 228
Wright, H. Stephen, 165
Wright, William, 171
Writer's Digest Books, 173
Writer's Market, 173, 291
Writing, 55-6, 253-77
 chronological structure, 268
 clarity, 261-4
 conclusion, 268-9
 continuity, 261-4
 copyright, 267
 development of narrative, 264-9
 first lines of narrative, 264-6
 footnotes, 269-74
 introduction, 266, 268
 literature review, 266
 narrative, 254-9
 paragraphs, 262, 263
 plagiarism, 272-3
 proofreading, 276-7
 quotations, use of, 274-5
 revision, 275-6
 scholarly, 266, 268-9
 sentences, 262
 thematic statement, 266
 topical structure, 268
 unity of composition, 259-61
 word choice, 262
Writing American History: Essays on Modern Scholarship, 306
Writing forms, 311-2
Writing of American History, The, 307
Writing of History, The: Literary Form and Historical Understanding, 255n, 258n, 312
Writings on American History: A Subject Bibliography of Articles, 153
Writings on American History: A Subject Bibliography of Books and Monographs 1962-73, 153
Writings on Christianity and History, 305
Wynar, Lubomyr Roman, 171

X, Y, Z

Xooxle National, State & Local Newspaper Archives, 209
Yale University Law School, 227
Yellow Journalism: Puncturing the Myths, Defining the Legacies, 119n
Yellow Press and Gilded Age Journalism, The, 43
Young Man Luther, 67
"Your Name in This Space: The Mysteries of Scholarly Publishing," 290n
Zammeto, John, 308
Zhou, Shuhua, 80n, 249n, 302